Lisbon

Julia Wilkinson

LONELY PLANET PUBLICATIONS
Melbourne • Oakland • London • Paris

Lisbon
2nd edition – April 2001
First published – April 1998

Published by
Lonely Planet Publications Pty Ltd ABN 36 005 607 983
90 Maribyrnong St, Footscray, Victoria 3011, Australia

Lonely Planet Offices
Australia Locked Bag 1, Footscray, Victoria 3011
USA 150 Linden St, Oakland, CA 94607
UK 10a Spring Place, London NW5 3BH
France 1 rue du Dahomey, 75011 Paris

Photographs
Many of the images in this guide are available for licensing from
Lonely Planet Images.
email: lpi@lonelyplanet.com.au

Front cover photograph
Complexo das Amoreiras was Lisbon's first foray into the modern
shopping mall phenomenon. (Paul Bernhardt)

Title page of map section
Not just an icon of Lisbon, the tram network is an ideal way to absorb
the feel of the city. (Paul Kennedy)

ISBN 1 86450 127 8

text & maps © Lonely Planet 2001
photos © photographers as indicated 2001

Printed by The Bookmaker International Ltd
Printed in China

Although the authors
and Lonely Planet try
to make the informa-
tion as accurate as
possible, we accept
no responsibility for
any loss, injury or
inconvenience sus-
tained by anyone
using this book.

Contents – Text

PLACES TO STAY   91

PLACES TO EAT   98

ENTERTAINMENT   111

SHOPPING   121

EXCURSIONS   127

LANGUAGE   153

GLOSSARY   160

INDEX   171

MAP SECTION   SEE BACK PAGES

MAP LEGEND   BACK PAGE

METRIC CONVERSION   INSIDE BACK COVER

Contents – Maps

The Author

Julia Wilkinson

The lure of the Orient set Julia off on her travel writing career. After university in England, she headed for Australia but got side-tracked in Hong Kong, where she worked in publishing and radio until going freelance as a writer and photographer. After years writing about South-East Asia, she returned to England and now concentrates on Europe. As well as co-authoring Lonely Planet's *Portugal* and *South West France*, Julia has helped update the Portugal chapters of LP's *Western Europe, Mediterranean Europe* and *Europe on a shoestring*. To get away from the road, she takes to the skies, flying hot-air balloons.

Julia lives in Wiltshire, south-western England, with her husband, LP author John King, and their two children.

From the Author

My thanks must first go to the Turismo de Lisboa, especially Miguel Gonzaga, Vitor Carriço, Rosário Gomes and Sandra Sequeira, for their hospitality and patient responses to my never-ending queries. Stalwarts Jorge Cosme and Pedro Ribeiro at Guidespy remained amazingly calm when faced with a stream of faxes and emails, as did Miranda Jessop of ICEP's PR outfit, KTA International, and Isabel Silva, Fátima Elias, Vera Morais and Catarinha Cunha of the Instituto Nacional de Estatistica. I'm also indebted to Geraldine Aherne at TAP Air Portugal and Amélia Paulo Vieira and Susana Lopez of Sintra's turismo who once again demonstrated their amazing efficiency.

Thanks are due also to Dra Helena Taborda and Sara Plácido of the Metropolitano de Lisboa for photos of the metro's modern art and to Lisbon transport expert, John Laidlar, for writing about it. The Fundação Calouste Gulbenkian's Alexandra Lopes Almeida kept me in touch with Gulbenkian goings-on while Parque das Nações spokespersons, João Paulo Velez and Katia Peres, made sure I left no *calzada portuguesa* (cobbled pavement) pattern un-turned in the park.

Without recommendations from journalist, Hans de Clercq, I would never have found some great restaurants in the Alfama – or been encouraged to discover the magic of José Saramago's poetical prose. Michael Collins of the Portuguese Arts Trust shared his vast knowledge of Lisbon's art world (particularly its fado) while Gareth Evans put me right on the state of Portugal's cinema industry.

Manuel Morais of ILGA-Portugal and António Serzedelo of Opus Gay both proved invaluable in providing information on Lisbon's gay and lesbian scene. David Sandhu stoically suffered a few hangovers to help update the Entertainment and Shopping chapters. And Clara Vitorino (LP's *Portuguese phrasebook* author) and husband Dionisio offered welcome companionship in Lisbon and help with my pidgin Portuguese.

Lastly, a special *obrigada* to my husband, John King, for his editorial eagle-eye, and for holding the fort at home.

This Book

Julia Wilkinson researched and wrote the 1st edition of *Lisbon* and also revised and updated this 2nd edition. In 2000, the Turismo de Lisboa – Visitors & Convention Bureau awarded the 1st edition of *Lisbon* with one of five 'Best Travel Guide Awards' to the city.

From the Publisher

This 2nd edition of *Lisbon* was edited in Lonely Planet's Melbourne office by Yvonne Byron, with assistance from Anne Mulvaney. Design and mapping were coordinated by Adrian Persoglia. Quentin Frayne edited the Language chapter and Maria Vallianos designed the cover. Thanks also to Yvonne Bischofberger, Lisa Borg, Matt King, Gus Poó y Balbontin and Jacqui Saunders. Barbara Dombrowski and Valerie Tellini assisted with photographs from Lonely Planet Images.

Thanks

Many thanks to the following travellers who used the 1st edition of *Lisbon* and wrote to us with helpful hints, useful advice and interesting anecdotes:

Philip Agre, Marisa Alexandra, Dirk Beiersdorf, Terry Birtles, Duncan Brimmel, M Broch, Luis Costa, Ben De Pauw, Ana Sofia e Guilherme, Ines Fontes, Clara Gomes Kris Helsen, Miki Jablkowska, Gundorph K Kristiansen, Michelle Matsui, C LeMoiznan, Lucia Miele, Ippolito Nievo, Thomas Olsen, John Osman, Suzy Provost, Geri Ramos, Andrea Rogge, Ralph Scoggin, Ruth Siwinski, Michael Stringer, Ted Stroll, Karl Sutton, Wei Teng, Angelo Volandes, R Watts, Viktor Weisshaeupl, Peter Wheeler, Marjorie Willcody, Dorothee Winden.

Foreword

ABOUT LONELY PLANET GUIDEBOOKS

The story begins with a classic travel adventure: Tony and Maureen Wheeler's 1972 journey across Europe and Asia to Australia. Useful information about the overland trail did not exist at that time, so Tony and Maureen published the first Lonely Planet guidebook to meet a growing need.

From a kitchen table, then from a tiny office in Melbourne (Australia), Lonely Planet has become the largest independent travel publisher in the world, an international company with offices in Melbourne, Oakland (USA), London (UK) and Paris (France).

Today Lonely Planet guidebooks cover the globe. There is an ever-growing list of books and there's information in a variety of forms and media. Some things haven't changed. The main aim is still to help make it possible for adventurous travellers to get out there – to explore and better understand the world.

At Lonely Planet we believe travellers can make a positive contribution to the countries they visit – if they respect their host communities and spend their money wisely. Since 1986 a percentage of the income from each book has been donated to aid projects and human rights campaigns.

Updates Lonely Planet thoroughly updates each guidebook as often as possible. This usually means there are around two years between editions, although for more unusual or more stable destinations the gap can be longer. Check the imprint page (following the colour map at the beginning of the book) for publication dates.

Between editions up-to-date information is available in two free newsletters – the paper *Planet Talk* and email *Comet* (to subscribe, contact any Lonely Planet office) – and on our Web site at www.lonelyplanet.com. The *Upgrades* section of the Web site covers a number of important and volatile destinations and is regularly updated by Lonely Planet authors. *Scoop* covers news and current affairs relevant to travellers. And, lastly, the *Thorn Tree* bulletin board and *Postcards* section of the site carry unverified, but fascinating, reports from travellers.

Correspondence The process of creating new editions begins with the letters, postcards and emails received from travellers. This correspondence often includes suggestions, criticisms and comments about the current editions. Interesting excerpts are immediately passed on via newsletters and the Web site, and everything goes to our authors to be verified when they're researching on the road. We're keen to get more feedback from organisations or individuals who represent communities visited by travellers.

Lonely Planet gathers information for everyone who's curious about the planet – and especially for those who explore it first-hand. Through guidebooks, phrasebooks, activity guides, maps, literature, newsletters, image library, TV series and Web site we act as an information exchange for a worldwide community of travellers.

6

Research Authors aim to gather sufficient practical information to enable travellers to make informed choices and to make the mechanics of a journey run smoothly. They also research historical and cultural background to help enrich the travel experience and allow travellers to understand and respond appropriately to cultural and environmental issues.

Authors don't stay in every hotel because that would mean spending a couple of months in each medium-sized city and, no, they don't eat at every restaurant because that would mean stretching belts beyond capacity. They do visit hotels and restaurants to check standards and prices, but feedback based on readers' direct experiences can be very helpful.

Many of our authors work undercover, others aren't so secretive. None of them accept freebies in exchange for positive write-ups. And none of our guidebooks contain any advertising.

Production Authors submit their raw manuscripts and maps to offices in Australia, USA, UK or France. Editors and cartographers – all experienced travellers themselves – then begin the process of assembling the pieces. When the book finally hits the shops, some things are already out of date, we start getting feedback from readers and the process begins again …

WARNING & REQUEST

Things change – prices go up, schedules change, good places go bad and bad places go bankrupt – nothing stays the same. So, if you find things better or worse, recently opened or long since closed, please tell us and help make the next edition even more accurate and useful. We genuinely value all the feedback we receive. A well travelled team reads and acknowledges every letter, postcard and email and ensures that every morsel of information finds its way to the appropriate authors, editors and cartographers for verification.

Everyone who writes to us will find their name in the next edition of the appropriate guidebook. They will also receive the latest issue of *Planet Talk*, our quarterly printed newsletter, or *Comet*, our monthly email newsletter. Subscriptions to both newsletters are free. The very best contributions will be rewarded with a free guidebook.

Excerpts from your correspondence may appear in new editions of Lonely Planet guidebooks, the Lonely Planet Web site, *Planet Talk* or *Comet*, so please let us know if you *don't* want your letter published or your name acknowledged.

Send all correspondence to the Lonely Planet office closest to you:

Australia: Locked Bag 1, Footscray, Victoria 3011
USA: 150 Linden St, Oakland, CA 94607
UK: 10A Spring Place, London NW5 3BH
France: 1 rue du Dahomey, 75011 Paris

Or email us at: talk2us@lonelyplanet.com.au

For news, views and updates see our Web site: www.lonelyplanet.com

HOW TO USE A LONELY PLANET GUIDEBOOK

The best way to use a Lonely Planet guidebook is any way you choose. At Lonely Planet we believe the most memorable travel experiences are often those that are unexpected, and the finest discoveries are those you make yourself. Guidebooks are not intended to be used as if they provide a detailed set of infallible instructions!

Contents All Lonely Planet guidebooks follow roughly the same format. The Facts about the Destination chapters or sections give background information ranging from history to weather. Facts for the Visitor gives practical information on issues like visas and health. Getting There & Away gives a brief starting point for researching travel to and from the destination. Getting Around gives an overview of the transport options when you arrive.

The peculiar demands of each destination determine how subsequent chapters are broken up, but some things remain constant. We always start with background, then proceed to sights, places to stay, places to eat, entertainment, getting there and away, and getting around information – in that order.

Heading Hierarchy Lonely Planet headings are used in a strict hierarchical structure that can be visualised as a set of Russian dolls. Each heading (and its following text) is encompassed by any preceding heading that is higher on the hierarchical ladder.

Entry Points We do not assume guidebooks will be read from beginning to end, but that people will dip into them. The traditional entry points are the list of contents and the index. In addition, however, some books have a complete list of maps and an index map illustrating map coverage.

There may also be a colour map that shows highlights. These highlights are dealt with in greater detail in the Facts for the Visitor chapter, along with planning questions and suggested itineraries. Each chapter covering a geographical region usually begins with a locator map and another list of highlights. Once you find something of interest in a list of highlights, turn to the index.

Maps Maps play a crucial role in Lonely Planet guidebooks and include a huge amount of information. A legend is printed on the back page. We seek to have complete consistency between maps and text, and to have every important place in the text captured on a map. Map key numbers usually start in the top left corner.

Although inclusion in a guidebook usually implies a recommendation we cannot list every good place. Exclusion does not necessarily imply criticism. In fact there are a number of reasons why we might exclude a place – sometimes it is simply inappropriate to encourage an influx of travellers.

Introduction

Lisbon is an enticing tangle of times past and present. It's funky and old-fashioned, unpretentious and quirky, yet booming with new money and new confidence. Its position on seven low hills beside the Rio Tejo (River Tagus) was the main attraction for traders and settlers in centuries past, and it's still a stunning site. Add to that today's cultural diversity, its laid-back ambience and a time-warp of architecture, and you have one of the most enjoyable cities in Europe. And, despite recently rising prices, Lisbon is still an economical destination, worth considering as a base for several nearby day trips after you've meandered around the city.

Apart from its muscle-aching hills – most enjoyably tackled by a bevy of funiculars and a few cranky old trams that hiss and zing through the streets – Lisbon is small enough to explore on foot (don't even try to drive; roadworks, traffic and parking are a nightmare). At its heart are wide, tree-lined avenues graced by Art Nouveau buildings, mosaic pavements and street cafes, while the Alfama district below Castelo de São Jorge is a warren of narrow old streets redolent of Lisbon's Moorish and medieval past. Seen from the river – one of the city's many great viewpoints – Lisbon is an impressionist picture of low-rise ochre and pastel, punctuated by church towers and domes.

But it has also experienced some massive redevelopment in recent years. Although the Alfama and Chiado districts have seen some sensitive restoration projects, many fine old buildings have given way to office blocks. Once-sleepy old Lisbon is now on a helter-skelter ride to modernisation, thanks to an expanding economy, the attention it received as host to the millennium's last exposition, Expo '98, and the flurry of still more infrastructure projects in the lead-up to the country hosting the Euro 2004 Football Championships.

The resulting contrasts can be startling – among the jackhammers and new high-rises are still some seedy backstreets in Alfama and Cais do Sodré. And though the traffic is increasingly frenzied, the main squares of Lisbon retain a caravanserai character, with lingering lottery ticket-sellers, shoe-shiners, itinerant hawkers and pavement artists.

You'll still find plenty of history and culture, from the magnificent Manueline masterpieces at Belém to the world-class Calouste Gulbenkian Museum. But there are pulsating new rhythms here too, most noticeably in the African clubs popping up everywhere as the communities from Portugal's former African colonies respond to a growing demand for their music. Nothing could be further from the soul-searing strains of the uniquely Portuguese *fado* songs (which originated in the Alfama district). Traditionalists may be disappointed, but this is definitely a city on the move.

When you're ready for a break, you have the option of day trips to the massive monastery at Mafra or the rococo palace at Queluz, seaside frolics in Sesimbra, Ericeira, Costa da Caparica or Cascais, or walks in the enchanting wooded hills of Sintra, a Unesco World Heritage Site. You can get to any of these within an hour or two and still be back in time for tea at one of Lisbon's Art Deco street cafes, to watch the city's amazing world go by.

Facts about Lisbon

HISTORY
Pre-Roman, Roman & Moorish Periods

Legend has it that Lisbon was founded by Ulysses but it was probably the Phoenicians who first settled here some 3000 years ago, attracted by the fine harbour and strategic hill of São Jorge. They called the city Alis Ubbo ('delightful shore'). Others soon saw its delightful qualities too; the Greeks ejected the Phoenicians and were in turn booted out by the Carthaginians.

In 205 BC the Romans arrived in the city, known then as Olisipo, managing to hold onto it for the next two centuries. Julius Caesar raised its rank (and changed its name to Felicitas Julia), making it the most important city in Lusitania, the western region of the Iberian Peninsula. You are still able to see the remains of a Roman theatre just north of the cathedral, and a fascinating catacomb in the Baixa, which may have been a Roman spa or part of a temple's foundations (see the Things to See & Do chapter for details of visits).

Following the Romans, a succession of northern tribes – Alans, Suevi and Visigoths – occupied Lisbon, but in 714 the powerful Moors arrived from Morocco. They fortified the city they called Lissabona and repelled occasional attacks by Christian forces for the next 400 years. Among the Moors' significant contributions to the city were a mosque (built on the site of the present-day cathedral) and a rebuilt castle, surrounded by strong walls that snaked downhill via Largo das Portas do Sol through the Alfama to the riverfront. One of the few bits of this wall still clearly visible is a tower at Largo de São Rafael.

Age of Discoveries & Riches

Finally, in 1147, after a four-month siege, the Christians under Dom (King) Afonso Henriques recaptured the city (see the boxed text 'The Siege of Lisbon' in the Things to See & Do chapter). However it was another century before the Reconquista (the reconquest of Portugal by Christian forces) was completely successful. A few years later, in 1255, Afonso III asserted Lisbon's pre-eminence by making it the country's capital in place of Coimbra. Thanks to far-sighted rulers such as Dom Dinis (1279-1325) the city's development was swift and, despite plague and earthquakes, the population swelled as both maritime and inland trade surged.

During 1385, a showdown between the Portuguese under João, Grand Master of the Order of Aviz, and the far greater forces of the (Spanish) Castilians at Aljubarrota resulted in an extraordinary victory, sealing Portugal's independence and putting João on the throne. Dom João I's military commander, Nuno Álvares Pereira, later built the Convento do Carmo, whose ruins still stand as one of the most striking sights in central Lisbon.

The 15th century was without doubt the city's most glorious period, largely thanks to Prince Henrique ('Henry the Navigator', the son of Dom João I and his English wife Philippa of Lancaster). Determined to sap the power of Islam by finding a way around

Seeking the riches of the New World

LPP

it by sea, Henrique set about collecting the best sailors, map makers, shipbuilders and astronomers he could find. Funded by the Order of Christ (which had superseded the religious military order, the crusading Knights Templar) he sent his revolutionary caravels off into the unknown. His ships soon began returning with West African gold and slaves.

By the time Henrique died in 1460, he had set Portugal on course for its so-called Age of Discoveries, turning it into a wealthy maritime power. The climax came after his death, when in 1497 Vasco da Gama set sail from Belém and, during a two-year voyage, discovered the longed-for sea route to India. With spices from the East now adding to the riches from Africa, Lisbon became the opulent seat of a vast empire, its monarchy and nobility wallowing in riches. Merchants flocked to the city, trading in gold and spices, silks and precious stones. Under Dom Manuel I, the extravagant architectural style that came to be called Manueline – typified by the Mosteiro dos Jerónimos at Belém – complemented Lisbon's role as the world's most prosperous trading centre.

Spanish Rule

By the 1570s, the huge cost of expeditions and the maintenance of an overseas empire had begun to take their toll. The expulsion of commercially minded refugee Spanish Jews in 1496 and the subsequent persecution of converted Jews – New Christians, or *marranos* – during the Inquisition only served to worsened the financial situation.

The final straw came in 1557 when the young idealist prince Sebastião took the throne. Determined to bring Christianity to Morocco, he rallied a huge force and set off in 1578, but was disastrously defeated; he and 8000 others were killed, including most of the Portuguese nobility. Over the next few years, his aged successor, Cardinal Henrique, had to drain the royal coffers to ransom those captured.

On Cardinal Henrique's death in 1580, Sebastião's uncle, Felipe II of Spain, claimed the throne, defeated the Portuguese and was crowned Felipe I of Portugal. It was a bitter

Lisbon's Great Earthquake

It was 9.30 am on All Saints' Day, 1 November, in 1755 when the great earthquake struck. Many residents were caught inside churches, celebrating High Mass, as three major tremors hit in quick succession. So strong was the earthquake that its effects were felt as far away as Scotland and the Caribbean. In its wake came an even more devastating fire – helped on its way by the flickering church candles – and a tidal wave that submerged the quay and destroyed the lower town.

At least 13,000 of the city's 270,000 people perished (some estimates put it at three times as many) and much of the city was devastated. Although Lisbon had suffered previous earthquakes – notably in 1531 and 1597 – there had been nothing on this scale.

Dom João I's minister, the redoubtable Marquês de Pombal, proved to be the man of the moment, efficiently handling the catastrophe (though it was actually the Marquês de Alorna who uttered the famous words 'we must bury the dead, and feed the living') and rebuilding the city in a revolutionary new 'Pombal' style.

Lisbon recovered, but many of its glorious monuments and artworks were obliterated and it lost its role as Europe's leading port and finest city.

blow to national pride. Resentment finally exploded in 1640. A group of nationalist leaders forced the unpopular woman governor from her Lisbon office and drove out the Spanish garrisons. The Duke of Bragança reluctantly stepped into the hot seat and was crowned João IV. Preoccupied with wars elsewhere, Spain made only half-hearted attempts to recapture Portugal and finally recognised Portugal's independence in 1668.

Meanwhile, Lisbon was enjoying another period of profligate expenditure, thanks to the discovery of gold in Brazil. However the extravagance was short-lived. A massive earthquake in 1755 (see the boxed text 'Lisbon's Great Earthquake') turned everything to rubble, and Lisbon never regained its power and prestige.

Troubles of the Republic & Revolution

After Napoleon's forces occupied the city in November 1807 (they were finally repulsed in 1811 by a joint British and Portuguese force), Lisbon descended with the rest of the country into political chaos and military insurrection. A radical, nationalist republican movement started to sweep the lower middle classes in Lisbon, Porto and the south. In 1908, at the height of the movement, Dom Carlos and his eldest son were assassinated as they rode in a carriage through the streets of Lisbon. Following an uprising by military officers on 5 October 1910, a republic was declared. But hopes that this would stabilise the country were overly optimistic; the republican factions squabbled, the economy disintegrated into tatters (especially after the strain of military operations in WWI) and the military became increasingly powerful. Over the next 16 years there were 45 changes of government and another high-profile assassination (President Sidónio Pais, at Lisbon's Rossio train station in 1918).

A further coup in 1926 introduced a new name onto the scene: António de Oliveira Salazar, who quickly rose from finance minister to prime minister, a post he was to hold for 36 years. In 1933 he announced a 'New State' that was nationalistic, authoritarian, fascist and repressive. Political parties and strikes were banned. Censorship, propaganda and brute force kept society in order. The only good news was that the economy markedly improved. During WWII, Salazar played two hands, allowing the British to use airfield facilities in the Azores and authorising the transfer of Nazi-looted gold from Switzerland to Portugal, while claiming official neutrality. Not surprisingly, Lisbon developed a reputation as a nest of spies.

Salazar died in 1970, leaving a country again teetering on the brink of chaos thanks to increasingly unpopular military expeditions to put down independence movements in Portugal's African colonies. On 25 April 1974, a nearly bloodless coup, later nicknamed the Revolution of the Carnations (after victorious soldiers stuck carnations into the barrels of their rifles), ushered in independence to the colonies and yet another turbulent period at home, with more political turbulence.

Contemporary Lisbon

The immediate effect on Lisbon was the influx of hundreds of thousands of refugees *(retornados)* from the former African colonies, a social upheaval it eventually managed remarkably well. But social and political unrest continued. It wasn't until 1986 – when Portugal was admitted to the European Union (at that time the European Community) and the veteran socialist leader, Mário Saores, became the country's first civilian president in 60 years – that Lisbon finally began to shake off its depressed Salazar-era looks and lifestyle.

Membership of the EU coincided with a stable, centre-right government that lasted a record 10 years. It also led to massive EU funding (especially welcome in Lisbon after a major fire in 1988 destroyed the Chiado district). In 1994, the city returned to the limelight as European City of Culture. The following years of spectacular economic growth were boosted by some major infrastructure projects such as the Ponte de Vasco da Gama (the longest river crossing in Portugal). Redevelopment schemes have included restoration of historic neighbourhoods such as the Alfama.

The most spectacular developments have been along the Rio Tejo riverfront, where derelict warehouses have become chic restaurants and bars beside spanking-new marinas and promenades. Most notable of all, a 60-hectare polluted industrial wasteland on the north-eastern riverfront has been transformed into the focus of the largest urban regeneration project ever seen in Portugal. This is where Lisbon established its high-profile appearance as the host of Expo '98. In the run-up to the Expo, the metro was expanded, port facilities were extended, hotel construction went into high gear and leading architects were drafted in to create some stunning monuments.

Expo '98 – whose theme was 'The Oceans' – confirmed the city's re-emergence on the world stage and set the tone for the new millennium. Lisbon has now regained some pride in its past and, with a revitalised and vibrant urban life and more huge infrastructure projects planned (notably a new airport scheduled to open in 2010), looks forward to a future firmly within Europe.

GEOGRAPHY

Lisbon has a superb position on the north bank of the Rio Tejo, some 15km inland from the Atlantic Ocean. Just east of the city's Ponte 25 de Abril, the Tejo broadens into a bay 11km wide called the Mar de Palha (Sea of Straw), which forms Portugal's finest natural harbour.

The city is spread over seven low-lying hills, each providing splendid *miradouros* (viewpoints). But it's also built over several geological fault lines, which caused earthquakes during the 14th and 15th centuries, and the disastrous earthquake of 1755. There have been only slight seismic tremors during the past century.

On excursions from Lisbon, you'll find enormous varieties of landscape. To the south are the vast sandy coastline of the Costa da Caparica and the inland Mediterranean woods of the Serra da Arrábida; and to the north-west, the craggy cliffs of the Cabo da Roca (the westernmost point of Europe) and the lush forested hills of the Serra de Sintra.

CLIMATE

Lisbon lies in both the Atlantic and Mediterranean climatic zones, thereby enjoying a pleasantly temperate climate year-round. Its mean annual temperature is 17°C, with average temperatures in winter of 13°C and 27°C in summer. Even when summer temperatures reach the mid-30s, the proximity of the Atlantic Ocean insures some cooling breezes.

The city receives an average of 666mm of rain annually (not bad, considering the national average of 1100mm), most of it falling during the winter months. July and August are the hottest, driest months, while November to February are the wettest and coldest.

The granite Serra de Sintra (see Sintra in the Excursions chapter) hosts a series of

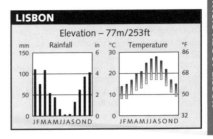

LISBON

Elevation – 77m/253ft

climatic phenomena that results in considerably cooler, damper conditions than in Lisbon, with frequent mists that occur even in midsummer.

ECOLOGY & ENVIRONMENT

Before Portugal joined the EU in 1986, Lisbon was one of the most run-down cities in Europe, its streets littered and potholed and several areas such as the Alfama suffering almost medieval living conditions. Some places (eg, around Cais do Sodré) are still pretty bad, but massive EU funding, increased demands from tourism and the infrastructural improvements for Expo '98 have resulted in huge changes. In historic areas such as the Alfama you'll still see major restoration works being undertaken by the Equipamentos dos Bairros Históricos de Lisboa (EBAHL).

Many *lisboêtas* are increasingly aware of their urban environment and are demanding continued improvements, although environmental issues are still low on the agenda. The booming economy, for example, has caused a surge in Lisbon's traffic (and air pollution), but there are few calls to restrict the use of private cars in the city.

One of the greatest environmental success stories is the Expo '98 site. Once a dangerously polluted factory area, it had a two-year clean-up before the event and now boasts a vast and spacious entertainment complex (Parque das Nações) dotted with gardens (see the Flora & Fauna section later in this chapter).

The Parque das Nações is at the core of the 340-hectare Expo Urbe regeneration project, which will continue until 2009. Already featuring residential, office and commercial buildings, and a recreational harbour, its latest addition is an 80-hectare 'green leisure zone', the Parque do Tejo e do Trancão, once a refuse landfill site. It's due for completion in 2002. Another new park is nearing completion on the northern fringes of Parque Eduardo VII, an area once threatened by encroaching development.

The World Heritage Site of Sintra is also taking some notable environmental steps forward. It has banned tour buses from its historical centre, reinstated an eco-friendly tram, and is now planning a traffic-free zone and electric buses.

Environmental Organisations

Portugal's most active environmental group is Quercus: Associação Nacional de Conservação da Natureza (National Association for the Conservation of Nature; ☎ 217 788 474, fax 217 787 749, **e** quercus@esoterica.pt), Bairro do Calhau, Parque Florestal de Monsanto, Apartado 4333, 1503-003 Lisbon (with a branch office at 139 Rua do Salitre 3-A that is open 3 to 7 pm weekdays only; Map 5).

Founded in 1985, Quercus has some 12,000 members, 19 branch offices, and a Web site at www.quercus.pt (Portuguese only). In addition to carrying out studies of Portugal's flora, fauna and ecosystems, and publishing environmental guides to specific areas, Quercus members bring issues to public and government attention through regular campaigns. Some branches arrange field trips, though information is hard to come by; low-budget and largely volunteer-run, Quercus has yet to develop an efficient public relations system.

Another activist group arranging weekend trips is GEOTA (Grupo de Estudos de Ordenomento do Território e Ambiente, or Environment Study Group; ☎ 213 956 120, fax 213 955 316, **e** geota@mail.telepac.pt), Travessa do Moinho de Vento 17, 1200-727 Lisbon. Also in the front line is the Liga para a Proteção da Natureza (League for the Protection of Nature; ☎ 217 780 097, fax 217 783 208, **e** lpn.natureza@mail .telepac.pt), Estrela do Calhariz de Benfica 187, 1500-124 Lisbon.

An organisation with a special brief is the Sociedade Portuguesa para o Estudo das Aves (Portuguese Society for the Study of Birds; ☎/fax 213 431 847, **e** spea@ip.pt), Rua da Vitória 53, 1100-618 Lisbon.

FLORA & FAUNA
Flora

Lisbon's city council, which recently planted 50,000 trees (mostly palms) along major avenues, has been working hard to boost the city's green space. In 2000, Lisbon won the Nations in Flower international prize for environmental management.

There's now a total of some 700,000 trees of around 200 different species, including plane trees and horse chestnuts, poplars (especially along Avenida 24 de Julho), elms (Avenida da Liberdade), jacarandas (Rua Castilho), and ancient olive trees (Belém). Some individual trees have become quite famous, such as the vast cedar in the Praça do Príncipe Real or the giant sequoia in Jardim de Parada.

The city's largest green lung is the 1000-hectare Parque Florestal de Monsanto, a densely wooded area west of the centre dating from the 1940s and thick with European pines and oaks. Several smaller parks in the city centre offer a surprising variety. Lisbon supports a mixture of Atlantic and Mediterranean (or European) floral species, as well as many other species of foreign origin, introduced during Portugal's colonisation era or in the 18th or 19th centuries

> ### National Parks
>
> The government agency responsible for the overall management, publicity and policy of the country's parks and nature reserves is the Instituto da Concervação Natureza (ICN; Map 2; ☎ 213 523 317, fax 213 542 501, **e** icn@icn.pt), Rua da Lapa 29-A, Lisbon. It has general information on the parks (and a Web site at www.icn.pt, in Portuguese only), but most individual park offices are better equipped and staffed and have maps, brochures and information on trails and accommodation.

when it was fashionable to sport a thuja fir or two in the back garden.

Charming, subtropical Jardim Botânico, which was established in 1874, has cacti and palms filling its small hillside site. The venerable and more formal Jardim Botânico da Ajuda (opposite the Palácio Nacional da Ajuda) was created even earlier. In the largest central park, the Parque Eduardo VII, you'll find two greenhouses dedicated to exotic species and rare tropical plants, ranging from palms and poinsettias to pineapple plants.

Some of the most recent additions to the city's flora can be found in the Parque das Nações. Here, in the Jardins Garcia de Orta (named after a 16th-century Portuguese doctor who spent 30 years in India studying plants and their medicinal uses), 10 regions of the world are represented by 2300 plants from 420 different species.

Not far from the city are several other areas to delight botanists, including Parque Natural da Arrábida and Parque Natural de Sintra-Cascais (see the Excursions chapter for details).

Fauna

The nearest place to catch sight of some wildlife is Parque Florestal de Monsanto, which harbours wild ferrets, weasels, bats and a fairly new colony of squirrels (once extinct in Portugal). There's a wide range of birds including woodpeckers, finches, owls and crows. Within the park is the 50-hectare Parque Ecológico (☎ 217 743 224), open 9.30 am to 5 pm Tuesday to Saturday and 2 to 5 pm on Sunday. This restricted zone has wetland areas hosting many species of flora and fauna and a visitor centre (largely geared to local schoolchildren). Visits must be booked in advance.

For birdlife on a grand scale, arrange a visit to the Reserva Natural do Estuário do Tejo, upriver from Lisbon. A vitally important wetland area, it hosts around 40,000 migrant wading birds during the winter, including avocets and teals. The reserve's headquarters (☎ 212 341 742, fax 212 341 654, e rnet@icn.pt), Avenida dos Combatentes da Grande Guerra 1, Alcochete, is accessible from Montijo (a ferry ride from Lisbon's Terreiro do Paço terminal).

On the Setúbal Peninsula south of Lisbon, Reserva Natural do Estuário do Sado is great for spotting storks and little egrets as well as migrant flamingos. And if you're into insects (especially beetles and butterflies) you'll love the peninsula's Parque Natural da Arrábida. Mammal life includes the wild cat, mongoose and bat. Lording over it all are some magnificent birds of prey. Setúbal's Sado Estuary is home to a community of some 30 bottlenose dolphins.

Parque Natural de Sintra-Cascais hosts a variety of birdlife including razorbills, gannets and puffins. In the wilder parts of the Serra de Sintra fly buzzards and tawny owls. Animal species are less varied, though there are plenty of foxes, rabbits, snakes and lizards.

Fancy seeing one of Portugal's most endangered species? If you're lucky you may catch a glimpse of one of 26 Iberian wolves at the Iberian Wolf Recovery Centre near Mafra (some 40km north of Lisbon).

For more details on all of these wildlife havens (as well as information on dolphin-watching tours), see the Excursions chapter.

GOVERNMENT & POLITICS

The administrative Região de Lisboa e Vale do Tejo (RLVT) extends over an area of 11,890 sq km from Tomar in the north to Sesimbra in the south, and eastward as far as the Alentejo border. Within this region are 52 *concelhos* (municipal councils), run by an assembly (a mayor and 16 other members), elected by popular vote for a four-year term. These councils are comprised of 526 *freguesias* (parish councils); there are 53 alone in the council of the Cidade de Lisboa (City of Lisbon). These freguesias are also governed by an assembly elected by popular vote under a system of proportional representation. The national ruling left-of-centre Socialist Party (Partido Socialista, which was returned to power in the 1999 elections), under Prime Minister António Guterres, currently controls most of the councils.

The City of Lisbon concelho is the most important and densely populated within the region. It covers an area of 84 sq km, extending to the suburb of Charneca in the north, Benfica in the west, and all along the Tejo Estuary in the east. The concelho's responsibilities include road maintenance, water services and sanitation as well as urban redevelopment and care of the city's architectural heritage.

Its current mayor, João Soares, has been in office since 1993. The next elections will be held in December 2001.

ECONOMY

Not long ago, Portugal was among Europe's poorest nations, its economy a shambles, inflation and unemployment rates appalling and the trade deficit a nightmare. Today its growth rate (about 3.2%) outstrips the European average (2.8%), inflation flutters at around 2.5% and the unemployment rate (5%) is one of Europe's lowest. Since it joined the euro currency zone in 1999, Portugal has been one of its star performers. Lisbon, as the country's largest commercial and financial services centre, and with one of its most important ports, has benefited from this dramatically.

The turnaround started in 1985 when the centre-right Partido Social Democrata (PSD) came to power. Over the next decade the government introduced a wide range of reforms and launched an ambitious privatisation program (which continued even under the Socialist government), while the EU pumped massive funds into the country.

Fuelled by huge infrastructure investment, especially in Lisbon, in the late 1990s Portugal enjoyed growing prosperity and rapid development, particularly in the financial, services and communications sectors. With preparations under way for the Euro 2004 Football Championships and a new Lisbon airport creating further building projects and investment, the future looks rosy, especially for the capital.

But there are some grim realities. Years of rapid growth have widened the gulf between the rich and poor, with a growing incidence of urban poverty. Lisbon has several appalling shanty towns (eg, Casal Ventoso, west of Estrela) and depressing, drug-riddled housing estates. Despite a glossy public face, Portugal is in fact the poorest of the euro zone's founding members, with typical wages at the bottom of the EU scale.

Tourism, however, is booming. Some 10 million tourists visit Portugal each year (over two million visit Lisbon), contributing US$4.4 billion in foreign exchange earnings. Lisbon has witnessed an 8.8% increase in airport passenger traffic, a jump from 25th to eighth place in its ranking as a popular international congress centre, and a surge in the number of visiting cruise ships. Lisbon's port is now the top-ranking Atlantic seaport of Europe.

Lisbon's commercial port activity is also thriving. With its docks, warehouses and quays stretching some 20km along the Tejo riverside, it handles millions of tonnes of traffic a year. A major new container terminal is under construction at Xabregas (near Parque das Nações).

The city's biggest industrial development is focused south of the Tejo, all the way down to and including Setúbal (50km away). Here are steel, cork and plastics factories and one of the world's largest cement plants. But the action is now focussed on massive manufacturing projects funded by foreign investment. Just north of Setúbal, the Volkswagen-run Autoeuropa car plant employs over 10,000 people to produce around 150,000 Ford and VW minivans annually, 98% for export.

POPULATION & PEOPLE

The Lisboa e Vale do Tejo region has a population of 3.3 million, over one-third of the national population. Around 15% are under 24 years old and 15% over 65. The City of Lisbon accounts for only 535,740 of this population, and that number is continually falling; in 1981 there were more than 807,000 residents.

Migration to the suburbs (or even farther afield) is due to lack of housing within the city centre, the cost of existing housing and the growing dissatisfaction with Lisbon's run-down residential areas. Major urban regeneration and housing projects, such as Expo Urbe (see Ecology & Environment

St Anthony's Brides

In 1997, Lisbon's mayor, João Soares, revived a charming Lisbon tradition, the Noivas de Santo António (literally 'Brides of St Anthony'), offering couples the chance to marry around St Anthony's Day (13 June) in the Igreja de Santo António, with expenses paid by the municipal authorities and commercial sponsors.

In the past, the free marriage was offered only to less-well-off couples (and to virgin brides!). These days, the idea behind the revival is to lure youngsters back into living in Lisbon rather than heading for the suburbs. Two of the requirements are that the bride or groom must be living in Lisbon and that they will live in the city once they are wed.

earlier) will help to alleviate the problem, but the mayor of Lisbon is also resorting to some novel ideas, such as all-expenses-paid weddings (see the boxed text 'St Anthony's Brides'), to entice young people to stay in the city.

Although Lisbon's population was boosted in the 1960s by African immigrant workers (especially from Cape Verde; there are now 26,400 Cape Verdeans in Lisbon), the biggest recent jump in population was in the mid-1970s, with the influx of nearly one million retornados following the independence of Portugal's African colonies. Many settled in the Lisbon area. In the late 1970s African refugees from war-torn Angola and Mozambique also arrived, followed more recently by refugees from Guinea-Bissau and São Tomé e Príncipe. Brazilians also now make up a sizable community (20,000 nationwide).

Many Africans have picked up work in Lisbon's booming construction industry. However, the continuing poverty of their lives and living conditions (eg, in suburban slums such as Bairro das Fontainhas to the north) is a depressing indication of government and national neglect of the growing Afro-Portuguese community.

As a visitor, however, you're more likely to be aware of the vibrancy of this community than its hardships. African music and cuisine is now all the rage in many Lisbon nightclubs and restaurants. At the heart of town, the Rossio is a constant caravanserai of groups chatting or selling wares. There appears to be little overt racism. However, traditional rivalries between Angolans and Cape Verdeans is fanning ethnic tensions, resulting in a vicious turf war on the nightclub scene (see Dangers & Annoyances in the Facts for the Visitor chapter).

ARTS
Music
Lisbon's most internationally famous style of music is *fado*. These bluesy, melancholic chants – performed as a set of three songs, each one lasting three minutes – are said to have their roots in troubadour songs (although African slave songs have also had an influence). They're traditionally sung by one performer accompanied by a 12-string Portuguese *guitarra* (a pear-shaped guitar), and often a Spanish guitar as well. Fado emerged in the 18th century in Lisbon's working-class districts of Alfama and Mouraria and gradually moved upmarket. A more academic version developed later in the university town of Coimbra.

The greatest modern *fadista* – who brought fado international recognition – was Amália Rodrigues, who died in 1999, aged 79 (see the boxed text 'Amália'). Amália's recordings are still the best; listen to *Com Que Voz* or *O Melhor* to hear what fado should really sound like.

A notable contemporary artist is dynamic young Mísia, considered a leading exponent of a new fado style. She has experimented with instrumentation (including piano, accordion and violin in addition to the usual guitar) and commissioned lyrics by contemporary poets. Her *Garras dos Sentidos* (Claws of the Heart) CD is particularly fine.

Venues to experience live fado in Lisbon are recommended in the Entertainment chapter. See also the Facts for the Visitor chapter for details about the city's new Festival do Fado, and the Things to See & Do chapter for information about a museum dedicated to its history, the Casa do Fado e da Guitarra Portuguesa.

Amália

Amália Rodrigues, the world's greatest singer of fado, who died in 1999, was born in Lisbon in 1920 to a poor, working-class family. Her career took off when, at 18, she won a 'Queen of Fado' competition. A triumphant trip to Madrid and Brazil followed.

During her long career (she continued singing well into her seventies), Amália made hundreds of records and several films and was famous as far afield as Japan. Dark and sultry looking, with a memorably dramatic stage presence, she often reduced her audience to tears. ('I don't sing fado,' she once said, 'it sings me.')

So revered was she in Portugal that when she died the government declared three days of mourning and gave her a full state funeral. 'Amália Rodrigues was the voice of the Portuguese soul,' explained Prime Minister Guterres to account for the outpouring of grief. A monument in her honour (Map 1), along Belém's riverside promenade continues to attract fans and mourners.

MARTIN HARRIS

The great *fadista* Amália

Both fado and traditional folk songs – and, increasingly, 'foreign' strains from Europe and Africa – have shaped Portugal's modern folk music scene (called *música popular*). It began to attract attention in the 1960s when musicians like José Afonso joined poets in a new musical movement dealing with social and political issues. Often censored during the Salazar years, its lyrics became overtly political after 1974, with singers' performances supporting various revolutionary factions. Today's música popular has returned to its folk roots while adding some contemporary innovations, thanks to singer-songwriters like Júlio Pereira.

The Portuguese guitar, too, has taken on a new range of expression under modern masters such as Carlos Paredes and António Chaínho. Well known folk groups include the venerable Brigada Victor Jara, Trovante, Almanaque and the internationally known Madredeus.

A popular genre in Lisbon is contemporary African jazz and rock. African nightclubs and dance halls now resonate to the rhythms of the former colonies. Traditional sounds include the melancholic *morna* from Cape Verde (best exemplified by Cesária Évora) or swinging *semba* from Angola (listen out for Guem or Waldemar Bastos). Fernando Luís from Mozambique and Kaba Mane from Guinea-Bissau are other big names. Newer, zappier versions of African music, such as zouk and Afro-techno kuduro, are also taking over the disco scene.

Literature

Portuguese literature has been moulded by foreign influences since the 13th century, notably by Spain's literary styles and standards. Nonetheless, Portuguese literature retains a distinct temperament and individuality. Two major styles dominate the field: lyric poetry and realistic fiction. No figure is more dominant than Luís Vaz de Camões (1524-80). Not until after his death was Camões' genius recognised, largely thanks to his epic poem, *Os Lusiadas* (The Lusiads), published in 1572, which relates the historic sea voyage by Vasco da Gama to India in 1497 while praising the greatness of the Portuguese spirit. It is now considered the national epic, its poet a national hero.

In the 19th century a tide of romanticism swept the Portuguese literary scene. Chief figurehead of this movement was the poet, playwright and novelist Almeida Garrett (1799-1854), who devoted much of his life to stimulating political awareness in Portugal through his writings. *Viagens na minha terra* (Travels in My Homeland) mixes fact and fiction in presenting a romantic episode that serves as an allegory of contemporary political events.

Towards the end of the 19th century a number of other notable writers emerged, among them José Maria Eça de Queirós, who introduced realism to Portuguese literature with his powerful 1876 novel, *O Crime do Padre Amaro* (The Sin of Father Amaro). His other outstanding works include the fascinating narratives of 19th-century life *Os Maias* (The Maias) and *A Illustre Casa de Ramires* (The Illustrious House of Ramires). Lisbon (especially the elegant Chiado district and Avenida da Liberdade) and romantic Sintra frequently served as backdrops to these *fin-de-siècle* novels.

Another 19th-century figure who is closely associated with Lisbon is the republican poet Cesário Verde. Verde, who died at the tragically early age of 31, brilliantly portrayed ordinary life in the city. His collected works, *O Livro de Cesário Verde*, were finally published in 1991.

But it is Fernando Pessoa (1888-1935), posthumously regarded as the most brilliant writer of his generation, who is considered Lisbon's own special poet. He created four different poet-personalities (which he referred to as heteronyms) and these resulted in four quite distinct strains of poetry and prose. Born in Lisbon, Pessoa was an active member of the city's literary salons that gathered at various artistic cafes. He wrote prolifically (both prose and poetry, in Portuguese, English and French), but only one work, his 1934 *Mensagem* (Message), was actually published during his lifetime. See the Things to See & Do chapter for details of the Casa Museu de Fernando Pessoa and a Walking Tour following in his footsteps.

During the repressive Salazar dictatorship, several notable writers suffered. Today's more liberated post-Salazar literary

José Saramago's Lisbon

José Saramago, the son of farmers, was born in Azinhaga, a small village in the Ribatejo, in 1922. He moved to Lisbon with his family while still young and after leaving school at 16 – for financial reasons – he worked in a variety of jobs, including publishing. Although Saramago's first novel was published when he was 25, it wasn't until 1980 that his writing career really took off and not until 1988, when his most powerful novel, *Memorial do Convento*, was published in English as *Baltasar & Blimunda*, that his international fame was launched. He was awarded the Nobel Prize for Literature in 1998.

NICKY CASTLE

Several of Saramago's lyrical works are set in Lisbon, notably *História do Cerco de Lisboa* (The History of the Siege of Lisbon) and *O Ano da Morte de Ricardo Reis* (The Year of the Death of Ricardo Reis), a novel about one of the imaginary poet-personalities created by the early 20th-century writer, Fernando Pessoa. In *Viagem a Portugal* (Voyage to Portugal), an anonymous traveller discovers the city. The Alfama district, in particular, holds his fascination, an 'immense discourse of houses, people, stories, laughter and inevitable weeping'.

scene is dominated by José Saramago, winner of the 1998 Nobel Prize for Literature (see the boxed text 'José Saramago's Lisbon'). A committed communist with strong anti-Church sentiments, Saramago often faced criticism at home but eventually found world-wide acclaim with *Memorial do Convento* (*Baltasar & Blimunda* in the English translation), which combines realism, astute political comment and poetic fancy.

Other leading writers of the contemporary period include António Lobo Antunes whose works, including *Explicação dos Pássaros* (An Explanation of the Birds), are marked by fast-paced prose, and José Cardoso Pires, whose finest novel is *Balada da Praia dos Cães* (Ballad of Dog's Beach), a gripping thriller based on a real political assassination of the Salazar era.

Architecture

There's relatively little original pre-18th-century architecture left to admire in the city centre, due to the devastating earthquake of 1755. The most notable of the few major monuments that did survive (albeit with later restoration work) are the Romanesque Sé (cathedral); the Igreja de São Vicente de Fora, built by the Italian Renaissance master Felipe Terzi in the early 17th century; and his other work, the Igreja de São Roque. The best testimony to the earthquake itself are the formidable Gothic ruins of the Convento do Carmo in the Chiado district.

The most outstanding architecture is found at Belém, about 6km west of the city centre. Here is one of the country's finest expressions of the Manueline style (see the boxed text 'Manueline Masterpieces').

Nothing could possibly match the Manueline's imaginative flourish but, in terms of flamboyance, the baroque style surpassed it. Financed by the 17th-century gold and diamond discoveries in Brazil, and encouraged by the extravagant Dom João V, local and foreign artists created baroque masterpieces of mind-boggling opulence, notably the massive Convento do Mafra (see the Mafra section in the Excursions chapter). A hallmark of the architecture at this time was the awesome use of *talha*

Manueline Masterpieces

The uniquely Portuguese Manueline style of architecture marked the transition from Gothic to Renaissance. It flourished during the reign of Dom Manuel I (1495-1521) when Vasco da Gama and his peers were exploring the seas as distant as India and discovering new lands and new wealth for Portugal.

The confidence of this Age of Discoveries was expressed in sculptural creations of extraordinary inventiveness, drawing heavily on nautical themes: ropes, coral and anchors in twisted stone topped by ubiquitous armillary spheres (Dom Manuel's emblem) and the cross of the Order of Christ, the former Knights Templar religious-military order that largely financed the explorations.

The Mosteiro dos Jerónimos at Belém is a supreme example of the art form; its portals are dense with sculptures and its cloisters adorned with intricately carved arches.

dourada (gilded woodwork), which was lavished on church interiors throughout the land. Lisbon's finest examples are inside the Igreja de São Roque and the Igreja de Nossa Senhora da Madre de Deus.

It was only when the gold ran out that the baroque fad faded. At the end of the 18th century, architects quietly returned to a classical style (exemplified by Mateus Vicente de Oliveira's Palácio de Queluz, 5km northwest of Lisbon). After the 1755 earthquake, even more simplicity followed. The Marquês de Pombal invited architect Eugenio dos Santos to rebuild the city in a revolutionary new 'Pombal' style marked by plain houses and wide avenues. Walk through the Baixa district and you'll see Pombal's influence everywhere.

A similar architectural opportunity was recently given to Portugal's greatest contemporary architect, Álvaro Siza Vieira, who restored the historic Chiado shopping district following a major fire in 1988. A believer in 'clarity and simplism', Vieira's expressionist approach is clearly reflected in his most notable Lisbon project (originally built for Expo '98), the Pavilhão de Portugal in the Parque das Nações. The Parque boasts other stunning contemporary works, including Peter Chermayev's Oceanário and Santiago Calatrava's extraordinary, wave-like Gare do Oriente.

The 'postmodern' Amoreiras shopping complex, designed by Tomás Taveira, is among notable city-centre pieces. A fine Lisbon example of the need to preserve historic buildings, at the same time as making them functional, is the headquarters of the Association of Portuguese Architects, which combines an original neoclassical facade with a contemporary interior.

The city's most bizarre engineering feat is the Elevador de Santa Justa, built in 1902 by Raul Mésnier (a colleague of Gustave Eiffel), while the 18km-long Ponte de Vasco da Gama is the most recent and stylish engineering accomplishment.

Painting

Among early Lisbon artists, the most outstanding was the 15th-century court painter Nuno Gonçalves, whose polyptych of the *Adoration of St Vincent* (in Lisbon's Museu Nacional de Arte Antiga) is a tapestry-style revelation of Portuguese society during the 15th century .

The Manueline school produced paintings remarkable for their realism and luminous colours. Lisbon's best artists at this time included Jorge Afonso (painter to Dom Manuel I), Cristóvão de Figueiredo and Gregório Lopes.

The 17th century saw a female artist, Josefa de Óbidos (based at Óbidos, 82km north of Lisbon) make waves with her rich still lifes. In the late 18th century, Domingos António de Sequeira produced wonderful portraits. The 19th century experienced an artistic echo of the naturalist and Romantic movements, expressed particularly strongly in the works of Silva Porto and Marquês de Oliveira, while Sousa Pinto excelled in the early 20th century as a pastel artist.

Naturalism continued to be the dominant trend during the 20th century, although Amadeo de Souza Cardoso struck out on his own impressive artistic path of cubism and expressionism, and Maria Helena Vieria da Silva became noted as the country's finest abstract painter (although she lived and worked in Paris for most of her life). Two other eminent contemporary artists include Almada Negreiros (often called the father of Portugal's modern art movement) and Guilherme Santa-Rita. Their works and many others can best be seen in the Centro de Arte Moderna in Lisbon.

Sculpture

Sculptors have excelled in many periods of Portugal's history. Among the first memorable creations are the carved tombs of the 12th to 14th centuries, such as the beautifully ornate limestone tombs of Inês de Castro and Dom Pedro in the Mosteiro de Santa Maria de Alcobaça. During the Manueline era sculptors, including Diogo de Boitaca, went wild with uniquely Portuguese seafaring fantasies and exuberant decoration. At the same time, foreign influences were seeping in, such as Flamboyant Gothic and plateresque styles (named after the ornate Spanish work of silversmiths or plateros) from Spanish Galicia and Biscay.

The Biscayan artists João and Diogo de Castilho created the most outstanding work during this time; the fantastically carved south portal of the Mosteiro dos Jerónimos in Belém is one of João's finest works. The main entrance to the monastery, the west portal, was carved by Nicolas Chanterène, one of the leading French artists who settled in Portugal during the Renaissance period. Another of his works near Lisbon is the beautiful alabaster altarpiece in Sintra's Palácio Nacional da Pena.

Foreign schools continued to influence Portuguese sculptors in the 18th-century baroque era, when Dom João V took advantage of the assembly of foreign artists working on the Convento do Mafra to found a school of sculpture there. Its first principal was the Italian, Alexander Giusti, but its most famous Portuguese teacher was Joaquim Machado de Castro (who crafted José I's bronze equestrian statue in Lisbon's Praça do Comércio). Humbler works by Castro are the terracotta figures of his baroque manger scenes in the city's cathedral (the Sé) and in Basílica da Estrela.

In the early 19th century, the Palácio da Ajuda (north of Belém) was a centre of neoclassical artistic activity. Several sculptures from this period are on view here as well as in the Palácio de Queluz.

A century later, the work of António Soares dos Reis reflects more French and Italian influences. At the beginning of the 20th century, two prominent names were Francisco Franco and the prolific António Teixeira Lopes (Soares dos Reis' pupil).

Handicrafts & Indigenous Arts

Although Portugal's finest handicrafts are mostly produced in the provinces, Lisbon's *artesanatos* (handicrafts shops; see the Shopping chapter for details) stock items from practically everywhere. Look out for superb ceramics such as the popular cabbage leaf designs from nearby Caldas da Rainha or encrusted jugs and bowls from Estremoz. *Azulejos* (painted tiles) are the speciality of artisans in nearby Sintra.

Hand-embroidered linen is a flourishing handicraft in both mainland Portugal and Madeira, and widely available in Lisbon. Lace and filigree jewellery, often crafted in the northern Minho province, are also fine examples of Portuguese craftwork.

More rustic kinds of handicrafts include rush or willow baskets and tiny straw figures dressed in traditional rural costume. Estoril holds a major Feira do Artesanato (Handicraft Fair) every summer.

Cinema

Portugal has a distinguished history of film making, though poor foreign distribution has left the world largely ignorant of it. The only internationally famous director is Manoel de Oliveira. The nonagenarian ex-racing driver has made 20 films (all except three after he turned 60). Very often theatrical and controversial, they demand to be interpreted on different levels. One of his latest offerings, the Cannes award-winning *A Carta*, is based on the classic 17th-century French novel *La Princesse de Clèves*.

Azulejos

Portugal's favourite decorative art is undoubtedly the painted tiles called *azulejos* (probably after the Arabic 'al zulaycha', meaning polished stone). They cover everything from church interiors to train stations. The Portuguese can't claim to have invented the technique – they learned it from the Moors, who picked it up from the Persians – but it has been used more widely and inventively in Portugal than anywhere else.

The first truly Portuguese tiles – multicoloured and geometric – appeared in the 1580s, gracing churches such as Lisbon's Igreja de São Roque. The late 17th century brought a fashion for huge panels depicting everything from cherubs to hunters (eg, at the Quinta dos Marquêses da Fronteira). Quality eventually gave way to quantity, however, and the blue-and-white Delft tiles of the Netherlands took over the market.

In the 18th century the Portuguese masters António de Oliveira Bernardes and his son Policarpo revived the use of blue-and-white and polychrome tiles to brilliant effect. Rococo themes appeared, decorating fountains, stairways and sacristies (eg, the Convento da Madre de Deus). But by the end of the century, quality was again on the decline, partly because of the huge demand for tiles after the 1755 earthquake.

Imaginative azulejos made a comeback in the 19th century, including panels in restaurants such as the Cervejaria da Trindade. The Art Nouveau and Art Deco movements took the art further into the public domain. Azulejos still have a place in contemporary Portuguese life, with Maria Keil and Júlio de Resende responsible for some stunning wall mosaics and murals (eg, in some of Lisbon's new metro stations).

For a detailed look at the history of this uniquely Portuguese art, visit the Museu Nacional do Azulejo.

As well as other older, well-established film makers (notably João Botelho and João Cesar Monteiro), a new generation of directors is emerging. These include Pedro Costa (highly regarded for his film *Ossos*) and Teresa Villaverde *(Os Mutantes)*, whose works are often provocative and harrowing; both these films deal with the dispossessed in contemporary Lisbon. The country's best known actress, Maria de Medeiros, chose Portugal's 1974 Revolution of the Carnations as the theme for her recent *Capitães de Abril*. Significantly, this film was funded by the Portuguese Film Institute (ICAM; Instituto de Cinema, Audiovisual e Multimédia), which has recently grown more daring in its approach.

Performing Arts

The theatre scene has finally cast out the demons of the Salazar years. In addition to the venerable Lisbon-based Teatro Nacional Dona Maria II there are now numerous private theatre companies in the city, largely thanks to events such as Expo '98 and more funding from the Ministry of Culture. In 1999, the ministry initiated an ambitious theatre restoration and construction program aimed at establishing more facilities, but funding still remains a huge problem for independent or avant-garde groups such as the youth-geared Teatro O Bando.

The Fundação Calouste Gulbenkian (Calouste Gulbenkian Foundation), one of Portugal's most generous and wide-ranging private arts sponsors, supports the country's best contemporary ballet company, Ballet Gulbenkian. Classical ballet is performed by the Companhia Nacional de Bailado, based at Teatro Camões (but often on tour). The year's classical ballet highlight is the Noites do Bailado international festival in Sintra (see Sintra in the Excursions chapter for details).

SOCIETY & CONDUCT
Traditional Culture

Thanks to a strong Catholic influence and decades of repression under the dictatorship of Salazar, Portugal remains a largely traditional and conservative country. Although Lisbon is far less religious than the

---

Saudade

It has been described as a great nostalgia for the glorious past, a fathomless yearning, and a longing for home, but unless you're Portuguese you'll probably never really grasp the uniquely Portuguese emotion of *saudade*. Its musical form is the aching sorrow expressed in fado songs – a melancholic submission to the twists and turns of fate. In Portuguese and Brazilian poetry it's a mystical reverence for nature, a brooding sense of loneliness that became especially popular among 19th and early-20th-century poets who cultivated a cult of *saudosismo*. In tangible form it's the return of thousands of emigres to their home villages every August, drawn not just by family ties but by something much deeper – a longing for all that home and Portugal represents: the heroism of the past, the sorrows of the present and wistful hopes for the future.

---

northern provinces, it still honours certain religious customs and festivals – none more so than the Festa de Santo António (see Public Holidays & Special Events in the Facts for the Visitor chapter), which features solemn religious processions as well as music, dancing and all-night revelries.

It doesn't take much of an event, either, to feature some traditional folk dancing. Lisbon often imports leading groups from the provinces (especially Minho or central Alentejo) to spice up a festival. The only modern activity to rival the popularity of the folk dance is football; when a big match is being played you'll find customers in bars and restaurants glued to the TV sets.

Dos & Don'ts

Generally, the Portuguese people share characteristics of friendliness and an unhurried approach to life; in other words, expect smiles and warmth but not punctuality or brisk efficiency. Though this habitual lassitude may sometimes drive you mad, displays of anger will get you nowhere.

When asked for information, Portuguese have a tendency to save face by giving an answer even if they don't know whether it's right. This frustrating habit sometimes extends to tourist office staff. You'll rarely hear *não sei* (I don't know). Get multiple opinions if the answer is important to you.

Speaking Portuguese – however clumsily – will earn you lots of points. Politeness is highly valued, so be sure to address people correctly (*senhor* for men, *senhora* for women, *senhora dona* followed by the Christian name for an elderly or respected woman). A handshake is the norm when you're introduced to someone, although you may well get a light peck on each cheek from a young person.

Your style of dress can be a sensitive issue, even in Lisbon in certain situations. While beachwear (and even nudity on some beaches) is acceptable in coastal resorts such as nearby Costa da Caparica, shorts and skimpy tops on a visit to a church are a definite no-no (as is intruding during church services). If you need to visit police, immigration offices or other authorities, you'll get more help if you're well dressed.

Treatment of Animals

Bullfighting Although it is not as popular in Portugal as in Spain, bullfighting is still considered by many Portuguese to be a spectacular form of 'entertainment' and a noble cultural tradition dating back 2000 years. At least 300 *touradas* (bullfights) are held March to October (traditionally from Easter Sunday to All Saints' Day), including at Lisbon's *praça de touros* (bullring).

Supporters point out that the Portuguese tourada is far less brutal and bloody than the Spanish version. There's a good deal more skilled horsemanship, artistry, valour and bravado. The most obvious differences are that the bull is initially fought by a man on horseback (Portugal has no leading female bullfighters yet), then by a team of young men who tackle the bull by hand; and the fight is not to the death (at least, not in public). Another difference is that the bull's horns are covered in leather or capped with metal balls.

However, none of this can disguise the fact that bullfighting is basically a cruel

sport. The anti-bullfighting lobby in Portugal is vocal but small. Most Portuguese are either impartial or simply surprised at the protests. If you feel strongly enough, you could write to the *turismo* (tourist office) and *câmara municipal* (town hall) of places that hold touradas.

RELIGION

As freedom of religion is included in the constitution there is no state religion in Portugal, but Roman Catholicism is the dominant faith, adhered to by roughly 95% of Portuguese. Young lisboêtas, however, show a growing trend to ignore traditional religious practices such as going to church. Civil marriage and divorce are accepted more easily here than elsewhere in the country. There are many other Christian denominations represented in Lisbon as well as small communities of Muslims, Jews and Ismaelites.

Christianity has been a major force in shaping Portugal's history. It first reached Portugal in the 1st century, and the wealth and vast resources of the Knights Templar

MARTIN HARRIS

The Knights Templar standard

(later reorganised as the Order of Christ) largely financed Portugal's overseas explorations in the 15th century.

But the Church has also been responsible for some of Portugal's darkest moments, notably the Inquisition, which was started in the 1530s by João III and his staunchly Catholic Spanish wife. Thousands were tortured, imprisoned or burnt at the stake at public sentencing ceremonies known as *autos-da-fé* (in Lisbon, these were held in the Rossio). The terror was only really suppressed in 1820.

Today, the Catholic Church in Portugal is powerful and highly respected. One of the most important centres of pilgrimage in Europe is at Fátima (about 120km north of Lisbon), where up to 100,000 pilgrims congregate for two days every May and October.

Lisbon shows its religious colours each June when it celebrates with gusto the Festa de Santo António. For more details, see Public Holidays & Special Events in the Facts for the Visitor chapter.

LANGUAGE

Portuguese, along with French, Italian, Spanish and Romanian, is a Romance language closely derived from Latin. It is not only spoken in Portugal but also in Brazil and five African nations.

English is the most widely spoken foreign language in Lisbon, and you'll find that many service employees (eg, in tourist offices, hotels and restaurants) can usually speak some French and German too. See the Language chapter for a guide to useful Portuguese words and phrases.

Facts for the Visitor

WHEN TO GO

Portugal's climate is temperate, and you'll find agreeable weather in Lisbon almost year-round. The best time is probably spring (late April to June) and early autumn (late September and October), though even in high summer the proximity of the city to the Atlantic ensures some cool breezes.

The peak tourist season is roughly mid-June through August or September. During this time, *pensões* (guesthouses) and hotels are at their busiest (and most expensive) so it's wise to book ahead, especially for mid-range or top-end accommodation. In the low season, prices may drop by as much as 50% (prices in this book are for peak season).

During August, when many *lisboêtas* take their holidays, some shops, restaurants and theatres close and cultural events are limited. On the plus side, there are some great summer sales, offering big discounts.

ORIENTATION

Lisbon nestles against seven hills on the northern side of the Rio Tejo (Tagus River). One of the hills – São Jorge – is topped by Lisbon's famous castle, Castelo de São Jorge. Each of the others – Estrela, Santa Catarina, São Pedro de Alcântara, Graça, Senhora do Monte and Penha de França – sport a church or *miradouro* (lookout).

Other fine places to gaze over the city are the Elevador de Santa Justa (Map 6) and Parque Eduardo VII (Map 2). The city's highest point (at 230.5m) is within the military fortress in the huge Parque Florestal de Monsanto (Map 1), west of the centre.

At the river's edge is the grand Praça do Comércio (Map 7), the traditional gateway to the city. Behind it spread the latticework streets of the Baixa ('lower') district, up to the twin squares of Praça da Figueira and Praça Dom Pedro IV– the latter known to virtually everybody as Rossio or Largo Rossio (Map 6).

Here the city forks along two main arteries. Lisbon's splendid 'main street', Avenida da Liberdade – more a long park than a boulevard – reaches 1.5km north-west from Rossio to Parque Eduardo VII. The other fork is Avenida Almirante Reis, running arrow-straight north for almost 6km to the airport from Largo Martim Moniz (where it's called Rua da Palma), near Praça da Figueira.

From the Baixa it's a steep climb west, through the upmarket Chiado shopping district into the pastel-coloured mini-canyons of the Bairro Alto, Lisbon's traditional nightlife centre. Eastward from the Baixa it's another climb to the Castelo de São Jorge and the ancient, maze-like Alfama district below it.

River ferries depart from Praça do Comércio and, to the west, Cais do Sodré. Lisbon's long-haul train stations are Santa Apolónia, 1.5km east of Praça do Comércio (for northern Portugal and all international links); Cais do Sodré (for Cascais and the Estoril Coast); Rossio (for Sintra and Estremadura); and Barreiro (for southern Portugal), reached by ferry across the Rio Tejo. Gare do Oriente is Lisbon's newest and biggest intermodal terminal, combining bus, train and metro stations on the north-eastern outskirts of town.

The city has two main long-distance bus terminals: Arco do Cego, on Avenida João Crisóstomo, near Saldanha metro station; and Gare do Oriente (see the Getting There & Away chapter for more details).

In addition to the metro and buses, ageing trams clank picturesquely around the hills, and smart new trams run 6km west from Praça da Figueira to the waterfront suburb of Belém.

With the exception of Belém and Parque das Nações (the former Expo '98 site, on the north-eastern waterfront), Lisbon's main attractions are all within walking distance of one another. Public transport (when you need it at all) works well.

Lisbon is connected across the Tejo to the Costa da Caparica and Setúbal Peninsula by the immense, 70m-high Ponte 25 de Abril, Europe's longest suspension bridge, which also carries trains to the suburbs. The new Ponte de Vasco da Gama – at 18km Portugal's longest river crossing – reaches across the Tejo farther north, from near the Parque das Nações to Montijo, providing a convenient bypass for north-south traffic.

MAPS

Staff at the city *turismos* (tourist offices) dispense a free but microscopic city map. Decent maps for sale in bookshops include the colourful 1:13,000 Falk *Lisboa Plan*; GeoBloco's *Touristic Plan* with street index and text (but hard-to-read street names); and Michelin's regularly updated 1:10,000 *Lisboa Planta* with a separate street index. Kümmerly + Frey's 1:15,000 *Lisboa* map includes bus and metro routes.

The extremely detailed, 230-page, 1:500 *Guia Urbano* city atlas (2000$00) noses into every corner of the city and was updated in 2000. From turismos you are able to buy the glossy *Mapas Turísticos* booklet (1300$00), which packs in adequate maps of Lisbon, Oeiras, Cascais and Sintra as well as lists of accommodation, restaurants, bars and museums.

Map Sources

The Instituto Português de Cartográfia e Cadastro (Portuguese Institute of Cartography & Registry; Map 2; ☎ 213 819 600, fax 213 819 699, ⒠ ipcc@ipcc.pt), at Rua Artilharia Um 107, produces and sells 1:50,000 to 1:250,000 topographic maps of Portugal. You can also order maps from its Web site at www.ipcc.pt (Portuguese only). Each sheet costs 1000$00.

The Instituto Geográfico do Exército (IGeoE or Army Geographic Institute; ☎ 218 520 063, fax 218 532 119, ⒠ igeoe@igeoe.pt) sells military topographic maps at its headquarters on Avenida Dr Alfredo Bensaúde (Map 1), including a 1:10,000 *Lisbon* map. Its Web site is www.igeoe.pt.

Many road and topographic maps are available by mail order. The widest range of Portugal maps is available from GeoCenter ILH (☎ 0711-788 93 40, fax 788 93 54), Schockenriedstrasse 44, D-70565 Stuttgart, Germany. Other reliable mail-order firms are:

Omni Resources (☎ 910-227 8300, fax 227 3748) 1004 S Mebane St, PO Box 2096, Burlington, NC 27216-2096, USA
Web site: www.omnimap.com

Stanfords (☎ 020-7836 1321, fax 7836 0189, ⒠ sales@stanfords.co.uk) 12-14 Long Acre, Covent Garden, London WC2E 9LP, UK

The Travel Bookshop (☎ 02-9241 3554, fax 9241 3159) 6 Bridge St, Sydney , NSW, Australia 2000

TOURIST OFFICES
Local Tourist Offices

The Associação Turismo de Lisboa (ATL; ☎ 213 610 350, fax 213 610 359, ⒠ atl@mail.atl-turismolisboa.pt) has just opened a new information centre (CRIA; Centro de Representação, Informação e Animação de Lisboa; Map 7; ☎ 213 433 672) dealing specifically with Lisbon inquiries. It's in Praça do Comércio.

For national information, head for the turismo (☎ 213 466 307, fax 213 468 772) in Palácio Foz on Praça dos Restauradores run by Investimentos, Comércio e Turismo de Portugal (ICEP), the state's umbrella organisation for tourism. ICEP's head office (Map 2; ☎ 217 909 500, fax 217 935 028, ⒠ informacao@icep.pt) is at Avenida 5 de Outubro 101. Both CRIA and ICEP's turismo at Palácio Foz are open 9 am to 8 pm daily. There are also turismo desks at the airport to help with accommodation, transport etc (see the Airport section in the Getting Around chapter for more information).

Turismo de Lisboa also runs several 'Ask Me Lisboa' information kiosks, most usefully in Rua Augusta, Largo Martim Moniz, inside Santa Apolónia train station and at Castelo de São Jorge. Opening hours are generally 10 am to 6 pm daily.

Excellent free publications available at all these offices include *Follow Me Lisboa*, a twice-monthly Portuguese/English leisure guide; *Lisboa Step by Step*, a quarterly glossy; *Cultural Agenda*, the town hall's monthly guide to events; *Lisboa City Walks*; and a *Guia Gay e Lésbico* (Gay & Lesbian Guide to Lisbon) leaflet. Also available at all Turismo de Lisboa outlets is the Lisboa Card (see the boxed text in the Getting Around chapter).

Keep an eye out for the free, regularly updated *Your Guide: Lisboa* published by ANA, the airport authority, which has listings of shops, restaurants and nightlife (also available at the airport arrivals terminal); and *Tips*, an info-packed miniguide, more often available in hotels.

A multilingual freephone tourist information service (☎ 800 296 296) operates from 9 am to midnight daily (to 8 pm Sunday) to provide basic information on the sights, transport and accommodation.

Tourist Offices Abroad

ICEP-affiliated trade and tourism offices abroad include the following:

Canada (☎ 416-921 7376, fax 921 1353, ✉ iceptor@idirect.com) 60 Bloor St West, Suite 1005, Toronto, Ontario M4W 3B8
France (☎ 01 56 88 30 80, fax 01 56 88 30 89, ✉ icepar@worldnet.fr) 135 blvd Haussmann, 75008 Paris
Germany (☎ 069-234 094, fax 231 433, ✉ icepfra@portugal.f.uunet.de) Schäfergasse 17, 60313 Frankfurt Main
Ireland (☎ 01-670 9133, fax 670 9141, ✉ info@icep.ie) 54 Dawson St, Dublin 2
The Netherlands (☎ 070-326 2525, fax 328 0025, ✉ icephaia@mail2.icep.pt) Paul Gabriëlstraat 70, 2596 VG Den Haag
Spain (☎ 91 522 44 08, fax 91 522 23 82, ✉ icep-madrid@portugal.org) Gran Via 27, 1st floor, 28013 Madrid
UK (☎ 020-7494 1441, fax 7494 1868, ✉ iceplondt@aol.com) 22-25a Sackville St, London W1X 1DE
USA (☎ 212-354 4403, fax 764 6137, ✉ tourism@portugal.org) 590 Fifth Ave, 4th floor, New York, NY 10036-4785

TRAVEL AGENCIES

The city's leading youth-oriented travel agency, offering budget hotel, bus, train and air bookings (plus student and teacher cards) is Usit Tagus (Map 2; ☎ 213 525 986, fax 213 532 715), at Rua Camilo Castelo Branco 20. There is a branch office (Map 2; ☎ 218 491 531) at Praça de Londres 9-C. Tagus' Web site is at www.usittagus.pt.

Similar outfits are Wasteels (Map 8; ☎ 218 869 793, fax 218 869 797) at Rua dos Caminhos do Ferro 90 and Jumbo Expresso Viagens (Map 2; ☎ 218 161 190, fax 218

161 199, ✉ jumbotravel@mail.telepac.pt) on the 1st floor at Rua Palmira 66.

A good mainstream travel agency is the American Express representative, Top Tours (Map 2; ☎ 213 155 885, fax 213 155 827, ✉ tourism-dept@toptours.pt), at Avenida Duque de Loulé 108, Lisbon 1050-093. Holders of AmEx cards or travellers cheques can change money commission-free here and have mail and faxes held or forwarded. The Amex office is open 9.30 am to 1 pm and 2.30 to 6.30 pm weekdays.

DOCUMENTS
Visas

No visa is required for nationals of European Union (EU) countries. Nationals of Canada, New Zealand and the USA can stay for up to 90 days in any half-year without a visa. Others, including nationals of Australia and South Africa, need a visa unless they're the spouse or child of EU citizens. See also the boxed text 'Schengen Visas'.

To apply for an of your visa or 90-day period after arriving in Portugal, directly contact the Foreigners Registration Service (Serviço de Estrangeiros e Fronteiras; Map 2;

Schengen Visas

The general requirements for entry to Portugal also apply to other signatories of the 1990 Schengen Convention on the abolition of mutual border controls (Austria, Belgium, Denmark, Finland, France, Germany, Greece, Iceland, Italy, Luxembourg, the Netherlands, Norway, Spain and Sweden).

The standard tourist visa issued by most Schengen countries (a 'Schengen visa') is valid for up to 90 days. (You must apply for the visa from your country of residence.) A visa issued by one Schengen country is generally valid for travel through all the others, though individual Schengen countries may impose additional restrictions on certain nationalities. Unless you're a citizen of the UK, Ireland or a Schengen country, you should check with the consulate of each Schengen country you plan to visit.

☎ 213 585 545), Rua São Sebastião da Pedreira 15, open 9 am to noon and 2 to 4 pm weekdays.

Travel Insurance

A travel insurance policy to cover theft, loss and medical problems is recommended. You should cover yourself for the worst-case scenario, such as an accident or illness requiring hospitalisation and a flight home. If you can't afford to do that, you certainly can't afford to deal with an unexpected medical emergency abroad. A wide variety of policies is available; your travel agent will have recommendations. The international policies handled by youth/student travel agencies are often good value.

You may prefer a policy that pays the doctors or hospitals directly rather than one that requires you to pay and claim later, though in Portugal you'll usually find an immediate cash payment is expected. If you have to claim later, make sure you keep all documentation.

EU citizens are eligible to receive free emergency medical treatment if they have an E111 certificate. See the Predeparture Planning section under Health later in this chapter for details.

Driving Licence & Permits

Nationals of EU countries need only their home driving licences to operate a car or motorcycle in Portugal, although holders of the UK's old pre-EU green licences should also carry an International Driving Permit (IDP). Portugal also accepts licences issued in Brazil, Switzerland and the USA. Other visitors should get an IDP through an automobile licensing department or automobile club in their home country.

For information on insurance and documents see the Car & Motorcycle section in the Getting There & Away chapter.

Hostel Cards

Portugal's *pousadas da juventude* (youth hostels) are affiliated with the Hostelling International (HI) network, so an HI card from your hostelling association at home entitles you to the standard cheaper rates.

Student & Youth Cards

The international student identity card (ISIC) and teacher's identity card (ITIC) enable holders to get discounts on everything from airline fares and accommodation to museum admission fees. The Web site www.istc.org has more information. Other youth cards such as Euro<26 and Go25/IYTC provide even more discounts, eg, in shops and cinemas. Check Euro<26's Web site, at www.euro26.org. Further information on ISIC, ITIC and Go25 is at www.counciltravel.com. All these cards are valid for a year and available for the equivalent of about UK£6 from youth-oriented travel agencies, such as Usit Campus, STA Travel and Council Travel, and Portuguese youth-travel agencies Usit Tagus and Wasteels.

Portugal's own Euro<26 card, the Cartão Jovem (1200$00), is the most widely recognised throughout the country. It's available to documented foreign residents as well as Portuguese residents from the youth-travel agents, Movijovem and Instituto Português da Juventude (IPJ) (see Useful Organisations later in this chapter).

Three *Guia do Cartão Jovem* regional guides (available at IPJ offices) list all places in Portugal where discounts are available with Euro<26 cards; see the *Sul e Ilhas* edition for Lisbon and surroundings.

Seniors Cards

Senior travellers can get similar discounts to youths, and more. Domestic train travel is half-price on weekdays for anyone aged 65 or over (see under Train in the Getting Around chapter). With the Rail Plus Card, those aged 60 and over get up to 25% off any rail journey crossing international borders. To be eligible you first need a local senior citizens railcard, eg, the UK's Senior Railcard (UK£18), sold, along with Rail Plus Cards (around UK£10), at major train stations, through rail companies or from Rail Europe (☎ 08705-848848).

Camping Card International

Certain camping grounds run by local camping clubs or grounds affiliated to the Federation Internationale de Camping et de

Caravanning (FICC) may be used by foreigners *only* if they have a Camping Card International (CCI). The CCI guarantees third-party insurance for any damage you may cause during your stay, and is sometimes good for discounts.

The CCI is available to members of most national automobile clubs except in the USA; the RAC in the UK charges members UK£4 for a card. It's also available from FICC-affiliated camping clubs such as the Camping & Caravanning Club (☎ 024-7669 4995) in the UK, and the Federação Portuguesa de Campismo (Map 1; ☎ 218 126 890, fax 218 126 918, e info@fpcampismo.pt), with an office at Avenida Coronel Eduardo Galhardo 24-D, 1170 Lisbon.

Copies

All important documents (passport data page, credit cards, travel insurance policy, driving licence etc) should be photocopied before you leave home. Leave one copy with someone at home and keep another with you, separate from the originals. Other copies you might want to carry include travellers cheque numbers, birth certificate and any documents related to possible employment.

It's also a good idea to store details of your vital travel documents in Lonely Planet's free online Travel Vault just in case you lose the photocopies or can't be bothered with them. Your password-protected Travel Vault is accessible online anywhere in the world – create it at www.ekno.lonelyplanet.com.

EMBASSIES & CONSULATES
Portuguese Embassies & Consulates

Portuguese embassies and consulates abroad include the following:

Australia
Embassy: (☎ 02-6290 1733, fax 6290 1957, e embport@dynamite.com.au) 23 Culgoa Circuit, O'Malley, ACT 2606
Consulate General: (☎ 02-9262 2199, fax 9262 5991, e info@consulportugalsydney.org.au) Level 9, 30 Clarence St, Sydney NSW 2000

Brazil
Embassy: (☎ 061-321 3434, fax 224 7347) Avenida das Nações, Lote 2, CEP 70402, Brasilia

Canada
Embassy: (☎ 613-729 0883, fax 729 4236, e consulpt@linkxs.com) 645 Island Park Dr, Ottawa, Ontario K1Y OB8
Consulate: (☎ 514-499 0359, fax 499 0366) 2020 rue de l'Université, 17th floor, Montreal, Quebec H3A 2A5
Consulate: (☎ 604-688 6514, fax 685 7042) 904 Pender Place, 700 West Pender St, Vancouver, BC V6C 1G8

Cape Verde
Embassy: (☎ 62 30 32, fax 62 30 36) Achada de Santo António, Cidade da Praia CP 160

France
Embassy: (☎ 01 47 27 35 29, fax 01 44 05 94 02) 3 rue de Noisiel, 75116 Paris
Consulate: (☎ 01 44 06 88 90, fax 01 45 85 09 58) 187 rue de Chevaleret, 75013 Paris

Germany
Embassy: (☎ 0228-36 30 11, fax 35 28 64, e 101327.2272@compuserve.com) Ubierstrasse 78, 53173 Bonn 2
Embassy: (☎ 030-391 96 49, fax 392 23 66) Wilhelmstrasse 65, Berlin

Guinea-Bissau
Embassy: (☎ 20 12 61, fax 20 12 69) Avenida Cidade de Lisboa, Apartado 76, 1021 Bissau Codex

Ireland
Embassy: (☎ 01-289 4416, fax 289 2849) Knock Sinna House, Knock Sinna, Fox Rock, Dublin 18

Morocco
Embassy: (☎ 07-756 446, fax 756 450) 5 rue Thami Lamdouar, Souissi, Rabat

Mozambique
Embassy: (☎ 01-490 316, fax 491 172, e culmapd@mail.tropical.co.mz) Avenida Julius Nyerere 720, Maputo CP 4696

The Netherlands
Embassy: (☎ 070-363 02 17, fax 361 55 89) Bazarstraat 21, 2518 AG The Hague
Consulate: (☎ 010-411 15 40, fax 414 98 89) Willemskade 18, 3016 Rotterdam

São Tomé e Príncipe
Embassy: (☎ 012-21130, fax 21190) Avenida Marginal 12 de Julho, CP 173, São Tomé

Spain
Embassy: (☎ 91 561 78 00, fax 91 411 60 71) Calle de Castelló 128, 28006 Madrid
Consulate: (☎ 91 445 46 00, fax 91 445 85 69) Paseo del General Martinez Campos 11-1, Madrid

UK
Embassy: (☎ 020-7235 5331, fax 7245 1287, e portembassy-london@dialin.net) 11 Belgrave Square, London SW1X 8PP

FACTS FOR THE VISITOR

Consulate: (☎ 020-7581 8722, fax 7581 3085) 62 Brompton Rd, London SW3 1BJ

USA

Embassy: (☎ 202-328 8610, fax 462 3726, ℮ portugal@portugalemb.org) 2125 Kalorama Rd NW, Washington, DC 20008
Consulate: (☎ 212-246 4580, fax 459 0190) 630 Fifth Ave, Suite 310-378, New York, NY 10111
Consulate: (☎ 415-346 3400, fax 346 1440) 3298 Washington St, San Francisco, CA 94115

Embassies & Consulates in Lisbon

Your embassy or consulate is the best first stop in any emergency. Most can provide lists of reliable local doctors, lawyers and interpreters. If your money or documents have been stolen, they might help you get a new passport or advise you on how to have funds transferred, but a free ticket home or a loan for onward travel is unlikely.

Foreign embassies and consulates in Lisbon include:

Angola

Embassy: (Map 1; ☎ 217 967 041, fax 217 971 238) Avenida da República 68

Brazil

Embassy: (Map 1; ☎ 217 267 777, fax 217 267 623) Estrada das Laranjeiras 144
Consulate: (Map 7; ☎ 213 220 100, fax 213 473 926) Praça Luís de Camões 22

Canada

Embassy: (Map 5; ☎ 213 164 600, fax 213 164 691) Edifício Victoria, Avenida da Liberdade 196

Cape Verde

Embassy: (Map 10; ☎ 213 015 271, fax 213 015 308) Avenida do Restelo 33

France

Embassy: (Map 4; ☎ 213 939 100, fax 213 939 222) & *Consulate:* (☎ 213 939 292) Calçada Marquês de Abrantes 123

Germany

Embassy: (Map 5; ☎ 218 810 210, fax 218 853 846) Campo dos Mártires da Pátria 38

Guinea-Bissau

Embassy: (Map 10; ☎ 213 015 371), Rua de Alcolena 17
Consulate: (☎ 213 157 972, fax 213 157 975) Avenida Praia da Vitória 41

Ireland

Embassy: (Map 4; ☎ 213 929 400, fax 213 977 363) Rua da Imprensa à Estrela 1

Morocco

Embassy: (Map 1; ☎ 213 020 842, fax 213 020 935) Rua do Alto do Duque 21

Mozambique

Embassy: (Map 2; ☎ 217 971 994, fax 217 932 720) Avenida de Berna 7

The Netherlands

Embassy: (Map 4; ☎ 213 961 163, fax 213 966 436) Avenida Infante Santo 43

Spain

Embassy: (Map 5; ☎ 213 472 381, fax 213 472 384) & *Consulate:* (☎ 213 220 500) Rua do Salitre 3

UK

Embassy: (Map 4; ☎ 213 924 000, fax 213 924 185) & *Consulate:* (☎ 213 924 159, fax 213 924 188, ℮ consular@lisbon.mail .fco.gov.uk) Rua de São Bernardo 33

USA

Embassy: (Map1; ☎ 217 273 300, fax 217 269 109) *Consulate:* (☎ 217 702 409, fax 217 272 354) Avenida das Forças Armadas

There are no embassies for Australia or New Zealand in Lisbon. In emergencies, Australian citizens can call the Australian Policy Liaison Office at the Canadian embassy; the nearest Australian embassy is in Paris (☎ 00-33-1 40 59 33 00). New Zealand citizens can contact the honorary consul on ☎ 213 509 690 between 9 am and 1 pm on weekdays; the nearest New Zealand embassy is in Rome (☎ 00-39-6-441 7171).

CUSTOMS

There's no limit on the amount of foreign currency you can bring into Portugal. Customs regulations say visitors who need visas must bring in at least 10,000$00 plus 2000$00 per day of their stay, but this isn't strictly enforced.

The duty-free allowance for travellers over 17 years old from non-EU countries is 200 cigarettes or the equivalent; and 1L of alcohol over 22% alcohol or 2L of wine or beer. Nationals of EU countries can bring in 800 cigarettes or the equivalent, and either 10L of spirits, 20L of fortified wine, 60L of sparkling wine or a mind-boggling 90L of still wine or 110L of beer!

There's no duty-free shopping in Portugal's airports. See Taxes & Refunds under Money later in this chapter for information on sales-tax refunds.

FACTS FOR THE VISITOR

MONEY
Currency

The Portuguese *escudo* remains the national currency until January 2002, when it will be exchanged for the euro (€). See the boxed text 'Euroland' for details.

The escudo is divided into 100 *centavos*. Prices are usually denoted with a $ sign between escudos and centavos, eg, 25 escudos 50 centavos is written 25$50. Portuguese notes in circulation are 500$00, 1000$00, 2000$00, 5000$00 and 10,000$00. Coin denominations are 1$00, 2$50, 5$00, 10$00, 20$00, 50$00, 100$00 and 200$00, though coins smaller than 5$00 are rarely seen. Market prices tend to be rounded out to the nearest 10$00.

The Portuguese frequently refer to 1000$00 as *um conto*.

Exchange Rates

Approximate exchange rates at the time of printing were:

country	unit		escudos
Australia	A$1	=	123$66
Canada	C$1	=	149$35
euro	€1	=	200$48
France	1FF	=	30$56
Germany	DM1	=	102$51
Japan	¥100	=	204$68
New Zealand	NZ$1	=	96$20
Spain	100 ptas	=	120$49
UK	UK£1	=	330$72
USA	US$1	=	228$18

Exchanging Money

Portuguese banks and private exchange bureaus accept most foreign currencies, but are free to set their own fees and rates. Thus a bureau's low commission may be offset by an unfavourable exchange rate. If you're watching every penny or escudo, you'll have to shop around.

General banking hours are usually between 8.30 am and 3 pm on weekdays only. Among French banks in Lisbon are Banque Nationale de Paris (Map 1; ☎ 217 910 200) at Avenida 5 de Outubro 206, and Crédit Lyonnais (Map 2; ☎ 213 509 900) at Rua

---

Euroland

Since 1 January 1999 the escudo and the euro (€) – Europe's new currency for 11 EU countries – have both been legal tender in Portugal, with a fixed exchange rate. Euro coins and banknotes will be issued on 1 January 2002, but you can already get billed in euros and opt to pay in euros by credit card.

The euro should actually make travellers' lives easier. Euro coins (in denominations of one, two, five, 10, 20 and 50 cents, and €1 and €2) and notes (€5, €10, €20, €50, €100, €200 and €500) will be usable in all of Euroland's 11 countries (Austria, Belgium, Finland, France, Germany, Ireland, Italy, Luxembourg, the Netherlands, Portugal and Spain) and in any other country that accepts euros. So you won't need to change money between Euroland countries.

The Lonely Planet Web site, which is at www .lonelyplanet.com, has a link to a currency converter as well as up-to-date news on the integration process.

Camilo Castelo Branco 46. Barclays Bank is well represented in Lisbon, with its headquarters (Map 2; ☎ 217 911 100) at Avenida da República 50 and a central branch (Map 7) at Rua Augusta 119. The Grupo Deutsche Bank (Map 5; ☎ 213 111 200) is at Rua Castilho 20.

The most convenient private exchange services are two Cota Câmbios bureaus (both Map 6), one at Rossio 41 open from 9 am to 9 pm daily; and the other at Rua Áurea 283 open from 9 am to 7 pm weekdays and 9 am to 1 pm Saturday.

Travellers Cheques & Cash Travellers cheques are easily exchanged, at slightly better rates than for cash, but they're poor value in Portugal because banks charge around 2500$00 commission for each transaction, regardless of size; exchange bureaus typically charge around 1000$00. The only exception is American Express travellers cheques, which can be exchanged at reasonable rates, commission-free, at Top Tours

Summer dining, Rua Augusta

Escort for the Senhora da Saúde parade in Mouraria during May

Café A Brasileira, a literary fave

Museu Nacional dos Coches displays past regal travel options.

Teatro Nacional Dona Maria II

VITOR VIEIRA

PAUL BERNHARDT

OLIVER STREWE

MARTIN MOOS

OLIVER STREWE

JULIA WILKINSON

VITOR VIEIRA

Whether it's breakfast, dinner or just a coffee, Lisbon can relieve those hunger pangs. Markets, restaurants and cafes offer everything from eels to cheese and a fine drop to follow.

(see Travel Agencies earlier). Fees for ex-changing Eurocheques are sometimes lower than for other travellers cheques, though for these cheques and the accompanying card you must pay an annual subscription fee.

Foreign cash can also be changed (for higher commissions) in automatic 24-hour cash exchange machines at the airport, Santa Apolónia train station or Rua Augusta 24.

ATMs Nearly every bank has 24-hour Multibanco automated teller machines (ATMs), where you can use a Visa, Access/ MasterCard, American Express or similar card to get a cash advance in escudos. Your home bank will levy a charge of about 1.5% per transaction, and conversion rates are reasonable. Cards are also accepted by many shops, hotels and a growing number of guesthouses and restaurants.

Portuguese ATMs occasionally spit out cards with a message like 'communication failure' or tell you your PIN number is wrong. A second try or another ATM will often work, but bear in mind that three 'wrong PIN number' messages may invali-date your card; after two such warnings you should seek help from a bank. A small stash of cash (pounds sterling or US dollars) is useful in case of such an emergency.

Costs

While costs are beginning to rise as Lisbon becomes more prosperous and popular, this is still one of Europe's most reasonably priced cities. Staying in hostels or camping grounds and self-catering, you could get by on around US$25 daily. Two people travel-ling together in the off season can eat and sleep well for US$60 to US$70 per day.

The cost of most things is likely to rise in the run-up period to the Euro 2004 Football Championships.

Tipping & Bargaining

If you're satisfied with the service at a restaurant, a reasonable tip is 5% to 10%. The bill at a top-end restaurant may include a *serviço* (service charge). For a snack at a bar or cafe, a bit of loose change is enough. Taxi drivers appreciate 10% of the fare.

Good-humoured bargaining is acceptable in markets. You can often bargain down the price of accommodation for long stays or during the low season.

Taxes & Refunds

IVA (Imposto Sobre Valor Acrescentado) is a sales tax of 17% levied on a wide range of goods and services. Tourists who are not resident outside the EU can claim an IVA refund on goods from shops belonging to Europe Tax-Free Shopping Portugal (as displayed on a sign in the window or at the till).

The minimum purchase for a refund is 11,700$00 in any one shop. The shop assist-ant fills in a cheque for the refund (minus an administration fee). When you're leaving

---

Quanto Custa?

Following are some typical unit costs in Lisbon. Accommodation prices show the range between the low and high seasons.

Double room in a lower-end pensão	4000$00 to 6000$00	(US$17 to US$25)
Double in a mid-range hotel	6000$00 to 15,000$00	(US$25 to US$65)
Three-course meal in a mid-range restaurant (minus drinks)	1700$00 to 3000$00	(US$7 to US$13)
Big Mac	490$00	(US$2.10)
Portuguese draught beer (30cL) in a bar	150$00 to 200$00	(US$0.65 to US$0.85)
Portuguese table wine (1L)	400$00 to 1500$00	(US$1.70 to US$6.50)
Three-minute, economy call from a Credifone to UK/USA	203$00	(US$0.85)

Lisbon airport you present the goods, cheque and your passport at a special customs desk in the departures terminal for a cash, postal-note or credit-card refund. If you're leaving overland, contact customs at your final EU border point, or call Europe Tax-Free Shopping Portugal (☎ 218 408 813).

POST & COMMUNICATIONS
Post
The most convenient post office (Map 6; ☎ 213 238 700) is in the pink building on Praça dos Restauradores. It's open 8 am to 10 pm weekdays and 9 am to 6 pm at weekends. The central post office (Map 7), on Praça do Comércio (officially known as Terreiro do Paço), is open 8.30 am to 6.30 pm weekdays. There is also a 24-hour post office at the airport.

Sending Mail *Correio normal* (to be posted in red letter boxes) refers to ordinary post, including air mail, while *correio azul* (in blue letter boxes) refers to priority or express mail. Postcards and letters up to 20g cost 140$00 to points outside Europe and 100$00 within Europe (except 90$00 to Spain); those within Portugal cost 52$00. International correio azul costs a minimum of 350$00 for a 20g letter.

Stamps are available at post offices, at kiosks and shops with a red *Correios – selos* (stamps) sign, and from vending machines. 'By air mail' is *por avião* in Portuguese; 'by surface mail' is *via superfície*. Allow four to six days for delivery within Europe, and eight to 10 days to the USA or Australia.

A 4kg to 5kg parcel sent surface mail to the UK costs 4700$00 (about US$25). Economy air (or surface airlift; SAL) costs about a third less than ordinary air mail, but usually arrives a week or so later. Printed matter is cheapest to send in batches of under 2kg.

Courier Services Courier agencies include DHL (☎ 218 100 099), TNT (☎ 218 545 050) and FedEx (toll-free ☎ 800 244 144). All are open during normal business hours (DHL also until 3 pm Saturday) and will collect from any Lisbon address. A 200g parcel costs about 5000$00 to the UK (24-hour delivery) or 7000$00 to the USA (one to two working days).

Receiving Mail Lisbon's *posta restante* service is at the central post office on Praça do Comércio. Letters should be addressed with the family name first, c/o Posta Restante, Central Correios, Terreiro do Paço, 1100 Lisbon. To collect poste restante mail (usually from counter 13 or 14), you must show your passport and pay 65$00 per item. Unclaimed letters are normally returned after a month.

American Express card-holders can have mail (and faxes) sent to them at Top Tours (see Travel Agencies earlier).

Addresses Addresses in Portugal are written with the street name first, followed by the building number. An alphabetical tag on the number, for example 2-A, indicates an adjacent entrance or building. The floor numbers may be included, with a degree symbol, so 15-3° means entrance No 15, 3rd floor. The further abbreviations D, dir or Dta (for *direita*, right), or E, esq or Esqa (for *esquerda*, left), tell you which door to go to. Floor numbering is by European convention; the 1st floor is one flight up from the ground floor. R/C *(rés do chão)* means ground floor.

Telephone
In 1999 Portugal overhauled its telephone numbering system. Aside from a few assistance numbers, all domestic numbers now have nine digits. All digits must be dialled from any location, effectively rendering area codes obsolete.

All except local calls are cheaper during the *económico* periods (9 pm to 9 am), and international calls to certain countries are even cheaper on Saturday and Sunday.

The cheapest and most convenient way to call anywhere is from a card-operated Credifone, using a *cartão telefónico* (phonecard). These cards are available from post and telephone offices and many newsagents for 650$00 (50 beeps or time units), 1300$00 (100) or 1900$00 (150); a youth or student card should get you a 10% discount. A metered telephone in a hotel or cafe will cost three to five times more than a Credifone.

You can also call, at coin-phone rates, from booths in Portugal Telecom offices and post offices, where you pay over the counter after your call is finished.

Numbers starting with 800 (*linha verde*; green line) are toll-free. Those starting with 808 (*linha azul*; blue line) are charged at local rates from anywhere in the country. Portugal's directory inquiries number is ☎ 118.

At the beginning of the *Páginas Amarelas* (Yellow Pages) in the telephone directory is a list of useful headings. Yellow Pages also has a Web site at www.paginasamarelas.pt. There is a privately operated 'talking yellow pages' at ☎ 217 952 222.

International Calls Here are approximate charges for a three-minute international call, using a phonecard:

country	normal	economy	weekend
Spain	200$00	181$00	109$00
UK, USA	229$00	203$00	109$00
Australia	582$00	436$00	436$00

For international directory inquiries, call ☎ 177. To make a reverse-charge *(pago no destino)* call, with the help of multilingual operators, dial ☎ 172. From Portugal, the international access code is ☎ 00.

International Phonecards A number of international phonecards now on the market can offer – at certain times and for certain destinations – cheaper rates than Portugal Telecom's. One is Lonely Planet's eKno Communication Card, aimed at independent travellers and offering competitive international rates, messaging services, free email and travel information. You can join online at www.ekno.lonelyplanet.com, where you will find the latest local-access number for the 24-hour service. Once you have joined always check the eKno Web site for updates on numbers and new features.

Country-Direct Service Portuguese operators can help you make collect (reverse

charges) or credit-card calls, but for an extra charge you can dial direct to operators in certain countries. Among these are:

Brazil	☎ 800 800 550
France	☎ 800 800 330
Germany	☎ 800 800 490
Ireland	☎ 800 800 353
New Zealand	☎ 800 800 640
USA	
(AT&T)	☎ 800 800 128
(MCI)	☎ 800 800 123
(TRT)	☎ 800 800 188

Calls to Portugal To call Portugal from abroad, dial the international access code of the country you're in, plus ☎ 351 (Portugal's country code), plus the full number (there are no area codes).

Telephone Rental Telecel rents *telemóveis* (mobile phones) from its airport shop (☎ 218 435 670, fax 218 435 673), open 8 am to 7 pm weekdays and 9 am to 6 pm Saturday. Aside from a refundable 70,000$00 deposit you pay only for the calls you make, at 90$00 per minute (180$00 to other phone networks during normal periods). International calls cost 180$00 per minute to the EU; 230$00 to other European countries, the USA and Canada; and 460$00 to other countries.

Using the TMN network, Polirent (Map 2; ☎ 213 513 511, fax 213 143 488) at Avenida Fontes Pereira de Melo 35, rents phones for 234$00 per day (after a deposit of around 40,000$00) and charges 25/47$00 per impulse (30 seconds) to TMN/other network phones. International calls cost 47/124$00 per impulse to Europe/other countries.

Mobile phone numbers all start with '9'.

Fax

The post offices offer a domestic and international fax service called Corfax, costing 820$00 for the first page to Europe and 1250$00 to North America or Australia (slightly less using the post office's own, much smaller, form). Collecting a fax at the post office costs 275$00 per page. Guesthouses and some computer/photocopying shops charge considerably less, eg, Planet

Megastore (see Email & Internet Access) charges 420$00 a page to Europe/Australia and 500$00 to North America (and 120$00 to receive a page).

Email & Internet Access

If you have a Web-based email account such as Hotmail (www.hotmail.com) or Yahoo! Mail (www.yahoo.com), you're set to access or send email from any cybercafe. If you want to log on from your hotel room, your Internet service provider (ISP) must have a global roaming service (enabling access via a Lisbon telephone number).

With luck your room will have a telephone jack. Most hotel jacks in Portugal are USA standard (RJ-11); for those that aren't you'll need an adapter. Be sure the hotel doesn't have a digital telephone exchange, which can blow your modem. You can always plug safely into an analog data line such as the hotel's fax line. Another problem with ordinary lines in Portugal is the faint 'beeps' that mark *impulsos* (units) of calling time, which can interfere with modem connections. The solution to this problem is an in-line filter.

Filters, line testers, telephone and power adapters, and various other accessories are available from a number of Web-based dealers including Konexx (www.konexx.com), TeleAdapt (www.teleadapt.com) and Road Warrior (www.warrior.com).

Several reliable places to log on to the Internet in Lisbon are:

Café.Com (also called Ciber 25; Map 8; ☎ 218 865 786) part of Teatro Taborda, Costa do Castelo 75; 2 pm to midnight Tuesday to Sunday; cafe with panoramic views; 500$00/hour (free until 7 pm for those under 18)

Ciber Chiado (Map 7; ☎ 213 466 722) next to Café no Chiado, Largo do Picadeiro 10; 4 pm to midnight weekdays, 8 pm to midnight Saturday; 300$00 per half-hour

Espaço Ágora (Map 4; ☎ 213 940 170) Rua Cintura, Armazém 1, Santos (behind Santos train station); 2 pm to around 1 am daily; 100$00 per 15 minutes; 300$00 per hour

Net Center (Map 2; ☎ 213 522 292) is in the Edifício Portugal Telecom building; some technical help available; 9 am to 7 pm weekdays only; 200$00 per half-hour

Pavilhão do Conhecimento (Map 9; ☎ 218 919 333) Parque das Nações; 10 am to 6 pm daily except Monday; free (but meant for visiting school children)

Planet Megastore (Map 2; ☎ 217 928 100) Avenida da República 41-B; computer and photocopying store; 8 am to midnight daily (until 11.30 pm Friday and Saturday and from 9 am on Sunday); 200$00 per 15 minutes

PostNet (Map 2; ☎ 213 511 050, fax 213 511 109) Avenida António Augusto Aguiar 17-B; stationery store; 8 am to 8 pm weekdays, to 2 pm Saturday; 150$00 per 15 minutes

Web Café (Map 6; ☎ 213 421 181) Rua do Diário de Notícias 126; cyberbar; 4 pm to 2 am daily; 175$00 per 15 minutes

INTERNET RESOURCES

The World Wide Web is a rich travel resource. You can research your trip, hunt down bargain fares, book hotels, check the weather, and chat with locals and fellow travellers about things to do (or avoid!).

A good place to start is the Lonely Planet Web site (www.lonelyplanet.com). Here you'll find postcards from other travellers and the Thorn Tree bulletin board, where you can ask questions before you leave or dispense advice when you get back. The subWWWay section links you to useful resources elsewhere on the Web. You'll find Web page Lonely Planet's Portugal at www.lonelyplanet.com/dest/eur/por.htm.

Turismo de Lisboa's good bilingual Web site, at www.atl-turismolisboa.pt, includes upcoming events, accommodation and a visitors guide. Another comprehensive site, www.eunet.pt/Lisboa/i/lisboa.html, has museum, bar and club listings, restaurants and sights. John Laidlar's very detailed site, www.luso.u-net.com/lisbon.htm, describes every kind of transport operating in and around Lisbon. Carris, the city's main transport authority, includes route details of buses and trams on its site at www.carris.pt.

The leading entertainment venues have their own sites, notably the Centro Cultural de Belém (www.ccb.pt) and the Parque das Nações (www.parquedasnacoes.pt). It's also worth checking www.gulbenkian.pt, the Fundação Calouste Gulbenkian's site for events and exhibitions.

BOOKS
Lonely Planet
If you plan to journey more widely than just Lisbon, consider Lonely Planet's country-wide *Portugal* or one of its multicountry guides: *Europe on a shoestring*, *Western Europe* or *Mediterranean Europe*. And how's your Portuguese? Lonely Planet can help there too, with its *Portuguese phrasebook* or *Western Europe phrasebook*.

Guidebooks
The small-format *Landscapes of Portugal* series by Brian and Eilenn Anderson has one on Sintra, Cascais and Estoril, which would suit drivers and walkers who are interested in short tours of these areas. Fernando Pessoa's *O Que O Turista Deve Ver* (What the Tourist Should See) is a quaint tour of the city dating from 1925 (see Arts in the Facts about Lisbon chapter for more on Pessoa).

Travel
Rose Macaulay's entertaining and well known collections, *They Went to Portugal* and *They Went to Portugal Too*, follow the experiences of a variety of English visitors from medieval times until the 19th century. These are easy to enjoy in small doses.

Paul Hyland's *Backwards out of the Big Beyond* is the poetic account of a voyage of discovery encompassing Lisbon, Sintra and the far corners of Alentejo.

History & Politics
David Birmingham's *A Concise History of Portugal*, academic but very readable, comes to grips with Lisbon's role in the history of Portugal up to 1993. A classic reference on the Age of Discoveries is CR Boxer's *The Portuguese Seaborne Empire, 1415-1825*. For insights into the Salazar years, delve into António de Figueiredo's *Portugal: Fifty Years of Dictatorship*. The events of 1974 are well documented in *Revolution & Counter-Revolution in Portugal*, written by Martin Kayman.

Recent gripping historical thrillers include Robert Wilson's award-winning *A Small Death in Lisbon*, set in 1940s Lisbon; and the best-selling *The Last Kabbalist of Lisbon* by Richard Zimler, revealing the harrowing life of secret Jews in the 16th century.

Italian author (and Pessoa's biographer), Antonio Tabucchi, re-creates the chilling period of the Salazar years in *Declares Pereira*.

Food & Drink
In *The Taste of Portugal*, Edite Vieira flavours her recipes with cultural background information and lively anecdotes. Another good cookbook is Maite Manjon's *The Home Book of Portuguese Cookery*.

Richard Mayson's brisk, readable *Portugal's Wines & Wine-Makers: Port, Madeira & Regional Wines* is a great introduction to the country's favourite product. Another detailed resource is Jan Read's *The Wines of Portugal*.

A fictional tour of Lisbon's bars and restaurants is poetically recounted in *Requiem: A Hallucination* by Antonio Tabucchi.

General
One of the best all-round books on Portugal and the Portuguese is Marion Kaplan's perceptive *The Portuguese: The Land & Its People* (revised 1998), which ranges knowledgably from Lisbon to literature, and from agriculture to emigrants.

FILMS
Wim Wenders' film *A Lisbon Story* had its world premiere in Lisbon in 1994, the year the capital was named European City of Culture. Originally conceived as a documentary, it acquired a story line as it went along: a movie sound man wanders through the streets trying to salvage a film that its director has abandoned, recording the sounds of the city. In the film Wenders pays tribute to many cinema greats, including the Portuguese director Manoel do Oliveira. See Cinema under Arts in the Facts about Lisbon chapter for more on locally made films about contemporary Lisbon.

NEWSPAPERS & MAGAZINES
Portuguese-Language Press
The major Portuguese-language daily newspapers include *Diário de Notícias*, *Público*, *Jornal de Notícias* and the gossip tabloid

FACTS FOR THE VISITOR

Correio da Manhã, which licks all the others for circulation. Popular weeklies include *O Independente* and *Expresso*. *Público* (www .publico.pt), *Diário de Notícias* (www.dn.pt) and *Jornal de Notícias* (www.jnoticias.pt) also have online editions.

Newsstands groan under the weight of sports publications; the best one for football is *A Bola*. For entertainment listings, check local dailies, especially the Saturday edition of *Público*.

Sport or the state of the world: Read all about it!

Foreign-Language Press

Several English-language newspapers are published in Portugal by/for its expatriate population and feature very useful classified sections. The best known are *APN* (Anglo-Portuguese News), published Thursday, and the *News*, which is published twice monthly in regional editions. The *News* has an online edition (www.the-news.net).

At well-stocked newsagents such as Tabacaria Mónaco, Rossio 21, and Tabacaria Adamastor at Rua 1 de Dezembro 2 (both Map 6), you can also pick up a range of the foreign papers including the *International Herald xTribune*, *Le Monde* and the *Guardian*, and magazines such as *Paris-Match*, *Le Point*, *l'Express*, *Der Spiegel*, *Bünte*, *The Spectator* and *The Economist*.

RADIO & TV

Domestic radio in Lisbon is represented by the state-owned Rádiodifusão Portuguesa (RDP) stations Antena 1 on MW and FM, and Antena 2 and Antena 3 on FM; the private Rádio Renascença; as well as a clutch of local stations. Essentially all of the radio broadcasts are in Portuguese. The evening programming includes helpings of music, with jazz on Antena 1 and rock on Rádio Comercial. In Lisbon you'll find Antena 1 is at MW 666kHz, FM 95.7 or 99.4MHz. For Rádio Comercial try MW 1035kHz or FM 97.4MHz.

English-language broadcasts of the BBC World Service and Voice of America (VOA) can be picked up on various medium-wave and short-wave frequencies in Portugal, though BBC reception is generally poor. The best way to find out current frequency and schedule information, contact the BBC at fax 020-7257 8258 or check its Web site, www.bbc.co.uk/worldservice/index.shtml; VOA information is available at fax 202-619 0916, **e** voa-europe@voa.gov or its Web site, www.voa.gov.

Portuguese TV consists of the state-run Rádio Televisão Portuguesa (RTP) channels RTP-1 (VHF) and RTP-2 (UHF), plus the private channels Sociedade Independente de Communicação (SIC) and TV Independente (TVI). Football matches, lightweight entertainment, Portuguese and Brazilian soap operas *(telenovelas)* and subtitled foreign movies dominate.

There are at least 15 cable TV and satellite channels available in Lisbon. These feature mainly sports, music and movies. Some of the mid-range and many top-end hotels offer satellite TV in their rooms for the entertainment of guests.

VIDEO SYSTEMS

If you want to record or buy video tapes to play back home, you won't get a picture if the image registration systems are different. Portugal uses the PAL system, which is not compatible with either the French SECAM system or the North American and Japanese NTSC system. Australia and most of Europe use PAL.

PHOTOGRAPHY & VIDEO
Film & Equipment
All brands of slide and print film and 8mm video cassettes are widely available, plus video accessories (but bring the necessary battery charger, plugs and transformer plus a few cartridges).

Print film processing is as fast and cheap as anywhere in Europe. Slide and video processing are rarer.

Technical Tips
Except for the occasional indoor shot with something like 400 ASA/ISO film, you'll rarely need anything faster than about 100 ASA/ISO. Contrast between light and shadow is harshest at high noon; try to get out in the early morning or just before sunset for the gentlest light and the best panoramic shots from the hilltop *miradouros* (lookouts) that abound in Lisbon.

Video cameras have amazingly sensitive microphones. Filming beside a busy road may produce only a deafening roar as a soundtrack when you replay it at home.

Restrictions
Some museums and galleries forbid flash photography.

Photographing People
Older Portuguese often become frustratingly serious when you take their photos, but few will object to it and many will be delighted. Everybody seems to like having their own children photographed! Nevertheless, the courtesy of asking beforehand *(Posse tirar uma fotografia, por favor?)* is always appreciated. The same goes for video: ask first.

Airport Security
Even lead-lined 'filmsafe' pouches may not keep unprocessed film safe, as some international airports now use 'smart' CTX 5000 scanners on checked baggage; any film inside is certain to be ruined. The solution is to carry unprocessed film in your carry-on bags: scanners for carry-on bags at most major airports are relatively harmless, at least for slow and medium-speed films.

TIME
Portugal, like Britain, is on GMT/UTC in winter and GMT/UTC plus one hour during summer. This puts it an hour ahead of Spain year-round. Clocks are set forward by an hour on the last Sunday in March and back on the last Sunday in October.

ELECTRICITY
Electricity is 220V, 50Hz. Plugs normally have two round pins, though some have a third, projecting, earth pin. North American appliances without built-in voltage adjustment will need a transformer.

WEIGHTS & MEASURES
Portugal uses the metric system; see the inside back cover for a conversion guide. Decimals are indicated with commas, and thousands with points.

LAUNDRY
Most *lavandarias* (laundries) concentrate on dry cleaning *(limpar/limpeza a seco)*. Those that also do wash-and-dry *(lavar e secar)*, eg, Tinturaria (Map 2), on Avenida Praia da Vitória, usually need a day or two. Some may do ironing *(passar a ferro)* too. Count on 1500$00 to 2500$00 for a 5kg load, including drying. Your guesthouse proprietor may be willing to do small loads.

The only self-service laundry in Lisbon is Lave Neve (Map 6) at Rua da Alegria 37, open 10 am to 1 pm and 3 to 7 pm weekdays and till noon on Saturday.

TOILETS
Public toilets *(sanitários* or *casas de banho)* are rare, though coin-operated street toilets (20$00) are increasingly common. Most people just go to the nearest cafe for a drink or pastry and use the facilities there. Look for a 'WC' sign, or 'H' *(homens*; men) or 'S' *(senhoras*; women).

euro currency converter 100$00 = €0.50

LEFT LUGGAGE

There are left-luggage facilities at the airport and the main bus terminal at Arco do Cego (around 500$00 per day depending on size), but lockers are only at the major train stations (costing from 200$00 for the first two hours to around 650$00 for 48 hours).

HEALTH

Lisbon presents no serious health problems to the sensible traveller. Your main risks are likely to be an upset stomach from enjoying too much food and wine, or sunburn from the nearby beaches.

Predeparture Planning

Citizens of EU countries are covered for medical treatment throughout the EU on presentation of an E111 certificate, though fees are likely to be charged for medications, secondary examinations and dental work. The E111 form should be available at your local health services department (or, in the UK, at post offices). Most travel insurance policies include medical cover.

If you wear glasses, take a spare pair and your prescription. Similarly, take an adequate supply of any medication you need (eg, contraceptive pills) as it may not always be available (although most pharmacies are remarkably well equipped). The most widely available contraceptive in Portugal is condoms *(preservativos)*, which are available in all pharmacies and most supermarkets.

No vaccinations are required for entry into Portugal, although a yellow fever vaccination certificate is required from travellers coming from infected areas and arriving in or bound for the Azores or Madeira. There are a few routine vaccinations that are recommended, including up-to-date tetanus, polio and diphtheria immunisations.

Precautions

Beware of any ice cream that has melted and been refrozen. Take care with shellfish (eg, cooked mussels that haven't opened properly can be dangerous) and avoid undercooked meat, particularly minced meat. Tap water is almost always safe to drink in Lisbon. Bottled water is widely available.

Medical Services

Farmácias (pharmacies) are plentiful in Lisbon and often have English-speaking staff. They are typically open 9 am to 6 or 7 pm weekdays (closing at lunchtime), and Saturday morning. To find an open pharmacy, check the list posted on the door of a closed one, call directory inquiries (☎ 118) or check the daily *Público* newspaper. A competent central pharmacy is Farmácia Estácio (Map 6) at Rossio 62. For homeopathic remedies, you could try Farmácia Homeopática Santa Justa (Map 6) at Rua Santa Justa 6.

Lisbon has half a dozen *centros de saúde* (state-administered medical centres), typically open 8 am to 8 pm daily, though you're unlikely to find any English-speakers.

If you have more serious problems, the private Hospital Britânico (British Hospital, also called Hospital Inglês; Map 4; ☎ 213 955 067, 213 976 329) at Rua Saraiva de Carvalho 49, has English-speaking staff and doctors. See Emergencies later in this chapter for details of large state hospitals with 24-hour *serviço de urgência* (emergency wards). There are also numerous (and pricier) private clinics and physicians; ask at turismos.

WOMEN TRAVELLERS

Despite the official reversal of many traditional attitudes towards women after the 1974 revolution, Portugal remains a man's world. Although women make up over half the total labour force, there are still few women in positions of public trust. The ruling Socialist Party, which favours quotas for women in elected and state-appointed bodies, took the first step in 1999 by creating the new post of Minister for Equality, whose brief includes minority and women's rights issues. Lisbon's more emancipated women already enjoy a measure of equality, but this is not representative of the rest of the country.

Attitudes Towards Women

Portuguese machismo is more irritating than dangerous. Waiters, for example, may serve every man in the place before even glancing at you, and if you're travelling with a male partner, everyone will expect him to do all the talking and ordering.

Safety Precautions

Women travelling on their own in Lisbon report few serious problems but there are certain areas you should be cautious of visiting alone late at night, in particular the Alfama, Bairro Alto, Cais do Sodré areas. Flashers and cruisers can be a problem in Parque Eduardo VII, even during the day. Stoked-up male tourists in nearby seaside resorts such as Cascais may be unpleasant company, especially late on weekend nights. Hitchhiking is not recommended for solo women, anywhere in the city or elsewhere.

Organisations

The Comissão para a Igualdade e para os Direitos das Mulheres (Map 2; ☎ 217 983 000, fax 217 983 098), the country's leading advocate of women's rights, has a library of relevant material. Its office is at Avenida da República 32.

The Associação Portuguesa de Mulheres Empresárias (Association of Portuguese Women Entrepreneurs; Map 2; ☎ 213 872 148, fax 213 872 149, e apme@mail.telepac .pt), Rua Marquês de Fronteira 4B, lobbies for female entrepreneurs and career women nationally and internationally (especially in the Portuguese-speaking African countries) and for the full integration of women into all aspects of society.

GAY & LESBIAN TRAVELLERS

Attitudes towards gay lifestyles in Lisbon have changed dramatically in the last few years. Thanks to steady political lobbying by ILGA-Portugal (the country's first official gay and lesbian organisation) and a more liberal environment overall, the homosexual movement has rapidly developed. However, this trend has yet to reach rural areas where gay lifestyles are generally a source of bafflement and lesbians are more or less ignored. In overwhelmingly Catholic Portugal, there is still little understanding of homosexuality and negligible tolerance of it within families.

Gay Pride

Gays recall 1997 as a watershed for gay awareness in Portugal, when Lisbon city authorities backed the first Gay Pride Festival (Arraial Gay e Lésbico) and a Gay & Lesbian Film Festival (Festival de Cinema Gay e Lésbico), and the city's first Gay & Lesbian Community Centre was opened (see under Gay & Lesbian Travellers). The festivals now take place annually – Gay Pride on the Saturday closest to 28 June and the Film Festival over the last two weeks in September.

Still, Lisbon has more places for gay/lesbian socialising than anywhere else in Portugal, mostly concentrated in Bairro Alto and nearby Príncipe Real. Venues include restaurants, bars, discos and saunas (some may look closed from the outside, and you'll need to ring a doorbell to get in). The nearby beaches (especially Costa da Caparica) are popular too.

For listings of gay bars/clubs, news and information on the Lisbon Gay and Lesbian Film Festival, visit ILGA-Portugal's Web site (www.ilga-portugal.org/english/index .html). ILGA's Women's Group (see Organisations later in this section) has its own good site (www.geocities.com/WestHollywood/ Stonewall/9915), with links to other lesbian organisations. The Portugal Gay Web site (www.portugalgay.pt/guide_uk) includes an English-Portuguese message board. All three sites have English versions.

Legal Situation

Homosexuality is not illegal in Portugal, but there is still discrimination. The penal code recognises 16 as the age of consent between homosexual partners (but 14 for heterosexuals) and considers all homosexual acts between an adult and an adolescent aged 14 to 16 criminal offences, liable to a fine and/or a jail term of up to two years.

Organisations

ILGA-Portugal was founded in 1995, and is a member of the International Lesbian &

Gay Association (ILGA). Its Centro Comunitário Gay e Lésbico de Lisboa (the Gay & Lesbian Community Centre; Map 5; ☎ 218 873 918, fax 218 873 922, e ilga-portugal@ ilga.org), Rua de São Lazaro 88, is open 5 to 9 pm Monday to Saturday (closed during August), and has information on gay organisations and facilities as well as a cafe that's open on Saturday.

ILGA-Portugal publishes a bimonthly newsletter, *Boletim Informátivo*. A popular gay magazine is the quarterly *Korpus*. The Associação Opus Gay (Map 2; ☎ 213 151 396, fax 213 170 797, e opus@opusgay association.com), Rua da Ilha Terceira 34, 2nd floor, works with Turismo de Lisboa and the International Gay & Lesbian Travel Association to promote gay and lesbian tourism in Portugal (e opusgayturismo@ hotmail.com). Its visitor-friendly centre is open 10 am to 1 pm and 4 to 8 pm Monday to Saturday.

Clube Safo (e clube_safo@hotmail.com) at Apartado 95, 2000-029 Santarém, is the country's leading lesbian club; it organises meetings and debates and also publishes a bimonthly newsletter, *Zona Livre*. Another lesbian periodical is *Lilás* (e lilas@pobox .com), Apartado 6104, 2700 Amadora. The efficient Grupo de Mulheres or Women's Group (☎/fax 218 873 918, e gmulheres@ geocities.com), a part of ILGA-Portugal, works to promote lesbian rights and a sense of pride. It organises social gatherings at the Gay & Lesbian Community Centre every second Saturday of the month from 8 pm to midnight, and lesbian film screenings every fourth Saturday at 6 pm.

DISABLED TRAVELLERS

Relatively few places in Lisbon have facilities for disabled travellers. Lisbon airport is wheelchair-accessible and the major train stations have toilets with wheelchair access. Eleven metro stations (including Marquês de Pombal, Baixa-Chiado, Cais do Sodré and Oriente) have passenger elevators; all stations should feature them in the near future.

Special parking spaces are scarce and are routinely used by nondisabled drivers. An EU-wide Blue Badge scheme, entitling disabled people to on-street parking concessions, is supposed to be implemented by the end of 2002; for more information visit the Web site: www.mobility-unit.detr.gov .uk/bluebadge/index.htm.

ICEP offices abroad (see Tourist Offices earlier in this chapter) and the Turismo de Lisboa offices can recommend barrier-free accommodation (mainly at top-end hotels). Both of Lisbon's youth hostels have wheelchair facilities.

Organisations

The Secretariado Nacional de Rehabilitação (Map 2; ☎ 217 936 517, fax 217 965 182), Avenida Conde de Valbom 63, publishes the Portuguese-language *Guia de Turismo para Pessoas com Deficiências* (Tourist Guide for Disabled People), with sections on barrier-free accommodation, transport, shops, restaurants and sights. It's available only from the Secretariado's offices, open 10 am to noon and 2 to 7 pm weekdays.

Carris (Lisbon's public transport agency) has specially adapted minibuses for hire, with advance notice (☎ 217 585 676, fax 213 649 399), but few staff speak any English. For help with this type of information and other travel arrangements, contact the Cooperativa Nacional Apoio Deficientes (CNAD; Map 1; ☎/fax 218 595 332), at Praça Dr Fernando Amado, Lote 566-E, whose Turintegra department deals specifically with holidays for disabled travellers.

SENIOR TRAVELLERS

The Portuguese show great respect to their elders and treat senior travellers well. If you're over 65 you can get some attractive discounts, including reduced entry fees to museums and for sightseeing excursions and train fares. See the Documents section of this chapter for details of seniors cards.

LISBON FOR CHILDREN

Portugal is a splendidly child-friendly place. As Marion Kaplan observes in *The Portuguese: The Land & Its People*, 'To the Portuguese, small children, no matter how noisy and ill-behaved, are angels to be adored and worshipped, overdressed and underdisciplined'. Even teenage boys seem to have a soft spot for toddlers.

But actual facilities aren't always so generously supplied. Following are some tips for making a trip to Lisbon with kids easier for you and fun for them. For more detailed and wide-ranging suggestions, pick up the current edition of Lonely Planet's *Travel with Children*.

Supplies & Food

Pharmacies are a handy source of baby supplies of all kinds (including tinned food). Every decent *minimercado* (grocery) has disposable nappies while *supermercados* (supermarkets) stock toys and children's clothes, too.

All but the stuffiest restaurants tolerate kids well and can provide child-sized portions. One problem for younger kids is that restaurants only open for evening meals at 7 pm at the earliest. Some may let you in earlier and cook something simple. Lucky you if your child likes soup; there is often a pot of it ready to be served as soon as you walk in the door.

Locations with traffic-free space for kids to run around while you sip your port at nearby restaurants include Largo do Carmo, Praça das Flores, Parque das Nações, Belém, and the chic open-air restaurants at the Doca de Santo Amaro.

Accommodation

The best bets are self-catering flats (eg, in Sintra; see the Excursions chapter for details) or simple pensões. Most hotels and pensões can come up with a baby cot. Lisbon's nearby camping grounds and its youth hostels (which have private rooms as well as dormitories) are excellent places to meet other children and families.

Health, Hazards & Annoyances

Lisbon presents no significant health risks for kids other than the usual city hazards of traffic and pollution and too much sun at the nearby beaches (beware, too, of the Atlantic Ocean's strong undertow). The city's parks can sometimes be grubby and popular with down-and-outs.

Teddy Traumas

Is your child throwing a fit because her teddy's lost its eye or leg? Help is at hand, thanks to the unique Hospital das Bonecas (Dolls' Hospital), founded in 1830 and still going strong. The 'hospital' (☎ 213 428 574) is actually a small workshop that can repair and replace everything from dolls' eyes, limbs and hair to wigs, hats and clothes. Emergency repairs can be undertaken within hours if necessary. New supplies are also on sale at the 'hospital' entrance at Praça da Figueira 7 (Map 6).

Toilets with baby-changing facilities are annoyingly rare, even in kid-friendly Parque das Nações, although modern shopping malls are often better-equipped; ask for *fraldário*.

Childcare

Baby-Sitters Baby-sitting services are advertised in the yellow pages (under 'Baby-Sitters'), the classified pages of *Público* and by students on notice boards at Planet Megastore (see Email & Internet Access earlier in this chapter) and the IPJ (see Useful Organisations later). Clube dos Traquinas (☎ 217 933 571) charges around 1500$00 an hour for baby-sitting at a hotel or at home. Criança e Companhia (☎ 213 572 616) has similar rates.

Kindergartens Ludoteca, found all over Portugal, are privately funded play areas for four to 12-year-olds, staffed by professional kindergarten teachers and equipped with good-quality games, toys, art supplies etc. Established mainly for Portuguese children (the staff usually speak little English), they are open to visiting children too. Lisbon's most convenient Ludoteca are at the Calouste Gulbenkian's Centro Artístico Infantil (Map 2; ☎ 217 823 491; open 10 am to 12.30 pm and 2.30 to 5 pm weekdays between mid-July and September) and at Chapitô's Collectividade Cultural, Costa do Castelo 7 (Map 8; ☎ 218 861 410; similar hours but closed during school holidays in July and August, and at Christmas and Easter).

FACTS FOR THE VISITOR

Discounts & Children's Rates

Children under the age of eight are entitled to a 50% discount in hotels and guesthouses if they share their parents' room; budget places may charge nothing extra at all. Preschool children usually get into museums and other sights free. Kids under four travel free on all city transport (four to 12-year-olds get 50% discount with Portuguese Railways).

Entertainment

Lisbon may look like a pretty stuffy place to a child. But its *elevadors* (funiculars) and trams are great fun (especially those to Belém and the Alfama), the spacious Parque das Nações is refreshingly kid-friendly and several museums, such as the Museu da Marioneta, can be appealing. Even feeding the pigeons in the squares can keep toddlers happy for hours. There are plenty of day-trip attractions too, including the palaces, castle and toy museum at Sintra as well as the beaches of Estoril, Cascais, Costa da Caparica and Praia Grande (for details see the Excursions chapter).

The best city-centre *parques infantil* (playgrounds) are in the Jardim da Estrela and Parque Eduardo VII (near the wonderful greenhouses, which are shady and fun, too). You can rent bikes from the Parque das Nações and along Belém's broad riverfront promenade (see the Getting Around chapter for details), though beware of the unfenced water's edge. Both places also have electric 'minitrain'; the one in Belém does a short circuit for 500$00 (free for children under four), starting from opposite the turismo kiosk every hour after 10 am. In the Parque, the trains depart from near the Pavilhão Atlântico between 10 am and 10 pm for 100$00 (50$00 children under 12).

Perhaps the best single venue for kids is Parque das Nações, an accessible and largely traffic-free 2km-long riverside esplanade. As well as its Oceanário and entertainment pavilions, it also has a cable car, shady gardens and a bowling arena and 'adrenalin park'. The nearby air-conditioned Centro Vasco da Gama shopping mall can be a useful diversion too. The Shopping chapter provides details of other big malls where toddlers can run amok safely and pester you for coin-operated toy rides.

Lastly, keep an eye out for festivals that often come complete with parades, music, fireworks and dancing (see Public Holidays & Special Events later in this chapter). For older children interested in windsurfing, hiking or horse riding, see the Activities sections of the Excursions chapter.

The town hall's monthly *Cultural Agenda* (available at tourist offices) has a good children's section on events and venues. Take a look, too, at the Saturday edition of *Público,* which lists the week's forthcoming events and entertainment for kids. Here are some other suggestions:

Centro Artístico Infantil (Map 2; ☎ 217 823 491) at the Museu Calouste Gulbenkian; play area (see Kindergartens in the Childcare section earlier) and free art workshops *(ateliers)* at 3 pm on Saturday and Sunday for children aged four to 12

Centro de Pedagogia e Animação (Map 10; ☎ 213 612 400) in the Centro Cultural de Belém; weekend program of performances and workshops during term time

Feira Popular (Map 1; ☎ 217 934 435), Avenida da República, Entrecampos; vast fairground with roller coasters, big wheels, stalls and restaurants; 4 pm to midnight weekdays; 3 pm to midnight on weekends and holidays; 300$00 (free for children under 11)

Jardim Zoológico (Map 1; ☎ 217 232 900) Estrada de Benfica 158; depressingly commercialised zoo, but with a good new reptile house and entertaining dolphin show; 10 am to 8 pm daily (to 6 pm in winter); all-inclusive tickets cost 1990$00 (1500$00 children aged three to 11; 1200$00 students)

Museu da Marioneta (Puppet Museum; Map 8; ☎ 218 865 794) Largo Rodrigues de Freitas 13; puppet curiosities and occasional weekend puppet shows; 10 am to 1.30 pm and 2.30 to 7 pm daily except Monday; 500$00

Museu das Crianças (Children's Museum; Map 10; ☎ 213 622 828) 1st floor of Belém's Museu de Marinha; for school children aged four to 12, with interactive educational displays (in Portuguese only); 10 am to 5 pm weekends (10 am to 6 pm daily except Monday between August and mid-September); 800$00 (children 550$00) includes admission to the Museu de Marinha

Museu de Cera (Wax Museum; Map 3; ☎ 213 979 095) at Gare Marítima Rocha do Conde de

Óbidos, Doca de Alcântara; 11 am to 2 pm and 3 to 8 pm daily except Monday; 800$00 (600$00 children under 12)

Parque do Gil (Map 9; ☎ 218 940 276) at Parque das Nações; huge indoor adventure playground for the under-12s; 3 to 8 pm weekdays (2.30 to 7.30 pm in winter and 10 am to 8 pm weekends); 600$00 per hour

Parque Recreativo do Alto da Serafina (also known as Parque dos Indios; Map 1; ☎ 217 743 224); expansive children's playground surrounded by tons of open space in the Parque Florestal de Monsanto (bus No 2 or 13 from Praça do Comércio to Serafina, then a 15-minute uphill walk); Indian-style wigwams as well as slides, swings, etc; 9 am to 8 pm (6 pm in winter) daily

Planetário Calouste Gulbenkian (Map 10; see Belém in the Things to See & Do chapter) special children's session (for children over 6) at 11 am Sunday (admission free)

Playcenter (Map 1; ☎ 217 113 735) Centro Comercial Colombo; Portugal's largest indoor fun fair including roller coaster, simulators, bumper cars and go-kart track; noon to midnight (11 am to midnight on weekends)

Teatro Infantil de Lisboa (Map 1; ☎ 218 477 853) Avenida Frei Miguel Contreras 52 (at Teatro Municipal Maria Matos); special performances for children during term time

USEFUL ORGANISATIONS

The Instituto Português da Juventude (IPJ; Portuguese Youth Institute) is a state-funded network of youth centres offering a wide range of facilities to people under 30. Most have libraries (free Internet access), cafes and study rooms, and are good places to meet local young people. IPJ's Lisbon headquarters (Map 5; ☎ 213 522 694, ⓔ ipj.infor@mail.telepac.pt), Avenida da Liberdade 194, includes a Departamento de Informação aos Jovens (Youth Information Department) with stacks of information on courses and adventure activities, plus useful notice boards. The nearest other IPJ branch is in Setúbal (see the Excursions chapter). IPJ's Web site is at www.sejuventude.pt.

Movijovem (Map 2; ☎ 213 596 000, fax 213 596 001, ⓔ movijovem@mail.telepac .pt), Avenida Duque d'Ávila 137, is a leading youth organisation. It arranges youth activities, issues youth cards and acts as the central booking office for the youth hostels around Portugal.

LIBRARIES

The best for Lisbon's *bibliotecas* are the General Arts Library of the Fundação Calouste Gulbenkian (Map 2; ☎ 217 935 131), Avenida de Berna 56, and Biblioteca Nacional (Map 1; ☎ 217 982 000) at Campo Grande 83. The Biblioteca Municipal (Map 2; ☎ 217 971 326) is in the Palácio das Galveias, Campo Pequeno.

UNIVERSITIES

The vast Universidade de Lisboa (Map 1) is 5km north-west of Rossio, while the most prestigious university in Lisbon is the Universidade Católica, near Sete Rios. There are nearly a dozen other private universities as well.

A good central place to meet students and pick up information from the notice boards is the Departamento de Informação aos Jovens (see Useful Organisations later) and Espaço Ágora, which also has a 24-hour cafe with student discounts (see Email & Internet Access earlier in the chapter). A notice board advertising everything from flats and jobs to computers and cars for sale can also be found at Planet Megastore (for this, and Espaço Ágora, see Email & Internet Access earlier).

CULTURAL CENTRES

The British Council (Map 5; ☎ 213 476 141, fax 213 476 151, ⓔ isabel.lopes@britcounpt .org), at Rua de São Marçal 174, has a huge library including the latest English newspapers. Opening hours vary daily but 2 to 6 pm on weekdays is a sure bet.

At Avenida Luís Bívar 91 (Map 2) are the Alliance Française (☎ 213 111 483, fax 213 157 950, ⓔ a.f.lisbonne@clix.pt) and the Institut Franco-Portugais de Lisbonne (☎ 213 111 400, fax 213 111 463, ⓔ ifplisb@ esoterica.pt). The latter has regular cultural events (including films) and a library, Mediateca (☎ 213 111 421, ⓔ bibifp@ ibm.net), open at varying times but always 1 to 6 pm Monday to Thursday and 10 am to 2.30 pm Friday. The library at the Goethe Institut (Map 5; ☎ 218 824 511), at Campo dos Mártires da Pátria 37, is open 3 to 7 pm Monday to Thursday.

FACTS FOR THE VISITOR

DANGERS & ANNOYANCES

Crime

Lisbon has a low crime rate by European standards, but it's on the rise. Most crime against foreigners involves pickpocketing and bag-snatching (especially in rush-hour trains and buses). Use a money belt and keep cameras and other tourist indicators out of sight. Car break-ins are rife. Reportedly, the only safe bet is to park your car in a hotel's locked garage.

Late at night (especially on weekends), it's unwise to wander alone through the streets of Bairro Alto, Alfama and Cais do Sodré or wait in deserted metro stations. Some African clubs can also be the scene of tension. Suspected rivalry between gangs of Cape Verdeans and Angolans has led to a rash of recent attacks, including one in April 2000 when seven people died at the city's popular Luanda club after tear gas canisters were set off.

Other places in the Lisbon area with a small but growing reputation for violent crime are the Estoril-Cascais beach resorts and the Setúbal region.

Traffic

Driving a car in or around Lisbon can be nerve-wracking. Normally gentle, peace-loving Portuguese can become irascible, deranged speed-freaks on the road, especially when they hit motorways: tailgating at high speeds and passing on blind curves are the norm. It's not surprising that Portugal has Europe's highest annual per capita death rates from road accidents. One of the most dangerous highways is the A5 west to Estoril.

Air Pollution

Thanks to Lisbon's surge of development and increasing car use, air pollution has noticeably worsened recently. Plus, many Portuguese smoke, and few restaurants have no-smoking areas.

Beaches

If you escape to the beaches, beware of the strong Atlantic Ocean currents and waves, especially at popular surfing spots like Praia do Guincho near Cascais.

EMERGENCIES

There's a (poorly signed) 24-hour tourist police post (Map 6; ☎ 213 421 634) in the Foz Cultura building next to the turismo in Praça dos Restauradores. The headquarters of the Polícia de Segurança Pública (PSP) (Map 7; ☎ 213 466 141) is at Rua Capelo 13 in Chiado.

The country-wide emergency number is ☎ 112. Call this for police *(polícia)*, fire services *(bombeiros)* or ambulance *(ambulância)*. Operators do understand English, French and Spanish.

There's no specific rape crisis hotline, but the Commissão para a Igualdade e para os Direitos das Mulheres (see Organisations under Women Travellers earlier) operates a freephone number for victims of violence at ☎ 800 202 148.

Hospitals with 24-hour emergency wards include São José (Map 6; ☎ 218 860 848, 218 860 131), on Rua José António Serrano, and Santa Maria Hospital School (Map 1; ☎ 217 975 171, 217 901 315) on Avenida Professor Egas Moniz.

LEGAL MATTERS

Foreigners here, as elsewhere, are subject to the laws of the host country. If you're detained by the police, your embassy in Lisbon can provide information on local lawyers and on the Portuguese legal system, take up allegations of ill-treatment in detention, and serve as a liaison between you and your family.

Penalties for dealing in, possessing and using illegal drugs are stiff, and may include heavy fines or jail terms.

BUSINESS HOURS

Offices normally operate 9 am to 1 pm and 3 to 5 pm and banks 8.30 am to 3 pm (both on weekdays only). Most shops open 9 or 9.30 am to 1 pm and 3 to 6 or 7 pm (and often 10 am to 1 pm Saturday too). The big shopping centres stay open to around 10 or 11 pm daily. Clubs and bars stay open until at least 3 am (and even later on Friday and Saturday nights).

Museums are typically open 10 am to 6 pm Tuesday to Saturday. If the Monday is a public holiday, they're usually closed on the following day as well.

Don't plan on getting much done between 1 and 3 pm, when the Portuguese give lunch serious and lingering attention.

PUBLIC HOLIDAYS & SPECIAL EVENTS

Lisbon is launching new festivals and events almost every year. For a full listing and further details, ask at any Turismo de Lisboa outlets for its English-language *Lisboa InVites – Events Calendar*.

Religious Festivals

Like the rest of Portugal, Lisbon enjoys celebrating various *romarias* (religious pilgrimages), *festas* (festivals) and *feiras* (fairs). At the core of many of these events are religious processions. Following are some of the more important ones that take place in and near the city.

February/March

Carnaval Taking place over the last few days before the start of Lent (about six weeks before Easter), Carnaval is a big fun event of parades featuring lots of drag and weirdly made-up kids.

May

Fátima Two annual pilgrimages to Fátima (in Estremadura), from 12 to 13 May and 12 to 13 October, celebrate the first and last apparitions of the Virgin Mary to three shepherd children here in 1917. This is one of the Catholic world's major holy sites. Hundreds of thousands of pilgrims from around the world turn up.

June

Feira Nacional da Agricultura A grand farming and livestock fair, also with bullfighting, folk singing and dancing, is held in Santarém (in Ribatejo) during the first week of June.

Festas dos Santos Populares (Festivals of the Popular Saints) See the boxed text 'Festas dos Santos Populares' in this section, plus the boxed text 'St Anthony' in the Things to See & Do chapter. Celebrations include the **Festa de São Pedro (St Peter)**, on 28 to 29 June, best seen across the Rio Tejo at Montijo, where there's a blessing of the boats, bullfights and a running of the bulls; and the **Festa de São João (St John)** on 23 to 24 June.

Theme Festivals

The new Festival dos Oceanos (Oceans Festival), which is held for two weeks from mid-August, has expanded its nautical theme (regattas, water sports contests and naval exhibitions) to encompass big shows

National Public Holidays

On the following days, banks, offices, department stores and some shops and museums close and public transport services are reduced.

New Year's Day	1 January
Carnaval Tuesday (the day before Ash Wednesday)	February/March (variable)
Good Friday	March/April (variable)
Liberty Day (celebrating the 1974 Revolution of the Carnations)	25 April
Labour Day	1 May
Corpus Christi	May/June (variable)
Portugal Day, or Camões & the Communities Day	10 June
Feast of the Assumption	15 August
Republic Day (commemorating the declaration of the Portuguese Republic in 1910)	5 October
All Saints' Day	1 November
Independence Day (commemorating the restoration of independence from Spain in 1640)	1 December
Feast of the Immaculate Conception	8 December
Christmas Day	25 December

Festas dos Santos Populares

In June, Lisbon lets its hair down with the Festas dos Santos Populares (Festivals of the Popular Saints), Christianised versions of traditional summer solstice celebrations. As Lisbon is the birthplace of Santo António (known elsewhere as St Anthony of Padua), the highlight of the celebrations is the Festa de Santo António (sometimes called the Festa de Lisboa or Lisbon Festival) on 12 to 13 June. The Alfama district (and to some extent Mouraria and Bairro Alto) parties through the night of the 12th, with little *tronos* (thrones) for Santo António in every square, plus parades, music, dancing and fireworks. On the 13th, a municipal holiday, revellers rest and the devout go to church.

The city then goes on buzzing for the rest of June, with city-sponsored concerts, exhibitions and street theatre.

and parades, musical performances, unusual city tours and a gastronomic fair.

Another new event, the Festival do Vinho (first fortnight in November) features a wine fair with products from all over Portugal plus folk dances and handicrafts.

The popular BaixAnima Festival enlivens the streets and main squares of the Baixa district with free performances of song, dance, drama, games and circus acts on weekends from July to September.

Music, Film & Art Festivals

The Fundação Calouste Gulbenkian (see the boxed text in the Things to See and Do chapter) organises several annual international music festivals including Jornadas de Música Contemporânea (Journeys in Contemporary Music) in May, Jazz em Agosto (Jazz in August) in the foundation's gardens in early August, and Jornadas de Música Antiga (Journeys in Ancient Music) at various historical sites in October.

The new Festival das Músicas e dos Portos (Harbour & Music Festival, sometimes called Festival do Fado), held for 10 days in early February, showcases fado and other sea-inspired music from another port city (Athens and New Orleans were previous participants) with fado performances, concerts, films, drama and dance. The Noite de Fado competition, held annually (usually in June), attracts some big names in fado, and up-and-coming artistes.

Neighbouring Almada hosts the Festival Internacional de Teatro, the country's leading theatre festival in early July, with events both here and in Lisbon. The two-week Festival de Cinema Gay e Lésbico in late September is increasingly popular; more mainstream is the long-established Festival Internacional de Cinema de Tróia (near Setúbal) in early June.

Lisbon's biggest rock event, Super Bock Super Rock, features two weeks of 18 concerts in March, both here and in Porto.

Athletic Events

Lisbon hosts an international marathon, the Maratona Cidade de Lisboa (☎ 213 644 097, fax 213 643 525, e memotur@mail .telepac.pt), every late November, attracting some 5000 athletes. Details are available on www.pgsite.com/memotur. In late March or early April, the Meia Maratona Cidade de Lisboa (Half Marathon; ☎ 214 413 182, fax 214 413 073) starts from Almada with some 30,000 runners crossing the river into Lisbon via the Ponte 25 de Abril, finishing in Belém. Both events also feature a 7km minimarathon for kids.

DOING BUSINESS

Portugal is one of Europe's most attractive investment opportunities thanks to political and social stability, a fast-growing economy, a business-friendly government offering EU-backed incentives and generous tax rates (the second lowest in the EU), and a cost-competitive and productive labour force. Foreign direct investment (notably from Germany, Spain, France and the UK) between 1992 and 1997 totalled over US$25.9 billion, primarily in manufacturing, finance, real estate and tourism.

Lisbon is an increasingly attractive venue for business conferences, ranking seventh in European popularity stakes. In addition to the new Feira Internacional de Lisboa (FIL) trade centre at the Parque das Nações (Map 9) there's also a brand new Centro de Congressos de Lisboa, at Parque Junqueira (Map 1; near Belém).

Useful Contacts Abroad

First contact your nearest branch of ICEP, the state's umbrella organisation for investment, commerce and tourism (see Tourist Offices earlier in this chapter for addresses; or check the Web site at www.portugal.org). ICEP can provide detailed information about the Portuguese economy, laws and regulations, investment areas and incentive schemes and identify suppliers of specific goods and services in Portugal. On request, ICEP can also select contacts and prepare meetings with the Portuguese business community or financial institutions and coordinate negotiations with officials for major investment projects.

Other useful Portuguese Chambers of Commerce or trade commissions include the following:

Camara Hispano-Portuguesa de Comercio e Industria en Espana (☎ 1 442 2300, fax 442 2290, e camaraportugal@mad.servicom.es) Zurbana 67-5B, 28010 Madrid

Chambre de Commerce Franco-Portugaise (☎ 01 42 22 87 60, fax 01 42 22 54 59) 219 blvd Saint-Germain, 75007 Paris

Portugal-US Chamber of Commerce Inc (☎ 212-354 4627, fax 575 4737, e anaosori@ix.netcom.com) 590 Fifth Ave, 3rd floor, New York, NY 10036 Web site: www.portugal-us.com

Portuguese UK Chamber of Commerce (☎ 020-7494 1844, fax 7494 1822, e info@portuguese-chamber.org.uk) 22-25 Sackville St, London W1X 1DE; foremost organisation promoting two-way trade and investment between the UK and Portugal, offering a wide range of support services Web site: www. portuguese-chamber.org.uk

UK Department of Trade & Industry Portugal Desk (☎ 020-7215 4776, fax 7215 4711) 66-74 Victoria St, London SW1 6SW

Useful Contacts in Lisbon

The trade office of your own embassy can provide tips and contacts. Other useful organisations include:

Câmara de Comércio Americano (American Chamber of Commerce; Map 2; ☎ 213 572 561, fax 213 572 508) Rua Dona Estefânia 155, 5th floor

Câmara de Comércio Luso-Britanica (British-Portuguese Chamber of Commerce; Map 4; ☎ 213 942 020, fax 213 942 029, e bpcc@mail.telepac.pt) Rua da Estrela 8

Câmara do Comércio e Indústria Portuguesa (Portuguese Chamber of Commerce & Industry; Map 6; ☎ 213 224 050, fax 213 224 051, e port.chamber.ci@mail.telepac.pt) Palácio do Comércio, Rua das Portas de Santo Antão 89

Office Rental

The Lisboa Business Centre (Map 2; ☎ 213 175 800, fax 213 575 658, e cenese@mail .telepac.pt), at Rua Alexandre Herculano 5, has fully furnished offices for rent from 60,000$00 a month and meeting rooms (for up to 16 people) for 2000$00 per hour or 50,000$00 per day. Secretarial services (including translation) are available for 20,000$00 per month. Staff speak some English, French and Spanish. The centre is open 24 hours from Monday to Saturday noon.

The international business outfit, Regus (☎ 213 404 500, fax 213 404 575, e lisboa .liberdade.21@regus.pt), has a central office complex at Avenida da Liberdade 110 (Map 5) with fully serviced office accommodation (from about 150,000$00 a month), conference rooms (with full audiovisual facilities) for up to 12 people, and secretarial and PA services. For companies who simply need a prestigious address, Regus can also offer its 'Link' service, providing a dedicated phone number, with calls answered in your company name or forwarded as required. For further details, check the Regus Web site at www.regus.com.

Computer Rental & Other Services

Planet Megastore (see under Email & Internet Access earlier in this chapter) has PCs and Macs for 800$00 per hour. Both here and at Fercopi (Map 7; ☎ 213 431 468), Rua da Vitória 91, there are photocopying, fax and laser copying facilities. The best store for your stationery and office equipment is Papelaria Fernandes (Map 6), with a central branch at Rua Áurea 145.

FACTS FOR THE VISITOR

Business Protocol

Although Portugal's rapid economic growth over the last decade has produced a new breed of enthusiastic and competitive entrepreneurial managers, many traditional ways of doing business are still valued. Trust, loyalty and personal contacts are regarded as the most crucial elements in a business relationship: it's who you know that matters. Be aware, too, that bargaining is part of the culture, so allow room to be flexible when trying to clinch a deal. Credit terms are also very important, and most Portuguese businesspeople expect to work on 90-day terms.

Although long, leisurely business lunches are the norm, meetings can be formal (and style of dress conservative). Appointments should be arranged well in advance (but don't be surprised if you're then kept waiting).

WORK

EU nationals can compete for any job in Portugal without a work permit. Non-EU citizens are expected to get a Portuguese work permit before they arrive, with the help of their prospective employer.

Several organisations can help you search for a job in Portugal before you go, and even arrange your work permit. One of the best known is the Council on International Educational Exchange (CIEE; ☎ 212-822 2600, fax 822 2699, e info@ciee.org), 205 East 42nd St, New York, NY 10017-5706. Its Web site is at www.ciee.org.

The prospects for on-the-spot work in Lisbon are limited unless you have a skill that's scarce or you can speak passable Portuguese. The search will be easier if you bring along a curriculum vitae, references and certified copies of relevant diplomas or certificates. Except for work where you're paid in kind or in petty cash, you'll probably have to sign a work contract.

If you're prepared to stay for a few months, a realistic option is English teaching. A TEFL certificate is a big help, though you may find work without one. Check the Páginas Amarelas under Escolas de Línguas (Language Schools), and the classified ads in Portugal's English-language press or in dailies such as *Diário de Notícias* and *Público*. You can also try posting notices in student-oriented places (see under Universities earlier in this chapter) where there's a need for English tutoring (a reasonable rate to charge is about 1500$00/hour).

Summertime bar or restaurant work is another possibility. Ask around the tourist bars in nearby beach resorts such as Cascais.

Serious job hunters and potential long-term residents will find Sue Tyson-Ward's *Living and Working in Portugal* a useful resource. *Live and Work in Spain and Portugal* by Jonathan Packer, aimed at EU citizens, is similar.

Getting There & Away

Lisbon airport is the city's main international gateway (Portugal's other international airports are at Porto and Faro). All overland connections are through Spain, of course. The two main rail crossings are at Vilar Formoso (the Paris to Lisbon line) and at Marvão-Beirã (the Madrid to Lisbon line).

Buses remain the cheapest way to get to Portugal, but not by much. Prices for the alternatives are coming down fast, thanks to the growing attraction of rail passes (even over point-to-point tickets) and the rise of 'no-frills' airline services.

AIR

Portugal's flagship international airline is TAP Air Portugal. PGA Portugália Airlines is the main domestic airline. It also has some European connections. There are more than two dozen carriers that have scheduled international services to and from Lisbon (see the boxed text 'Airlines & Booking Numbers' for some of the major ones and contact information).

Lisbon airport (Aeroporto de Lisboa, also called Aeroporto da Portela) is 30 minutes from the city centre when there's no traffic, but 45 minutes or more in rush hour; see the

WARNING

The information in this chapter is particularly vulnerable to change. Prices for international travel are volatile, routes are introduced and cancelled, schedules get changed, special deals come and go, and rules and visa requirements are amended. Always check directly with the airline or a travel agent to make sure you understand how a fare (and ticket you may buy) works, and get opinions, quotes and advice from as many airlines and travel agents as possible before you part with your money. The details in this chapter should be regarded as pointers and are no substitute for careful research.

Getting Around chapter for information on getting to/from the airport. For flight arrival and departure information, call ☎ 218 413 700. A new international airport is due to open at Ota, about 50km north of the city, in 2010.

Buying Tickets

The world of aviation has never been so competitive, making air travel better value than ever. But you have to research the options carefully to make sure you get the best deal. The Internet is a useful resource for checking air fares, as most travel agencies and airlines now have Web pages. But a close watch on newspaper travel ads will turn up short-term bargains too.

In general there's little to be gained from going directly to the airlines. They release discounted tickets to selected travel agents and discount agencies, and these are often the best deals. For short-term travel you'll save by travelling midweek, staying away at least one Saturday night or going for promotional offers. Many discounted tickets for long-term travel are valid for 12 months, allowing multiple stopovers with open dates. Another money-saving tactic is an indirect flight with a third-country carrier. Some airlines offer student/youth fares. Round-the-World (RTW) tickets are comparable in price to ordinary long-haul return flights. A good travel agent can tell you about all such deals.

But travel agents are now getting a run for their money from the new breed of 'no-frills' airlines, which mostly sell direct – by telephone or online – and very often for knock-down prices. At the time of writing the only one flying to Lisbon was the British carrier Go. Unlike 'full-service' airlines, no-frills carriers often sell one-way tickets at half the return fare, making it easy to stitch together an 'open jaw' itinerary, flying into one city and out of another.

You may find some very cheap flights advertised by obscure agencies. Most such

Airlines & Booking Numbers

Following are booking numbers for major carriers serving Lisbon. Numbers starting with 800 are toll-free, and those starting with 808 are charged at local rates, from anywhere in the country.

Aeroflot	☎ 213 496 193	LAM (Linhas Aéreas de Moçambique)	☎ 213 219 960
Air France	☎ 808 222 324	Lufthansa	☎ 214 245 155
Alitalia	☎ 213 536 141	PGA Portugália	☎ 218 425 559
Lisbon		after business hours	☎ 213 855 562
British Airways	☎ 808 212 125	Royal Air Maroc	☎ 213 190 770
Continental Airlines	☎ 213 834 000	Sabena	☎ 213 465 572
Delta Air Lines	☎ 213 139 861	Swissair	☎ 808 205 701
Iberia	☎ 213 558 119	TAAG Angola Airlines	☎ 213 575 899
KLM	☎ 218 476 354	TACV Cabo Verde Airlines	☎ 213 230 555
		TAP Air Portugal	☎ 808 205 700
		Tunisair	☎ 218 496 346
		TWA	☎ 800 201 284
		Varig	☎ 213 136 830

firms are honest and solvent, but there are some rogue outfits, so keep your eyes open. Paying by credit card generally offers protection since most card issuers do provide refunds if you don't get what you paid for. If you feel suspicious about a firm, steer clear – or pay only a deposit until you get your ticket, then ring the airline to confirm that you're actually booked on the flight before paying the balance.

Unless otherwise noted, fares quoted here are approximate return fares during peak air-travel season, based on advertised rates at the time of writing. None of them constitutes a recommendation for any airline.

Fares tend to be considerably cheaper outside of peak season. In North America and Europe, peak season is roughly from June to mid-September plus Christmas; 'shoulder' season is April to May and mid-September to October. In Australia and New Zealand, peak season is roughly December to January.

Travellers over 50 can get bargain fares with SAGA Holidays (☎ 1 800 414 383 in the USA; or ☎ 01303-773 532 in the UK); check its Web site at www.saga.co.uk.

Travellers with Special Needs

If you have special requirements (eg, you're in a wheelchair) let the airline know when you book and be sure to restate your needs when you reconfirm.

Guide dogs for the blind are subject to the same stiff quarantine laws as any other animal entering or returning to rabies-free countries such as Britain or Australia. Recent modifications to British quarantine laws allow animals arriving from elsewhere in the EU via certain routes to avoid quarantine, provided they meet strict vaccination and other requirements (for more details contact the UK Ministry of Agriculture, Fisheries & Food at ☎ 0870-241 1710, @ pets@ahvg.gsi.gov.uk).

Airport Taxes

International airport taxes for return flights between Portugal and other European countries are included in the price of any ticket from a scheduled carrier, but payable at check-in in the case of a charter flight. They currently range from about 5300$00 to the Netherlands to 9200$00 to the UK.

Domestic departure tax depends on your destination; it's 780$00 for a Lisbon-Faro flight. This is also included in the ticket price.

Other Parts of Portugal

Portugália and TAP both have multiple daily Lisbon-Porto and Lisbon-Faro flights (taking under one hour) year-round, plus additional Faro links from April to October. A high-season, one-way fare (including taxes) with Portugália is 17,100$00 for Lisbon-Porto or 16,300$00 for Lisbon-Faro. There are no discounts on return tickets.

An under-26 card gets you a 50% discount with PGA Portugália Airlines and limited

Air Travel Glossary

Cancellation Penalties If you have to cancel or change a discounted ticket, there are often heavy penalties involved; insurance can sometimes be taken out against these penalties. Some airlines impose penalties on regular tickets as well, particularly against 'no-show' passengers.

Lost Tickets If you lose your airline ticket an airline will usually treat it like a travellers cheque and, after inquiries, issue you with another one. Legally, however, an airline is entitled to treat it like cash and if you lose it then it's gone forever. Take good care of your tickets.

Open-Jaw Tickets These are return tickets where you fly out to one place but return from another. If available, this can save you backtracking to your arrival point.

Promotional Fares These are officially discounted fares, available from travel agencies or direct from the airline.

Reconfirmation If you don't reconfirm your flight at least 72 hours prior to departure, the airline may delete your name from the passenger list. Ring to find out if your airline requires reconfirmation.

Restrictions Discounted tickets often have various restrictions on them – such as needing to be paid for in advance and incurring a penalty to be altered. Others are restrictions on the minimum and maximum period you must be away.

Round-the-World Tickets RTW tickets give you a limited period (usually a year) in which to circumnavigate the globe. You can go anywhere the carrying airlines go, as long as you don't backtrack. The number of stopovers or total number of separate flights is decided before you set off and they usually cost a bit more than a basic return flight.

Travel Periods Ticket prices vary with the time of year. There is a low (off-peak) season and a high (peak) season, and often a low-shoulder season and a high-shoulder season as well. Usually the fare depends on your outward flight – if you depart in the high season and return in the low season, you pay the high-season fare.

discounts from TAP Air Portugal. See Money in the Facts for the Visitor chapter for information on where to get these cards.

The USA & Canada

Discount travel agents in the USA and Canada are called consolidators, and they can be found through the Yellow Pages or major newspapers. Ticket Planet is one leading consolidator, with a Web site at www.ticketplanet.com. The *Los Angeles Times*, *New York Times*, *San Francisco Examiner*, *Chicago Tribune*, *Globe & Mail* (Toronto), *Montreal Gazette* and *Vancouver Sun* have weekly travel sections with ads and information.

There are direct links to Lisbon daily from New York (TWA and TAP from JFK, and Continental and TAP from Newark), Washington (British Airways; BA) and Los Angeles (Continental). TAP operates direct flights from Boston twice a week. You can save money, and fly from a wider range of cities, by taking an indirect flight such as Air France via Paris or BA via London. Adult/youth return fares start at around US$890/680 from New York or around US$1130/830 from Los Angeles.

There are no direct flights between Canada and Portugal. The cheapest option is to travel via a European hub city. Fares start at around C$1500 from Montreal or Toronto, or about C$1800 from Calgary, Edmonton or Vancouver.

Two air-fare specialists in the USA are STA Travel (☎ 1 800 777 0112), with a Web site at www.statravel.com, and Council Travel (☎ 1 800 226 8624), whose Web site is at www.counciltravel.com. Canada's best bargain-ticket agency is Travel CUTS/ Voyages Campus (☎ 1 800 667 2887); its Web address is www.travelcuts.com.

GETTING THERE & AWAY

Australia & New Zealand

Check travel agency ads in the Yellow Pages, and the Saturday travel sections of the *Sydney Morning Herald*, Melbourne *Age* or *New Zealand Herald*.

There are no direct flights from Australasia to Portugal, but dozens of indirect routes via third countries. At the time of research Lufthansa was offering return flights from Sydney to Lisbon for around A$2120. An alternative is a bargain flight to London (eg, A$1520 from Sydney with Garuda) plus an onward no-frills or charter flight. Another possibility is a RTW ticket for around A$2260. The only Asian carrier serving both Australasia and Portugal is Thai Airways.

Flight Centres International and STA Travel, both with offices across Australia and New Zealand, are major dealers in cheap air fares. For the nearest office, contact STA at its Australia-wide number, ☎ 131 776, or its Web site, www.statravel .com.au; and Flight Centres Australia-wide at ☎ 131 600 or Web site www.flightcentre .com.au or www.flightcentre.com/nz.

The UK

Thanks to Britain's long love affair with Portugal, and the UK's discount air-travel business, there are some excellent deals. Cheap fares appear in the weekend national papers and, in London, in *Time Out*, the *Evening Standard* and *TNT* magazine.

Scheduled daily direct flights to Lisbon are operated from Heathrow by BA (☎ 0845-722 2111) and TAP (☎ 0845-601 0932); from Gatwick by BA; and from Stansted by Go (☎ 0845-605 4321). Less competitive routes include Manchester-Lisbon with Portugália (☎ 08707-550 025).

Midsummer return fares for a direct London-Lisbon connection start at about UK£160 from Go and UK£200 from full-service carriers. Discounted adult/youth fares for other routes include UK£185/160 for London-Paris-Lisbon (Air France). Charters operate from all over the UK (though mostly to Faro) with high-season return fares starting at around UK£170.

The UK's best known bargain-ticket agencies are Trailfinders (☎ 020-7937 5400),

Usit Campus (☎ 0870-240 1010), Travel CUTS (☎ 020-7792 3770) and STA Travel (☎ 020-7361 6145). The best Web sites – where you can track down, book and pay for flights – are those of Usit Campus (www.usitcampus.co.uk) and STA Travel (www.statravel.co.uk).

Continental Europe

The no-frills Spanish airline Air Europa (☎ 902 401 501), codesharing with TAP, flies Madrid-Lisbon several times daily for about 19,000 ptas return. Others with daily links on this route are Portugália (☎ 902 100 145), Iberia (☎ 902 400 500) and Lufthansa (☎ 902 220 101). Portugália and TAP also go to Lisbon from Barcelona. A reliable airfare specialist with offices all over Spain is Usit Unlimited (☎ 902 25 25 75).

Carriers with multiple daily nonstop Paris-Lisbon connections are TAP (☎ 08 02 31 93 20), mostly from Orly, and Air France (☎ 08 02 80 28 02) from Charles de Gaulle. Portugália flies to Lisbon daily from Bordeaux, Nice, Lyon and Toulouse, and TAP almost daily from Nice and Lyon. Expect to pay at least 1850FF return for Paris-Lisbon; TAP and Air France also have youth/student prices.

Bargain-flight specialists with branches around France include AJF (☎ 01 42 77 87 80) and OTU (☎ 01 40 29 12 12). AJF has a Web site at www.otu.fr. Others to check out in Paris are Usit Connect (☎ 01 42 44 14 00), with a Web site at www.usitconnect .fr, and STA affiliate Voyages Wasteels (☎ 08 03 88 70 04) whose Web site is www .voyages-wasteels.fr.

Lufthansa and TAP have daily direct flights to Lisbon from Munich and Frankfurt. Adult/youth fares from Frankfurt start at about DM600/520. Other direct links with Germany are from Berlin, Cologne, Hamburg and Stuttgart (with Portugália). Air-fare specialists with branches around Germany include Frankfurt-based STA Travel (☎ 069-70 30 35), Cologne-based Usit Campus (☎ 0221-925 9670) and SRS (☎ 030-283 30 94) in Berlin.

From Amsterdam, KLM and TAP fly direct to Lisbon daily; expect to pay at least f630. Try the official student travel agency NBBS Reizen (☎ 020-624 09 89), or Malibu Travel (☎ 020-626 32 30).

From Brussels, TAP and Sabena codeshare a number of daily direct flights to Lisbon; fares start at about Bf10,400. A recommended agency is Acotra Student Travel Agency (☎ 02-512 86 07) or Usit Connections (☎ 02-550 01 00); in Antwerp try Wats Reizen (☎ 03-226 16 26).

Africa

The most frequent direct links to/from Africa are four weekly flights between Lisbon and Casablanca (Morocco) by TAP (Royal Air Maroc codeshare; US$260) and two by Portugália. TAP also flies to Lisbon from several of its former colonies: Mozambique (at least three weekly codeshares with Linhas Aéreas de Moçambique), Guinea-Bissau and São Tomé e Princípe (each once weekly). Civil war has effectively put Angola out of reach. Other TAP flights go once or twice weekly from Abidjan, Dakar (US$410) and Johannesburg (US$670), and Tunisair flies twice weekly from Tunis. The best option for most other points in Africa is to fly via another European city.

South America

Historically, Lisbon was an important stop on the air route between Europe and South America; in fact the first-ever flight between Heathrow and South America stopped there. Nowadays, direct flights to Lisbon include Varig daily and TAP almost daily from Rio de Janeiro (US$820), and TAP three times weekly from Caracas (US$780). Most of the indirect flights to these and other capitals go via Madrid or Rio with Spanish airlines Iberia, Air Europa and Spanair.

BUS
Other Parts of Portugal

A network of small, private bus operators, most amalgamated into regional companies, crisscrosses the country. Among the largest operators are Renex, Rede Expressos (Web site: www.rede-expressos.pt/index_uk.htm), and the Algarve line EVA (Portuguese-only Web site: www.eva-bus.com).

Bus services are of three general types: *expressos* are comfortable, fast, direct coaches between major cities; *rápidas* are fast regional buses; and *carreiras* stop at every crossroad. EVA also offers a fast deluxe category called *alta qualidade*.

Expressos are generally the most convenient way to get between Lisbon and other parts of Portugal (particularly good value for long trips, where per-kilometre costs are lowest). Even in summer you'll have little problem booking a ticket for the next or even the same day. An under-26 card should get you a discount of around 20%, at least on long-distance services. Senior travellers can often get up to 50% off.

Don't rely on turismos for accurate timetable information. Most bus companies have printed timetables *(horários)* or will give you a computer printout of fares and services at the ticket desk. If you're counting escudos, be sure to ask about cheaper slower services too.

Here are some sample expressos fares from Lisbon:

Faro	2500$00	4 to 5 hours
Porto	2350$00	3½ to 4 hours
Coimbra	1500$00	2½ hours
Évora	1500$00	1¾ hours
Viana do Castelo	2400$00	5½ hours

Bus Stations

Be sure to check which terminal to use in Lisbon. The new Gare do Oriente (with train, metro and bus stations) is gradually taking over services from all the other city centre terminals, although Arco do Cego near Saldanha remains the base for the two largest carriers.

Gare do Oriente This glorious architectural masterpiece, adjacent to Parque das Nações (Map 9), is Lisbon's newest and most important intermodal station. It looks wonderful, as if it's about to take flight. Inside, however, its bus station is bewildering with lousy signs, useless video information screens and no central information desk.

Within the building's rib-cage there's the basement metro level with banks, shops, cafes and a police post, next to which is a

GETTING THERE & AWAY

Where's My Bus?

The Gare do Oriente is the terminal for a dozen or so bus companies; ticket booths are above the bus lanes on the terminal's 1st floor (see Bus Stations). You can also get tickets on the bus. Other bus services (eg, those currently based at Praça de Espanha) may eventually move to Gare do Oriente too.

Booth No	Company	Major Destinations	Bus Lane
1	AVIC (☎ 218 940 238)	Figueira da Foz, Viana do Castelo, Valença, Monção, Melgaço	D-31
2	Tamega & Joaquim Martins da Fonseca (☎ 218 956 913)	Chaves, Viseu, Coimbra, Vila Real	D-32 or E-41
3	Rodonorte (☎ 218 956 850)	Amarante, Chaves, Miranda do Douro, Mirandela, Vila Real, Viseu, Régua	D-33 or 34
4	Berrelhas & Cidade Berço (☎ 218 956 844)	Viseu, Guimarães	D-35
5	Turilis (☎ 218 956 796)	Viana do Castelo, Melgaço, Monção	E-44
6	Joalto & EAVT (☎ 217 959 099)	Fátima, Viseu, Vila Nova de Foz Côa, Castelo Branco	D-36 to 40
7	Santos (☎ 218 956 890)	Coimbra, Porto, Vila Real, Mirandela, Bragança	E-42 or 43
8	Asadouro Expressos & Empresa Guedes (☎ 218 870 725)	Régua, Coimbra, Lamego	E-45 and 50
9 & 10	Renex, which includes the southern bus lines Caima, Frota Azul and Resende (☎ 218 874 871, 218 882 829)	Faro, Albufeira, Lagos, Portimão, Braga, Porto	E-46 to 49
none	Setúbalense (☎ 265 525 051)	Setúbal and Setúbal Peninsula	C-21

tiny left-luggage locker room. The street level has more shops, a post office, and Avis and Europcar car-rental offices (opposite the bus terminal). On the 1st floor you'll find main-line train ticket booths with the train platforms above.

Also on the 1st floor, above the actual bus terminal, you'll find a row of ticket booths for each different bus company. Most booths are open from around 9 am to 5.30 pm on weekdays (to 7 or 7.30 pm Friday and closing daily at lunchtime), but the smaller companies only open when there's a bus about to go. All close at weekends (you can usually buy tickets on the bus on these days, but it's wise to phone ahead for a seat reservation). See the boxed text 'Where's My Bus' for a rundown of the companies operating from here.

Arco do Cego Arco do Cego on Avenida João Crisóstomo (Map 2) is the base for all long-distance coaches operated by Rede Expressos (☎ 213 103 111), which includes Rodoviária do Tejo, Belos Transportes and a host of smaller companies; and EVA/Mundial Turismo (☎ 213 147 710). Between them these companies cover the whole country. There's a general information desk here (☎ 213 545 439).

Next to this desk is an Intercentro office (Eurolines; ☎ 213 159 277) for international coach tickets; it's open 8 am to 12.30 pm and 1.30 to 5 pm weekdays and to 1 pm on Saturday (closed Sunday). The adjacent left-luggage room is open 8 am to 7 pm weekdays and 8 am to 1 pm and 2 to 6 pm weekends.

Campo Grande & Praça de Espanha

Several small regional companies with destinations in the north, including Mafrense (for Ericeira and Mafra), Barraqueiro Oeste (for Malveira and Torres Vedras) and Rodoviária do Tejo (for Peniche), currently operate from outside Campo Grande metro station (Map 1). Buses heading for Costa da Caparica and Sesimbra and some Setúbal services use the open-air terminal at Praça de Espanha (Map 2).

International

The two major options for long-distance coach travel are Eurolines and Busabout. Though a coach trip from the UK to Portugal can be pretty tedious, you get reclining seats, on-board toilets and stops for meals. Try to book at least a week ahead in summer.

Eurolines Eurolines is a consortium of coach operators with offices across Europe. There's a 10% discount for travellers aged under 26 and at least 60. A Eurolines Pass will give you unlimited travel between 48 European cities for 30 days (high-season price UK£245 for adults, UK£195 for youth and seniors) or 60 days (UK£283/227) – although Madrid is currently the closest city to Portugal covered by the pass.

Among some 200 Eurolines offices are the following:

Amsterdam Eurolines (☎ 020-560 8787, fax 560 8717) Rokin 10, and Amstel Bus Station, Julianaplein 5
Frankfurt Deutsche Touring/Eurolines (☎ 069-790 350, fax 790 3219) Am Romerhof 17
Web site: www.deutsche-touring.com
London Eurolines (bookings ☎ 08705-143 219, information ☎ 020-7730 8235, fax 7730 8721) 52 Grosvenor Gardens, London SW1W 0AU
Web site: www.eurolines.co.uk
Madrid SAIA (☎ 91 327 1381, fax 91 327 1329) Estación Sur de Autobuses
Paris Eurolines (☎ 08 36 69 52 52, fax 01 49 72 51 61, Minitel 3615 EUROLINES) Gare Routière Internationale de Paris, 28 ave du Général de Gaulle, Bagnolet
Web site: www.eurolines.fr

Portugal's main Eurolines affiliates are Internorte, Intercentro and Intersul which, as the names suggest, are based in northern

(Porto), central (Lisbon) and southern Portugal (Faro and Setúbal). Lisbon's main Intercentro office (☎ 213 571 745, fax 213 570 039), at Rua Actor Taborda 55, is open 9 am to 1 pm and 2 to 6 pm weekdays only. There's also a ticket office at the Arco do Cego bus terminal (see details under Arco do Cego earlier).

Information and tickets for international departures are scarce at weekends, so avoid that last-minute Sunday dash out of Portugal.

Busabout Busabout is a hop-on-hop-off network linking some 70 European cities. Coaches run from April to October, and travellers can move freely around the network using one of two passes.

The Consecutive Pass is good for a set period from 15 days (UK£155; UK£139 for youth or student card-holders) to seven months (UK£659/589). The Flexi-Pass lets you choose the number of travel days you want, from 10 days within two months (UK£235/209) to 30 days within four months (UK£609/549). The passes are available from Busabout (☎ 020-7950 1661 in London) or from its Web site at www .busabout.com, or from suppliers such as Usit Campus and STA Travel.

The coach stop in Lisbon is at Lisboa Camping – Parque Municipal. At certain 'bonus stops' passengers can look around for a few hours or get off; the bonus stop in Portugal is at Óbidos (95km north of Lisbon). Busabout also offers an add-on, round-trip London-Paris shuttle by coach and ferry.

The UK, France & Germany From April to October, Eurolines runs five weekly London to Lisbon services (UK£108/168 one way/return, 42 hours) via Channel ferry (and a 7½-hour stopover and change of coach in Paris); and five to six coaches weekly from Paris to Lisbon (735/1180FF, 26 hours). Coaches of the French operator IASA (Paris ☎ 01 43 53 90 82, Lisbon ☎ 213 143 979) also run five times weekly from Paris to Lisbon (640/990FF). They all stop at intermediate French, Spanish and Portuguese cities.

GETTING THERE & AWAY

From across Germany, Eurolines runs to Lisbon (eg, from Hamburg DM 270/436) twice weekly.

Spain Spain-Portugal fares noted here are for one-way journeys.

Eurolines runs twice weekly coaches (four weekly from July to September) from La Coruña to Lisbon (4480 ptas/5390$00, 9½ hours) and three weekly from Madrid (5700 ptas/6860$00, eight hours). Another Lisbon service starts at Barcelona (11,440 ptas/13,790$00) every Sunday from April to October.

In addition, AutoRes (☎ 902-19 29 39, Lisbon ☎ 217 961 778) and the Spanish line ALSA (Madrid ☎ 91 754 6502) each has a Madrid-Lisbon service two times a day via Badajoz and Mérida for around 5645 ptas/6775$00 (AutoRes' terminal in Lisbon is at Entrecampos Rotunda 37-B). SAIA Eurolines has a Salamanca to Lisbon service twice a week for 4000ptas/4820$00.

From Seville, Eurolines goes via Elvas and Évora to Lisbon (4870 ptas/5870$00, 14½ hours) twice weekly (four times weekly from July to October). A piecemeal alternative is via twice-daily bus from Seville to Ficalho in Portugal; from there, frequent local buses go to Serpa (390$00, 55 minutes) where there are express coaches on to Lisbon (1700$00, four hours). There's also one daily direct Ficalho-Lisbon coach (1900$00, 4½ hours) leaving at 1.45 pm. Another snail's-pace Alentejo crossing is on local buses from Badajoz to Caia and Caia to Elvas (220$00, 20 minutes, twice daily) plus an Elvas-Lisbon express (1700$00, 3½ hours, seven daily).

Eurolines also runs from Seville through the Algarve to Lagos (2630 ptas/3170$00, 5¼ hours) four to six times weekly from April to October. The Algarve carrier EVA and the Spanish line Damas (Huelva ☎ 959 25 69 00) jointly link Seville and Faro (1700 ptas/2050$00, five hours) twice daily (except Sunday in winter), with swift onward connections to Lisbon.

The Spanish line Transportes Agobe (☎ 902 154 568, Lisbon ☎ 217 966 148) runs three times weekly from Granada via

Seville and Albufeira to Lisbon (return run leaves on Tuesday, Thursday and Saturday from Gare do Oriente). Seville-Albufeira (2410 ptas/2900$00) takes four hours, Seville-Lisbon (4800 ptas/5800$00) 10 hours and Granada-Lisbon (8300 ptas/ 10,000$00) 14 hours.

TRAIN
Other Parts of Portugal

Travelling with the state railway company, Caminhos de Ferro Portugueses (CP), is cheaper (though generally slower) than going by bus, thanks partly to state subsidies. There are three main types of service: *regional* trains (marked R on timetables), which stop everywhere; reasonably fast IR *interregional*; and express IC *intercidade* (or *rápido*) trains. *Alfa* is a marginally faster, considerably pricier IC service on the Lisbon-Coimbra-Porto main line. *Suburbano* trains run on both suburban and regional lines. Most trains have both 1st and 2nd-class carriages and all have a no-smoking section somewhere.

Serious rail-riders may want to buy the *Guia Horário Oficial* (360$00), containing CP's complete domestic and international timetables. It's available from ticket windows at major stations, at least in Lisbon.

Here are some sample 2nd-class fares from Lisbon. Note that for travel to Faro (Algarve) or the Alentejo, you first have to catch a ferry (180$00) from the Terreiro do Paço terminal (by Praça do Comércio; Map 5) to reach Barreiro station.

destination	Alfa	IC	IR
Faro	–	2100$00	1930$00
Porto	3150$00	2650$00	2080$00
Coimbra	2300$00	1900$00	1510$00

Discounts Children under four years travel free; those aged four to 12 go for half-price. A Euro>26 card gets you a 30% discount on R and IR services on any day, and on IC services from Monday midday to Friday midday. Travellers aged 65 and over can get a *cartão dourado* (senior card) at ticket counters, entitling them to half-price travel on weekdays, except on suburban commuter trains at rush hour.

Train Stations

For details of Gare do Oriente, see under Bus Stations, earlier in the chapter. Note that nearly all train services (including international ones) now stop at Gare do Oriente, conveniently linked to the city centre by metro and to the airport by bus No 44.

Santa Apolónia Santa Apolónia (Map 8) has a helpful CP information desk (☎ 218 884 025 to 027 or 218 867 555, fax 218 816 088) at door No 8, open 6.45 am to 10 pm weekdays (from 7.30 am on weekends).

The international section at door No 47, open 8 am to 8 pm daily, has a ticket desk, a bank, Europcar and Avis car-rental desks, snack bar and seating area. Also in this section is a Wasteels travel agency (see Facts for the Visitor – Travel Agencies) where you can buy Inter-Rail and other youth-geared travel tickets. It's open Monday to Saturday. Opposite this is a Turismo de Lisboa (☎ 218 821 604) open 8 am to 1 pm and 2 to 4 pm daily (in summer the opening hours may be longer).

Bye-Bye Barreiro

The Rio Tejo has always been a hurdle for rail services linking Lisbon with southern Portugal. At present, if you want to catch a train to the Algarve, you must first catch a Soflusa ferry from the Terreiro do Paço terminal (Map 5; by Praça do Comércio) to the Barreiro train station across the Tejo. But that's all set to change.

In 1999, the Ponte 25 de Abril started carrying swish, air-conditioned, double-decker trains from Roma/Areeiro across the Rio Tejo to Fogueteiro (about 10km south-east of Almada). Designed initially for commuters, the line, run by Fertagus, is only useful at the moment for hopping across to this part of the Setúbal Peninsula. However it will eventually link up at Pinhal Novo with the main line to the Algarve. A second rail crossing over the Tejo is now planned to connect the north-eastern suburb of Chelas directly with Barreiro. The quaint but slow Soflusa ferries chugging across the river will soon be a thing of the past.

On the platform immediately outside is a cash exchange machine and credit-card ATM; luggage lockers are nearby. There are two other cafes at the station, at doors 16 and 52, both open 8 am to midnight.

Rossio At the time of research, Rossio (Map 6) was still a mess of redevelopment. But its information office is a flashy affair on the platform called Gabinete de Apoio ao Cliente (☎ 213 433 747 or free phone ☎ 800 200 904). It's open 8 am to 8 pm weekdays only. There are left-luggage lockers nearby.

International

Trains are a very popular way to get around Europe – comfortable, frequent and generally on time. But unless you have a rail pass (eg, Inter-Rail or Eurailpass) or a senior rail card (see Discounts under Money in the Facts for the Visitor chapter) the cost can be higher than flying. Most rail passes are available through youth-oriented travel agents such as STA Travel or Wasteels or in the UK through Rail Europe (see the following UK section). Note that even with a pass you must still pay for seat and couchette reservations and express-train supplements.

There are two standard long-distance rail routes into Portugal via the *TGV Atlantique* from Paris to Irún (Spain), where you must change trains. From there the *Sud-Expresso* crosses into Portugal via Vilar Formoso to Coimbra and Lisbon; some coaches change at Coimbra for Porto. The other journey runs from Irún to Madrid, with a change to the *Talgo Lusitânia*, into Portugal via Marvão-Beirã to Lisbon. To reach Portugal from elsewhere in Europe you must go via Paris.

The UK The cheapest UK-Portugal rail route from London is from Charing Cross station to Paris on a 'rail-sea-rail' ticket, crossing the Channel by ferry or SeaCat, with a change of trains (and stations) in Paris for the onward journey. Tickets for this route can be purchased from travel agents, larger main-line stations or Connex South Eastern (☎ 0870-001 0174). A 2nd-class adult/youth ticket from London to Lisbon costs UK£175/166.

GETTING THERE & AWAY

For speed and convenience, however, the best route is on the Eurostar service from London Waterloo to Paris via the Channel Tunnel. This can shorten the journey by some six hours (making a London-Lisbon trip possible in about 25 hours), but it is costs more. A 2nd-class London-Lisbon adult/youth Apex return fare costs UK£242/218, including TGV supplements. Tickets are available from travel agents, larger stations, Connex or Rail Europe (☎ 08705-848848).

The overnight Irún-Lisbon section costs about UK£15 more for a couchette in a six-person sleeper.

Travellers aged under 26 can get youth discounts through specialists such as Usit Campus (see the UK section under Air earlier in this chapter).

France The daily train journey from Paris (Gare d'Austerlitz) to Lisbon takes about 20 hours. A 2nd-class adult/youth ticket costs about 1780/1550FF return, plus 150FF for a couchette on the overnight Irún-Lisbon section. Reserve at least several days ahead in the high season. Booking 30/eight days ahead gets you a 50/20% reduction on the Paris-Irún section.

In France, SNCF (French Railways) has a nationwide telephone number (English speakers ☎ 08 36 35 35 39) and its Web site is at web.sncf.fr.

Spain The main rail route is from Madrid to Lisbon via Marvão-Beirã on the *Talgo Lusitânia* (10½ hours). A 2nd-class reserved seat costs 6640 ptas/8000$00 one way, a berth in a (sex-segregated!) *turista* (four-person sleeper) 9630 ptas/11,200$00 or 14,248 ptas/17,170$00 in a 1st-class double.

Another well-used route is Vigo-Porto, crossing into Portugal at Valença do Minho (three expresses daily). The Badajoz-Caia-Elvas-Lisbon route is tedious (five hours; two regional services daily, with a change at Entroncamento), but the scenery through the Serra de Marvão is grand.

USA & Canada You can book rail tickets in advance with Rail Europe – in the USA at ☎ 1 800 4 EURAIL, fax 432 1FAX; and

in Canada at ☎ 1 800 361 RAIL, fax 905-602 4198; or on the Web at www.raileurope.com.

CAR & MOTORCYCLE
Other Parts of Portugal

Thanks to European Union subsidies, the country's road system has been extensively upgraded; beyond Lisbon you'll quickly encounter a rapidly expanding network of *estradas* (highways). Top of the line are *auto-estradas* (motorways), all of them *portagens* (toll roads). The longest, the 304km Lisbon-Porto motorway, has a toll of 2950$00.

Main roads are sealed and generally in good condition. Minor roads in the countryside get better every year, and often have surprisingly little traffic.

The downside of driving here is your road-mates. On the whole, Portuguese drivers, men and women alike, are aggressive and breathtakingly reckless. Portugal's annual per capita death rate from road accidents is Europe's highest. The closer you get to Lisbon the worse it gets: the Lisbon-Cascais A5 is particularly hair-raising.

Assistance Automóvel Club de Portugal (ACP), Portugal's national auto club, provides medical, legal and breakdown assistance for its members. Road information and maps are available to anyone at ACP's Lisbon head office (Map 5; ☎ 213 180 100, fax 213 180 227) at Rua Rosa Araújo 24.

Baffling Highways

Portugal's highway nomenclature can be baffling. Main two-lane *estradas nacionais* or national roads are usually (but not always) prefixed by N. Motorway numbers prefixed with an E are Europe-wide designations. Toll-roads get an A. Highways in the country's main network are prefixed IP (*itinerário principal*) and subsidiary ones are labelled IC (*itinerário complementar*). Some highways have several designations and numbers that change in mid-flow; eg, the Lisbon-Porto road is variously called E80, E01, A1 and IP1.

If you're a member of certain national auto clubs (eg, AA and RAC in the UK, and the Australian, New Zealand, Canadian or American Automobile Associations) you can also use ACP's emergency services. The ACP emergency help number for Lisbon and the south is ☎ 219 429 103.

Rules & Regulations You may not believe it after seeing what Portuguese drivers do, but there are rules. To begin with, driving is on the right, overtaking is on the left and most signs use international symbols, as in the rest of continental Europe.

Except when marked otherwise, speed limits for cars (without a trailer) and motorcycles (without a sidecar) are 50km/h in towns and villages, 90km/h outside such built-up areas and 120km/h on motorways. If you've held your driving licence for less than a year, you're restricted to 90 km/h even on motorways and your vehicle must display a '90' disk, available from any ACP office.

By law, car safety belts must be worn in front and back seats, and children under 12 years old may not ride in the front seat. Motorcyclists and their passengers must wear helmets, and motorcycles must have their headlights on day and night.

Police are authorised to impose on-the-spot fines (in escudos) for speeding and parking offences, and must issue receipts for them. Typical parking fines are about 5000$00.

Fuel The cost of fuel is high: 185$00 or more for a litre of 95-octane *sem chumbo* (unleaded petrol) and 120$00 for *gasóleo* (diesel). Unleaded petrol is readily available and there are plenty of self-service stations. Major credit cards are accepted at most, but not all, stations.

Drinking & Driving

The maximum legal blood-alcohol level for anyone behind the wheel is a mere 0.05%. If you drink and drive and are caught, you can expect to spend the night in a lockup, and the next morning in a courtroom.

Airport Trap

Lisbon's chaotic airport can be a trap for car-rental drivers. Keep a sharp eye out for the yellow signs directing you into the rental-car lot. If you go into the regular car park instead, you'll have to pay to get out!

Motorail CP has Motorail service (car transport by rail) on major lines, including Lisbon-Porto and Lisbon-Faro. Fifteen days' notice at the departure station is required, and return tickets are valid for two months.

Insurance & Documents If you drive your own car or motorcycle into Portugal, in addition to passport and driving licence (see the Documents section in the Facts for the Visitor chapter) you must carry vehicle registration (proof of ownership) and insurance documents. If people other than the registered owner are to drive, they'll need written authorisation from the owner.

Motor vehicle insurance with at least third-party cover is compulsory throughout the EU. It's wise (though not a legal requirement) to carry a Green Card from your home insurer, confirming that you have the correct coverage.

Spain, France & UK

Roads cross the Portugal-Spain border in at least 30 places, most notably at Valença do Minho, Feces de Abajo (Chaves), Vilar Formoso (Guarda), Elvas, Vila Verde de Ficalho (Serpa) and also Vila Real de Santo António. Land border controls between the two countries have disappeared.

The quickest, easiest driving route to Lisbon from the UK is to bypass France and Spain by taking a ferry to northern Spain – with P&O Portsmouth from Portsmouth to Bilbao (29 to 35 hours) or, from mid-March to mid-November, with Brittany Ferries from Plymouth to Santander (24 hours). Both sail twice weekly. From Santander it's roughly 1000km to Lisbon.

Return tickets with Brittany Ferries, for weekdays in the high season, start at about

GETTING THERE & AWAY

UK£770/520 for a car/motorcycle including driver and passenger (slightly more with P&O). Contact Brittany at ☎ 0870 536 0360 or its Web site at www.brittany-ferries.com; or P&O at ☎ 0870 600 3300 or its Web site at www.poportsmouth.com.

An alternative is to catch a ferry across the Channel (or use the Eurotunnel vehicle service underneath it) to France and motor down the coast. From the channel ports of France it's roughly 1900km to Lisbon.

BICYCLE
Other Parts of Portugal

If you're travelling to Lisbon by train, note that you can no longer take bikes on Portuguese trains as accompanied baggage (the Lisbon-Sintra service is an exception). Bikes as baggage are not allowed on Eurolines coaches either, and are at the discretion of the driver with Busabout. Most national bus lines will accept your bike, unboxed, subject to space and sometimes for an extra 1000$00 or so.

The alternative is to use a collapsible bike, or to send your machine on ahead as cargo. Transporte de Encomendas Expresso (TEX), a shipping company with offices at or near the main train stations in over 40 Portuguese towns and cities, will ship a boxed-up bicycle between any two of those stations for about 4100$00 including tax.

International

Bicycles can travel by air. You can take yours to pieces and put it in a bag or box, but it's much easier to simply wheel it to the check-in desk, where it should be treated as baggage. But check this with the airline well in advance. Let much (but not all) of the air out of the tyres to prevent them from bursting in the low-pressure baggage hold.

Before you leave home, fill your repair kit with every imaginable spare.

For its members, Cyclists' Touring Club (CTC; ☎ 01483-417217, fax 426994, ℮ cycling@ctc.org.uk) in the UK publishes a useful, free information booklet on cycling in Portugal, plus touring notes for half a dozen routes around the country. The CTC Web site is at www.ctc.org.uk.

HITCHING

Hitching is never entirely safe anywhere, and we don't recommend it. Travellers who hitch should understand that they're taking a small but potentially serious risk. In any case it's not an easy way to get around Portugal. Almost nobody stops on major highways, and on smaller roads drivers tend to be going short distances. You can meet some interesting characters, but you may only advance from one field to the next!

BOAT
Other Parts of Portugal

Other than its river cruises, Lisbon's only water transport are Transtejo commuter ferries across the Tejo (see the Getting Around chapter) and Transado ferries across the mouth of the Sado between Setúbal and Tróia (see the Excursions chapter).

International

Lisbon is the foremost European Atlantic seaport, with hundreds of cruise ships calling here every year. Several cargo boats with passenger space also stop here: the German-registered *OPDR Tejo* (☎ 04503-73675, fax 74437) sails between Rotterdam and the UK via Portugal; and several ships of P&O Containers in London (☎ 020-7836 6363, fax 7497 0078) return from Australia and New Zealand via Portugal. See the earlier Car & Motorcycle section for details on ferry services from the UK to the continent.

ORGANISED TOURS

There are any number of flight and accommodation packages on offer; any travel agency worth its salt can find a cheap deal through mass-market operators such as Airtours and Thomson of Britain or LTU and Hapag Lloyd of Germany.

The UK's best specialist tour operators are listed in *AITO Holiday Directory*, a free annual index of the Association of Independent Tour Operators. It's available from AITO (☎ 020-8744 9280, ℮ aito@martex .co.uk). Most overseas offices of ICEP, the Portuguese state tourism organisation, publish their own directories (in the UK it's called the *Portugal Tour Operators Guide*).

For domestic tours and activity programs, see Organised Tours in the Getting Around chapter, and Activities in the Facts for the Visitor chapter.

Lisbon City Breaks

Typical city-break packages to Lisbon by UK operators, including air fare and accommodation, start from around UK£350 for a high-season, two-night stay in a two-star hotel. Some of the best deals are available from Mundi Color Holidays (☎ 0870 444 3485); Osprey Holidays (☎ 0870 605 605); Time Off (☎ 0870 584 6363) and also Kirker Travel (☎ 020-7231 3333, e cities@kirker.itsnet.co.uk).

Look out, too, for promotional airline deals, eg, from BA or TAP Air Portugal and its Caravela Tours (☎ 020-7630 9223); their low-season, three-night packages can be as little as UK£170. The Portuguese Abreu Travel Agency (☎ 020-7229 9905) often has good flight and accommodation deals.

Special offers at many of the hotels include free accommodation for children under 12 and a 'free' night if you stay more than three or four nights.

Lisbon & Elsewhere

Several UK operators, such as Travelscene (☎ 020-8427 8800), offer 'twin centre' packages featuring, for instance, Lisbon and the Estoril Coast or Sintra from around UK£320 for three nights including air fare. Mundi Color Holidays (see the Lisbon City Breaks section) has a 10-day fly/drive package from Lisbon to the Alentejo and Estremadura. Other agencies offering fly-drive and accommodation packages include Portuguese Affair (☎ 020-7385 4775) and The Magic of Portugal (☎ 020-8741 1181).

There are UK companies that cater for special-interest groups, including Individual Travellers Portugal (☎ 08700-773773, e holidays@indiv-travellers.co.uk), Destination Portugal (☎ 01993-773269, e info@destination-portugal.co.uk) as well as Simply Portugal (☎ 020-8541 2207, e portugal@simply-travel.com). For more information check out Destination Portugal's Web site at www.destination-portugal.co.uk.

Reliable Portugal-specialist tour operators in France include Lusitania (☎ 01 42 89 42 99, e lusitania.portugal@lusitania.fr) and Donatello (☎ 01 44 58 30 60, e donatello@donatello.fr).

Walking Tours

In the UK, ATG Oxford (☎ 01865-315678, e info@alternative-travel.co.uk) offers a five-day walking tour to Lisbon and Sintra with deluxe bed and board. Week-long jaunts with Headwater (☎ 01606-813333, e info@headwater.com) include Parque Natural da Arrábida, Lisbon and Sintra.

Lisbon-based Rotas do Vento (Map 3; ☎ 213 649 852, fax 213 649 843, e rotas@rotasdovento.pt), Rua dos Lusíadas 5, organises weekend guided walks (in Portuguese, with English or French-speaking guide) for groups of six to 18, to nearby and remote corners of Portugal.

Cycling Tours

UK-based Bike Rides (☎ 07000 560749) offers one-week, off-road tours from Lisbon to Faro; also check out its Web site at www.bike-rides.co.uk.

In the USA, Easy Rider Tours (☎ 978-463 6955, toll-free ☎ 1 800 488 8332, fax 978-463 6988, e info@easyridertours.com) specialises in small-group itineraries including one heading down the south-west coast from Lisbon.

Toronto-based Butterfield & Robinson (☎ 416-864 1354, toll-free ☎ 1 800 678 1147, fax 416-864 0541) offers combined biking and walking from the Alentejo to Sintra, with deluxe accommodation.

Botanical Tours

One-week 'garden holidays' in Estoril and around Lisbon are offered for seniors by SAGA Holidays (UK ☎ 01303-773 532; USA ☎ 1 800 343 0273). Its Web site is at www.saga.co.uk.

Golf, Tennis & Horse-Riding Holidays

UK specialists 3D Golf (☎ 0800 333 323, e sales@3dgolf.co.uk) offers Estoril Coast golfing packages including car hire and

GETTING THERE & AWAY

discounted green fees. Longshot Golf Holidays (☎ 01730-268621, ✉ longshot@meontravel.co.uk) offers three to seven-night packages including prebooked rounds at the major courses near Lisbon.

Two Web sites worth checking for other golf tours around the Lisbon area are www.ecs.net/golf and www.latitude40.net.

Need to improve your dressage? Contact Equitour (☎ 01865-511642, fax 512583, ✉ eqtours@aol.com) for its week-long program on Lusitano horses at Alcainça near Mafra. It also offers a one-week riding tour in Estremadura and along the 'dolphin coast' south of Setúbal.

Upmarket accommodation in Lisbon, Sintra or Estoril with tennis centres, golf courses or horse-riding facilities can be arranged by EHS Travel (☎ 01993-700600, ✉ info@ehstravel.co.uk).

Art & Architecture

UK-based Martin Randall Travel (☎ 020-8742 3355, ✉ info@martinrandall.co.uk) arranges five-day upmarket architecture and art tours in Lisbon and Sintra.

Cristo Rei reaches out to all.

Ponte Vasco da Gama is a striking testament to modern Lisbon.

Stepping into the world of Portugal's Age of Discoveries.

Padrão dos Descobrimentos

Writer Fernando Pessoa

Oriente station is Lisbon's newest, most stunning transport terminal.

VITOR VIEIRA

A cobbled Alfama street

PAUL BERNHARDT

The defensive capabilities of the Torre de Belém on display.

CARLOS COSTA

The rooftops of Lisbon with Castelo do São Jorge above the city.

PAUL KENNEDY

Weathered walls in Bairro Alto

MARTIN MOOS

On guard at Rossio station

MARK DAFFEY

Manueline arches of Mosteiro dos Jéronimos

Getting Around

THE AIRPORT

Aeroporto de Lisboa (also called Aeroporto da Portela) is about 4km north-east of the city centre. In the arrivals hall you'll find two turismos: the larger ICEP desk (☎ 218 492 343) open 6 am to 2 am daily, which dispenses information and maps but little else; and the smaller Turismo de Lisboa desk opposite (☎ 218 450 660) open 6 am to midnight, which can advise on taxis and other transport and make hotel reservations. It also sells the Lisboa Card (see the boxed text later in this chapter).

Telecel (see Post & Communications in the Facts for the Visitor chapter) has a shop nearby for renting mobile/cellphones. The useful *Your Guide – Lisboa*, published by the airport authority, ANA, is worth picking up from display racks or the ANA desk.

Among car rental agencies at the airport are Sixt, Avis and Europcar. See Rental in the Car & Motorcycle section for contact details.

TO/FROM THE AIRPORT

The Aero-Bus departs from outside the arrivals hall roughly every 20 minutes from 7 am to 9 pm. It takes around 30 to 45 minutes (depending on traffic) to get from the airport to Cais do Sodré station, with a stop near the turismo on Praça do Comércio (both Map 7). It's 460/1075$00 for a one/three-day Bilhete Turístico that you can continue to use on all city buses, trams and funiculars. Note that the Passe Turístico (see the following Bus, Tram & Funicular section) is for some reason not valid for this bus. For TAP Air Portugal passengers who show their boarding pass (not just the air ticket), the ride into the city is free. Collect a voucher from the airline's Welcome Desk if you've lost the pass.

Local bus Nos 8, 44, 45 and 83 also run from the city centre to the airport but they're a nightmare in rush hour if you have baggage. A more convenient option (especially if you're arriving in Lisbon by train just to get to the airport) is to take bus No 44 from Gare do Oriente (Map 9). It runs

---

Lisboa Card

Holders of this card get free travel on nearly all city transport, including the metro (and the train to Belém); free or discounted admission to many of the city's museums and monuments (including some in Sintra); and also discounts of up to 65% on bus and tram tours, river cruises and other admission charges. There are 24, 48 and 72-hour versions costing 2100$00, 3500$00 and 4500$00 respectively (or 850$00, 1300$00 and 1700$00 for children from five to 11 years) – reasonable value if you plan on cramming lots of sights into a short stay. You validate the card when you want to start it.

The Lisboa Card is sold at all Turismo de Lisboa offices and kiosks.

---

until 9.30 pm. Also see the Excursions chapter for a direct airport-bus service to/from Cascais and Estoril.

For a taxi to the city centre, expect to pay at least 1500$00, plus an extra 300$00 if your luggage needs to go in the boot. Avoid long taxi queues by flagging down a taxi at Departures. Rip-offs are common on the airport-to-city route; you can buy a prepaid Táxi Voucher from the Turismo de Lisboa desk in the arrivals terminal at set prices for specific destinations. Only those taxis involved in the scheme (marked with a coloured sticker) will accept the vouchers.

BUS, TRAM & FUNICULAR

Companhia Carris de Ferro de Lisboa, or Carris (☎ 213 613 060, 213 613 038), operates all transport except the metro. Its buses and trams run from about 5 or 6 am to 1 am; there are some night bus and tram services.

You can get a transport map, *Planta dos Transportes Públicas da Carris* (including a map of night-time services) from the turismo or from Carris kiosks. Carris' Web site, www.carris.pt, also has timetables and route details.

Funicular Fun

The city has three funiculars (*elevadors* or *ascensors*), which labour up and down the steepest hills around the Baixa and Bairro Alto, plus the extraordinary **Elevador de Santa Justa** (Map 6), a huge wrought-iron lift at the end of Rua de Santa Justa.

Santa Justa is more popular with tourists (though the queues can quickly sap enthusiasm), but the most charming ride is on the **Elevador da Bica** (Map 5) through the Santa Catarina district, at the south-western corner of Bairro Alto. The other two funiculars are the **Elevador da Glória** (Map 6), which provides stately entrance to the Bairro Alto, climbing up from the Praça dos Restauradores to the superb São Pedro de Alcântara viewpoint atop one of Lisbon's seven hills; and the **Elevador do Lavra** (off Map 6) from Largo de Anunciada, on the eastern side of Restauradores.

The Elevador de Santa Justa operates 7 am to 11.45 pm daily (9 am to 11 pm Sunday and holidays); the Elevadors da Bica and do Lavra run 7 am to 10.45 pm; and the Elevador da Glória works 7 am to 1 am daily. They're not for anyone in a hurry!

BETHUNE CARMICHAEL

Individual tickets cost 160$00 on board or half that price if you buy a BUC (*Bilhete Único de Coroa* – a one-zone ticket just for the city centre) beforehand. These prepaid tickets are sold at Carris kiosks, most conveniently at Praça da Figueira, at the foot of the Elevador de Santa Justa (both Map 6), and at Santa Apolónia (Map 8) and Cais do Sodré stations.

From these kiosks (open 8 am to 8 pm daily) you can also get a one-day (460$00) or three-day (1075$00) Bilhete Turístico, valid for all buses, trams and funiculars. Another type of pass is the Passe Turístico (1720$00/2430$00 for four/seven days), available from all Carris kiosks and metro stations, and valid for buses (except the Aero-Bus), trams, funiculars *and* the metro. You must show your passport to get the (nontransferable) Passe Turístico.

Tram

Clattering, antediluvian trams *(eléctricos* or *tranvías)* are an endearing component of Lisbon. Don't leave Lisbon without riding tram No 28 through the narrow streets of the Alfama district, and back around to Largo Martim Moniz (Map 6). You should catch it in the Largo to get the full run. Westbound, it clanks through Bairro Alto to Estrela peak.

Two other useful lines are the No 15 from Praça da Figueira (Map 6) and Praça do Comércio (Map 7), via Alcântara to Belém; and the No 18 from Praça do Comércio to Alcântara to Ajuda. The No 15 line features huge, modern space-age articulated trams, which also have machines on board for tickets and one and three-day passes. Tram stops are usually marked by a small *paragem* sign hanging from a lamp post or the overhead wires.

Over 100km of additional fast tram routes are in the pipeline; the old trams will survive only where 'tourist interest justifies their preservation'.

TRAIN

Lisbon has three major train stations. Santa Apolónia (Map 8) is the terminal for IC and IR trains from northern and central Portugal, and all international services. Over the river, Barreiro (Map12) is the terminal for *suburbano* services to Setúbal and all long-distance services to the south of Portugal; frequent connecting ferries leave from the pier at Terreiro do Paço (Map 5). At this pier, you need to buy two tickets: a 180$00 ferry ticket to Barreiro plus your onward train ticket (see the boxed text 'Bye Bye

Tram Tips

Don't be alarmed if your tram driver suddenly stops the tram and jumps out. He's probably only *mudar as agulhas* (changing tracks). Or he might be judging whether he can get past a badly parked car. This is a particular hazard along the narrow streets of the No 28 tram's route and one which often causes long delays. You might even be asked to help budge the offending vehicle!

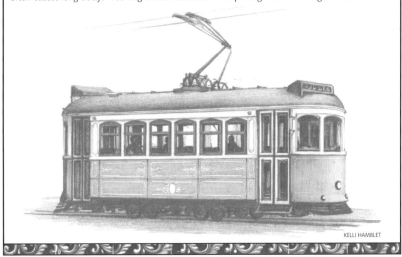

KELLI HAMBLET

Barreiro' in the Getting There & Away chapter). Lisbon's newest and most useful major station is the intermodal Gare do Oriente (Map 9); all services to/from Santa Apolónia pass through here.

There are four smaller stations: Cais do Sodré (Map 7) is the terminal for Cascais and Estoril; Rossio (Map 6) serves Queluz-Belas, Cacém and Sintra; and the newly modernised Entrecampos (Map 1) station (at Avenida 5 de Outubro) serves the northern Azambuja Line as well as Fertagus trains across the Ponte 25 de Abril. Entrecampos Poente, 200m east of Entrecampos, serves the suburban line to Cacém.

For more information about the major stations, see the entries in the Getting There & Away chapter.

METRO

The rapidly expanding *metropolitano* (underground) system (Map 11), which currently has 28km of track and 40 stations, is useful not only for short hops across the city, but also to reach the intermodal Gare do Oriente and nearby Parque das Nações (Map 9). By 2003 – when a Santa Apolónia link is expected to be completed – there will be 47km of track and 60 stations. Many stations are adorned with fantastic modern art (see the boxed text 'Metro Art').

Individual tickets are 100$00, a *caderneta* of 10 tickets costs 850$00. Tickets can be purchased from windows or automatic dispensers in metro stations. Single tickets must be validated in the little machine at the

There's Rossio & Rossio

Rossio metro station, beneath the square called Rossio (Praça Dom Pedro V), is *not* the closest one to the Rossio train station. For the train station you will need to get off at Restauradores metro station.

euro currency converter 100$00 = €0.50

Metro Art

Metro journeys in Lisbon are brightened by striking tile and marble-work on most platforms. Each station, designed by a celebrated modern artist, reflects a local or historical theme: the literary designs at Entrecampos, by Bartolomeu Cid dos Santos, reflect the nearby Biblioteca Nacional; Campo Pequeno's ceramics evoke the nearby bullring and boast an imposing marble tableau, by Francisco Simões, representing the rural inhabitants of this once outlying area. Martim Moniz station is perhaps the most attractive of all, with José João Brito's stylised representations of Crusaders, who spearheaded the liberation of Lisbon from the Moors in 1147. There is even an underground waterfall in the atrium of Cais do Sodré's metro station!

John Laidlar

entrance to the platform; don't forget to do it – there *are* ticket inspectors. A one-day metro pass will cost 270$00 (940$00 for seven days). If you have bought a Passe Turístico or Lisboa Card, both are are valid on the metro.

The system operates 6.30 am to 1 am. Entrances are marked by a big red M. Travel is quite straightforward. Useful signs include *correspondência* (transfer between lines) and *saída* (exit to the street). Pickpockets can be a nuisance at any time. And computer diskettes are at risk; wrap them in silver foil to avoid harmful magnetic interference. The metro's Web site is at www .metrolisboa.pt.

CAR & MOTORCYCLE

Don't even think about driving in Lisbon: it's no fun at all, thanks to heavy traffic, metro roadworks and manic drivers. There are two ring roads, both of which are useful for staying *out* of the centre. On maps the inner one is marked CRIL (Cintura Regional Interna de Lisboa), the outer one CREL (Cintura Regional Externa de Lisboa).

If you do venture into the city centre you'll find that parking spaces are scarce

and car parks expensive. All-day rates in the underground car parks (eg, at Praça Marquês de Pombal; Map 2) are around 1250$00. Upmarket hotel car parks can be twice that. Hotels with (free) street car parking are mentioned in the Places to Stay chapter. Free parking is also possible in Campo dos Mártires da Pátria (Map 5). As elsewhere in Portugal, down-and-outers (nicknamed *arrumadores* or 'arrangers') often loiter in parking areas to 'help' you find a spot. A tip of 50$00 or 100$00 is expected. Always lock the car and don't leave any valuables inside; theft from cars is common.

For details about required documents and national rules and regulations, see the Car & Motorcycle section of the Getting There & Away chapter.

Rental

To rent a car in Portugal you must be at least 25 years old and have held your driving licence for over a year (some companies do allow younger drivers, at higher rates). The best deals are often part of 'fly-drive' packages, the worst tend to be those done with international firms after you arrive.

Daily rates (including unlimited mileage, tax and insurance) for a small car range from 6000$00 to 9000$00 per day in the high season; it's worth shopping around. Local operators with reasonable multiday rates include Sixt (☎ 219 405 247, fax 219 405 248), Mundirent (☎ 313 93 60, fax 313 93 69) and Solcar (☎ 213 139 070, fax 213 560 504). International firms include Avis (toll-free ☎ 800 201 002, fax 217 547 852), Europcar (☎ 219 407 790, fax 219 425 239) and Hertz (toll-free ☎ 800 238 238, fax 219 400 490).

The nearest place to rent a motorcycle or scooter is Transrent in Cascais (see the Excursions chapter).

TAXI

Compared with the rest of Europe, Lisbon's *táxis* are quick, reasonably cheap and plentiful. Pick one up at a rank (hailing one can be difficult); useful ranks are at Rossio, Praça dos Restauradores (both Map 6), near all train and bus stations, at Terreiro do Paço ferry terminal (Map 5) and at top-end hotels.

Street Names

Street names in Lisbon (and throughout Portugal) provide a potted history of the country. Here are some of the most important.

Rua/Avenida

25 de Abril	the date when the 1974 Revolution of the Carnations began
5 de Outubro	the date in 1910 when the monarchy was overthrown and a republic established
1 de Dezembro	the date in 1640 when Portuguese independence was restored after Spanish rule
da Liberdade	referring to the freedom established by the 1974 revolution
dos Restauradores	the restorers of independence after Spanish rule
Afonso de Albuquerque	the viceroy of India who expanded Portugal's empire; he conquered Goa in 1510, Malacca in 1511 and Hormuz in 1515
Luís de Camões	Portugal's most famous 16th-century poet
João de Deus	a 19th-century lyric poet
Almeida Garrett	a 19th-century poet, playwright and novelist
Alexandre Herculano	a 19th-century historian
Alexandre Serpa Pinto	a late-19th-century African explorer
Gil Vicente	a 16th-century court dramatist
Martim Moniz	valiant Christian solider who broke the three-month siege of the Moors' Castelo de São Jorge in 1147 by scaling the walls
Rosa Araújo	19th-century president of Lisbon's Câmara Municipal (town hall) responsible for the creation of the Avenida da Liberdade

You can also telephone for one (at an extra charge of 150$00). Try Rádio Táxis de Lisboa (☎ 218 119 000), Autocoope (☎ 217 932 756) or Teletáxis (☎ 218 111 100, fax 218 151 790). The latter one or Os Unidos de Lisboa (☎ 218 160 000, fax 218 160 009) can arrange excursions, usually in meterless taxis marked T (for *turismo*), at fixed rates and with drivers who are used to dealing with tourists. Or you can make your own arrangements: for a chauffeur who speaks English, French or Italian, call Dantas on ☎ 966 800 211 or Almeida on ☎ 964 055 397. Machado (☎ 931 253 917) has staff that speak German.

The fare on weekdays during daylight hours is 380$00 flag fall plus a complex formula based on distance and elapsed time. It'll cost about 1000$00 for a jaunt across town. Rates are about 20% higher at night (10 pm to 6 am) and weekends and holidays. Once a taxi leaves the city limits you also pay a surcharge or higher rate, and possibly the cost of a return trip (whether you take it or not). It's best to insist on the meter, although it's possible to negotiate a flat fare. Tips are voluntary; 10% is the norm.

All taxis have meters, but rip-offs do happen, in particular with some taxis that haunt the airport (see To/From the Airport earlier for details about a prepaid taxi voucher scheme). If you think you may have been cheated, get a receipt from the driver (and note the car's registration number and your time of departure and arrival) and make a claim with Inspecção-Geral das Actividades Económicas (Map 4; ☎ 213 831 523), Rua São Bento 347. The police or turismo should also be able to help.

BICYCLE

Lisbon traffic is a nightmare for cyclists. You're better off stashing your bike with the left-luggage office at the bus station or airport and seeing the city by public transport. Better hotels and pensões may have a storage

GETTING AROUND

room. See the Bicycle section in the Getting There & Away chapter for information on transporting your bike between cities.

The only pleasant places to ride a bike are Parque das Nações (see the Things to See & Do chapter) and a 5km stretch along the Rio Tejo from 1km west of Doca de Santo Amaro (Map 3) to Belém and Praia d'Algés. Tejo Bike (Map 1; ☎ 218 871 976) has a bike-rental stall on this riverfront promenade just west of Café In; charges are 750$00 per hour (5000$00 for 10 hours). Tandems and child bikes are also available. It's open 10 am to 8 pm daily in summer (to 7 pm weekends only in winter).

You can also rent bikes (as well as motorbikes) from Transrent in Cascais (for details see the Excursions chapter).

BOAT

The Transtejo ferry line has several riverfront terminals (estações fluviais). From the eastern end of the Terreiro do Paço terminal (off Praça do Comércio; Map 5), swanky catamarans ferry passengers across the Rio Tejo to Montijo (300$00, 30 minutes) and Seixal (220$00, 30 minutes) every hour or so (every 15 minutes during rush hours and less often at weekends). From the main part of the terminal, called Estação do Sul e Sueste, Soflusa ferries run every 30 to 60 minutes to Barreiro (180$00, 30 minutes), where you pick up rail connections to the Alentejo and Algarve. Next door, at Cais da Alfândega, passenger ferries go every 10 minutes to Cacilhas (110$00, 10 minutes). In late 2000, these transferred temporarily to the pier at Cais do Sodré (Map 7) due to metro works. Car (and bicycle) ferries also go from Cais do Sodré to Cacilhas.

Farther along, in Belém, ferries depart every 30 to 60 minutes for Trafaria and Porto Brandão (110$00), about 3.5km and 5km respectively east of Costa da Caparica.

ORGANISED TOURS
Bus & Tram Tours

Carristur, part of the municipal transport company, Carris (☎ 213 613 000), runs city tours; the 1½-hour Eléctrico das Colinas tram tour of the hills around the Baixa runs four or five times daily between March and October and is 3000$00 (children 1500$00). Between May and August, Carris also runs a Circuito Tejo (Tagus Tour) of the city and Belém by open-top bus every half-hour from 11 am to 4 pm (to 5 pm in August); and an Expresso Oriente (Orient Express) tour of north-eastern Lisbon, including the Parque das Nações, six times daily in July and August. Both cost 2000$00 (children 1000$00). These tours are arranged so you can get off, explore the area and pick up the next bus an hour later. Taped commentaries are multilingual. The tours depart from Praça do Comércio.

Cityrama (☎ 213 191 091), Portugal Tours (☎ 213 522 902) and Gray Line (☎ 213 522 594) run more or less identical sightseeing bus tours of Lisbon and the surrounding region. Typical Lisbon itineraries include a 5½-hour city day tour (5250$00); Lisbon by night (10,500$00, four hours), with a restaurant meal; and Lisbon plus Sintra and the Estoril Coast (12,500$00, full day). All of the tour buses depart from Marquês de Pombal (Map 2; you can hop aboard there without prebooking if there's space) but also pick up passengers at selected hotels. Check the Web site at www.cityrama.pt for more details.

Walking Tours

The Centro Nacional de Cultura (☎ 213 466 722, fax 213 428 250, ⓔ ino@cncpt) offers three-hour themed walks (eg, Monumental and Artistic Lisbon) for a minimum of five people (3500$00 per person). Advance booking is essential.

River Cruises

Transtejo (☎ 218 820 348) runs two-hour, multilingual cruises on the Tejo (Cruzeiros no Tejo) at 11 am and 3 pm daily except Monday between April and October (3 pm only in winter) from the eastern end of the Terreiro do Paço ferry terminal (Map 5). Tickets cost 3000$00 (children 1500$00).

Things to See & Do

Lisbon is the kind of place where you can be as indolent as you like, sitting at street cafes watching the world go by or meandering through old neighbourhoods such as Alfama or Bairro Alto, sampling food or fado. Other attractively lazy options include taking a tram to the end of the line, a ferry across the Rio Tejo, or watching the sun set from the city's various hilltop *miradouros* (viewpoints).

But for the eager there are also plenty of cultural activities. In addition to architectural masterpieces at Belém (some 6km west of the city centre), Lisbon also has 50 or so museums, ranging from obscure house-museums to the world-class Gulbenkian (not to be missed). And at the Parque das Nações (Nations Park) you'll find the quite stunning Oceanário and other high-tech and kid-friendly activities.

WALKING TOURS

As long as you don't mind the occasional muscle-aching steep street, Lisbon is a joy for walkers. It's generally easy to find your way around, small enough to explore over a few days and is visually pleasing almost everywhere. An added bonus is the proliferation of cafes and restaurants where you can stop for refuelling. Even if you're not a walker you should allow a few hours to stroll in the Alfama, one of Lisbon's most rewarding areas.

You can find clear descriptions and maps of five walks (in Belém, Alfama, Bairro Alto & Cais do Sodré, Baixa & Chiado and Estrela & Docas) in the Turismo de Lisboa's *Lisboa City Walks* (available free at all its outlets – see Tourist Offices in the Facts for the Visitor chapter). Here are a few more suggestions, with two on a literary theme (see the Arts section in Facts about Lisbon for more about these two famous writers). For information about guided walking tours available in the city, see Organised Tours in the Getting There & Away and Getting Around chapters.

Highlights

The pick of Lisbon's many highlights is:

- the Mosteiro dos Jerónimos at Belém, a Manueline masterpiece
- the Oceanário, Europe's largest aquarium, and other spectacular architectural attractions in the Parque das Nações
- the world-class Museu Calouste Gulbenkian, plus the Museu Nacional de Arte Antiga and the Museu Nacional do Azulejo
- the tram No 28 ride from Largo Martim Moniz, east into the Alfama or west into the Bairro Alto
- fado music in a fado house of the Bairro Alto
- the atmospheric lanes of the medieval Alfama district
- Castelo de São Jorge and its panoramic views
- riverside hotspots such as Doca de Santo Amaro for restaurants and late-night clubs

Fernando Pessoa Walk (Maps 7 & 6)

The famous writer and poet, Fernando Pessoa (1888-1935) is closely associated with Lisbon, where he was born and where he died. This walk – which will admirably suit those who like lingering at cafes – starts at one of his favourite haunts, **Café A Brasileira** (Map 7) on Rua Garrett in the suburb of Chiado, where a bronze statue of him sits among the tables outside. A little farther east along Rua Garrett is the church where Pessoa was baptised, the 18th-century **Basílica da Nossa Senhora dos Mártires**. It was originally built to commemorate the soldiers killed during the 1147 reconquest of Lisbon from the Moors. Follow Rua Serpa Pinto south of here to reach **Largo de São Carlos**, described by Pessoa as 'the village in which I was born'; his birthplace is the house opposite the Teatro Nacional de São Carlos.

In neighbouring Baixa (Map 7), reached via Rua Nova do Almada from Rua Garrett, Pessoa spent his creative hours. It was in **Rua Áurea** and neighbouring **Rua da Prata** that he was employed to write business correspondence in English for various commercial firms, although he was also working privately on a vast body of poetry, essays and texts. Walk down to nearby Praça do Comércio to find another cafe that Pessoa often frequented to find inspiration, the famous **Martinho do Arcada**. The table at which he scribbled his now famous work, *Mensagem* (Message), is still there, the cafe walls now adorned with photos of the great man.

From here you can head north up Rua da Prata and along **Rua dos Douradores** (Pessoa's favourite lunchtime haunt) to the **Rossio** (Map 6), where Pessoa would meet his intellectual buddy, Mário de Sá Carneiro, at another cafe long favoured by literati, the renowned **Nicola**.

José Saramago Walk (Maps 4, 5 & 7)

Nobel Prize winner, José Saramago, who now lives in Lanzarote, spent much of his life in Lisbon and portrayed the city in several of his novels. This long walk (which can be supplemented by hops on Tram No 28) starts in **Praça da Estrela** (Map 4). The neoclassical style of the **Basílica da Estrela** was inspired by the Convento (now Palácio Nacional) de Mafra on which Saramago based his memorable novel, *Memorial do Convento*.

Follow Calçada da Estrela past Rua dos Ferreiros à Estrela (Saramago lived at No 32) to Avenida Dom Carlos I, passing the grandiose **Palácio da Assembleia da República** on the corner. Downhill a bit, turn left into Rua do Poço dos Negros (named after the *poço*, or well, which served as a mass grave for black slaves during the 16th and 17th centuries). Your goal from this point is the **Miradouro de Santa Catarina** (Map 5), reached via Travessa Condessa do Rio. The miradouro is dominated by a roughly hewn **monument to Adamastor**, the mythical giant feared by the 15th-century Portuguese

explorers on their sea voyages. Saramago made this place the beginning and end of his novel *The Year of the Death of Ricardo Reis*.

From the miradouro, wend your way through the atmospheric Santa Catarina neighbourhood along backstreet Travessas da Laranjeira and da Guilherme Coussul (Map 7) to follow Ricardo Reis' example and stop before a statue of another famous writer, Eça de Queiroz, in **Largo do Barão de Quintela**. From here it's an easy walk down Rua do Alecrim to **Cais do Sodré**, passing the former Hotel Bragança, right at the bottom on the left, where Reis is described as staying.

Stagger on a few more minutes along Rua Bernardino Costa to reach **Praça do Comércio** (Map 7) and Martinho da Arcada cafe. In the novel, Reis tries to persuade Fernando Pessoa to stop there. 'That would be unwise, the walls have ears and a good memory...' replies Saramago's Pessoa. But for weary walkers on a literary trail, there's no better place to rest.

Alfama Walk (Map 8)

From the Baixa (Map 7), it's an easy stroll from Rua da Conceição up to the Alfama's most important religious monument, the Sé or cathedral (this and other sights are described later in the Alfama, Castelo & Graça section). From here you can strike uphill for the Castelo de São Jorge or downhill into the heart of the Alfama from the nearby viewpoint of Largo das Portas do Sol.

From the Sé to the Castelo Following Rua Augusto Rosa uphill from the cathedral you'll pass the unmemorable ruins of a **Roman theatre** (apparently consecrated by Nero in 57 BC) off to the left in Rua de São Mamede, before reaching two of the area's most stunning viewpoints. The **Miradouro de Santa Luzia** with its attractive garden and pond and, a little farther on, the **Largo das Portas do Sol** (the 'sun gateway', originally one of the seven gateways into the Moorish city), which has a tempting outdoor cafe with great views over the Alfama. Nearby is the **Igreja da Santa Luzia**, with azulejos depicting the capture of the castle from the Moors.

From here, follow Travessa de Santa Luzia and stagger up the steep Travessa do Funil into Rua do Chão da Feira, which leads to the entrance of the castle. Bus No 37 can take you directly back to Praça da Figueira (Map 6) from here.

From the Largo das Portas do Sol to Alfama This is one of the easiest and most picturesque routes to follow through the Alfama's dense network of alleys and stairways, starting with Beco de Santa Helena (turn right just uphill from the Largo das Portas do Sol). Where it meets Rua do Castelo, turn left and then right into the pretty **Beco das Cruzes**, with its azulejo panels and archway. When this meets the main Rua da Regueira, turn right into Rua de São Miguel. In this street there are lots of little shops and restaurants for you to linger over.

You then have two choices: drop down into Largo do Chafariz de Dentro via Beco do Mexias, and then back westward along Rua de São Pedro, which joins Rua de São Miguel at the Largo de São Rafael; or continue westward along Rua de São Miguel itself. The second option gives you the chance to explore some more *becos* (alleys), in particular the **Beco da Cardosa** with its attractive 16th and 18th-century houses. Along Rua de São Miguel and Rua de São Pedro, as far as Largo do Chafariz de Dentro ('fountain within the walls'), are most of the Alfama's shops, restaurants and cafes.

At Largo de São Rafael, pause to look at a ruined **Moorish tower**, part of the Moors' original town wall. The old **Jewish quarter** is adjacent, marked by tiny Rua da Judiaria. From here you can continue along Rua de São João da Praça, which will take you back to the cathedral. Hop on tram No 28 to reach the Baixa district again, or you can continue walking downhill.

BAIXA & THE RIVERFRONT

Following the 1755 earthquake, one of the few people who kept his head was the autocratic Marquês de Pombal, Dom José I's chief minister. He took the opportunity to rebuild the city centre as quickly as possible, in a severe and simple, low-cost style.

The entire area from the riverside to the Rossio was reborn as a grid of wide, commercial streets (with pavements), with each dedicated to a trade. The memory of these districts lives on in the Baixa's trade-related street names – Áurea (formerly Ouro; gold), Sapateiros (shoemakers), Correeiros (saddlers), Prata (silver), Douradores (gilders) and Fanqueiros (cutlers).

This lower town remains the de facto heart of Lisbon. Down the middle runs pedestrianised Rua Augusta, the old street of the cloth merchants, now overflowing with cafes, shops and banks.

A number of the city's bus and tram lines funnel through Praça do Comércio (Map 7) at the Baixa's riverside end, or Rossio and Praça da Figueira (both Map 6) at its upper end. And several of the city's most charming funiculars, including the Eiffel-inspired Elevador de Santa Justa, can hoist you above the Baixa to superb viewing spots. (See the boxed text 'Funicular Fun' in the Getting Around chapter.)

Praça do Comércio (Map 7)

Before the earthquake, Praça do Comércio was called Terreiro do Paço (Palace Square), after the royal Palácio da Ribeira that overlooked it until the fateful morning of 1 November 1755. Most visitors coming by river or sea in bygone days would have arrived here. The huge square still feels like the entrance to the city, thanks to Joaquim Machado de Castro's bronze **equestrian statue** of Dom José I, arcaded 18th-century **ministries** along three sides and Verissimo da Costa's **Arco da Vitória**, the arch opening onto Rua Augusta.

Just off the north-western corner of the square is a smaller square, the recently restored **Praça do Município**, dominated by Lisbon's 1874 Paços do Concelho (town hall) on the eastern side, the former marine arsenal on the southern side and a finely carved, 18th-century *pelourinho* (pillory) at the centre.

For the route east of Praça do Comércio, see the Alfama, Castelo & Graça section later.

Cais do Sodré (Map 7)

Continuing west for another 400m along Rua do Arsenal from Praça do Comércio, you arrive at Lisbon's other main riverfront plaza, Praça do Duque da Terceira, better known by its riverfront name, Cais do Sodré, where you'll find the Transtejo car ferry and the Cais do Sodré metro and train stations.

A few short blocks west is the domed **Mercado da Ribeira**, the city's former main market (officially the Mercado Municipal 24 de Julho), which is now being converted into a flower and craft market.

From here, Avenida 24 de Julho runs for 3km along the river to the Port of Lisbon and the warehouse district of Alcântara and Doca de Santo Amaro. This strip is a major axis for Lisbon's nightlife (see the Entertainment chapter). A pleasant way to return to Praça do Comércio is along the breezy riverfront promenade.

Núcleo Arqueológico (Map 7)

Under the streets of the central Baixa is this web of tunnels, which may be the remnants of a **Roman spa** (or possibly the foundations of a temple) and probably dating from the 1st century AD. You are able to descend into the mouldy depths, via the offices of the modern Banco Comércial Portuguesa, at Rua dos Correeiros 9, on a guided tour that is run by the Museu da Cidade (see the Greater Lisbon section later in this chapter). Tour times are at 3, 4 and 5 pm on Thursday and hourly 10 am to noon and 3 to 5 pm on Saturday (admission free).

Elevador de Santa Justa (Map 6)

You can rise above the Baixa in the most unique mode of transport in the city: a huge, wrought-iron lift designed by Raul Mésnier du Ponsard (a follower of Gustave Eiffel) and completed in 1902. It hoists you 32m above Rua de Santa Justa to a crammed viewing platform and cafe at eye level with the Convento do Carmo ruins in the Chiado district. Be prepared for long queues for this antiquated lift.

It operates 7 am to 11.45 pm daily (9 am to 11 pm Sunday and holidays); a ticket (available from the Carris kiosk at the back of the elevador) costs 160$00.

Rossio & Praça da Figueira (Map 6)

This pair of plazas forms the gritty heart of the Baixa, with lots of cafes from which to watch a cross-section of Lisbon's multicultural population, and hustlers and hawkers preying cheerfully on visitors.

In the middle of the Rossio is a **statue**, allegedly of Dom Pedro IV, after whom the square is formally named. The story goes the statue is actually of Emperor Maximilian of Mexico and was abandoned in Lisbon en route from France to Mexico after news arrived of Maximilian's assassination. On the northern side of the square is the restored 1846 **Teatro Nacional de Dona Maria II**, its facade topped by a statue of 16th-century playwright Gil Vicente.

In the city's less orderly times the Rossio was the scene of animal markets, fairs and bullfights. The theatre was built on the site of a palace in which the unholiest excesses of the Portuguese Inquisition took place from the 16th to 19th centuries. In the nearby **Igreja de São Domingos**, the Inquisition's judgments, or *autos-da-fé*, were handed down.

Rolling Motion Square

This was the nickname given to the Rossio by early English visitors because of the undulating mosaic pattern of its pavements. Such cobbled pavements – constructed from handcut white limestone and grey basalt cubes (originally installed by prison-labour gangs in the 19th century) – are still much in evidence everywhere, painstakingly pounded by hand into a bed of sand.

The pavements in the Rossio practically disappeared during recent metro and roadworks and are now being relaid. Meanwhile, for Lisbon's best contemporary 'rolling motion' pavement art, take a look at the creations in the Parque das Nações (see the boxed text 'Art in the Parque' later in this chapter).

CHIADO & BAIRRO ALTO

These two districts, lying above the Baixa to the west, make a perfect pair for day and night exploration. The Chiado, which is a wedge of wide streets roughly between Rua do Crucifixo and Rua da Misericórdia, is the posh place for shopping and loitering in cafes. The gutted buildings that pockmarked the Chiado after a massive fire in 1988 have now been restored and redesigned by architect Álvaro Siza Vieira into swanky shopping malls.

The Bairro Alto, a fashionable residential district in the 17th century (and still boasting some fine mansions), is now better known as the raffish heartland of Lisbon nightlife.

Convento do Carmo (Map 6)

Uphill from Rua Garrett, the ruins of this convent stand as stunning testimony to the 1755 earthquake. Only the Gothic arches, walls and flying buttresses remain of what was once one of Lisbon's largest churches. It was built in 1423 under the orders of Nuno Álvares Pereira, Dom João I's military commander (who became religious after a life of war and spent his last eight years in this Carmelite retreat).

The convent once housed the Museu Arqueológico, an open-air collection of rather intriguing items including Egyptian mummies and ancient Peruvian skulls, but it's been closed so long *para obras* (for repairs) it seems unlikely ever to reopen.

A striking view of the ruins can be seen from the top of Elevador de Santa Justa (see Baixa & the Riverfront earlier).

Teatro Nacional de São Carlos (Map 7)

This theatre, on Rua Serpa Pinto, is one of the very few survivors of the 1988 fire. It's Lisbon's opera house and the city's largest, most handsome theatre, built in the 1790s in imitation of the San Carlos Theatre in Naples. It stands opposite the smaller Teatro Municipal de São Luís.

Museu do Chiado (Map 7)

Nearby, housed in the former Convento de São Francisco at Rua Serpa Pinto 4, is the

A typical *beco* of Bairro Alto

Chiado Museum (☎ 213 432 148), which has a respectable collection of Portuguese art dating from approximately 1850 to 1950. It also hosts changing exhibitions. Among the painters represented are Rafael Bordalo Pinheiro, José de Almada Negreiros, Amadeo de Souza Cardoso and Maria Helena Vieira da Silva. The museum's opening hours are 2 to 6 pm Tuesday and 10 am to 6 pm Wednesday to Sunday; admission is 450$00 (seniors and students 225$00; free on Sunday morning).

Jardim Botânico (Map 5)

Strike uphill along Rua Dom Pedro V to this venerable botanical garden, a great place for a picnic. It's open 9 am to 8 pm (from 10 am at weekends, and closing at 6 pm in winter); admission costs 200$00 (seniors 100$00). The main entrance is on Rua da Escola Politécnica 58, with another entrance on Rua da Alegria.

Igreja de São Roque (Map 6)

It's a short walk downhill from Elevador da Glória to Largo Trindade Coelho and this late-16th-century Jesuit church whose dull facade is one of Lisbon's biggest deceptions. Inside are chapels stuffed with gold, marble and Florentine azulejos. The *pièce de résistance* is the more restrained but exquisite **Capela de São João Baptista**, to the left of the altar. Commissioned in 1742 by Portugal's most extravagant king, Dom João V, this chapel was designed and built in Rome using the most expensive materials possible, including amethyst, alabaster, agate, lapis lazuli and Carrara marble. After its consecration by Pope Benedict XIV it was dismantled and shipped to Lisbon for what was then a staggering UK£225,000.

Santa Catarina (Map 5)

From the southern end of the Bairro Alto (walking distance from Cais do Sodré) the **Elevador da Bica** creeps up to Rua do Loreto, a few blocks west of Praça de Luís Camões. Riding this gives you a chance to explore the unsung Santa Catarina neighbourhood, a compact, maze-like district bright with fluttering laundry, and alive with balcony gossip, chattering kids and caged songbirds. The district's name comes from the 17th-century **Igreja de Santa Catarina** in Calçada do Combro, largely rebuilt after the 1755 earthquake but still full of pre-earthquake gilded woodwork and with a gloriously ornate baroque organ.

Downhill, at the end of Rua Marechal Saldanha, on another of Lisbon's seven hills, is the **Miradouro de Santa Catarina** (with cafe-kiosk), offering a bird's-eye view of the river and the Ponte 25 de Abril. See the José Saramago walking tour earlier for a description of a route through this area.

ALFAMA, CASTELO & GRAÇA

This area east and north-east of the Baixa is Lisbon's oldest and most historically interesting district with a warren of medieval streets and outstanding views from three of Lisbon's seven hills – São Jorge, Graça and Senhora do Monte (see Alfama Walk earlier for a description of a route through this area).

As far back as the 5th century, the Alfama was inhabited by the Visigoths, and remnants of a Visigothic town wall remain. But it was the Moors who gave the district its shape and atmosphere, as well as its name. The Arabic *alhama* means springs or bath, probably a reference to hot springs found near Largo das Alcaçarias. In Moorish times this was an upper-class residential area. After earthquakes brought down many of its mansions (and post-Moorish churches) it reverted to a working-class and fisherfolk quarter. It was one of the few districts to ride out the 1755 earthquake.

Plunging from the castle to the river, the Alfama's tangled alleys and vertiginous stairways are a sharp contrast to the Baixa's prim streets. With narrow lanes of residential houses and grocery stores, it has a distinct village atmosphere; you can quickly feel like an intruder if you take a wrong turn into someone's backyard. Becoming more gentrified (renovation projects are in full swing), it's now a popular dining area with dozens of tiny restaurants. Early morning is the best time to catch a more traditional scene, when women sell fresh fish from their doorways. For a real rough-and-tumble atmosphere, visit during the Festas dos Santos Populares in June (see Public Holidays & Special Events in the Facts for the Visitor chapter).

Igreja da Conceição Velha (Map 8)

Walking east from the Praça do Comércio in Baixa, you'll come to this church on the north side of Rua da Alfândega. Its finely carved Manueline facade was rebuilt and reattached to the church after the earthquake.

Casa dos Bicos (Map 8)

Where Rua dos Bacalhoeiros merges with Rua da Alfândega is the startling early-16th-century 'House of Points' – a folly built by Afonso de Albuquerque, a former viceroy of India. Its prickly facade was restored in the early 1980s. It's now the offices for the Comemorações dos Descobrimentos organisation; in the lobby you can buy Age of Discoveries souvenirs and see bits of the old Moorish city wall and brick streets.

Sé (Map 8)

This Romanesque cathedral (on the route of tram No 28) is the Alfama's most important religious monument. It was built in 1150, soon after the city was recaptured from the Moors by Afonso Henriques. He was wary enough to want the church built like a fortress (its French architects designed a similar fortress cathedral for Coimbra). It's been extensively restored and is now rather dull, but check out the baroque organs and intricate baroque crib by the 18th-century sculptor, Joaquim Machado de Castro, in a chapel off the north aisle.

The Gothic cloister – whose centre reveals a deep archaeological excavation – is open 10 am to 6 pm daily except Sunday; admission costs 100$00. Religious paraphernalia on display in the treasury (same hours; 400$00) includes São Vicente relics in a mother-of-pearl casket.

Igreja de Santo António (Map 8)

Across the road from the cathedral is the Church of St Anthony, built in 1812. A tiny crypt inside (the entrance is through the second door on the left) claims to be the site of the saint's birthplace (admission free). A small museum (entrance next to the church) features statues, books and engravings from the 18th to 20th centuries; all are devoted to Lisbon's most popular saint. It's open 10 am to 1 pm and 2 to 6 pm daily except Monday (admission 180$00).

Casa do Fado e da Guitarra Portuguesa (Map 8)

In Largo do Chafariz de Dentro is one of Lisbon's newest museums, the House of Fado & Portuguese Guitar (☎ 218 823 470). It presents an excellent audiovisual display of fado's history, including some fascinating recordings of both fado and guitar music, and various dioramas including one of a traditional fado house. It's open 10 am to 6 pm daily except Tuesday; admission costs 450$00 (students and seniors 225$00, youth card-holders 180$00).

Museu-Escola de Artes Decorativas (Map 8)

On Largo das Portas do Sol 2, this museum-school of decorative arts (☎ 218 862 183, e fressmuseu@mail.telepac.pt) is owned and run by the private Fundação Ricardo do Espírito Santo Silva, founded in 1953 to

St Anthony

Although St Vincent is officially Lisbon's patron saint, lisboêtas show far greater affection for St Anthony, despite the fact that he spent most of his life in France and Italy. Born in Lisbon in 1195 and baptised in the cathedral, he eventually joined the Franciscan order. After illness forced him back from an African trip, he divided his time between France and Italy, dying near Padua in 1231.

Revered in Italy as St Anthony of Padua, or simply Il Santo, his humanistic preachings and concern for the poor made him internationally famous. A day after his death he was canonised (the fastest canonisation on record). Many miracles are attributed to him but he's especially renowned for his help in fixing marriages. Many single women and newly wed couples still leave gifts at the Alfama's Igreja de Santo António, built in 1812 allegedly on the site of his birthplace, and containing a museum devoted exclusively to the saint's life.

The best time to feel the fervour of affection for this saint is during the Festa de Santo António on 12 to 13 June. See Public Holidays & Special Events in the Facts for the Visitor chapter for details.

MARTIN HARRIS

showcase banker Espírito Santo Silva's striking collection of 16th to 19th-century furniture and other decorative articles. The foundation also provides workshop space to artisans working with traditional methods. Housed on several floors of the elegant 18th-century Palácio Azurara (which itself sports some fine original azulejos), it's open 10 am to 5 pm daily except Monday. Admission costs 800$00 (seniors and youths 400$00; it's free to art students and children under 12).

Castelo de São Jorge (Map 8)

A short, steep climb from Largo das Portas do Sol via Travessa de Santa Luzia (or catch bus No 37 from Rossio) will bring you to Lisbon's magnificent castle (open 9 am to 9 pm daily in summer and to 6 pm in winter; admission free).

From its Visigothic beginnings in the 5th century, the castle was later fortified by the Moors in the 9th century and surrounded by a 2km-long wall. After it was sacked by Christians in the 12th century (see the boxed text 'The Siege of Lisbon'), the Moorish governor's residence, Paço de Alcáçova, was transformed into a royal residence, particularly favoured by Dom Dinis. But by the 17th century, when attention had shifted to the waterfront area, this had fallen into ruins.

What remains of the castle has now been considerably tarted up for tourists. At the time of research, major restoration works were still in progress, closing off certain areas. Despite this there's still plenty to enjoy – notably the fantastic panoramas.

Near the entrance is **Olissipónia** (☎ 218 877 244), an excellent multimedia exhibition with a rapid-fire, multilingual headphone commentary about Lisbon's history and demography. Don't miss the best display in the last room (ask the reception staff to switch it on if necessary). There are also computers available for accessing more multilingual information about Lisbon's sights or history. It's all open 10 am to 5 pm daily except Wednesday; admission costs 600$00 (under-26s 300$00).

The inner walled area – part of which was once an elite residential neighbourhood for

The Siege of Lisbon

The recapture of Lisbon from the Moors in 1147 is one of the more unsavoury chapters in Portugal's early history. Afonso Henriques, Count of Porto, had already thrashed the Moors at Ourique in 1139 (and started calling himself King of Portugal) and now set his sights on Lisbon. Short of experienced troops, he persuaded a ruffian band of English, French, Flemish and German adventurers-crusaders on their way to Palestine to give him a hand. 'Do not be seduced by the desire to press on with your journey,' begged the Bishop of Porto on the king's behalf, 'for the praiseworthy thing is not to have been to Jerusalem, but to have lived a good life while on the way'.

It sounded an attractive idea (they were offered all the enemy's loot if the city was taken) and in June 1147 the siege of the Castelo de São Jorge began. The Moors were at first contemptuous – 'How many times within your memory have you come hither with pilgrims and barbarians to drive us hence?' – and managed to hold out for 17 weeks. But in October the castle's defences finally gave way and the 'Christian' forces (described more correctly by a contemporary reporter as 'plunderers, drunkards and rapists ...men not seasoned with the honey of piety') showed their true colours by raping and pillaging their way through the city, despite assurances of leniency for the losers from Afonso himself. The only good man among them appears to have been one Gilbert of Hastings, an English priest who later became Bishop of Lisbon.

the Moors, whose mosque stood on the site of the nearby Igreja de Santa Cruz – has another attraction, the **Câmara Escura** (signposted Tower of Ulysses). A periscope, featuring a mirror and two lenses, has been placed on top of the Tower to reflect 360° images of Lisbon inside. The 15-minute sessions take place every half-hour between 11 am and 2 pm daily except Tuesday. Admission costs 300$00 (free for children under 14) and there's commentary in English and French.

Marvellous Miradouros

Uphill from Largo de Rodrigues de Freitas, Calçada da Graça leads you to two splendid *miradouros* (viewpoints; Map 5). The first is **Miradouro da Graça** (with cafe-kiosk), atop one of Lisbon's seven hills. To the right is a former Augustinian convent, which is now a barracks, and about 700m north-west of the convent (turn up Calçada do Monte) is another major viewpoint, on another of Lisbon's hills, the **Miradouro da Senhora do Monte**. This is the best point in town for views of the castle, Mouraria and city centre.

Mouraria (Map 8)

To the north of the castle is this quarter where the Moors lived after the Christian Reconquista. It's now a rather sombre area, though Rua da Mouraria has been modernised and pedestrianised.

Museu da Marioneta (Map 8)

This intriguing Puppet Museum (☎ 218 865 794), at Largo de Rodrigues de Freitas 13, uphill from Largo das Portas do Sol, is crammed full with everything from finger puppets to life-size creations, including traditional 19th-century Portuguese puppets and an Asian collection (check out the great elephant puppets from Myanmar). A tiny theatre has occasional weekend performances for groups of school children.

The museum is open 10 am to 1.30 pm and 2.30 to 7 pm daily except Monday; admission costs 500$00.

Panteão Nacional (Map 8)

East of Largo de Rodrigues de Freitas (tram No 28 also passes close by) you can spot the huge dome of the Igreja de Santa Engrácia, officially known as the Panteão Nacional (National Pantheon; ☎ 218 876 629). When work began on this church in 1682, it was to be one of Lisbon's grandest. After almost three centuries of dithering and neglect, it was inaugurated as the national pantheon in 1966, featuring marble cenotaphs to historic and literary figures (among them Vasco da Gama and Henry the Navigator), tombs of former presidents. The best about it is the view from the roof.

It's open 10 am to 5 pm daily except Monday, and hosts occasional exhibitions; admission costs 300$00.

Mosteiro de São Vicente de Fora (Map 8)

This impressive monastery, just west of the Panteão Nacional, was built in Mannerist style by master of the Italian Renaissance, Felipe Terzi, between 1582 and 1627. Its wide nave and coffered vault are striking in their simplicity. Also notable is the sacristy, richly decorated in polychrome marble, and the former refectory which is now a mausoleum containing the sombre marble tombs of almost the entire Bragança dynasty, from João IV (died 1656) to Manuel II (died 1932, in exile in England).

Most memorable are the 18th-century azulejos that cover practically every wall of the place including in the two tranquil cloisters. On the 1st floor is a special display of 38 azulejo panels depicting La Fontaine's fables, accompanied by excellent text in English and French.

You can climb to the very top of the monastery for especially good views of the river, then enjoy a coffee or meal in its pretty open-air courtyard (see the Pastelarias, Cafes & Confeitarias section in the Places to Eat chapter). The monastery is open 10 am to 6 pm daily except Monday. Admission costs 500$00 (seniors and under-26s 250$00).

SANTA APOLÓNIA

Best known for its international train station, this area also hosts three museums and an up-and-coming riverside complex, Doca do Jardim do Tabaco, which boasts some spiffy restaurants (see the Alfama section in the Places to Eat chapter).

Museu Militar (Map 8)

Just west of Santa Apolónia station, on Largo do Museu de Artilharia, the Military Museum (☎ 218 842 569) claims to have the world's biggest artillery collection. War freaks can also look at other armaments,

...aintings. It's open 10 ...t Monday; admission

Map 5)

...izarre subject for a museum, but this Water Museum (☎ 218 135 522), devoted to Lisbon's water supply over the centuries, won the Council of Europe's Museum Prize in 1990. Lisbon only got a dependable water supply in the 18th century and what an amazing project it was (see the boxed text 'The Aqueduct of Free Waters' later in this chapter).

The museum, in a former pumping station (Estação Elevatória dos Barbadinhos), is one of four water-related museums in the city run by EPAL, the municipal water company. It's open 10 am to 6 pm Monday to Saturday; admission costs 350$00 (students 175$00). Take bus No 104 or 105 from Praça do Comércio; get off four stops after Santa Apolónia station and walk up Calçada dos Barbadinhos; turn right into Rua do Alviela and walk to the end.

Museu Nacional do Azulejo (Map 1)

The National Azulejos Museum (☎ 218 147 747), at Rua Madre de Deus 4, is probably Lisbon's most attractive museum. A splendid array of tiles from as early as the 15th century (plus displays on how they're made) is integrated into the elegant buildings of the former convent of Igreja de Nossa Senhora da Madre de Deus. Among the highlights are a 36m-long panel depicting pre-earthquake Lisbon and a lovely mural, *Our Lady of Life* by Marçal de Matos (dating from about 1580). There are also some charming 20th-century azulejos.

The church, with its own beautiful tiles, the Manueline cloister, and the stupendous baroque chapel and adjacent rooms of carved, gilded wood are highlights in their own right. The complex was founded for the Poor Clare order of nuns in 1509 by Dona Leonor, wife of Dom João II.

The museum is open 2 to 6 pm Tuesday and 10 am to 6 pm Wednesday to Sunday; the admission charge is 450$00 (seniors and

under-26s 250$00; free on Sunday morning). There's also a pleasant restaurant here (see the boxed text 'Azulejos for Lunch?' in the Places to Eat chapter). Take bus No 104 or 105 from Praça do Comércio (weekdays) or No 59 from Rossio (weekends).

ESTRELA, LAPA & DOCA DE ALCÂNTARA

The attractions in this district west of Bairro Alto are limited, though getting here on westbound tram No 28 from Largo Martim Moniz (Baixa) is fun (you can also take bus No 13 from Praça do Comércio).

Palácio da Assembleia da República (Map 4)

This imposing 17th-century former convent, in Largo de São Bento, now houses Portugal's parliament (also called the Palácio da Assembleia Nacional) and the national assembly has convened here since 1833. Behind are several other buildings, including the official residence of the prime minister.

Basílica da Estrela (Map 4)

Even seen through a tangle of tram wires, the massive dome and belfries of this church are still impressive. Completed in 1790 by order of Dona Maria I (whose tomb is here) in gratitude for bearing a male heir, the church is all elegant neoclassicism outside and chilly, echoing baroque inside. Its best feature is the view across Lisbon from the dome, the weight of which was ingeniously spread over three concentric structures by architect Mateus Vicente de Oliveira. You should also check out the life-size Christmas manger, with figures carved by Joaquim Machado de Castro (better known for the bronze equestrian statue of Dom José I in Praça do Comércio). The church is open 7.30 am to 1 pm and 3 to 8 pm daily (admission free).

Across the road is a big, beautiful public park, the **Jardim da Estrela**, with a good children's playground.

Cemitério dos Ingleses (Map 4)

Beyond the Jardim da Estrela lies a patch of heresy in this Catholic land: the Protestant

BETHUNE CARMICHAEL

DAMIEN SIMONIS

Ride to the top of Elevador de Santa Justa.

Travelling the tourist route by tram

DAMIEN SIMONIS

Don't miss a trip on tram No 28 around all the sights of Lisbon from the Sé to the Baixa.

Castelo de São Jorge is illuminated above the darkened suburbs like a beacon to returning sailors.

Neoclassical Basilica da Estrela

Torre de Belém stands guard on the Rio Tejo.

Dom Jose I on Praça do Comércio, the former gateway to the city

Padrão dos Descobrimentos

English Cemetery, founded in 1717 under the terms of the Treaty of 1654 with England. Among expatriates at rest here are novelist Henry Fielding (author of *Tom Jones*), who died during a visit to Lisbon for his health in 1754. At the far corner is all that remains of Lisbon's old Jewish cemetery.

Casa Museu de Fernando Pessoa (Map 4)

Lisbon's favourite poet, Fernando Pessoa, had about 30 different lodgings during his working life. The one where he spent the last 15 years, at Rua Coelho da Rocha 16 in Campo de Ourique, and just up the road from the Cemitério dos Ingleses, is now a museum (☎ 213 968 190) dedicated to the writer's life and work. It's open 10 am to 6 pm weekdays (1 to 8 pm on Thursday). Admission is free.

Museu Nacional de Arte Antiga (Map 4)

To the south of the elegant Lapa district, this first-class National Museum of Ancient Art (☎ 213 964 151) is housed in a 17th-century palace at Rua das Janelas Verdes 9. Here is the official national collection of works by Portuguese painters, the largest such collection in the country. Also on display are other 14th to 20th-century European works, including some by Hieronymus Bosch, Piero della Francesca and Albrecht Dürer, and an extensive collection of applied art.

The most outstanding item is undoubtedly the *Adoration of St Vincent* by Nuno Gonçalves, most brilliant of the Flemish-influenced Portuguese painters prominent in the 15th century. The six extraordinarily detailed panels show a crowd of contemporary Portuguese figures from every level of society (including the Duke of Bragança and his family) paying homage to Portugal's patron saint, São Vicente. You may recognise the frequently reproduced central panels, which include Henry the Navigator in his floppy hat. Gonçalves is thought to have painted himself in the far left corner of the central left panel.

Japanese *namban* screens are the most interesting items in the museum's new wing.

Namban (meaning southern barbarians), the Japanese name for the Portuguese who landed on Tanegaxima Island in southern Japan in 1543, has come to refer to all Japanese art inspired by this encounter. The 16th-century screens show the Portuguese arrival in intriguing detail. Other items from this era include Afro-Portuguese carved tusks and Indo-Portuguese chests inlaid with mother-of-pearl.

Don't overlook the fantastic silverware collection, with dozens of masterpieces by the French silversmith Thomas Germain and his son François-Thomas, made in the late 18th century for the Portuguese court and royal family.

The museum is open 2 to 6 pm Tuesday and 10 am to 6 pm Wednesday to Sunday (closed Monday). Admission costs 500$00 (under-26s and seniors 250$00; free to teachers and journalists; and free to everyone on Sunday morning). Take bus No 40 or 60 from Praça da Figueira or tram No 15 west from Praça do Comércio. From Estrela, take tram No 25 from in front of the basilica.

Museu da Carris (Map 3)

In the Alcântara district, west of Lapa, is a funky alternative to high culture, the Carris Museum (☎ 213 613 087), housed in the Carris headquarters at Rua 1 de Maio. It details the fascinating history of Lisbon's transport system (Carris is Lisbon's main transport carrier), including its lovable trams. It's open 10 am to 5 pm weekdays and 10 am to 1 pm and 2 to 4.30 pm Saturday. Tram No 15 passes right by. Admission costs 350$00 (under-26s and seniors 175$00).

RATO, MARQUÊS DE POMBAL & SALDANHA

Northern and north-western Lisbon has a hotchpotch of attractions, from hothouses to high culture, reachable on foot via Avenida da Liberdade or by metro or bus.

Museu Calouste Gulbenkian (Map 2)

This museum (☎ 217 823 418), the jewel in the crown of the Fundação Calouste

Museu Calouste Gulbenkian Highlights

Among the classical and oriental art collections, some of the most memorable items are in the **Egyptian Room**: an exquisite 2700-year-old alabaster bowl, small female statuettes (each with a different hairstyle), and a series of bronze cats. In the adjoining **Greek and Roman** section, note especially the 2400-year-old Attic vase, Roman glassware in magical colours and an absorbing collection of Hellenic coins with finely carved heads and figures.

In the **Oriental Islamic Art** collection are some 16th and 17th-century Turkish faïence glowing with brilliant greens and blues, and 14th-century mosque lamps from Syria with strikingly sensuous shapes. The adjoining **Armenian collection** includes illuminated manuscripts and books from the 16th to 18th centuries.

The **Chinese and Japanese** collection features a rich display of porcelain, lacquer, jade and celadon. Especially lovely are the 19th-century Japanese prints of flowers and birds by Sugakudo.

The huge **European Art** section is arranged in chronological order, from medieval ivories and manuscripts to paintings from the 15th to 19th centuries. All the big names are here, including Rembrandt, Van Dyck and Rubens. Particularly lovely is the 15th-century *Portrait of a Girl* by Ghirlandaio and a white marble *Diana* by Houdon.

Eighteenth and 19th-century European art is comprehensively represented with Aubusson tapestries, fabulous if often fussy furniture (including items from Versailles), Sèvres porcelain and intricate clocks. Outstanding paintings in the collection are Gainsborough's *Mrs Lowndes*, two atmospheric La Tour portraits, some typically turbulent Turners and a passionate *Spring Kiss* by Rodin.

Finally, fans of Art Nouveau will appreciate the magical jewellery of French designer **René Lalique**, featuring fantasies in the form of coronets and hair combs, brooches and necklaces.

MARTIN HARRIS

***Henut Taoui*, an Egyptian artefact**

Gulbenkian, is a Lisbon must-see. One of Europe's unsung treasures, and definitely Portugal's finest museum, it's set in a peaceful, landscaped garden at Avenida de Berna 45-A. It was recently completely revamped after a year's renovation. The collection spans every major epoch of Western art and much Eastern art, with hardly an unappealing item in it (see the boxed text 'Museu Calouste Gulbenkian Highlights'). Spend at least a full day here if you can.

The Museu Calouste Gulbenkian and the Centro de Arte Moderna (see later) also host changing exhibitions and a comprehensive program of live music and other performances. Both museums are open 2 to 6 pm Tuesday and 10 am to 6 pm Wednesday to Sunday. Admission costs 500$00 (free to children, students, teachers and seniors; free to everyone Sunday). There is a snack bar in the main museum building and a restaurant in the Centro de Arte Moderna. Take the metro to São Sebastião station or bus Nos 31, 41 or 46 from Rossio. The museum's Web site is at www.gulbenkian.pt.

Centro de Arte Moderna (Map 2)

The Fundação Calouste Gulbenkian's adjacent Modern Art Centre (☎ 217 823 474) boasts the country's best collection of 20th-century Portuguese art, including pieces from Amadeo de Souza Cardoso, José de Almada Negreiros and Maria Helena Vieira da Silva.

Calouste Gulbenkian

Calouste Sarkis Gulbenkian, born to Armenian parents in Istanbul in 1869, was one of the 20th century's wealthiest men and best known philanthropists. He was an astute and generous patron of the arts years before he struck it rich in Iraqi oil. His great artistic coup was the purchase of works from Leningrad's Hermitage in 1928-30, when the young Soviet Union desperately needed hard currency.

In his later years he adopted Portugal as his home and bequeathed to it his entire, stupendous art collection – snubbing Britain (though he had British citizenship) after it labelled him a 'technical enemy' for working as an economic adviser in Paris at the time of the Vichy government. He lived in Portugal from 1942 until his death in 1955. In 1969 his art collection was moved into its own purpose-built quarters, Lisbon's Museu Calouste Gulbenkian.

Gulbenkian also bestowed on Portugal an extraordinary artistic, educational, scientific and charitable foundation that has become Portugal's main cultural life force. Fundação Calouste Gulbenkian, with assets now exceeding US$1 billion and a budget bigger than some Portuguese government ministries, funds architectural restoration and the construction of libraries, museums, schools, hospitals, and centres for disabled people all over the country. In Lisbon it administers the Museu Calouste Gulbenkian and has endowed the adjacent Centro de Arte Moderna, built galleries and concert halls, and supports its own orchestra, choir and contemporary dance ensemble.

The foundation's main offices (Map 2; ☎ 217 823 000, fax 217 823 032, e info@gulbenkian.pt) are at Avenida de Berna 45-A, 1067 Lisbon.

Also based in the foundation's garden complex is **ACARTE** (Serviço de Animação, Criação Artística e Educação pela Arte, or Department of Animation, Artistic Creation & Education through Art), which promotes contemporary Portuguese performance and other arts. ACARTE operates the **Centro Artístico Infantil** (Children's Art Centre) here; although it is designed for Portuguese-speaking children, the exhibitions and related activities may also be of interest to young foreign visitors.

Parque Eduardo VII (Map 2)

When you need a breather, head for this stately park (named after England's Edward VII, who visited Lisbon in 1903), at the top of Avenida da Liberdade. The park, and a recent addition on its northern fringe (the Jardim Alto do Parque), provides an escape, especially in its gorgeous **estufas** (greenhouses), the *estufa fria* (cool) and *estufa quente* (hot). These have exotic collections of tropical and subtropical plants and romantically inspiring paths (favoured by courting couples) that meander right up to the glass or latticed roof. There's an outdoor area, too, with a large pond. This and the estufa

quente are open 9 am to 5.30 pm (4.30 pm in winter) daily; the estufa fria closes at 6 pm (5 pm winter). Admission to all of this area costs 210$00 (free to children under 10); access is from Rua Castilho on the western side of the park. There's also a great playground nearby.

GREATER LISBON

You'll need metro or bus transport to reach the sights in this area – and a dose of enthusiasm for its rather specialised museums.

Jardim Zoológico (Map 1)

Lisbon's zoo (☎ 217 232 900) is right by the metro station of the same name, three stops north of Parque. Criticised in the past for the appalling conditions in which it kept its animals and for its overriding concern for 'profit and the amusement of people', the zoo has recently introduced some improvements, notably a new reptile house.

There are a variety of shows, including a dolphin show (rather heavy on chatter and slapstick). It's open 10 am to 8 pm daily (to 6 pm in winter). An all-inclusive ticket costs 1990$00 (1500$00 for children aged three to 11; 1200$00 students).

duct of Free Waters

Lisbon's major attractions, the extraordinary Aqueduto das Águas Livres (Aqueduct of Free Waters, is curiously overlooked by visitors nowadays. Its 109 grey stone arches lope south across the hills into Lisbon from Caneças, over 18km away.

The aqueduct was built to bring the city its first clean drinking water, by order of Dom João V, who laid the inaugural stone at Mãe d'Água (Mother of Water), the city's main reservoir at Praça das Amoreiras. Its cost was borne by the populace through a tax on meat, olive oil and wine. Most of the work was done between 1728 and 1748, under the gaze of engineer Manuel da Maia and architect Custódio Vieira. Its construction was interrupted by the 1755 earthquake (though little was damaged) and it was not completed until 1835.

This massive Mãe d'Água reservoir, which can hold 5500 cubic metres of water, is still impressive. Its cool, echoing chamber (from where you can see the start of the narrow aqueduct passage) now hosts art exhibitions and is open 10 am to 6 pm Monday to Saturday. Admission costs 350$00 (175$00 students). For details of other aqueduct-related sights in the city, contact the Museu da Água da EPAL (the municipal water company; ☎ 218 135 522). Its main museum is covered separately in this chapter.

The aqueduct itself is at its most impressive at Campolide, where the tallest arch is about 65m high. Take any train from Rossio station to the first stop.

Quinta dos Marquêses da Fronteira (Map 1)

A 10-minute walk south-west of the zoo, this 17th-century mansion (☎ 217 782 023), at Largo de São Domingos de Benfica 1, is renowned for its garden of box hedges and statues and its abundant azulejos, most notably a panel of mounted cavaliers with plumed hats overlooking a pond. At the time of research, the mansion had closed for restoration but the garden was still open (10.30 am to noon daily except Sunday; admission free).

Museu da Cidade (Map 1)

Farther to the north, the City Museum (☎ 217 591 617) offers the visitor a good telescopic view of Lisbon's history. The exhibits include an enormous model of pre-earthquake Lisbon and azulejo panels of city scenes. The museum occupies the 18th-century Palácio Pimenta (said to have been built by Dom João V for one of his mistresses) at Campo Grande 245. It's open 10 am to 1 pm and 2 to 6 pm daily except Monday; admission costs 370$00 (free on Sunday morning). To reach the museum by publoic transport, take the metro to Campo Grande or bus No 1 or 36 from Rossio.

Museu Nacional do Traje & Museu Nacional do Teatro (Map 1)

The National Costume Museum (☎ 217 590 318) and National Theatre Museum (☎ 217 567 410) both occupy 18th-century palaces in the grounds of the beautifully lush Parque de Monteiro Mór (take bus No 7 from Praça da Figueira or bus No 3 from Campo Grande metro station). The Costume Museum (open 10 am to 6 pm daily except Monday) features changing exhibits of court and common dress from the Middle Ages to the present. The Theatre Museum (open 2 to 6 pm Tuesday and 10 am to 6 pm Wednesday to Sunday) has theatrical costumes, props, posters and lots of photos of actors. Both charge 400$00 for admission.

PARQUE DAS NAÇÕES

The former Expo '98 site on the riverfront, north-east of the city has been renamed Parque das Nações ('naz-**oish**', Nations Park; Map 9). In addition to its famous Oceanário and other family-geared attractions, it features some stunning modern architecture (see the Arts section in the Facts about Lisbon chapter for details), relaxing gardens, restaurants, bars and huge entertainment venues.

Surrounded by continuing construction work relating to Expo Urbe, a major urban regeneration project (see Ecology & Environment in the Facts about Lisbon chapter), Parque das Nações still feels a bit raw. Many locals, who still refer to the area as 'Expo', have yet to be won over to the possibilities and benefits. Come on a Monday morning and you'll probably find the whole place is deserted. The main complaint is the expense, both for entrance fees to the attractions and for the costs of the restaurants (don't forget to pack your own munchies if you're counting your escudos).

The easiest way to get here is to take the metro to Gare do Oriente (another impressive Expo '98 architectural project). Walk through the Centro Vasco da Gama shopping mall opposite the station and you'll immediately find the park's Posto de Informação (information desk; ☎ 218 919 333), open 9.30 am to 8 pm daily. It provides free maps and detailed information on events that are happening and it also provides a free left-luggage facility. Check out the park's informative Web site at www.parquedasnacoes.pt, with details on all facilities.

There's a Turismo de Lisboa kiosk near the Pavilhão de Portugal open 10 am to 6 pm daily (closing for lunch at weekends).

The concession prices quoted below apply to children aged six to 17, seniors over 65 or students with a youth card. A Cartão do Parque (Park Card), which is sold at the Posto de Informação and turismos, offers free admission to certain facilities (including the Oceanário) and also discounts at restaurants. It costs 5500$00 (for a family of four), 2250$00 (adult) and 900$00 (senior). The following sites are all on Map 9.

Oceanário

The Parque's big attraction is Europe's largest aquarium (☎ 218 917 002 to 006), which boasts some 25,000 fish, birds and mammals in a strikingly designed, two-storey facility that re-creates the entire global scene. It's open 10 am to 7 pm daily (6 pm in winter); admission costs 1700$00 (concession 900$00) and has a Web site at www.oceanario.pt.

Bike, Train, Lift or Cable Car?

The most exciting way to get from the northern to the southern end of the Parque das Nações is on the **Teleférico** (cable car). It runs along the riverside from noon to 7 pm (10 am to 8 pm on weekends), and costs 500$00 (concession 250$00). The **Torre Vasco da Gama** lifts you to spectacular heights for the same price. It's open 10 am to 8 pm daily (to 10 pm Friday to Sunday and in summer).

The **Comboios de Passeio** electric train runs from 10 am to 10 pm (to midnight on Saturday) roughly every half-hour on a circular route round the Parque (there's a stop by the Centro Vasco da Gama) for 100/50$00 (children under four go free).

Bikes can be rented (from noon to 8 pm daily), for use only within the park, from in front of the Centro Vasco da Gama and Oceanário and by the Parque Adrenalina (from 2 to 8 pm daily). Costs are 500/750/1125$00 per junior/adult/tandem bike per hour, or 1000/1550/2325$00 for three hours. See the Activities section in this chapter for more on the park's sports facilities.

Pavilhão da Realidade Virtual

The park's Virtual Reality Pavilion (☎ 218 917 002) includes a virtual reality presentation (accompanied by English and Spanish translations) on the life of Luís de Camões, Portugal's national poet. The show incorporates a dramatic simulator experience. The pavilion is open 10 am to 7 pm daily except Monday (to midnight on Thursday, Friday and Saturday); admission costs 1500$00 (concession 750$00).

Pavilhão do Conhecimento

Science nerds and school children love this Knowledge Pavilion (☎ 218 917 112), with its interactive displays about science and technology and its cybercafe. It's open 10 am to 6 pm daily except Monday (11 am to 7 pm weekends; the last admission is one hour before closing time) and costs 800$00 (concession 400$00).

Art in the Parque

The Parque das Nações features some amazing contemporary architecture – notably the Pavilhão de Portugal by Álvaro Siza Vieira, Portugal's greatest contemporary architect (see Arts in the Facts about Lisbon chapter for details). But there's also some notable if less immediately noticeable urban artworks by 24 international artists, including distinctive *calzada portuguesa* cobbled pavement patterns; check out the amazingly wave-like *Mar Largo* by Fernando Conduto beside the Pavilhão Atlântico; *Monstros Marinhos* by Pedro Proença beside the Oceanário; and the fabulous colourful mosaics by the marina, *Rio Vivo*, by Rolando Sá Nogueira. On quite a different level, the shining, delicate *Reflexo do Céu Navegante* (Sky-Reflecting Compass) by Sasumu Shingu, is an enchanting distraction, opposite the Teatro Camões.

Gardens

The green and frog-croaking **Jardins da Água** is a most delightful place to relax, with its water wheel, whistling wooden levers and wall fountain. Next to it, **Jardim das Ondas** (Wave Garden) is an undulating expanse of greenery that perfectly reflects its name.

BELÉM

The district of Belém (Map 10), 6km west of Rossio, was one of the main launching pads for Portugal's Age of Discoveries. Most famously, this was the place from which the great explorer Vasco da Gama set sail on 8 July 1497 for the two-year voyage on which he discovered a sea route to India.

On da Gama's safe return, Dom Manuel I ordered the construction of a monastery on the site of the riverside chapel (founded by Henry the Navigator) where da Gama and his officers had kept an all-night vigil before their historic voyage. Mosteiro dos Jerónimos, like its predecessor, was dedicated to the Virgin Mary, St Mary of Bethlehem (Belém) – hence the district's name.

The monastery, and the offshore watchtower, Torre de Belém, also commissioned by Manuel I (both Unesco World Heritage

Sites), are essential viewing for every visitor to Lisbon. They are definitely among the finest remaining examples of the exuberant Portuguese brand of Renaissance-Gothic architecture called Manueline (see the Arts section in the Facts about Lisbon chapter).

This peaceful suburb also boasts several other historical monuments and a clutch of worthwhile museums. It makes a good full-day outing from central Lisbon – but don't go on a Monday, when nearly everything is closed. In summer, a Turismo de Lisboa kiosk sets up opposite the monastery.

The most interesting way to get here is on the No 15 modern tram from Praça do Comércio; otherwise take bus No 14 from Rossio or Praça da Figueira. Trains go from Cais do Sodré station to Oeiras via Belém three to five times an hour weekdays (slightly fewer on weekends). Unless indicated otherwise, the following sites are all on Map 10.

Mosteiro dos Jerónimos

Manuel I ordered this monastery to be built in memory of Vasco da Gama's discovery of a sea route to India and, while he was at it, arranged that its church be made a pantheon for himself and his royal descendants (many of whom are now entombed in its chancel and side chapels).

Huge sums were funnelled into the project, including the so-called 'pepper money', a 5% tax levied on all income from the spice trade with Portugal's expanding African and Far Eastern colonies.

Work began in about 1502, following a Gothic design by architect Diogo de Boitaca, considered one of the originators of the Manueline style. After his death in 1517, building resumed with a Renaissance flavour under Spaniard João de Castilho and, later, with classical overtones under Diogo de Torralva and Jérome de Rouen (Jerónimo de Ruão). The monastery was only completed towards the end of the 16th century. The huge neo-Manueline western wing and the domed bell tower, which date from the 19th century, seem out of keeping with the rest.

The monastery was populated by monks of the Order of St Jerome, whose spiritual job was to give comfort and guidance to sailors – and, of course, to pray for the king's soul. When the order was dissolved in 1833, the monastery was used as a school and orphanage until about 1940.

The facade of the **church** is dominated by João de Castilho's fantastic south portal, dense with religious and secular carvings. Enter through the west portal, designed by the French sculptor Nicholas Chanterène and now obscured by a modern passage. In contrast to the extravagant exterior, the interior is sparsely adorned, spacious and lofty beneath an unsupported 25m-high baroque transept vault. Vasco da Gama is interred in the lower chancel, in a place of honour opposite the revered poet Luís de Camões.

The central courtyard of the monastery's **cloisters** is a magically peaceful place, even when crowded. In the old refectory to the west of the cloisters, an azulejo panel depicts the biblical story of Joseph. The sarcophagus in the echoing chapter house on the northeastern corner is that of the 19th-century Portuguese historian Alexandre Herculano.

The monastery and church are open 10 am to 1 pm and 2 to 5.30 pm daily except Monday and holidays (to 5 pm in winter). Entry to the cloisters costs 500\$00 (under-26s and seniors 200\$00; free 10 am to 2 pm Sunday). There is no charge to see the church.

Torre de Belém

The Tower of Belém sits just offshore, roughly 1km from the monastery. This hexagonal chesspiece – perhaps Portugal's most photographed monument – has come to symbolise Lisbon and the Age of Discoveries. Manuel I intended it as a fortress to guard the entrance to Lisbon's harbour. Before the shoreline slowly shifted south, the tower sat right out in mid-stream (and the monastery sat on the river bank).

Designed by the brilliant Arruda brothers, Diogo and Francisco, the tower is an arresting mixture of early Gothic, Byzantine and Manueline styles. Admission price and opening times are the same as for the monastery.

Padrão dos Descobrimentos

The huge Discoveries Monument was inaugurated in 1960 on the 500th anniversary of the death of Henry the Navigator. Made of limestone, it is shaped like a stylised caravel and crowded with important Portuguese figures. At the prow is Henry the Navigator; behind him are explorers Vasco da Gama, Diogo Cão and Fernão de Magalhães, poet Luís de Camões, painter Nuno Gonçalves and 27 others. Opposite the entrance is a wind rose (a device for determining the direction of the wind). Inside are exhibition rooms, and a lift and stairs to the top, which offers a bird's-eye view of the monastery and river. The monument is open 9 am to 5 pm daily except Monday; admission to the top-floor viewpoint costs 350\$00 (under-26s and seniors 175\$00).

Centro Cultural de Belém

The massive Belém Cultural Centre (☎ 213 612 400), on the western side of Praça do Império, is one of Lisbon's main cultural venues, with a full program throughout the year. Recently opened inside is the brilliant **Museu do Design** (☎ 213 612 934), which houses a fascinating collection of 20th-century furnishings (lip-shaped chairs, stainless-steel sofas and a number of other mind-boggling items) and design items in three sections (Luxury, Pop and Cool) from the collection of Francisco Capelo. It's open 11 am to 8 pm daily (last entrance 7.15 pm). Admission costs 500\$00 (under-26s and seniors 250\$00). Other exhibition halls feature changing displays of modern art.

Museu Nacional de Arqueologia

First opened in 1893, the National Museum of Archaeology (☎ 213 620 000), in the west wing of the Mosteiro dos Jerónimos, has exhibits from prehistory through to Moorish times and a large collection of antique gold jewellery from the Bronze Age through to Roman times. It's open 2 to 6 pm Tuesday and 10 am to 6 pm Wednesday to Sunday; admission costs 400\$00 (under-26s and seniors 200\$00; free on Sunday mornings).

Museu de Marinha

This Naval Museum (☎ 213 620 019) is stuffed full with model ships from the Age of

Discoveries onward, and cases full of astro-labes and navy uniforms. It's open 10 am to 6 pm daily except Monday (to 5 pm in winter); admission costs 500/200$00 per adult/youth aged 10 to 19 (free for children under 10).

Planetário Calouste Gulbenkian

This planetarium (☎ 213 620 002), by the Museu de Marinha, has 40-minute shows at 11 am and 2.30 and 4 pm on Wednesday and Thursday, and at 3.30 and 5 pm on Saturday and Sunday. Admission costs 500$00 (200$00 for children and 200$00 extra for headphone translations in English or French).

Museu Nacional dos Coches

The National Coach Museum (☎ 213 610 850), in the former royal riding school on Praça Afonso de Albuquerque, has one of the world's best collections of royal, aristo-cratic and ecclesiastical coaches from the 17th to 19th centuries, illustrating clearly the ostentation and staggering wealth of the old Portuguese elite. There are enough gilded, painted and truly over-the-top vehi-cles here to numb the senses. The museum is open 10 am to 5.30 pm daily except Monday; admission costs 450$00.

Other Museums

Museu de Arte Popular (Folk Art Museum; ☎ 213 011 282) on Avenida de Brasília houses a charming collection from around the country. Among items you're unlikely to spot anywhere else are bagpipes from Mirando do Douro, toby jugs from Aveiro and huge spiked dog collars for the beasts of Castelo Branco. The museum (closed at the time of research for renovation) is normally open 10 am to 12.30 pm and 2 to 5 pm daily except Monday; admission costs 300$00.

The often overlooked **Museu Nacional de Etnológia** (Map 1; National Ethnological Museum; ☎ 213 015 264) on Avenida Ilha da Madeira, a short walk north of Belém, mounts excellent temporary exhibitions on Portugal's former African and Asian colonies and tradi-tional textiles and weaving techniques from around the world. It's open 2 to 6 pm on Tuesday and 10 am to 6 pm Wednesday to Sunday; admission costs 400$00. It's on the

route of the electric tourist train that does a circuit of the museums from the Mosteiro dos Jerónimos. Alternatively, take bus No 32 from Praça da Figueira.

AJUDA

Ajuda is a former royal quarter on a hilltop above Belém. The present official National Palace (Palácio Nacional de Belém) and the Presidential Palace (Presidência da Repúb-lica), just beyond the Museu Nacional dos Coches on Calçada da Ajuda, are not open to the public.

Igreja da Memória (Map 10)

A 500m walk (or take bus No 27) up Calçada do Galvão from Largo dos Jerónimos is a little marble basilica, built by order of Dom José I on the site of an unsuccessful attempt on his life and now the resting place of his chief minister, the Marquês de Pombal.

Museu do Palácio Nacional da Ajuda (Map 1)

If you bear right at the church and then head left up Calçada da Ajuda (or take bus No 14 from Praça Afonso de Albuquerque in Belém or tram No 18 from Praça do Comércio), you will come to the oversize Palácio da Ajuda. Begun in the late 18th century, left in limbo

What's Free

Many museums are free on Sunday morning (10 am to 2 pm), as noted in the text. Free music and dance performances are held at the Centro Cultural de Belém's Bar Terraço from 7 to 9 pm on winter weekdays, and on Friday and Saturday nights (from 10 pm) during July and August in its outdoor Jardim dos Oliveiras.

During the Festa de Santo António (12 to 13 June) and on other summer weekends, free concerts are often held at churches (eg, the Basílica da Estrela, Igreja de São Roque and the Sé) and Teatro de São Carlos.

The popular BaixAnima Festival enlivens the streets of the Baixa district with free per-formances between June and September (see Public Holidays & Special Events in the Facts for the Visitor chapter).

when the royal family fled to Brazil, used as a royal residence from 1861 to 1905 but never quite finished, it has now been converted into a museum (☎ 213 637 095).

The museum's vast collection of kitsch royal belongings is dominated by the furnishings of Dona Maria II and her husband Dom Ferdinand, whose lack of taste will be familiar to any visitor to Sintra's Palácio Nacional da Pena, their summer retreat (see the Excursions chapter).

The opening hours are 10 am to 5 pm daily except Wednesday; admission costs 400$00 (seniors and under-26s 200$00). The one-hour accompanied visits are at set times, every half-hour.

Jardim Botânico da Ajuda (Map 1)

A short walk from the palace is this delightful botanical garden, Lisbon's oldest and one of its most elegant. Established in the 18th century it features some exotic trees including a vast South African *Schotia afra* under whose shade stroll white peacocks.

The garden, on Calçada da Ajuda, is open 9 am to 6 pm daily except Wednesday (admission free) and also houses a rather pricey restaurant.

ACTIVITIES

The idea of deliberately exerting yourself to get fit has yet to seriously catch on among the food-and-wine-loving Portuguese. The only sport that inspires passion is football. But Portugal's success in athletics may prove inspirational. The latest coups include António Pinto winning the 2000 London Marathon (and setting a European record) and Fernanda Ribeiro winning bronze in the women's 10,000m event at the 2000 Olympics. Lisbon plays host to the World Indoor Athletics Championships in 2001.

Swimming

Many of Lisbon's top hotels have their own swimming pools (or access to pools at adjacent clubs). Among municipal indoor public pools are those at Areeiro (Map 1; ☎ 218 486 794), Avenida de Roma 28, and Olivais (Map 1; ☎ 218 514 630), Avenida

Dr Francisco Luís Gomes. Opening hours are 8 am to 3 pm and 8 to 9.30 pm. Admission costs 240$00 (under-26s 120$00).

Privately run, rooftop Piscina do Ateneu (Map 6; ☎ 213 430 947), at Rua das Portas de Santo Antão 102, is open to the public 1.30 to 4.30 pm daily and charges 650$00.

Kids may prefer the Piscina do Alvito (Map 1; ☎ 213 635 940), Estrada do Alvito, at Parque Infantil do Alvito, a children's park within the Parque Florestal de Monsanto (bus No 24 from Alcântara). It's open 9 am to 8 pm (closing at 6 pm in winter).

See the Excursions chapter for details of the best local surfing and windsurfing spots.

Golf

Golfers are spoilt for choice. There are six major courses in the area (see boxed text 'Golf on the Estoril Coast' in the Excursions chapter), as well as the 18-hole course at the Lisbon Sports Club (☎ 214 321 474, fax 214 312 482) at Casal da Carregueira, Belas (just north of Queluz). Expect to pay green fees of around 9000$00 (more at weekends).

South of the Tejo are the following golf courses:

Clube Golf Aroeira (☎/fax 212 971 314) A 6040m par 72 course, in an estate of pine woods and lakes, designed by Frank Pennink.
Clube Golf Montado (☎ 265 706 648) An 18-hole par 72 course near Setúbal designed by Duarte de Sottomeyer, in a natural landscape of cork oaks, streams and lakes.
Quinta do Perú (☎ 212 134 300, fax 212 134 321) An 18-hole par 72 course near Vila Nogueira de Azeitão designed by Rocky Roquemore.
Tróia Golf (☎ 265 441 112, fax 265 44) A 6337m par 72 course just across the estuary from Setúbal; bordered by sand and set among pine trees, this Robert Trent Jones course is considered the most difficult in Portugal.

Tennis

You'll need to book well ahead if you want to reserve a court at popular sports centres such as the Centro Desportivo Universidade de Lisboa (Map 1; ☎ 217 932 895) at the university; Instalações de Ténis de Monsanto (Map 1; ☎ 213 648 741) in Parque Florestal de Monsanto (bus No 24 from Alcântara); or the newer (but also pricier) Lisboa Racket

Centre (Map 1; ☎ 218 460 232), Rua Alferes Malheiro, Alvalade (bus No 44 from Rossio).

Bowling

At Parque das Nações, Bowling Internacional de Lisboa (Map 9; ☎ 218 919 193) is Portugal's biggest bowling centre, open noon to 2 am (to 3 am on Friday and 10 am to 3 am on Saturday). It costs 650$00 (750$00 after 8 pm, and 850$00 after 8 pm on Friday and after 3 pm on weekends).

The similarly priced Playcenter (see the Lisbon for Children section in the Facts for the Visitor chapter) has a 24-lane bowling alley (plus Extreme Bowling, to be played in darkness), open noon to 1 am daily.

Skateboarding

The coolest spots for rollerblades, skateboards and the like are in Parque das Nações and along the riverside promenades of Belém and neighbouring Junqueira. There are special tracks available at Pedrouços in Oeiras and at the riverfront in Algés (accessible by train from Cais do Sodré).

Sports Centres & Health Clubs

Parque Adrenalina (Map 9; ☎ 218 922 300) at Parque das Nações boasts everything from exercise machines to 35m-high swings. It's open 4 pm to midnight (from 2 pm Sunday, to 2 am Friday and 2 pm to 2 am Saturday).

A swanky club with tennis courts, swimming pools and health and exercise facilities is Clube VII (☎ 213 865 818, fax 213 865 820) at Parque Eduardo VII (Map 2).

COURSES
Language

All of the following offer private lessons (for around 5200$00 per hour) as well as group courses; be sure to check if there's an additional enrolment fee. The standard 'hour' in Portuguese language lessons is actually 50 minutes.

The Cambridge School (Map 5; ☎ 213 124 600, fax 213 534 729, ✉ cambridge@mail.telepac.pt), at Avenida da Liberdade 173 (and three other branches), offers an intensive group course (for three to six students) of 40 hourly lessons costing 98,800$00; private lessons start at 220,800$00 for a 20-lesson course. Web site: www.cambridge.pt

The Centro de Línguas e Informática da Costa do Sol (CLICS; ☎ 214 671 304, fax 214 671 577, ✉ clics@mail.telepac.pt), at Rua Mello e Sousa 9, Estoril, offers monthly group courses costing 9500$00 (for two hours per week), plus intensive two-week (42-hour) group courses in July and August, for 51,000$00.

CIAL-Centro de Línguas (Map 2; ☎ 217 940 448, fax 217 960 783, ✉ portuguese@cial.pt), Avenida da República 41, 8th floor, has group courses from 45,000$00 weekly. Social and cultural activities (eg, visits to museums) are included in the price. Web site: www.cial.p

Instituto IPFEL (Map 2; Instituto Particular de Formação e Ensino de Línguas; ☎ 213 154 116, fax 213 154 119, ✉ instituto@ipfel.pt), Rua Camilo Castelo Branco 44, 4th floor, runs intensive two-week group courses at a cost of 58,000$00 (discounts for students).

Other Courses

Among other things you can learn while in Lisbon are:

Afro-Brazilian martial dance, dramatic expression, juggling and photography Monthly evening courses at Chapitô, the Collectividade Cultural e Recreativa de Santa Catarina (Map 8; ☎ 218 861 410, fax 218 861 463, ✉ chapito@ip.pt), Costa do Castelo 1

Arts and crafts Courses in ceramic pottery, azulejos as well as traditional Arraiolos carpet-making at the Associação dos Artesãos da Região de Lisboa (☎ 217 957 374, fax 217 957 823), Rua de Entrecampos 66; an eight-hour course in ceramics and azulejo-making at CIAL-Centro de Línguas (see Language courses)

Portuguese gastronomy Eight-hour course at CIAL-Centro de Línguas (see Language courses)

Riding Portugal's famous Lusitano horses Escola de Equitacao de Alcainça (☎ 219 662 122, fax 218 686 117), Rua de São Miguel, Alcainça (near Mafra)

Scuba diving Three-week courses with Nautilus-Sub (☎ 212 551 969, fax 212 553 900, ✉ nautilus.sub@mail.telepac.pt) with dives at Sesimbra; instructors speak English, French and German.

Zen meditation, yoga and tai chi (weekday evenings) Centro de Alimentação e Saúde Natural (☎ 213 150 898), Rua Mouzinho da Silveira 25

For information on US universities with exchange programs in Portugal, check out the Web site at www.studyabroad.com.

Places to Stay

There's a huge range of places to stay in Lisbon, from camping grounds to former palaces. But during the high season (mid-June to September) many are booked out, so it's imperative to book ahead, especially for middle and upper-range accommodation near the city centre.

Most budget accommodation is to be found in the Baixa and Rossio areas, while mid-range and top-end hotels tend to be in the Saldanha, Marquês de Pombal and Avenida da Liberdade districts. Most rooms, even in budget pensões, now have private bathrooms and televisions. Pricier ones will feature telephones, air-con, minibars and/or refrigerators.

For a room with a double bed, you should ask for *um quarto de casal* or *um quarto de matrimonial*; for twin beds (nearly always more expensive) ask for *um duplo*; and for a single room, ask for *um quarto individual*.

Among useful Web sites offering help with guesthouse and other accommodation in Lisbon and beyond are the following:

Portugal Travel & Hotels Guide Thousands of hotels, villas and apartments, plus online reservations at up to 65% off official prices. Web site: www.portugal-hotels.com
Portugal Holiday Homes Accommodation, golfing packages and car rental, especially around Ericeira. Web site: www.portugal-villa.com

TYPES OF ACCOMMODATION
Camping
This is easily the cheapest option. Depending on facilities, high-season prices per night are about 300$00 to 700$00 per adult, plus 300$00 to 700$00 for a small tent and 300$00 to 700$00 per car. Lower prices often apply in the low season.

Portugal's best-equipped, biggest (but priciest) camping grounds are run by Orbitur. Bookings can be made through Orbitur's central booking office (☎ 218 117 000, fax 218 158 045, ⓔ info@orbitur.pt) in Lisbon.

The annual *Roteiro Campista* (900$00), sold in larger Portuguese bookshops, is an excellent multilingual guide with details of,

and directions to, nearly every camping ground in the country. For information about the Camping Card International (CCI), see the Documents section in the Facts for the Visitor chapter.

Hostels
Portugal has a network of 38 *pousadas da juventude* (youth hostels), all affiliated with Hostelling International (HI).

In the high season, dorm beds cost 1700$00 to 2900$00. Most hostels also offer basic doubles for 3800$00 to 4600$00 (without bathroom) or 4100$00 to 6500$00 (with). Rates are highest in popular hostels such as those in Lisbon and Porto. There are no single-room rates. Bed linen and continental breakfast are included in the price; lunch or dinner costs 950$00. Many hostels have kitchens where you can do your own cooking, plus TV rooms and social areas.

How Much?

Prices in Portugal are always per room, not per person. Single-room rates are usually about two-thirds the price of a double room, partly because few budget or mid-range places actually have dedicated single rooms. There's often a range of prices (eg, for rooms with/without a window); it's always worth asking. Many give discounts for longer stays but, again, you must ask. At upmarket hotels also ask about any special discounts; cheaper rates are also often available if you book on-line or through a travel agent (see the Hotels section in this chapter). Be prepared for prices at nearly all places to escalate during the high season or for special events (eg, the Euro 2004 Football Championships).

In this book we use the following price categories for an establishment's most basic double with toilet and shower or bath: budget (up to 6000$00); mid-range (from 6000$00 to 15,000$00); and top end (over 15,000$00).

Advance reservations are essential during summer, especially for doubles. The central HI reservations office is at Movijovem (Map 2; see Useful Organisations in the Facts for the Visitor chapter). There's a reservation charge of 300$00 per set of bookings (although you can call ahead from one hostel to your next one for nothing).

If you don't already have a HI card from your national hostel association, you can get a 'guest card', which will be stamped at each of the first six hostels where you stay (for 400$00 each time), after which you've effectively paid for your membership.

Only the Lisbon and Porto hostels are open 24 hours a day; most are open 8 am to midnight. You can usually stash your bags and return at official check-in times, typically 8 am to noon and 6 pm to midnight.

Nine hostels, often called by the old name of *centro de alojamento* (accommodation centre), are connected to branches of the Instituto Português da Juventude (IPJ; see Useful Organisations in the Facts for the Visitor chapter). The IPJs usually have facilities such as cafes, libraries (often with Internet access) and information resources for young people. On the other hand, the standard of these centros is generally lower than the others and opening hours limited to the official check-in times.

Want a Room?

If you get approached by a matronly lady in a popular tourist resort (eg, Ericeira), chances are she's going to ask if you want a room. A *quarto particular* (or simply *quarto*, meaning room) is usually just a room in a private house and can be an excellent deal: clean and cheap (from around 5000$00 a double in the high season, with shared bathroom), and the owners are often friendly and informative.

Some turismos keep lists of these unofficial quartos (Cascais and Sintra turismos contact the owners for you directly), though others ignore them. If you don't get approached in the street or at the bus station, look out for 'quartos' signs.

Guesthouses

The most common guesthouses, the Portuguese equivalent of bed and breakfasts (B&Bs), are the *residencial* (plural *residenciais*) and *pensão (pensões)*. High-season rates for a double with private bathroom in the cheapest pensão are about 5000$00; you'll pay slightly more for a residencial, where breakfast is often included in the price. Cheaper rooms with shared bathrooms are becoming increasingly scarce as owners upgrade their properties. Some places confusingly advertised as 'Pensão Residencial' are usually pensões with pretensions to being residenciais.

Pensões and residenciais are probably Lisbon's (and Portugal's) most popular form of tourist accommodation, and they fill up in summer; try to book at least a week ahead. During the low season, rates drop by at least a third.

A step down are boarding houses, called *hospedarias* or *casas de hóspedes*, where prices are lower and showers and toilets are usually shared.

Hotels

Hotels (*hotel*, plural *hotéis*) are graded from one to five stars. For a double room in the high season you'll pay about 12,000$00 to 15,000$00 at the lower end and 20,000$00 to 40,000$00 at the upper end. In the same category, but more like upmarket inns, are *albergarias* and pricier *estalagens* (both unstarred). In the low season the prices drop spectacularly, with doubles in spiffy hotels going for as little as 10,000$00. Breakfast is usually included.

In popular resorts (eg, along the Estoril Coast) you'll also find *aparthotels* – whole blocks of self-contained apartments for rent to tourists, managed as hotels.

Prices in this book are official walk-in rates, though you can often get discounted or promotional rates with some chain hotels by booking online or through a travel agent; eg, see the Web site of Best Western hotels (www.bestwestern.com). UK-based Room Service (☎ 020-7636 6888, fax 7636 6002, e rooms@netcomuk.co.uk) can reserve rooms at mid-range and top-end hotels and

Pousadas de Portugal

These are deluxe, government-run former castles, monasteries or palaces (plus some new establishments), over 60 in all, usually in areas of natural beauty or historical significance. Most pousadas offer professional service and a friendly welcome, though visitors describe some as aloof, disproportionately overpriced and sited purely for the Grand View. In the Lisbon area you can find them in Queluz, Óbidos and Setúbal.

Doubles at a pousada cost 16,300$00 to 35,700$00 in high season, 12,900$00 to 26,500$00 in low season. For more information and/or reservations, contact Pousadas de Portugal (☎ 218 442 001, fax 218 442 085, e guest@pousadas.pt), Avenida Santa Joana Princesa 10, 1749-090 Lisbon, or check out the Web site at www.pousadas.pt.

This logo is used to indicate Turismo de Habitação properties

resorts in Lisbon, the Estoril Coast and elsewhere. Check out the Web site at www.room-service.co.uk.

Turismo de Habitação

Under a private but government-monitored scheme called Turismo de Habitação, and smaller schemes known as Turismo Rural and Agroturismo (often collectively called Turihab), you can stay in anything from a farmhouse to a mansion as the guest of the owner. Some have self-contained cottages, though owners prefer stays of at least three or four days in these. Turihab properties include some of Portugal's finest middle and upper-range bargains, and are invariably welcoming and relaxing places with tactful and helpful hosts.

For a double in the high season you'll pay a minimum of 18,500$00 in a Turihab manor house, but just 9500$00 in a farmhouse. In the low season, and/or if you book directly with the owner, prices can drop significantly.

A hefty, multilingual book, *Turismo no Espaço Rural*, describing most of the possibilities, is available for 2500$00 from ICEP tourist offices abroad and in Lisbon and

Porto. Unless you plan on Turihabbing every night of your trip and want to book each one, you may not need this book, as nearly all turismos have lists of Turihab properties in the local area.

PLACES TO STAY – BUDGET
Camping

Six kilometres west of Rossio in the Parque Florestal de Monsanto is the big, well-equipped facility, *Lisboa Camping – Parque Municipal (Map 1; ☎ 217 623 100, fax 217 623 106)*. It's open year-round. A site in the high season costs 840/840/540$00 per person/tent/car. Bungalows for two to six people are also available. Take bus No 43 from Cais do Sodré.

Next nearest is a pricey site run by *Clube de Campismo de Lisboa (☎ 219 623 960)*, 20km north-west of Lisbon at Almornos; prices are 850/900/850$00 per person/tent/car (640/675/640$00 with a CCI card). There are a couple more on the other side of the Tejo along the Costa da Caparica, and others to the west at Praia Grande and Praia do Guincho (see the Excursions chapter).

Hostels

Lisbon's 24-hour, but not very helpful, *pousada da juventude (Map 2; ☎ 213 532 696, fax 213 537 541, Rua Andrade Corvo 46)*, is near Picoas metro (or take bus No 46 or 90 from Santa Apolónia or the Rossio, or the Aero-Bus from the airport). A dorm bed/double with bathroom will cost 2900/6500$00. There are no cooking facilities.

The newer *casa da juventude (Map 1; ☎ 218 920 890, fax 218 920 891, Via de Moscavide)*, affiliated to the IPJ, is near Parque das Nações, 1km north of Gare do Oriente. It has a restaurant, plus cooking

PLACES TO STAY

and laundry facilities. A dorm bed/double with bathroom costs 2100/5100$00. Reception is open 8 am to midnight.

There are other pousadas da juventude across the Tejo River at *Almada (☎ 212 943 491, fax 212 943 497, Quinta do Bucelinho, Pragal)* and near the beach at *Catalazete (☎ 214 430 638, fax 214 419 267, Estrada Marginal)* in Oeiras, 12km west of Lisbon, accessible by frequent trains from Cais do Sodré station. Reservations are essential – at least a month ahead in summer. There's also a pousada in Sintra, 45 minutes by train from Rossio station (see the Excursions chapter).

Pensões & Residenciais
Rossio & Praça dos Restauradores (Map 6) Climb up three floors lined with fragmented azulejos to reach *Pensão Santo Tirso (☎ 213 470 428, Praça Dom Pedro IV 18)*, which has pleasant, plain rooms and friendly management. Doubles without/with bathroom cost 4000/5500$00.

Similarly priced is the bright and clean *Residencial Nova Avenida (☎ 213 423 689, Rua de Santo António da Glória 87)* near Praça da Alegria, and the less attractive *Pensão Lafonense (☎ 213 467 122, Rua das Portas de Santo Antão 36, 2nd floor)*, which also has budget triples. Several other cheapies are along this road and even seedier options on Rua da Glória, near the Elevador da Glória. Near the top of the elevador, the more salubrious *Pensão Globo (☎ 213 462 279, Rua do Teixeira 37)* offers doubles from 5500$00 (4500$00 without shower).

Others falling in the upper price bracket are the popular *Pensão Duque (☎/fax 213 463 444, @ pensao_duque@yahoo.com, Calçada do Duque 53)*, which has nice vibes (and its owner speaks both English and French), the slightly noisier *Pensão Estrela de Ouro (☎ 213 465 110, Largo Trindade Coelho 6)* and less appealing but conveniently central *Pensão Estação Central (☎ 213 423 308, Calçada do Carmo 17)*, by Rossio station.

Baixa (Map 6) Many cheap places in the Baixa are on upper floors of old residential flats, with grotty stairwells and thin-walled

rooms. The best of these places is *Pensão Norte (☎ 218 878 941, fax 218 868 462, Rua dos Douradores 159, 2nd to 4th floors)*, whose clean, modern doubles (with phone and TV) cost 5000/6000$00 with shower/bathroom. Similarly priced are the *Pensão Prata (Map 7; ☎ 213 468 908, Rua da Prata 71, 4th floor)* and the rather less welcoming *Pensão Arco da Bandeira (☎ 213 423 478, Rua dos Sapateiros 226, 3rd floor)*.

Alfama (Map 8) Among several waterfront cheapies, the best choice is cheerful *Pensão Varandas (☎ 218 870 519, Rua dos Bacalhoeiros 8, 2nd floor; also accessible from Rua Afonso de Albuquerque 7)*, which has doubles (with a shower cubicle) for around 6000$00, the best with balconies overlooking Campo das Cebolas.

Arroios (Map 2) Three blocks to the east of Arroios metro station, *Pensão Louro (☎ 218 133 422, Rua Morais Soares 76)* is a student hostel during the school year, but in July and August some spartan rooms with showers are available, including doubles for 5000$00 without bathroom.

PLACES TO STAY – MID-RANGE
Rossio, Praça dos Restauradores & Baixa (Map 6)
In the 6000$00 to 7000$00 per double room price range are several good choices including the cheery *Pensão Imperial (☎ 213 420 166, Praça dos Restauradores 78, 4th floor)*. *Hospedaria Bons Dias (☎ 213 471 918, Calçada do Carmo 25)* has nice, brightly decorated rooms (with separate bathroom), some with a small balcony, and a lift to get to you to its 5th floor. On the 2nd floor of No 25 is the pricier *Residencial Estrela do Mondego (☎ 213 467 109)*, which has spacious rooms (some with fridge), all with air-con and telephone, from 7500$00. Old-fashioned *Pensão Residencial Alcobia (☎ 218 865 171, fax 218 865 174, Poço do Borratém 15)* offers spacious, quiet doubles for 8000$00 (7000$00 without bathroom) including breakfast.

For a similar price is the smart *Pensão Residencial Florescente (☎ 213 463 517, fax 213 427 733, Rua das Portas de Santo Antão 99)* with a huge range of rooms; and security-conscious **Pensão Residencial Gerês** *(☎ 218 810 497, fax 218 882 006, Calçada do Garcia 6)*. The **Hotel Suiço-Atlântico** *(☎ 213 461 713, fax 213 469 013, Rua da Glória 3)*, in a rather seedy neighbourhood, offers adequate doubles costing 10,000$00 including breakfast.

In the Baixa's pedestrianised district, popular **Residencial Duas Nações** *(Map 7; ☎ 213 460 710, fax 213 470 206, Rua da Vitória 41)* offers decent doubles with bathroom for 8500$00, while nearby **Albergaria Insulana** *(☎ 213 427 625, fax 213 428 924, Rua da Assunção 52)* has simple, pleasant rooms with bathroom and breakfast that cost 11,000$00.

Bairro Alto & Chiado

Best value in this neighbourhood and price bracket is **Pensão Londres** *(Map 6; ☎ 213 462 203, fax 213 465 682, e pensaolondres@ mail.telepac.pt, Rua Dom Pedro V 53)*. There's a big range of rooms (somewhat noisy facing the street) costing from 7200$00 to 11,500$00 (with bath), all including breakfast. This popular place gets booked out a month ahead in summer.

In the Rato district, **Casa de São Mamede** *(Map 5; ☎ 213 963 166, fax 213 951 896, Rua Escola Politécnica 159)* is a small traditional hotel in quite an elegant townhouse. Doubles (including safe and telephone) are 15,000$00, breakfast included.

Alfama (Map 8)

Just below the Castelo de São Jorge, a long climb up from the street, is **Pensão Ninho das Águias** *(☎ 218 854 070, Costa do Castelo 74)*. It's not always very welcoming but its stunning city views, garden and 14 elegant rooms mean it gets booked up a month ahead in summer. Doubles/triples cost 8000/10,000$00 (7000/8000$00 without bathroom).

Behind the cathedral are two appealing if rather overpriced places at Rua São João da Praça 97: the popular **Pensão São João da Praça** *(☎/fax 218 862 591, 2nd floor)* has doubles from 8500$00 (without bath) to

10,500$00 (with). **Sé Guest House** *(☎ 218 864 400, 1st floor)* has a gentle ambience and doubles from 12,000$00 including breakfast.

Saldanha & Avenida da Liberdade (Map 2)

Residencial Lisbonense *(☎ 213 544 628, fax 213 544 899, Rua Pinheiro Chagas 1)* has bright rooms on four upper storeys; doubles with breakfast cost 8000$00. In the quieter Rua Filipe Folque, at No 19, is similarly priced **Residencial Marisela** *(☎/fax 213 160 423)*. **Pensão Residencial Princesa** *(☎ 213 193 070, Rua Gomes Freire 130)*, in Estefânia, has comfortable doubles/triples for 10,000/12,000$00 including breakfast; take bus No 100 from Praça da Figueira. The popular **Pensão Residencial 13 da Sorte** *(Map 5; ☎ 213 531 851, fax 213 956 946, Rua do Salitre 13)* has doubles/triples with bathroom, TV and telephone costing 9000/12,000$00.

PLACES TO STAY – TOP END
Rossio & Praça dos Restauradores (Map 6)

The discreet and low-key **Hotel Métropole** *(☎ 213 219 030, fax 213 469 166, e almeida .hotels@ip.pt, Praça Dom Pedro IV 30)* is a renovated but wonderfully old-fashioned hotel with spacious rooms featuring original 1950s furnishings. Doubles cost 25,000$00. The **Hotel Lisboa Tejo** *(☎ 218 866 182, fax 218 865 163, Calçada Poço do Borratém 4)* is a new hotel in a fine old building. The double rooms, nicely decorated with azulejos, cost 18,000$00.

An aparthotel called **Orion Eden Lisboa** *(☎ 213 216 600, fax 213 216 666, e eden .lisboa@mail.telepac.pt, Praça dos Restauradores 24)* has studio apartments costing 16,500$00 and flats for up to four people (with kitchen, satellite TV and telephone) for 19,500$00. Three are wheelchair accessible.

Alfama

At the Miradouro da Senhora do Monte, **Albergaria Senhora do Monte** *(Map 5; ☎ 218 866 002, fax 218 877 783, Calçada do Monte 39)* has comfortable rooms that

PLACES TO STAY

PLACES TO STAY

Pick of the Best

At Rua das Janelas Verdes 47, near the Museu Nacional de Arte Antiga (Map 4), there's an aristocratic 18th-century mansion which once belonged to the famous Portuguese novelist, Eça de Queirós. It's now a luxurious little hotel, *As Janelas Verdes* (☎ 213 968 143, fax 213 968 144, e jverdes@heritage.pt). Richly furnished doubles cost 31,900$00, including breakfast served in room. The Web site, www.heritage.pt, features other properties in this exclusive chain.

Almost opposite, at No 32, you climb an ivy-trellised stone stairway to the enchanting little garden of *York House* (☎ 213 962 435, fax 213 972 798, e yorkhouse@mail.telepac.pt), a former 17th-century convent. The 36 rooms, furnished with antiques from Portugal and England, cost 34,000$00.

Also in this elegant district of Lapa is the very exclusive *Lapa Palace* (☎ 213 950 005, fax 213 954 003, e reservas@hotelapa.com, Rua do Pau de Bandeira 4). The former residence of a noble Portuguese family in the 19th century, it has an abundance of marble, stucco and azulejos, a beautifully landscaped garden, health club and swimming pools and even a presidential suite if you've won the lottery. Doubles cost a breathtaking 50,000$00.

Another special place, in the far north of the city (near Alto dos Moinhos metro station) is Lisbon's only Turismo de Habitação – the *Quinta Nova da Conceição* (Map 1; ☎/fax 217 780 091, Rua Cidade de Rabat, 5). Set in a large garden, this 18th-century house (once the residence of the Count of Benfica) has just three rooms (24,000$00 including breakfast) and a grand piano in the lounge.

cost 21,000$00 (plus pricier ones with spectacular views). Free car parking is available on the quiet street, and tram No 28 runs close by.

At the time of research, *Solar do Castelo*, a deluxe addition to the Heritage Hotels chain, was being created inside the castle (Map 6). Check out the Heritage Web site (www.heritage.pt) for the latest details.

Marquês de Pombal & Rato (Map 2)

Best Western Hotel Eduardo VII (☎ 213 568 800, fax 213 568 833, toll-free reservations ☎ 800 839 361, e sales@hotel .eduardovii.pt, Avenida Fontes Pereira de Melo 5) is a long-established, classic hotel with a panoramic rooftop restaurant. Nonsmoking rooms are available and all feature a fridge and safe. Doubles cost 19,700$00. Check out the Best Western Web site (www .bestwestern.com) for seasonal discounts. *Hotel Fénix* (☎ 213 862 121, fax 213 860 131, e h.fenix@ip.pt, Praça Marquês de Pombal 8) has a similar atmosphere; with double rooms that cost 25,000$00.

In a quieter location, overlooking the park, the *Hotel Miraparque* (☎ 213 524 286, fax 213 578 920, e miraparque@ esoterica.pt, Avenida Sidónio Pais 12) retains a personal touch despite tour groups. Plain rooms cost a reasonable 14,500$00; metered car parking spaces are outside.

Hotel Real Parque (☎ 213 570 101, fax 213 570 750, e info@hoteisreal.com, Avenida Luís Bívar 67) is a posher outfit with spacious doubles (six equipped for the disabled) costing 21,000$00. There's an exclusively nonsmoking floor and garage parking. Not far away on busy Rua Castilho, at No 74, the friendly *Hotel Diplomático* (☎ 213 839 020, fax 213 862 155, e reservas@ hotel-diplomatico-mailpac.pt) has doubles that officially cost 26,000$00 (although you can often get them for lower than this).

Top of the range is the modern high-rise *Sheraton Lisboa Hotel & Towers* (☎ 213 575 757, fax 213 547 164, e lisboasheraton@ sheraton.pt.com, Rua Latino Coelho 1), with 384 rooms, including 63 executive-club rooms and 23 'smart' rooms designed for the business traveller. There's a health club including a swimming pool, gym and sauna. Doubles cost 46,000$00 (buffet breakfast costs 3000$00).

Avenida da Liberdade (Map 5)

Just off Avenida da Liberdade, the nicely old-fashioned *Hotel Jorge V* (☎ 213 562 525, fax 213 150 319, Rua Mouzinho da Silveira 3) has doubles costing from 14,500$00. A three-star hotel with the facilities of a four-star is the **Hotel Presidente** *(Map 2; ☎ 213 173 570, fax 213 520 272, Rua Alexandre Herculano 13)*; doubles with air-con, minibar and great breakfasts cost 16,000\$00. Nearby, the modern **Hotel Lisboa** *(☎ 213 554 131, fax 213 554 139, e reservdep@hlisboa .mailpac.pt, Rua Barata Salgueiro 5)* is twice as slick and expensive (25,000\$00 or 35,000\$00 for an executive room with office).

Hotel Britania *(☎ 213 155 016, fax 213 155 021, e britania.hotel@heritage.pt, Rua Rodrigues Sampaio 17)*, designed by Portuguese modernist architect Cassiano Branco in the 1940s, has masses of charm. Its 30 rooms, costing 24,600\$00 a double, are huge but the atmosphere is pleasantly intimate. Another classy little 1950s hotel in the same chain with the same prices is the **Hotel Lisboa Plaza** *(☎ 213 463 922, fax 213 471 630, e plaza.hotels@ heritage.pt, Travessa do Salitre 7)*.

Cheaper and blander but tucked away in a quiet location, is **Hotel Botânico** *(Map 6; ☎ 213 420 392, fax 213 420 125, Rua Mãe d'Água 16)*, where doubles (featuring air-con and minibar) cost 18,000\$00. Free parking is available outside.

Top of the range is **Hotel Sofitel Lisboa** *(☎ 213 228 300, fax 213 228 310, e sofitel .lisboa@mail.telepac.pt, Avenida da Liberdade 127)*, where doubles (not including breakfast) cost 45,000\$00. Parking in the hotel's garage costs 2500\$00 daily.

Belém

If you want to wake up in the presence of the Mosteiro dos Jerónimos in Belém, the **Hotel da Torre** *(Map 10; ☎ 213 630 161, fax 213 645 995, Rua dos Jerónimos 8)* is just around the corner. Doubles with breakfast cost 27,900\$00.

LONG-TERM RENTALS

If you just need a room, your best bet would be to negotiate a long-term price with your preferred hotel or residencial. For a studio room with kitchenette, there's **Hotel Impala** *(Map 2; ☎ 213 148 914, fax 213 575 362, Rua Filipe Folque 49)*, which has apartments for two to four people costing 15,000\$00, with discounts for longer stays.

Pricier, but very central, is **Orion Eden Lisboa** (see Places to Stay – Top End, Rossio & Praça dos Restauradores). Every studio flat or larger one-bedroom apartment here has a small desk, direct phone line with private number, satellite TV and kitchen facilities. Fax and photocopying services are available at reception. Cheaper rates for long periods can be negotiated.

The best choice of other aparthotels are in Cascais or Estoril (see the Excursions chapter). For more aesthetic surroundings, consider renting a private apartment in nearby Sintra. Daily rates for a one or two-bedroom place with kitchen average 8500\$00, but for extended periods it could be much cheaper, especially in the low season. Contact Sintra's turismo for details.

For basic student flats in or near the city centre, check the notice boards at the IPJ (see Useful Organisations in the Facts for the Visitor chapter) or Planet Megastore (see Email & Internet Access in the Facts for the Visitor chapter). For more upmarket, long-term rentals, check the classified section of the *Público* daily newspaper.

PLACES TO STAY

Places to Eat

FOOD

Without a shadow of doubt the Portuguese is the most refined, the most voluptuous and succulent cuisine in the world...We did acquire – thanks to the spices from the Orient, the tangy bits from Brazil and the art of using sugar from sweet-toothed countries, Turkey, India and the Moors of northern Africa – culinary skills, foods, delicacies, recipes, which turned us into a foremost gastronomic people. There is no other country that can boast such an array of national dishes...

Fialho de Almeida, *Os Gatos,* 1893

Olive oil, wine and friendship, the older the better.
Portuguese proverb

Don't get your hopes up; most travellers' experiences of Portuguese cuisine don't come close to Almeida's lyrical description. There's no doubt that eating and drinking get serious attention here, but traditional Portuguese cuisine is far from fancy; it is basically the honest fare of farmers and fisherfolk. And that means hearty portions (at cheap prices), lots of fish and meat, rice and potatoes, and a few scraps of lettuce as the standard 'vegetable'.

The only meal that may fail to fill your stomach is *pequeno almoço* (breakfast), which is traditionally just coffee and a bread roll. *Almoço* (lunch) is generally a far bigger affair, often lasting at least two hours (usually 1 to 3 pm), although the trend in Lisbon is increasingly for shorter, cheaper lunches. Both lunch and *jantar* (the evening meal) traditionally feature three courses, including a hot main dish, invariably served with potatoes (and sometimes rice). As most main dishes in the cheaper eateries cost less than 1200$00 each, you'll find it easy to gorge yourself on a full three-course meal for under 1800$00.

Restaurants open at about 7 pm for dinner (last orders at around 10.30 pm), with most people eating around 8 pm. Restaurants are usually closed between 4 and 7 pm, even if they do say they're open all day. But you'll always be able to find something to eat somewhere. In addition to the *restaurantes*, hordes of cafes serve snacks throughout the day; some may serve simple meals at lunchtime, often at the bar counter as well as at tables. Some apparently tiny cafes may even have a big *sala de jantar* (dining room) upstairs. Several packed-out lunch eateries in Lisbon are almost entirely stand-up.

Another popular option, especially for lunch, is a *casa de pasto*, a casual eatery with cheap, simple meals. Slightly more up-market and popular with locals for both lunch and dinner is a *tasca*, a simple tavern, often with rustic decor. A *cervejaria*, literally 'beer house', serves food as well as drinks, while a *marisqueira* specialises in seafood (and is therefore often expensive). The *churrasqueira* (or *churrascaria*), literally a barbecue or grill, is actually a popular family-style restaurant serving grilled foods, especially chicken.

If you can't face the standard huge servings in many resturants, you can ask if a *meia dose* (half-portion) is available. This is a standard practice in Portugal (less so for evening meals), although the cost usually works out to be about two-thirds of a *dose*, not one-half. A better bargain is the *prato do dia* (dish of the day), often an excellent deal at about 800$00.

Many restaurants also advertise an *ementa turística* (tourist menu), which is a set meal with a choice of dishes and a glass of beer or half-bottle of wine. Not necessarily geared to tourists, these can occasionally be good value.

Often served at the start of a meal are tempting little titbits such as olives or cheese spread. If you start nibbling, you'll be charged extra for them (they're usually listed as a *couvert* on the bill, or as *pão e manteiga*, ie, bread and butter). If you don't want them, play it safe and send them back at the outset.

Finally, be prepared for two very common features of Portuguese restaurants: a TV blaring in the corner (especially in budget or mid-range restaurants); and widespread smoking. Few restaurants have nonsmoking sections so all nonsmokers can do is avoid the dining rush hour.

To order the bill, ask for *a conta, se faz favor*. Cafes don't usually charge for service (a tip of small change is acceptable). In restaurants, you can add 5% to 10% of the total if you're happy with the meal and service. The bill at an upper-end restaurant may already include a *serviço* (service charge).

Snacks

Snacks include delicious *sopas* (soups); *sandes* (sandwiches), typically with *queijo* (cheese) or *fiambre* (ham); *prego no pão* (a slab of meat sandwiched in a roll, often with a fried egg as well); *pastéis de bacalhau* (cod fishcakes); and *tosta mista* (toasted cheese-and-ham sandwich). Prices start at about 250$00. Keep an eye out for cafes advertising lunchtime *combinados*, tasty miniature portions, costing about 700$00, of a regular meat or fish dish, invariably served with chips (and sometimes salad).

Main Meals

Before delving into the menu (*a ementa* or *a lista*) it's always worth asking if there's a prato do dia or *especialidade da casa* (speciality of the house). Greedy tourist-geared eateries may simply suggest the expensive *arroz de marisco* – a rich seafood and rice stew, usually for a minimum of two – but elsewhere you could well end up with an unusual or home-made dish.

Among *entradas* (starters), the best value are the excellent home-made soups. Especially popular is *caldo verde*, a jade-green potato and cabbage soup (see the boxed text 'Caldo Verde'). In upmarket restaurants, you may find local cheeses or the occasional *queijo fresco* (fresh goat's cheese).

An Order of Bull, Please

Be careful not to get *uma torrada* and *uma tourada* mixed up: the first means a piece of toast; the second, a bullfight!

Caldo Verde

This is the most typical of Portugal's soups and is made with kale or cabbage. The stalk and tough parts of the kale are removed and the rest is shredded finely so that it resembles grass. The soup is sometimes served with a slice of maize bread and a side dish of small black olives.

Serves 4

500g (1lb) floury potatoes, peeled and cut into quarters
1L (4 cups) water
salt
3 tablespoons olive oil
1 onion, finely chopped
250g (8 oz) kale or cabbage leaves, very finely shredded
1 small clove of garlic (optional)
freshly ground black pepper
4 thin slices of chouriço (optional)

Cook the potatoes in salted water until they are soft enough for mashing. Remove, mash and return to the water, along with the oil, onion and shredded cabbage, and boil for three to four minutes (the cabbage should not be over-cooked or mushy). Season and serve hot. Place a slice of chouriço (a Portuguese spicy pork sausage) in each soup bowl if desired.

Portugal has the highest per capita consumption of fish in all of Europe, and for main meals *peixe* (fish) and seafood offer exceptional value. The variety is amazing, from *linguada* (sole) and *lulas* (squid) or *pescada* (hake) to *bife de atúm* (tuna steak) and *espadarte* (swordfish, sometimes confused in translation with *peixe espada*, or scabbard fish).

The cheapest fish are *sardinhas assadas* (charcoal-grilled sardines), delicious with salad and chilled white wine or port. And you won't get far before discovering Portugal's favourite fish dish: *bacalhau* (salted cod), which has been a Portuguese culinary obsession for 400 years (see the boxed text 'Bacalhau, the Faithful Friend').

PLACES TO EAT

'Bacalhau, The Faithful Friend'

The Portuguese have had an obsession with *bacalhau* – salted cod – since the early 16th century. It was at this time that Portuguese fishing boats started to fish for cod around Newfoundland, Canada (claimed by the Corte Real brothers in 1500). The sailors salted and sun-dried their catch to make it last the long journey home, thereby discovering the perfect convenience food for their compatriot seafaring explorers (who were sailing as far as India at the time) and for their fish-loving but fridgeless folk back home. Indeed, so popular did bacalhau become throughout Portugal that it soon became known as *fiel amigo*, the faithful friend.

Most of today's cod is imported from Norway and is fairly expensive, but as it more than doubles in volume after soaking, keeps well and is extremely nourishing, it's still widely popular. If you join the fan club, you're in for a treat – there's said to be a different bacalhau recipe for every day of the year.

It takes a few centuries to become addicted – try the *bacalhau à Gomes de Sá*, a tastier version than most of the 364 other recipes (this one features flaked cod baked with potatoes, onions, hard-boiled eggs and black olives).

Some more exotic fish specialities include popular but expensive *caldeirada* (fish stew – *açorda de marisco* if it's bread-based); *cataplana* (a combination of shellfish and ham cooked in a sealed pan, typical of the Algarve region); and all of the varieties of shellfish, from *camarões* (shrimps) and *amêijoas* (clams) to *lagostins* (crayfish) and *chocos* (cuttlefish).

The Portuguese are voracious meat-eaters but choosing a good *carne* (meat) or *aves* (poultry) dish is often hit-and-miss. Strike it lucky and you'll find delicious specialities such as *leitão assado* (roast suckling pig), *borrego* (lamb) and *presunto* (smoked ham). *Carne de porco à alentejana* is an inspired combination of pork and clams. Even the lowliest menu invariably features *vitela* (veal) and *bife* (beef steak),

while *coelho* (rabbit) and *cabrito* (kid) are unexpected culinary delights. The most popular poultry is *frango* (chicken), widely available grilled on a spit *(frango assado)*, and a perfect takeaway meal.

Strike it unlucky, however, and you'll get *tripas* (tripe), a speciality of Porto; *migas alentejanas*, a stodge of corn bread and fatty pork; an impossibly meaty *cozido à Portuguesa* stew; or a bloody, bready slop called *papas de sarrabulho*.

Desserts & Pastries

Sobremesas (desserts) tend to be fairly unimaginative, though you're in for a treat if a home-cooked *doce* (sweet pudding) such as a *leite creme* (custard) or *mousse de chocolate* is available. More likely you'll be offered *pudim* (creme caramel), *arroz doce* (sweet rice) or *gelado* (ice cream, usually the overpriced Olá or Motta commercial varieties).

A variety of fresh fruit is usually available – the best are strawberries and seasonal figs. There's also cheese; the best and most expensive is *queijo da serra*, a soft white variety made from ewe's milk, which comes from the Serra da Estrela region.

Pastelarias or *casas de chá* (teahouses) have the sweetest concoctions imaginable, made from egg yolks and sugar. Nuns of the 18th century created many of the recipes, and presumably gave them their present, tongue-in-cheek names, like *papos de anjo* (angel's breasts) and *barriga de freira* (nun's belly). Local specialities include almond pastries *(travesseiros)* from Sintra. Sweet *pasteis de nata* (custard tarts) are a ubiquitous favourite, at their famous best from the Pasteis de Belém shop in Belém.

Vegetarian Food

If you're a vegetarian who can eat fish, you'll have little trouble in Portugal. But strict vegetarians can have a miserable time in this carnivorous country, where vegetables just don't figure in the traditional cuisine. Lisbon itself has a fair selection of vegetarian restaurants (plus some other restaurants that offer a few token vegetarian dishes). Elsewhere, though, exclusively vegetarian restaurants are rare. It's an enduring mystery why markets groan under fresh vegetables in season but so little ends up in restaurants, other than pureed into soups.

Mind you, these soups are delicious and grace every menu. But beware – even popular caldo verde is often topped with *chouriço* (spicy pork sausage) or bits of fatty pork, and there's no telling whether the stock was made with meat.

In addition to the standard international vegetarian fare that's widely available (eg, omelettes and salads), there's also some traditional Portuguese specialities that do avoid meat, notably the simple peasant *migas* (bread soup) dishes such as *migas do Ribatejo*. They look disgusting (their main ingredient is soaked maize bread, with lots of olive oil and garlic to taste), but fit the bill when you're ravenous.

Keep an eye out, too, for *arroz de tomate* (tomato rice) or *favas com azeite* (broad beans with olive oil). If nothing on the menu looks suitable, it's always worth asking the waiter if they just have vegetables *(tem alguma hortaliça, por favor?)*.

Alternatively, you can shop for yourself. In addition to excellent fruit and vegetables, markets usually have freshly baked bread and local cheeses. Markets are best on Saturday, worst on Monday and closed on Sunday. They're open from early morning to about 6 pm.

DRINKS
Nonalcoholic Drinks
Many cafes have fresh orange juice *(sumo de laranja)* and/or stock the local bottled varieties labelled Tri Naranjus. Portuguese *água mineral* (mineral water) is also excellent and widely available, either *com gás* (carbonated) or *sem gás* (still).

Coffee drinkers are in for a high time. Coffee is freshly brewed, even in the humblest cafe, and comes in all varieties with its own convoluted nomenclature. For a small black espresso (the most popular form) just ask for *um café* (or *uma bica* to be more precise; many waiters don't believe foreigners want the real thing – strong, black and punchy). You may soon graduate to a

double dose, *um café duplo*, or retreat ᴠ something weaker, *um carioca*. If you want milk, ask for *um garoto* (small size) or *um café com leite*. Popular at breakfast time is the caffe latte-style *um galão*, a large milky coffee served in a glass (usually with a good deal more milk than coffee). For equal portions (in a cup) ask for *um meia de leite*. Uma bica usually costs 80$00, but it does depend where you drink it: a typical Lisbon pastelaria might charge 80$00 if you drink your coffee standing up by the *balcão* (counter), 120$00 at the *mesa* (table) or as much as 200$00 outside at the *esplanada* (street tables).

Chá (tea) is usually served rather weak, in the style of Catherine of Bragança, who is best remembered not for being the wife of Charles II but for setting England on its long love affair with tea (and toast). You can ask for tea *com leite* (with milk) or *com limão* (lemon), but if you ask for *um chá de limão*, you'll get a glass of hot water with a lemon rind (which is actually quite refreshing).

Also available in cafes and teahouses is *um chocolate quente* (hot chocolate), or simply *um copo de leite* (a glass of milk).

Alcoholic Drinks
Portuguese people like their tipple. At cafes, restaurants and bars throughout the day (and most of the night) you can pick up anything from a glass of beer or wine to a shot of *aguardente* (firewater). A mixture *(traçado)* of alcoholic drinks is common, including the morning-only *Martini com cerveja* (Martini topped with beer). The bartenders aren't stingy with their tots – most of them don't even bother with such things as spirit measures. A single brandy here often contains the equivalent of a double in the UK or the USA.

In most places you pay when you're ready to leave (as in a restaurant), but in some foreign-owned bars there's a pay-as-you-order system *(pronto pagamento)*.

Wines Portuguese wine offers great value in all its varieties – red, white or rosé; mature or young (and semisparkling). You can find decent some *vinho da casa* (house wine)

y of Wines & Their Labels

	winery or cellar
ano	year
branco	white
bruto	extra dry
colheita	a single-harvest vintage tawny port, aged for at least seven years
doce	sweet
engarrofado por ...	bottled by ...
espumante	sparkling
garrafeira	wines of an outstanding vintage, at least three years old for reds and one year for whites
generoso	fortified wine
LBV	late-bottled vintage; a vintage port aged for four to six years in oak casks before bottling
licoroso	sweet fortified wine
meio seco	medium dry
quinta	a country property or wine estate
região demarcada	officially demarcated wine region
reserva	wine from a year of outstanding quality
ruby port	the cheapest and sweetest port wine
seco	dry
tawny port	sweet or semisweet port, the best of which has been aged for at least 10 years; less likely than a vintage port to give you a hangover
tinto	red
velho	old
vinho branco/tinto	white/red wine
vinho da casa	house wine
vinho do Porto	port wine
vinho maduro	wine matured for more than a year
vinho regionão	a new classification for superior country wines, similar to the French *vins de pays*
vinho verde	young (literally 'green wine') wine, slightly sparkling and available in red, white and rosé varieties
vintage character porto	a cheap version of a vintage port, blended and aged for about four years
vintage port	the unblended product of a single harvest of outstanding or rare quality, bottled after two years and then aged in the bottle for up to two decades, sometimes more
white port	usually dry, crisp and fresh; popular as an aperitif

everywhere, for as little as 300$00 for a 350mL bottle or jug. And for less than 800$00 you can buy a bottle to please the most discerning taste buds.

Restaurant wine lists differentiate not only between *tinto* (red) and *branco* (white), but also between *maduros* (mature wines) and *vinhos verdes* (semisparkling young wines). As there are more than a dozen major regional wines (usually produced by cooperatives), with new ones coming onto the market all the time, you're spoilt for choice.

The most famous of the maduros are probably the red *Dão* table wines produced just north of the Serra da Estrela. Sweet and velvety, they resemble a Burgundy. Other maduros worth trying are the increasingly popular wines from the Alentejo (the reds from Reguengos are excellent); the reds and whites of Buçaco, near Coimbra; the dry, straw-coloured whites of Bucelas in Estremadura; and the table wines of the Ribatejo, especially the reds of Torres Vedras and the whites from Chamusca. The expensive but venerable reds of Colares (famous since the 13th century) near Sintra are made from vines grown on sand dunes, and never touched by phylloxera (a fungus that has ravaged many a European wine region over the years).

The vinho verde (literally 'green wine') of the northern Minho and lower Douro Valley area is also very popular. Young (hence its name) and slightly sparkling, it has a low alcohol content and comes in red, white and rosé varieties. The white is undoubtedly the best (especially with some shellfish). The best known vinho verde label is Casal Garcia.

Portugal's best known rosé is the sweet, semisparkling Mateus rosé. The Portuguese themselves prefer their bubbles either in vinho verde form or as *espumantes naturais* (sparkling wines). The best of these are from the Bairrada region near Coimbra and the Raposeira wines from Lamego. Sweet dessert wines are rare – the *moscatel* from Setúbal and the Carcavelos wine from Estremadura offer the fruitiest flavours.

Port & Madeira *Vinho do Porto* (port), a fortified wine made exclusively from grapes grown in the northern Douro Valley, is Portugal's most famous export. Fortified by adding grape brandy, it is matured in casks or large oak vats, traditionally at Vila Nova de Gaia, across the Rio Douro from Porto – from which it took its name. Port can be red or white, dry, medium or sweet. The main difference in price and quality is between blended ports taken from a number of different harvests and vintage port from a single high-quality harvest. All the genuine ports carry the seal of the Port Wine Institute.

You can sample hundreds of port eties at the institute's palatial Lisbon loun (see the boxed text 'Solar do Vinho do Porto' in the Entertainment chapter). Any cafe, bar or restaurant can also serve you a glass for about 200$00. A bottle of humble port in a supermarket can cost as little as 800$00 (but at least 2500$00 for the better-quality vintage brews).

Cheapest and sweetest are the ruby and red ports, made from a blend of lesser wines, bottled early and drunk young (after about three years). Also blended are semisweet or sweet tawny ports, named after the mahogany colour they gain after years aged in wooden oak casks, and very popular as an aperitif (especially with the French, who drink several million cases of it every year). Check out the label ('10 Years Old', '20 Years Old' etc) for an indication of the best-quality tawnies. Vintage-character port is a cheap version of a vintage (but with similar characteristics), blended and aged for about four years.

The single harvest ports range from the *colheita* port, a tawny made from high-quality wines and aged for at least seven years before bottling, to late-bottled vintage (LBV) ports, which are produced from an excellent harvest and aged for four to six years before bottling. The most sublime (and most expensive) port of all – vintage

Cherry Delights

Just off the Rossio, on Largo de Domingos, is a tiny and historic bar-cum-shop, *A Ginjinha* (Map 6), devoted solely to selling Espinheira ginjinha, a cherry liqueur. The drink actually takes its name from the original Galician owner of the shop.

The recipe for the extremely sweet but addictively potent drink came from a local friar who advised Espinheira to let cherries ferment in brandy before sugar, water and cinnamon were added. It became hugely popular (and still is), thanks to its cheapness and sweetness.

At the bar's sticky counter (open 9 am to 10.30 pm daily) you can stand and enjoy a glass for 110$00 (including a couple of cherries), or buy a 70cL bottle for 1200$00.

PLACES TO EAT

in a year of outstanding ...hin two years and aged es, sometimes more. Lit- ...Portugal but well worth ...y...g a... w...... ports, ranging from dry to rich and sweet. The dry variety is served chilled with a twist of lemon.

Vinho da Madeira (Madeira) is one of the oldest fortified wines of all. Vines were first introduced to this Atlantic Ocean island province of Portugal soon after it was claimed by Portuguese explorers in 1419. The English (who called the sweet version of the wine 'malmsey') became particularly partial to it (the Duke of Clarence, brother of Richard III, drowned in a butt of the stuff). In addition to the malmsey dessert wine, there's a dry aperitif version called *sercial* and a semisweet *verdelho*.

Spirits Portuguese whisky, brandy and gin are all much cheaper than elsewhere in Europe, although the quality isn't as good. If you fancy something with a more unique taste and punch, try some of the aguardente firewaters: *medronho* (made from arbutus berries), *figo* (figs), *ginjinha* (cherries; see the boxed text 'Cherry Delights') and *licor beirão* (aromatic plants) are all delicious – and safe in small doses. For some rough stuff that nearly destroys your throat, ask for a *bagaço* (made from grape husks).

Beer Stronger and cheaper than in the UK or the USA, Portugal's *cerveja* (beer) amounts to three fairly indistinguishable lagers: Sagres, Cristal and Super Bock.

You can order beer in bars by the bottle or on draught. A 20cL glass of draught beer is called *um imperial*, 33cL is *um principe*, 50cL is *uma caneca* and 1L is *um girafe*. Many Lisbon bars also have popular foreign brews such as bitter or stout.

PLACES TO EAT

Lisbon has hundreds of restaurants, many offering great value for money, especially at lunchtime, when generous daily specials cost as little as 800$00. Note that popular Bairro Alto restaurants can fill by 8 pm and that many places close on Sunday night.

Azulejos for Lunch?

One of the finest settings for a light lunch is the restaurant of the Museu Nacional do Azulejo (Map 1), in the old convent of Nossa Senhora da Madre de Deus Church. Choose from a small menu of salads, crepes or meat and fish dishes and eat in the bright, traditional kitchen (tiled with azulejos, of course) or the plant-filled garden.

The Turismo de Lisboa's Restaurant Card (available at all its outlets) offers discounts of between 10% and 15% in more than 40 quality restaurants. Valid for 72 hours and available at turismo outlets and some hotels, the card costs 1000$00 per person, 1400$00 per couple or 1900$00 for a family of two adults and two children under 14.

PLACES TO EAT – BUDGET
Rossio & Praça dos Restauradores

Rua da Glória has several locally popular budget places, including *O Brinco da Glória (Map 6; ☎ 213 468 635)* at No 23. The food is not great but portions are generous. *Restaurante Solar do Duque (Map 6; ☎ 213 426 901, Rua do Duque 67)*, described by a reader as a 'cracking restaurant', has a comfortably laid-back atmosphere. The nearby Calçada do Duque has several other more touristy restaurants, most with outdoor seating. Meat-lovers might particularly fancy *Casa Transmontana (Map 6; ☎ 213 420 300, Calçada do Duque 39)*, which serves at least one strong-tasting northern Portuguese speciality for under 1200$00.

Nearer the Alfama, try *A Galera (Map 8; ☎ 218 872 489, Rua dos Bacalhoeiros 24)*, where the lunchtime dishes can cost less than 800$00.

Bairro Alto & Chiado

Mention Bairro Alto and most tourists think fado, although most casas de fado are better known for their music than their menus. See the Entertainment chapter for several good fado houses with adequate food, most of them in the Bairro Alto.

A favourite budget restaurant here is venerable *A Primavera (Map 6; ☎ 213 420 477, Travessa da Espera 34)*, where a family ambience is complemented by honest, good cooking at modest prices. Another friendly place is *O Cantinho da Rosa (Map 6; ☎ 213 420 376, Rua da Rosa 222)*, which has lunchtime pratos for around 1000\$00. *Hau Lon (Map 6; ☎ 213 420 683, Rua do Norte 100)* can fill you with noodles and rice dishes for under 1000\$00.

If you get tired of waiting for the Elevador da Bica on Rua da Bica Duarte Belo, pop into *Restaurante Alto Minho (Map 7; ☎ 213 468 133)* at No 61, which does cheap and wholesome fare.

A great outdoor spot for a quiet, shady meal is *Leitaria Académica (Map 6; ☎ 213 469 092, Largo do Carmo)*. The indoor version of the restaurant at No 13 is so small it's like eating in a cell but the prices are cheaper (around 700\$00 for daily specials) than outside.

Similarly short on atmosphere but with daily specials is the plain *Cafetaria Brasil (Map 6; Rua de São Pedro de Alcântara 51)*. Nearby *Tascardoso (Map 5; ☎ 213 427 578, Rua do Século 244)*, another popular lunchtime haunt, offers reasonable dishes for less than 1000\$00.

On the western edge of Bairro Alto, the African neighbourhood of Rua do Poço dos Negros hosts the popular *Cantinho do Paz (Map 5; ☎ 213 908 638)* at No 64. It serves Indian and African food (evenings only) with live music at weekends.

Saldanha, Marquês de Pombal & Rato

The bright and cheerful *Bella Italia III (Map 2; ☎ 213 528 636, Avenida Duque d'Ávila 40-C)* is a pastelaria-cum-restaurant, with pizzas and half-portions of Portuguese fare for under 1000\$00. Two other cheapies, both near the youth hostel, are *Casa Mourisca (Map 2; Avenida Fontes Pereira de Melo 23)* and the *Restaurante António (☎ 213 538 780, Rua Tomas Ribeiro 61)*.

East of Avenida da Liberdade, Rua de Santa Marta is a good hunting ground for unpretentious restaurants (crammed for lunch). Go early if you want to get a seat at *Estrela de Santa Marta (Map 5; ☎ 213 548 400)* at No 14-A, where daily specials are less than 1000\$00, or *O Coradinho (Map 5; ☎ 213 555 950)*, at No 4, where generous half-portions are even cheaper (700\$00).

A popular cafe for snacks and cheap lunches is *Balcão do Marquês (Map 2; ☎ 213 545 086, Avenida Duque de Loulé 119)*. Eating is mainly stand-up (the *balcão* of the cafe's name means counter).

Alfama

As the Alfama becomes gentrified it is harder to find cheap local restaurants. *Solar do Vez (Map 8; ☎ 218 870 794, Campo das Cebolas 48)* still has an appealing simplicity and dishes for only 1000\$00 or so. *Snack-Bar Arco Iris (Map 8; ☎ 218 864 536, Rua São João da Praça 17)* is another reasonably priced place, with half a dozen outdoor tables.

There are pricier tourist-geared places around Largo do Chafariz de Dentro, but *Restaurante Cais d'Alfama (Map 8; ☎ 218 873 274)* at No 24 attracts the locals, too, with its extensive menu (including fresh sardines grilled outdoors) and prices under 1200\$00. The nearby *Barracão de Alfama (Map 8; Rua de São Pedro 16)* is also recommended. At *Restaurante Tolan (Map 8; ☎ 218 872 234, Rua dos Remédios 134)* dishes cost less than 900\$00 (the bacalhau is especially good).

In the Mouraria area, the fashionable *Algures na Mouraria (Map 6; ☎ 218 872 470, Rua das Farinhas 1)* offers Portuguese and African dishes at reasonable prices. Nearby *São Cristóvão (Map 6; ☎ 218 885 578, Rua de São Cristóvão 30)* is a bustling, family-run place famous for its effervescent mum who cooks up great Cape Verdean and other African dishes. Check out the delicious *moamba de galinha* (Angolan chicken stew).

Cais do Sodré & Belém

Caneças (Map 7; Rua Bernardino Costa 34-36), open from 6 am, is a great breakfast and lunch spot, serving cakes and snacks.

In Belém, a fine place for an outdoor snack is *Cafetaria Quadrante (Map 10)* on

PLACES TO EAT

Chic & Open-Air

Doca de Santo Amaro (Map 3) in the Alcântara area of western Lisbon is the most popular of the recently revamped waterfront areas, with a dozen restaurants-cum-bars. Overlooking the yachts in the marina and with a view of the massive Ponte 25 de Abril above, it's a great place for open-air dining and late-night boozing. In addition to the following (all open till at least 5 am at weekends), see the Entertainment chapter for more bar-oriented places.

Doca de Santo Esplanada (☎ 213 963 522); large outdoor dining area, extensive menu of dishes (including some great salads) for under 1200$00 (plus pricier dishes at night)

Havana (☎ 213 979 893); colourful decor and a simple menu of hamburgers, salads or tapas; live music from Tuesday to Friday. The 'mínimo consumo 10,000$00' sign outside is simply to deter 'undesirables'!

Tertúlia do Tejo (☎ 213 955 552); one of the strip's poshest, with traditional Portuguese fare from 2500$00 to 7000$00 per dish

Cosmos (☎ 213 972 747); specialises in pizzas, salads and pastas for under 1500$00

Celtas & Iberos (☎ 213 976 037); as you'd expect of a Celtic bar, serves dishes with Guinness additions

Zonadoca (☎ 213 972 010); zany decor and classy music, plus a stylish menu of salads, crepes and ices (pricier after 11 pm)

Pasta Caffé (☎ 213 079 607); enticing pastas and pizzas for under 1400$00, in a bright, cheerful setting

To get here, take a train from Cais do Sodré to Alcântara Mar station and then follow the *marítima* signs, turning right to Doca de Santo Amaro. Alternatively, catch tram No 15 from Praça da Figueira, alighting at Dock's Club at Doca de Alcântara.

the roof of the Centro Cultural in Belém. And don't miss the custard tarts at *Pasteis de Belém* (Map 6; see the Pastelarias, Cafes & Confeitarias section later in this chapter).

PLACES TO EAT – MID-RANGE

For a rundown of restaurant-bars in the trendy Doca de Santo Amaro area, see the boxed text 'Chic & Open-Air'.

Rossio & Praça dos Restauradores

Casa do Alentejo (Map 6; ☎ 213 469 231, Rua das Portas de Santo Antão 58) has so-so food (including Alentejan specialities, of course) but an extraordinary setting in a 19th-century melange of Franco-Arabic decor, with a huge ballroom of faded glory and two azulejo-adorned dining rooms (including a cafe). Prices are surprisingly modest. It's closed Monday and summer Saturdays.

Along this same road are cafes and restaurants galore, many specialising in expensive seafood. Nearby *Pinóquio* (Map 6; ☎ 213 465 106, Praça dos Restauradores 79) is less pretentious than most.

Off Avenida da Liberdade is the nicely down-to-earth *O Fumeiro* (Map 6; ☎ 213 474 203, Rua da Conceição da Glória 25), devoted to the cuisine of the mountainous Beira Alta and Serra da Estrela region; even the pictures on the walls are of sausages.

Cervejaria Ribadouro (Map 5; ☎ 213 549 411, Rua do Salitre 2) is a traditional (though modernised) beer hall popular with locals; it has great fare, with prices from around 1300$00.

Baixa

Rua dos Correeiros has lots of good-value places, catering to Portuguese at lunchtime and tourists at night. The pleasantly simple *Restaurante Adega Regional da Beira* (Map 6; ☎ 213 467 014) at No 132 has half-portions for 1000$00. Also popular is the slightly pricier *João do Grão* (Map 6; ☎ 213 424 757) at No 228 and *Lagosta Vermelha* (Map 6; ☎ 213 424 832) at No 155. Up the price scale are *Ena Pãi* (Map 6; ☎ 213 421 759) at No 180, and *Restaurante Múni* (Map 7; ☎ 213 428 982) at No 115.

The popular *Hua Ta Li* (Map 8; ☎ 218 879 170, Rua dos Bacalhoeiros 109) has an East-meets-West menu and more traditional Chinese dishes for around 1000$00 each.

Bairro Alto & Chiado

Tasca do Manel (Map 6; ☎ 213 463 813, Rua da Barroca 24) serves a number of tasty standards from about 1200$00 a dish. Slightly pricier is smart the *Sinal Vermelho*

(Map 6: ☎ 213 461 252, Rua das Gáveas 89); make sure you leave room for its great desserts. Popular places in the same price bracket are *Vá e Volta (Map 6; ☎ 213 427 888, Rua Diário de Notícias 100)* and *Bota Alta (Map 6; ☎ 213 427 959, Travessa da Queimada 35)*. Recommended by an LP reader is nearby *O Barrigas (Map 6; ☎ 213 471 220, Travessa da Queimada 31)*, where prices start at around 1800$00. The small and homy *Mastiga na Tola (Map 6; ☎ 213 477 195, Travessa da Cara 20)* – named after a contemporary bandit (though he doesn't know it) – offers classical music and smiles along with home-cooked fare (dinners only, Tuesday to Saturday) from around 1600$00.

Fancy a couscous? Two places on Rua da Atalaia specialise in Moroccan-style fare: *Ali-a-Papa (Map 6; ☎ 213 472 116)* at No 95 and the newer (slightly cheaper) *Pedro das Arábias (Map 6)* at No 70. Tiny *Tendinha da Atalaia (Map 7; ☎ 213 461 844, Rua da Atalaia 4)* specialises in fish grilled on the spot, while nearby *Sinal Verde (Map 6; ☎ 213 421 601, Calçada do Combro 42)* serves fare from north-eastern Portugal; try the delicious *lulas recheadas* (stuffed squid).

The cavernous *Cervejaria da Trindade (Map 6; ☎ 213 423 506, Rua Nova da Trindade 20-C)* is a former convent building with gorgeous 19th-century azulejos and a robust, busy atmosphere. This cervejaria has been serving food for over 150 years. The beef and seafood grilled dishes (from 1400$00) are especially famous.

Praça das Flores has a couple of places with outdoor tables. *Taberna Espanhola (Map 5; ☎ 213 972 225)* at No 40 is as much a bar as a restaurant, and cheaper *Pão de Panela Pastelaria (Map 5; ☎ 213 972 220)* at No 27 serves lunches for around 1000$00.

Saldanha, Marquês de Pombal & Rato

Popular *Li Yuan (Map 2; ☎ 213 577 740, Rua Viriato 23)* offers enticing Chinese dishes for under 1800$00. The attractive *O Campos (Map 2; ☎ 213 577 196, Rua Filipe Folque 19-A)* offers slow service but good Portuguese fare from around 1300$00.

At *Mãe Preta (Map 2; Avenida António José de Almeida 5-D, 1st floor)*, in the Centro Comercial São João de Deus, you can sample Angolan fare such as *muzongué* (fish broth with sweet potatoes) for around 1400$00.

One of the Rato's artiest eateries is the bar and restaurant *Real Fábrica (Map 4; ☎ 213 872 090, Rua Escola Politécnica 275)*. This converted 19th-century silk factory, famous for its home-brewed beer, serves surprisingly low-cost lunchtime specials (under 1500$00). There's a pleasant outdoor terrace, too, and occasional live music or dance (eg, Sevillian flamenco).

Alfama
The Alfama is an increasingly popular dining area. Among the tempting waterfront restaurants with outdoor seating is *Solar dos Bicos (Map 8; ☎ 218 869 447, Rua dos Bacalhoeiros 8)*, where lunchtime prices start at 800$00 (pricier at night). Brazilian *picanha* (popular dish of grilled, finely sliced beef) is on the menu at *Pincho's (Map 8; ☎ 218 868 008)* in the revamped riverside Doca do Jardim do Tabaco.

In Alfama proper, unpretentious *O Bêco Restaurante Típico (Map 8; ☎ 218 869 945, Rua de São Miguel 87)* is reasonable, despite attracting tourists for its nightly, amateur fado performances. Highly recommended by one reader, the floral-decorated *Malmequer Bemmequer (Map 8; ☎ 218 876 535, Rua de São Miguel 23)* has 'unbelievable food deserving a Michelin star'. A smarter place, with its own lovely shaded courtyard, is *Lautasco (Map 8; ☎ 218 860 173, Beco do Azinhal 7)* where dishes cost from 1400$00. *Mestre André (Map 8; ☎ 218 871 487, Calcadinha Santo Estevão 6)* is a well-hidden, chic little nook with a few outdoor tables and with evening dishes from 1300$00.

Up by the castle, modestly priced *Castelo Mourisco (Map 8; ☎ 218 867 852, Rua Santa Cruz do Castelo 3)* has an unusual *bife à café* (beefsteak with coffee) on its menu. *Gargalhada Geral (Map 8; ☎ 218 878 225, Costa do Castelo 7)*, part of Chapitô, an arts cooperative, offers a refreshingly imaginative menu and an open-air terrace with spectacular views.

PLACES TO EAT

North of Alfama, in the Graça district, popular *Restaurante O Pitéu (Map 5; ☎ 218 871 067, Largo da Graça 95)* has an extensive menu of Portuguese fare for under 1400$00. It's closed Sunday.

Alcântara & Lapa

Assóporco (Map 4; ☎ 213 951 800, Rua das Janelas Verdes) has a one-dish *entrecosta grelhado* deal – marinated grilled pork ribs with potatoes, salad and beans for 1450$00.

As Ilhas (Map 4; ☎ 213 930 934, Calçada Marquês de Abrantes 38) is a recommended Cape Verdean restaurant, serving tasty dishes from 1400$00.

Cais do Sodré & Belém

Traditional *Porto de Abrigo (Map 7; ☎ 213 460 873, Rua dos Remolares 18)* has good seafood and other dishes from 1100$00. Huge helpings (for around 1400$00) are available at *Cervejaria Solar do Kadete (Map 7; ☎ 213 427 255, Cais do Sodré 2)*; the outdoor tables are a bonus. Along Rua do Alecrim are the upmarket *Cervejaria Alemão (Map 7; ☎ 213 422 916)* at No 23, which serves German cuisine as well as Portuguese fare, and *A Charcutaria (Map 7)* at No 47; prices at both start at around 2000$00.

In Belém, head for the row of restaurants on Rua Vieira Portuense, all with outdoor seating overlooking the park. The most reasonably priced place is *Restaurante Floresta (Map 10)* at No 2. *A Cápsula (☎ 213 648 768)* at No 72 is fancier. For cheaper snacks, try *Nau de Belém (Map 10; ☎ 213 638 133, Rua de Belém 29)*. *Adamastor (Map 10; ☎ 363 61 16, Rua de Belém 83)* has a cosy 1st-floor dining area as well as its more casual street-level restaurant.

Parque das Nações

Food and drink is expensive here – even a coffee in a tiny plastic cup costs 100$00. On the plus side, there's airy outdoor seating and great riverside views. Cheapest is the self-service *Oceanário Café (Map 9; ☎ 218 950 204)*, which has soup and sandwiches (and main dishes from 1400$00). *Peter Café Sport (Map 9; ☎ 218 950 060)*, a branch of the legendary outlet in the Azores, also serves bar snacks as well as main meals. Other good bets are the row of restaurants opposite the Marina, catering to office workers, including *Mestre Doce (Map 9; ☎ 218 9446 043)*, where lunchtime dishes cost from 850$00.

If money's no problem, there are some enticing ethnic choices. *Macau (Map 9; ☎ 218 957 204)* has lunchtime specials from 950$00. *Restaurante del Uruguay (Map 9; ☎ 218 955 445)* serves hearty meat dishes including very good *espetada do chefe* (skewered meat) for 1900$00. The adjacent *Os Alentejanos (Map 9; ☎ 218 956 116)* is a lively, fun place where tapas plates cost from 750$00 and main dishes from 1700$00.

You can make reservations at any Parque restaurant by calling ☎ 218 919 666 between 9.30 am and 8.30 pm daily.

PLACES TO EAT – TOP END

For a selection of the best VIP places to eat, see the boxed text 'Celebrity Haunts'.

Bairro Alto & Chiado

La Brasserie de l'Entrecôte (Map 7; ☎ 213 428 344, Rua do Alecrim 117) is high on style and ambience. This spacious modernist venue offers a simple French menu – entrecote, salad and chips (2550$00) – cooked to perfection, accompanied by some superb herb and nut sauces.

The more intimate *Conventual (Map 5; ☎ 213 909 196, Praça das Flores 45)* charges at least 4000$00 per dish for superb and often unusual Portuguese food. It's closed all day Sunday, and Saturday and Monday evening.

Alcântara & Lapa

Alcântara Café (Map 3; ☎ 213 637 176, Rua Maria Luisa Holstein 15) is a design eye-opener, combining neoclassical and Art Deco. It's open evenings only, serving international fare. *Sua Excelência (Map 4; ☎ 213 903 614, Rua do Conde 38)* is small and deluxe; dishes cost at least 4000$00. It's closed Wednesday and weekend lunchtimes.

Brazilian grill house *Churrascaria Porção (Map 5; ☎ 213 932 090, Cais do Santos)* specialises in skewered grilled meat, sushi and live music. It has a zany Californian-style decor and swish service.

Celebrity Haunts

If you want to rub shoulders with the rich and famous (or simply those aspiring to be famous) these are the places to head for. Expect to pay at least 3500$00 a dish.

Belcanto *(Map 7; ☎ 213 420 607, Largo de São Carlos 10)*; favourite haunt of bankers and politicians; famous for its bacalhau dishes; closed weekends

Farinelli *(Map 4; ☎ 213 900 111, Rocha Conde de Óbidos, Cais das Oficinas)*; chic new riverside restaurant dedicated to opera, beautiful people and fine food; closed Sunday

Gambrinus *(Map 6; ☎ 213 421 466, Rua das Portas de Santo Antão 23)*; popular with the elite for over 70 years; refined ambience; superb fish and roast beef (prices from 6000$00)

Pap' Açorda *(Map 6; ☎ 213 464 811, Rua da Atalaia 57)*; startling minimalist decor, excellent, expensive *açorda* (bread and shellfish stew served in a claypot) and legendary chocolate mousse served from a huge tureen; closed Saturday evening and Sunday

Restaurante Japanês Bonsai *(Map 6; ☎ 213 462 515, Rua da Rosa 244)*; elegant and traditional decor, with tatami mats and rice-paper screens; special lunch menu of Japanese specialities; open for lunch Tuesday to Friday and for dinner Monday to Saturday (closed Sunday)

Tagide *(Map 7; ☎ 213 420 720, Largo da Academia Nacional de Belas Artes 18)*; river views outside and 17th-century azulejos inside; Portuguese and French menu; closed Saturday evening and all day Sunday

Tavares Rico *(Map 6; ☎ 213 421 112, Rua da Misericórdia 35)*; strong on tradition (it was founded in 1784) and palatial-style chandeliers; closed for lunch on Saturday and Sunday

Alfama

Top of the range, on both the geographic and culinary scale, is *Casa do Leão (Map 8; ☎ 218 875 962)*, right inside the castle, with a terrace offering panoramic views. Expect to part with at least 3000$00 per dish.

The riverside Doca do Jardim do Tabaco boasts several flashy restaurants including *Jardim do Marisco (Map 8; ☎ 218 824 242)*, where you can feast on lobster (13,500$00), crab and other seafood delicacies. The nearby *Bica do Sapato (Map 5; ☎ 218 810 320, Cais da Pedra à Santa Apolónia)*, another revamped warehouse, is now a vast modernist venue with grand riverside views.

Belém

Well known, upmarket *Restaurante São Jerónimos (Map 10; ☎ 213 648 979, Rua dos Jerónimos 10)* serves very fine food in an artistic setting. It's closed Sunday and Saturday lunchtime.

Portugália (Map 10; ☎ 213 032 700, Edifício Espelho d'Água), right by the water's edge, serves pricey seafood and steaks.

A short walk eastward along the broad riverfront promenade brings you to trendy *Café In (Map 1; ☎ 213 626 249, Avenida de Brasília, Pavilhão Nascente)*, opposite the new congress centre. Dishes cost around 2000$00 (200$00 just for a coffee), but the setting is unbeatable.

VEGETARIAN

Thankfully in a country that so loves its meat, the capital has some good, modestly priced vegetarian restaurants. Most lunchtime dishes start at around 800$00. Our choice for value is *Restaurante Os Tibetanos (Map 5; ☎ 213 142 038, Rua do Salitre 117)*, part of a school of Tibetan Buddhism in an old house topped with prayer flags. It's closed weekends.

Restaurante Espiral (Map 2; ☎ 213 573 585, Praça da Ilha do Faial 14-A) serves macrobiotic rice and vegetable dishes plus lots of desserts – and sometimes live music.

Centro de Alimentação e Saúde Natural (Map 2; ☎ 213 150 898, Rua Mouzinho da Silveira 25) has a peaceful courtyard and a small selection of vegetarian and macrobiotic dishes; it's open weekdays and Saturday until 2 pm.

Celeiro (Map 6; Rua 1 de Dezembro 65) is a health-food shop with a self-service macrobiotic restaurant downstairs (☎ 213 422 463), open 9 am to 7 pm weekdays. Busy *O Sol (Map 6; Calçada do Duque 23)*

PLACES TO EAT

and modest *Yin-Yang* *(Map 7;* ☎ *213 426 551, Rua dos Correeiros 14)* offer macrobiotic and other fare to office workers.

The *restaurant* at the Centro de Arte Moderna in the Gulbenkian museum (Map 2) is open daily for lunch, and serves some great salads. The no-frills self-service canteen, *Superfrutas* *(Map 2; Avenida António Augusto de Águiar 58-H)* has a wide range of salads, fruit platters and *tostas* (toasted sandwiches).

PASTELARIAS, CAFES & CONFEITARIAS

Lisbon has enough pastry shops and coffee shops to keep you buzzing all day. Many also serve cheap lunches. Note that you'll pay quite a lot more to have your coffee or snack outside.

Plain but conveniently located cafes are *Chiadomel* *(Map 6;* ☎ *213 474 401, Rua de Santa Justa 105)*, right by the Elevador de Santa Justa, and gay-friendly *Caffé Rosso* *(Map 7;* ☎ *213 471 524, Rua Garrett 19)* in its own quiet courtyard. Serenaded by seagulls, *Café Atinel* *(Map 5)* is on the water's edge at Cais da Alfândega.

For a great view over the Alfama, the outdoor tables at *Bar Cerca Moura* *(Map 8;* ☎ *218 874 859, Largo das Portas do Sol 4)* are worth the extra escudos. Less touristy cafe-kiosks with similarly fantastic views are at the *miradouros* (viewpoints) of Largo da Graça and Santa Catarina (both Map 5).

Beloved by students and old dears from the neighbourhood is *Confeitaria Císter* *(Map 5; Rua da Escola Politécnica 107)*.

Sweet Treats

Since it first opened in 1829, the *Confeitaria Nacional* on Praça da Figueira (Map 6) has been providing diet-busting pastries and cakes to its patrons. This landmark establishment (it is believed that *bolo-rei*, the Portuguese Christmas cake, was re-created here from an ancient Roman recipe) buzzes with office workers refuelling on sugar and caffeine before and after work.

Somewhat quieter, in cultured surroundings, is the open-air courtyard of Mosteiro de São Vicente de Fora's *Monasterium Café* *(Map 8;* ☎ *218 885 652)*.

The classiest and most famous cafes are in the city centre, many with tempting outdoor seating. Art Deco *Café Nicola* *(Map 6; Rossio 24)* is considered the grande dame of Lisbon's cafes. More long-established *Casa Suiça* *(Map 6; Rossio 96 & Praça da Figueira 3-A)* does a brisk trade with the tourists outside and elderly locals inside. Venerable *Confeitaria Nacional* *(Map 6; Praça da Figueira 18)* nearby has a dizzying array of pastries and sweets. Another attractive place for a stand-up coffee is *Casa Chineza* *(Map 6; Rua Áurea 274)*.

For artistic elegance and public attention, head for *Café A Brasileira* *(Map 7;* ☎ *213 469 547, Rua Garrett 120)*. It has strong literary associations – the bronze statue sitting outside is of the poet and writer Fernando Pessoa, a frequent habitué of the cafe in his day. Nearby *Café Bénard* *(*☎ *211 373 133)* at No 104 is an equally salubrious alternative. You can get (pricey) evening meals here and at *Martinho da Arcada* *(Map 7;* ☎ *218 879 259, Praça do Comércio 3)*. In business since 1782, the latter was once a haunt of Pessoa, too, and other literary notables.

One of the grandest pastelarias in the city – also serving rather expensive meals – is *Versailles* *(Map 2;* ☎ *213 546 340, Avenida da República 15-A)*, with splendidly over-the-top chandeliers and marble columns.

Finally, when you go to Belém, don't miss *Pasteis de Belém* *(Map 10; Rua de Belém 88)*, where the traditional custard tarts called *pastéis de Belém* are made on the premises and consumed in vast quantities.

SELF-CATERING

The there are supermarkets and groceries *(minimercados)* scattered everywhere. The most convenient is the well-stocked *Celeiro* *(Map 6)*, near Rossio station. It even has freshly grilled chicken, as well as foreign brands of cereal, chocolate and other luxuries. The big shopping complexes such as Amoreiras, Colombo and Vasco da Gama also have supermarkets.

Entertainment

Probably the most famous form of entertainment in Lisbon (though not necessarily among lisboêtas themselves) is listening to *fado* – the haunting, melancholy Portuguese equivalent of the blues (see the Arts section in the Facts about Lisbon chapter). Much of it has been expensively packaged for tourists, although you can still find some authentic places. More in tune with local tastes are the city's bars, clubs and discos. Lisbon is as lively as its European neighbours when it comes to nightlife and there are dozens of venues, especially in the traditional nightlife neighbourhood of Bairro Alto, which heaves with revellers at weekends, and the booming riverside dock area of Doca de Santo Amaro, where the local crowd is dressed-down cool. The clubs in the two other popular nightlife areas – Alcântara and Avenida 24 de Julho – are more about flash and cash, often with admission prices to match.

At any club, drinks can be expensive (around 500$00 a beer). Doormen may tell you there's a *consumo mínimo* (minimum consumption) charge – anything from 1000$00 to 5000$00 depending on whether the club is busy, or even how they like the look of you. Some clubs have set admission prices which include a couple of drinks. A few may ask an extortionate amount as a deterrent (they can be unpredictably choosy about their clientele) or simply refuse you entry. Don't be put off – simply move on to the next venue. And the later you move, the better. Evening revels everywhere start late – 11 pm at the earliest – and stagger to a stop any time up until dawn. The Bairro Alto area shuts down earlier than the *docas* (dock areas), where many clubs party till 7 am at weekends. Most places close on Sunday and/or Monday.

Clubs come and go at an amazing pace. Your best bet may be to do what everybody else does: trawl the neighbourhoods to find what appeals to you. Up-and-coming areas benefiting from the official drive to move

Information & Tickets

For information on forthcoming events, check the Turismo de Lisboa's *Follow me Lisboa* free twice-monthly publication, the municipal *Agenda Cultural*, daily listings in *Público* or the Portuguese-only What's On hotline (☎ 217 901 062). The Centro Cultural de Belém (☎ 213 612 444) and Fundação Calouste Gulbenkian (☎ 217 935 131) publish their own monthly programs and have their own Web sites (see under Internet Resources in the Facts for the Visitor chapter).

Tickets for most events are available at Turismo de Lisboa's CRIA centre in Praça do Comércio (Map 7); at the ABEP ticket kiosk (especially for sporting events) in Praça dos Restauradores (Map 6; ☎ 213 475 824); or the Ticket Line agency at the Centro Vasco da Gama shopping mall (Map 9; or at the FNAC store in Centro Comercial Colombo (Map 1; ☎ 217 114 200). The Centro Vasco da Gama shopping mall also has a booking kiosk (Map 9; ☎ 217 120 300).

Ticket agencies specialising in music and theatre shows can be found at the Valentim de Carvalho store (Map 6; ☎ 213 241 570) in Rua do Carmo; FNAC stores in Rua Nova do Almada (Map 7; ☎ 213 221 800) or Centro Comercial Colombo (Map 1; ☎ 217 114 237); or Virgin Megastore (Map 6; ☎ 213 460 309) in Praça dos Restauradores.

Discoteca Bi-Motor at Loja 2044, Amoreiras shopping centre (Map 2; ☎ 213 831 133), specialises in pop-rock concerts and has an online ticket-sales service (Portuguese only) at www.bimotor.pt.

revellers away from residential Bairro Alto include Parque das Nações and the Santa Apolónia waterfront district which boasts the new Lux club (see the boxed text 'John, I'm Only Dancing' later in this chapter).

The bar scene is casual, and even the cooler places are laid-back. Some of the late-night bars in the Bairro Alto now have DJs and are open as late as clubs (and have cheaper drinks).

Although Lisbon has few problems with violence in its bars and discos, there have been recent troubles at some of the African clubs (see Dangers & Annoyances in the Facts for the Visitor chapter). This has undoubtedly cast a shadow over what was previously a very vibrant music scene.

Concerts and shows take place in several main performance halls plus half a dozen other theatres (see the later Classical Music, Opera & Ballet section). Many pop or rock bands choose to kick off their European tours in Lisbon (eg, at the Sony Plaza in the Parque das Nações) as local fans have a reputation as one of the best – meaning wildest – crowds. Admission can be reasonable, too: around 7000$00 to see top names such as Oasis.

Traditional Portuguese entertainment – such as folk music and dancing, parades and processions – can best be enjoyed during the month-long Festas dos Santos Populares (see the boxed text in the Facts for the Visitor chapter) or other festivals both in the city and nearby towns such as Sintra and Estoril. For details of these and other cultural events, see the Public Holidays & Special Events section in the Facts for the Visitor chapter and the boxed text 'What's Free' in the Things to See & Do chapter.

FADO

Listening to Portugal's 'blues' in its authentic form is a wonderfully melancholy way to drink your way through the night, and the Alfama district is said to be its true home. But the sad truth is that many of Lisbon's *casas de fado* offer pale imitations – 'tourbus meets Greek taverna', as one travel writer put it – often packaged with folk dancing and warm-up acts, and at prices to make you moan along with the *fadista*. Nearly all are restaurants and insist that you spend a minimum of around 3000$00 (this usually includes two drinks) or at least 5000$00 for dinner in order to stay and hear the music.

Following are some better known fado houses and an indication of the minimum

CHICO ARAGÃO

Contemporary *fado* **singer,** *Mísia*

charges. All are in Bairro Alto (Map 6) unless otherwise noted.

Adega do Machado (☎ 213 224 640, *Rua do Norte 91)*; long-established venue but rather touristy; 2800$00; music 9.30 pm to 3 am (closed Monday)

Adega do Ribatejo (☎ 213 468 343, *Rua Diário de Notícias 23)*; reasonable food prices and great atmosphere; 2000$00; music 8.30 pm to midnight (closed Sunday)

Adega Mesquita (☎ 213 219 280, *Rua Diário de Notícias 107)*; well known venue with fine fado; 2000$00; 8 pm to 3.30 am

Café Luso (☎ 213 422 281, *Travessa da Queimada 10)*; venerable fado house where Amália began her career; now rather casual with jazz on Thursday and Friday; 3500$00; 9 pm to 3.30 am

Clube do Fado (Map 8; ☎ 218 882 694, *Rua de São João da Praça 92, Alfama)*; small and informal, popular with locals; 2000$00; 8.30 pm to 2 am

Lisboa à Noite (☎ 213 462 603, *Rua das Gáveas 69)*; 2750$00; 8 pm to 3 am (closed Sunday)

euro currency converter **€1 = 200$48**

Moorish-style *quinta* in Monserrate Gardens

A feast of *azulejos* in Palácio Nacional de Sintra

Sintra's exotic Palácio Nacional da Pena

Estoril's beaches are popular with sun-seekers.

Castelo dos Mouros' walls weaving above Sintra

Coastal Cascais is a favourite haunt of *lisboêtas*.

Magnificent Palácio de Queluz

The port of Setúbal is a base for water and land adventure.

Aqueduto das Águas Livres survived the great earthquake of 1755 to carry fresh water to Lisbon.

Palácio-Convento de Mafra was built for Dom João V in the 1700s.

Basilica, Convento de Mafra

NICKY CASTLE

A 12-string *guitarra* – a pear-shaped fado guitar

Nono (☎ 213 468 625, Rua do Norte 47); casual place with atmosphere but no big-name fadistas; 2000$00; 8 pm to 3.30 am

O Bêco Restaurante Típico (Map 8; ☎ 218 874 914, Rua de São Miguel 87, Alfama); small restaurant featuring amateur fadistas; reasonable menu prices, plus 500$00 extra per person for the music; 8.30 pm to midnight

O Forcado (☎ 213 468 579, Rua da Rosa 219); very touristy but often features some excellent fadistas after 11 pm; 3000$00; 8 am to 2 am

Os Ferreiras (Map 5; ☎ 218 850 851, Rua de São Lázaro 150); 2500$00; 9 pm to 2 am Friday and Saturday

Parreirinha de Alfama (Map 8; ☎ 218 868 209, Beco do Espírito Santo 1, Alfama); a favourite with loyal fans; 2000$00; 8 pm to 3 am

Senhor Vinho (Map 4; ☎ 213 972 681, Rua do Meio à Lapa 18, Lapa); you get what you pay for: excellent fado; 3000$00 (dinner from 7000$00); 8.30 pm to 3 am (closed Sunday)

Taverna do Embuçado (Map 8; ☎ 218 865 088, Beco dos Cortumes 10, Alfama); cosy venue that attracts some famous fadistas; 4000$00; 9 pm to 2 am (closed Sunday)

Tímpanas (Map 3; ☎ 213 972 431, Rua Gilberto Rola 24, Alcântara); low-key venue popular with local fado enthusiasts; 2000$00; 8 pm to 2 am (closed Wednesday)

Voz do Operário (Map 8; ☎ 218 862 155, Rua Voz do Operário 13, Alfama); workers' club featuring amateur fado (and folk music) on an occasional Saturday (except August) from 11 pm; 1000$00

DISCOS & CLUBS

Lisbon has scores of discos and clubs, some with occasional live bands, although the main emphasis is on DJs and dance music. Rua Nova do Carvalho (near Cais do Sodré) is the traditional den of discos; most are sleazy dives, although ***Jamaica*** (Map 7; ☎ 213 421 859) at No 6 often features good reggae sounds (especially on Tuesday). Trawl the following areas for better possibilities.

Bairro Alto

This area (Map 6) is a popular starting point for later club-hopping in the docas. The most famous venue here is ***Frágil*** (☎ 213 469 578, Rua da Atalaia 126), the influential club that pioneered the area's nightlife scene in the 1980s. It's still going strong (with a mainly gay clientele), open 11 pm to 4 am (closed Sunday). The doorman may try to put you off by asking for a 5000$00 entry fee.

Another original is ***Os Três Pastorinhos*** (☎ 213 464 301, Rua da Barroca 111-113); one of the first discos in the area, now playing mostly house but occasional acid jazz excursions. It's open 11 pm to 4 am. A place that's popular with the alternative and hard techno crowd is ***Incógnito*** (Map 5; ☎ 213 908 755, Rua dos Poiais de São Bento 37), open 11 pm to at least 4 am (closed Sunday and Monday).

Fun for a quick boogie to cheesy house music is ***espaço fátima lopes*** (☎ 213 240 540, Rua da Atalaia 36), an extremely kitschy disco house in the middle of a boutique. It's open 11.30 pm to 4 am (closed Sunday and Monday).

Avenida 24 de Julho

Before Doca de Santo Amaro stole its thunder, this was the liveliest nightlife area in town (Map 4). Its famous clubs still draw eager clubbers hoping to get past the doorman. Dress smart to try your luck at ***Kapital*** (☎ 213 955 963, Avenida 24 de Julho 68), a hip and happening disco, bar and roof terrace attracting an older, affluent crowd for excellent garage. It's open 11.30 pm to 4 am (closed Monday and Wednesday). ***Kremlin*** (☎ 216 087 768, Escadinhas da Praia 5),

ENTERTAINMENT

notorious for its strict door policy, plays acid and techno to the young and ravey. It's open 1 am to 7 am (to 8 am Friday and Saturday; closed Sunday and Monday).

Less challenging options are *Absoluto* *(Map 5; ☎ 213 955 009, Rua Dom Luís I 5)*, playing music for all tastes, midnight to 4 am Thursday to Saturday (it has a restaurant and bar, too); *Trifásica (Avenida 24 de Julho 66)*, a hip new club/bar with stylish wood curves, open 11.30 pm to 4 am (closed Sunday); and *Indústria (Map 5; ☎ 213 964 841, Rua do Instituto Indústrial 6, Santos)*, a converted factory hugely popular with a fun-loving mixed crowd; open midnight to 6 am (closed Sunday and Monday).

Alcântara

The Doca de Alcântara (Map 4) has a string of converted warehouses providing lots of chic space for party-goers.

Alcântara Mar (Map 3; ☎ 213 636 432, Rua da Cozinha Económica 11); flashy, long-established venue with lingering hints of outrageous flavour,

rock on Wednesday and Thursday, funk on the weekends; plus a stylish cafe *(☎ 213 637 176)*; 11.30 pm to 6 am (closed Monday and Tuesday)

Blues Café (☎ 213 957 085, Rua da Cintura do Porto de Lisboa); a hot spot for those with a penchant for Cajun food; New Orleans-style trad jazz on Thursday; closed Sunday

Discoteca Kings and Queens (☎ 213 977 699, Rua da Cintura do Porto de Lisboa); loud and proud gay club; 10.30 pm to 5 am (closed Sunday)

Dock's Club (☎ 213 950 856, Rua da Cintura do Porto de Lisboa 226); brash, pretentious venue; 10 pm to around 4 am (closed Sunday and Monday)

Gartejo (Map 3; ☎ 213 955 977, Rua João de Oliveira Miguens 38); attracts a young and very trendy crowd; occasional live bands; 10 pm to at least 4 am (closed Sunday)

Indochina (☎ 213 955 875, Rua da Cintura do Porto de Lisboa); impressive, modern, Oriental-themed club, the hippest in the area; 10 pm to around 4 am (closed Monday and Tuesday)

BARS

This section is for people in search of watering holes. Many of these places also have music (sometimes live, sometimes supplied by a DJ) but if you're specifically after dancing see the sections on Discos & Clubs and Live Music.

Alfama

The Alfama (Map 8) is more a place for dining than bar-hopping, but if you're in the area, check out **Costa do Castelo** (☎ 218 884 636, Calçada do Marquês de Tancos 1-B), a bar-restaurant with great city views and live music on Thursday and Friday. It's open 4 pm to 2 am (closed Monday). Other options include **O Esboço** (☎ 218 877 893, Rua do Vigário 10), a plain local bar (ring for entrance) open 11 pm to 2 am (closed Sunday); and **Ópera** (Map 5; ☎ 218 862 318, Travessa das Mónicas 65), open 10 pm to 2 am (Friday and Saturday nights to 3.30 am) and featuring occasional art exhibits.

Bairro Alto & Chiado

Dozens of bars line the narrow streets of this hilly quarter. Check out some of the following (all venures are found on Map 6 unless otherwise noted):

A Capela (☎ 213 470 072, Rua da Atalaia 45); one of the liveliest bars in the area, especially very late; 10 pm to 2 am (Friday and Saturday to 4 am)

Arroz Doce (☎ 213 462 601, Rua da Atalaia 117); cheap, cheerful, boozy and unpretentious; 6 pm to 2 am (closed Sunday)

Café Suave (Map 7; ☎ 213 471 144, Rua do Diário do Notícias 6); friendly, arty crowd; a summertime favourite; 9 pm to 2 am

Cena de Copos (Rua da Barroca 103); heaving with youngsters, especially late; 9 pm to 2 am

Clube Da Esquina (☎ 213 427 149, Rua da Barroca 30); currently one of the most popular bars attracting a flirty young crowd that spills onto the pavement outside; DJs on Friday and Saturday; 10 pm to 4 am

Fremitus (☎ 213 433 632, Rua da Atalaia 78); hip but often pretty quiet; 8.30 pm to 3.30 am nightly

Ma Jong (Map 7; ☎ 213 421 039, Rua da Atalaia 3); often the first stop on a bar-crawl for Lisbon's creative types who dig its minimalist decor; 11 pm to 2.30 am

Nova (☎ 213 462 834, Rua da Rosa 261); scruffy trendy; the back room plays host to Lisbon's cognoscenti; 10 pm to 2 am (Friday and Saturday to 2.30 am)

Pavilhão Chinês (☎ 213 424 729, Rua Dom Pedro V 89); idiosyncratic, early 20th-century decor; pool tables make this a good spot for an early start, although quite touristy; 6 pm to 2 am (from 9 pm Sunday)

Play Bar (Rua da Rosa 225); recently opened style bar so hip it almost hurts; Balearic house music and indie hits from local DJs, funky furniture and a sense of humour make this an essential late stop; midnight to 4 am

Portas Largas (☎ 218 466 379, Rua da Atalaia 105); converted old tavern; casual atmosphere; popular with both straights and gays; a focal point of the Bairro Alto; 8 pm to 4 am

Primas (☎ 213 425 925, Rua da Atalaia 154); noisy, basic local pub with pinball machines and cheap booze; 9.30 pm to 2 or 3 am

Snob Bar (Map 5; ☎ 213 463 723, Rua do Século 178); favourite watering hole (serving meals until about 11 pm) for journalists and the advertising crowd; 4.30 pm to 3 am

Soul Factory Bar (Map 7; Rua das Salgadeiras 28); mainly hip hop but also some reggae, soul, hip hop and funk; 9.30 pm to 3.30 am (closed Tuesday)

Sudoeste (☎ 213 421 672, Rua da Barroca 129); slightly naff cocktail bar and small disco; 6 pm to 3 am weekends only

Work in Progress (Map 7; ☎ 218 866 532, Rua da Bica Duarte Belo 47); bizarre combination of clothes shop and bar, with live music on Wednesday; 10 pm to 4 am

Solar do Vinho do Porto

The Instituto do Vinho do Porto (Port Wine Institute) is an autonomous, Porto-based agency with the job of maintaining the reputation of the port-wine appellation by controlling its quality and output, as well as promoting it generically. Among other things, it runs **Solar do Vinho do Porto** (Map 6; ☎ 213 475 707, fax 213 478 392, e solarlisboa@ivp.pt, Rua de São Pedro de Alcântara 45), in an old palace right at the top of the Elevador da Glória, in the Bairro Alto.

Here, in a refined, living-room-like setting, you can select from around 200 varieties of port wine, costing from 250$00 to 800$00 (or more) a glass. Snacks such as cheese (especially queijo de Serra), nuts and even chocolate cake (which apparently goes very well with port) are also available. You can also peruse (or buy) books and other information on port wine. It's open from 2 pm to midnight daily except Sunday. The institute has its own Web site at www.ivp.pt.

Cais do Sodré

This is a rather seedy area (Map 7), but Brits may like to check out *British Bar* (☎ *213 422 367, Rua Bernardino Costa 52)* for its traditional pub paraphernalia and choice of 42 beers (open 10 am to 2 am). Guinness-lovers can head for *Hennessy's Irish Pub* (☎ *213 431 064, Rua Cais do Sodré 38)*, open noon to 1 am (4 am at weekends); or the cheerier *Ó Gilíns Irish Pub* (☎ *213 421 899, Rua dos Remolares 8-10)* open 11 am to 2 am. This also has live traditional Irish music on most Thursday and Saturday nights and live jazz with brunch on Sunday.

Considerably slicker is *Bar do Rio* (☎ *213 467 279, Armazém 7, Cais de Santos)*, a small, exclusive bar open 11 pm to 6 am; you'll probably have to fork out a 5000$00 minimum consumption charge.

Avenida 24 de Julho

Useful watering holes for late-night club-bers (all on Map 4) include *Cervejinhas e Comidinhas* (☎ *213 908 050, Avenida 24 de Julho 78-B)*, popular with a youngish crowd (closed Sunday); *Décibel* (☎ *213 961 729, Avenida 24 de Julho 90-B/C)*, which has psychedelic rock and visuals to match; and *Paulinha* (☎ *213 964 783, Avenida 24 de Julho 82-A)*, attracting all ages nightly except Sunday and Monday. All are open from around 11 pm to 3 am. *Gringo's Café* (☎ *213 960 911, Avenida 24 de Julho 116)* is a typical Tex-Mex theme cafe-bar with spicy eats until 1 am (closed Sunday).

Doca de Santo Amaro

This strip of bar-restaurants (all on Map 3) can be pricey but their location is unbeatable. *Celtas & Iberos* (☎ *213 976 037)*, open 12.30 pm to 2 am (closed Monday) will appeal to homesick Dubliners. *Hawaii* (☎ *213 958 110)* is a hedonistic venue, identifiable by the giant surfboard sticking through its roof. At the end of the strip is *Cafe da Ponte* (☎ *213 957 669)*, a chic drinking den.

GAY & LESBIAN VENUES

There are many gay bars and clubs clustered in the hills of Rato and the northern Bairro Alto (Map 5). For up-to-date listings,
check the Web sites mentioned in the Gay & Lesbian Travellers section of the Facts for the Visitor chapter.

Bar Água no Bico (☎ *213 472 830, Rua de São Marçal 170)*; crowded, friendly cyberbar popular with students; 9 pm to 2 am

Bar 106 (☎ *213 427 373, Rua de São Marçal 106)*; one of the best and busiest, with a friendly atmosphere; 9 pm to 2 am

Bric-a-Bar or *O Brica* (☎ *213 428 971, Rua Cecilio de Sousa 84)*; oldest and one of the largest gay bars in town, with two floors and two bars; 9 pm to 4 am

Finalmente (☎ *213 479 923, Rua da Palmeira 38)*; famous drag shows nightly (around 2 am); gets crowded; 10 pm to 5 am

Memorial (☎ *213 968 891, Rua da Gustavo de Matos Sequeira 42-A)*; very popular; predominantly lesbian; 11 pm to 3.30 am (closed Monday

Mister Gay (☎ *962 586 803, Quinta Silveira, Via Rápida, Monte da Caparica)*; large popular disco across the river near Costa da Caparica (see Map 12); transvestite shows on Friday and Saturday

Portas Largas (Map 6; ☎ *213 466 379, Rua da Atalaia 105)*; converted old tavern, also quite popular with straights; often patronised by fashion-world types; 8 pm to 4 am

Sétimo Céu (Map 6; ☎ *213 466 471, Travessa da Espera 54)*; small, with an easy-going atmosphere and mixed youthful crowd, gay icon music, occasionally fado; 10 pm to 2 am

Trumps (☎ *213 971 059, Rua da Imprensa Nacional 104-B)*; largest, best known gay club in town, with a huge dance floor (striptease shows twice weekly), pool tables, cafe and three bars; 10 pm to 6 am

LIVE MUSIC

Young Lisbon may be more interested in the dance floor beats right now, but there are still places in the city playing live music.

Rock & Pop

Lisbon's biggest live rock (plus occasional heavy metal) venue is *Rock City (Map 5; ☎ 213 428 640, Rua Cintura do Porto de Lisboa, Armazém 225)*, a huge – and hugely popular – club with a restaurant and four bars (two in a tropical garden), open midnight to 4 am (closed Monday).

Live rock and dancing also features at *Álcool Puro (Map 4; ☎ 213 967 467, Avenida Dom Carlos I 59)*, open from 11 pm to 4 am

ENTERTAINMENT

(closed Sunday); and *Até Qu'Enfim* (Map 4; ☎ 213 965 939, Rua das Janelas Verdes 2, Lapa), open 10 pm to 2 am daily. At the club *Anos 60* (Map 5; ☎ 218 873 444, Largo do Terreirinho 21) you can bop to live 60s music between 9.30 pm and 3 am on Friday and Saturday (closed Sunday).

Jazz
The *Hot Clube de Portugal* (Map 5; ☎ 213 467 369, Praça da Alegria 39) is the city's only dedicated jazz club, featuring live acts (mostly modern) at 11 pm and 1.30 am, at least three or four nights weekly. Check out the club's Web site at www.isa.utl.pt/HCP/HCPhome.html. It's open 10 pm to 2 am (closed Sunday and Monday).

Smaller, more casual venues include *Tertúlia* (Map 6; ☎ 213 462 704, Rua Diário de Notícias 60), with some live jazz plus a piano for anyone to tinkle (open 10.30 pm to 2 am except Sunday); and *Café Luso* (see under Fado earlier), a fado house featuring live jazz 8 pm to 3.30 am on Thursday and Friday. *Speakeasy* (Map 4; ☎ 213 957 308, Cais da Rocha do Conde de Óbidos, Doca do Alcântara) is bigger, if less atmospheric, with live blues and jazz jam sessions 6 pm to 4 am (closed Sunday).

The Fundação Calouste Gulbenkian and Hot Clube de Portugal jointly organise an excellent international jazz festival at the foundation's open-air amphitheatre (Map 2) in early August.

African
The African music scene (with its roots predominantly in Cape Verdean, but also Mozambique, Guinea-Bissau and Angola) bops in bars all over town. Some of the better known venues include:

B.leza (Map 5; ☎ 213 963 735, Largo do Conde Barão 50); atmospheric venue in historic building, with Creole and Cape Verde music; 10.30 pm to 5 am (closed Monday)
Café Be Pop (Map 6; ☎ 213 421 626, Rua Luz Soriano 18); live Latin-African (eg, from Guinea-Bissau) and jazz sounds, especially Saturday nights; closed Sunday and Monday
Discoteca A Lontra (Map 4; ☎ 395 69 68, Rua de São Bento 15); well known venue with music after midnight (closed Monday)

Enclave (Map 4; ☎ 213 888 738, Rua do Sol ao Rato 71-A); long-established informal Cape Verdean haunt, best on Saturday; 9 pm to 4 am (closed Sunday and Monday)
Kussunguila (Map 3; ☎ 213 633 590, Rua dos Lusíadas 5); one of the hippest African clubs; 11 pm to 6 am nightly (live music Monday and Thursday)
Luanda (Map 3; ☎ 213 633 959, Travessa de Teixeira Junior 6); newish addition to the African music boom; midnight to 6 am
Mussulo (Map 2; ☎ 213 556 872, Rua Sousa Martins 5-D); hugely popular Angolan club (especially on Sunday) with some sensual beats and great DJs; 11 pm to dawn (closed Monday and Tuesday)
Ritz Clube (Map 6; ☎ 213 465 998, Rua da Glória 57); mainly Cape Verdean; late meals; 10 pm to 4 am (closed Sunday)

Latin American
For live Brazilian rhythms, ring the bell at *Pé Sujo* bar (Map 8; ☎ 218 865 629, Largo de São Martinho 6, Alfama); it's closed Monday. Other options include *Havana* (Map 3; ☎ 213 979 893, Doca de Santo Amaro), a Cuban bar and restaurant (open noon to 4 am daily) with live Brazilian music on Friday; the *Salsa Latina* (Map 3; ☎ 213 950 550, Gare Marítima de Alcântara), a restaurant-cum dance hall with live music nightly and a salsa dance teacher at hand on Friday; and *Pilom* (Map 3; ☎ 213 648 640, Rua do Alvito 10), which provides lively salsa beats and samba 11 pm to 6 am nightly except Sunday.

CLASSICAL MUSIC, OPERA & BALLET
Thanks to the 1755 earthquake (which destroyed venues and music libraries), and 20th-century political upheavals, cultural repression and later government apathy to the arts, Lisbon's classical music scene is pretty paltry. Portugal's only major orchestras are the Orquestra Gulbenkian and the state-sponsored Orquestra Sinfônica Portuguesa (based at Teatro Camões). Lisbon also has its own Orquestra Metropolitana de Lisboa. None of them is world class.

Opera performances take place in the city's handsome 18th-century opera house, *Teatro Nacional de São Carlos* (Map 7;

☎ *213 465 914, Rua Serpa Pinto 9)*. The two leading dance companies are the contemporary dance group, Ballet Gulbenkian, and the largely classical Companhia Nacional de Bailado (based at Teatro Camões).

Most classical music and dance performances are held at one of the three halls of the **Fundação Calouste Gulbenkian** *(Map 2;* ☎ *217 935 131)*, the **Centro Cultural de Belém** *(Map 10;* ☎ *213 612 444)*, **Teatro Camões** *(Map 9;* ☎ *218 917 725)* or **Teatro Municipal de São Luís** (see later).

Theatres & Concert Halls

Lisbon's fanciest theatres are the **Teatro Nacional de Dona Maria II** *(Map 6;* ☎ *213 422 210)*, the historic city centre theatre dominating Praça Dom Pedro IV, and the equally venerable **Teatro Municipal de São Luís** *(Map 7;* ☎ *213 427 172, Rua António Maria Cardoso 54)*, which also has a studio theatre, **Teatro Estúdio Mário Viegas** *(*☎ *213 471 279)*. Check its Web site at www.cteatralchiado.pt.

Major new venues in the Parque das Nações (Map 9) include the **Sony Plaza** *(*☎ *218 918 409)*, Lisbon's largest open-air theatre, used for concerts and special events; the **Pavilhão Atlântico** *(Atlantic Pavilion;* ☎ *218 918 471)*, Portugal's largest indoor arena, catering to big shows (and sporting events); and the modernist **Teatro Camões** (see earlier).

Other places where you can catch drama, music, pop-rock or more bizarre events are:

Agência 117 Theatre *(Map 6;* ☎ *213 461 270, Rua do Norte 117)*; one of the more unusual venues, doubling as a clothes shop and hairdresser's salon as well as an ad-hoc venue for off-beat performances

Aula Magna da Reitoria *(Map 1;* ☎ *217 967 624, Alameda da Universidade)*; university venue used mainly for pop and rock concerts

Coliseu dos Recreios *(Map 6;* ☎ *213 240 580, Rua das Portas de Santo Antão 92)*; long-established venue for all kinds of music events or shows

Cordoaria Nacional *(Map 1;* ☎ *213 630 796, Avenida da India)*; 200-year-old former rope and sail-making factory now hosting exhibitions and special events

Culturgest *(Map 2;* ☎ *217 905 155, Edifício Caixa Geral de Depósitos, Rua do Arco do Cego)*; art gallery and exhibition venue as well as theatre (galleries open 10 am to 5.30 pm weekdays except Tuesday, and 3 to 7 pm weekends); theatre often hosts unusual performances

Espaço Oikos *(Map 8;* ☎ *218 866 134, Rua de São Tiago 9)*; an attractive building hosting art exhibits, drama and dance performances

Institut Franco-Portugais de Lisbonne *(Map 2;* ☎ *213 111 477, Avenida Luís Bívar 91)*; occasional performances by visiting French artists and companies

Paradise Garage *(Map 3;* ☎ *213 957 157, Rua João Oliveira Miguens 48)*; pop and rock concerts (especially for the Super Bock Super Rock festival)

Teatro Aberto *(Map 2;* ☎ *217 970 969, Praça de Espanha)*; specialises in classical (eg, German) plays

Teatro Municipal Maria Matos *(Map 1;* ☎ *218 497 007, Avenida Frei Miguel Contreras 52)*; Teatro Infantil de Lisboa (Lisbon Children's Theatre) plays during term time

Teatro da Trindade *(Map 6;* ☎ *213 423 200, Rua Nova da Trindade 9)*; dance, jazz and popular musical shows

Teatro Taborda *(Map 8;* ☎ *218 854 190, Rua Costa do Castelo 75, Alfama)*; small new venue (with cybercafe) often featuring young, independent drama groups

CINEMAS

Lisbon has some 60 cinemas, most showing current blockbusters (subtitled, not dubbed). Swankiest are the Warner-Lusomundo and other multiplexes in the shopping malls of **Galerias Monumental** *(Map 2;* ☎ *213 531 859)*, **Amoreiras** *(Map 2;* ☎ *213 878 752)* and **Centro Comercial Colombo** *(Map 1;* ☎ *217 113 200)*. One of the oldest remaining central cinemas is **São Jorge** *(Map 5;* ☎ *213 579 144, Avenida da Liberdade 175)*.

A ticket at these complexes costs 850$00 to 950$00, with prices often reduced to 600$000 on Monday in an effort to lure audiences away from home videos. **Instituto da Cinemateca Portuguesa** *(Map 5;* ☎ *213 546 279, Rua Barata Salgueiro 39)*, shows international classics twice daily for a bargain 400$00. You can find comprehensive listings in *Público*.

SPECTATOR SPORTS

If you're into athletics, check to see if any major championships are taking place in venues such as the Pavilhão Atlântico at the

Man, Bull & Horse

A typical *tourada* (bullfight) starts with a huge bull charging into the ring towards a *cavaleiro*, a horseman dressed in elaborate 18th-century-style costume and plumed tricorn hat (so far, there's only one female *cavaleira* or mounted bullfighting woman in the world, the 24-year-old Portuguese Marta Manuela). The 500kg bull has his horns capped with metal balls or leather, but he's still an awesome adversary. The cavaleiro sizes him up as his backup team of *peões de brega* (footmen) distract and provoke the bull with capes. Then, with incredible horse-riding skills, he gallops within inches of the bull's horns and plants a number of short, barbed *bandarilha* spears into the bull's neck.

The next phase of the fight, the *pega*, features a team of eight young, volunteer *forcados* dressed in breeches, white stockings and short jackets, who face the bull barehanded, in a single line. The leader swaggers towards the bull from across the ring, provoking it to charge. Bearing the brunt of the attack, he throws himself onto the animal's head and grabs the horns while his mates rush in behind him to try and immobilise the beast, often being tossed in all directions in the process. Their success marks the end of the contest and the bull is led out of the pen among a herd of steers. Though the rules for Portuguese bullfighting prohibit a public kill, the hapless animal is usually dispatched in private afterwards.

Another style of performance (often the final contest in a day-long *tourada*) is similar to the Spanish version, with a *toureiro* challenging the bull – its horns uncapped – with cape and bandarilhas. Unlike in Spain, however, there's no *picador* on horseback to weaken the bull with lances. It's man against beast. And, unlike in Spain, the kill is symbolic, a short bandarilha feigning the thrust of a sword.

MICK WELDON

Parque das Nações. The Turismo de Lisboa will have information.

Football

Lisboêtas are as obsessed as everybody else in Portugal with football (soccer). Of Portugal's major three club sides, two – SL Benfica (Sport Lisboa e Benfica) and rival team, Sporting (Sporting Club de Portugal) – are based in Lisbon.

Despite the more illustrious history of Benfica (one of Europe's most famous footballing names), the 2000 season saw a Sporting renaissance (for many in Lisbon, the team of the people) when it became the national champion after a five-year winning streak by arch-rivals FC Porto. Benfica, recently plagued by financial scandals, now appears to be in decline.

The season runs from September to mid-June, and most league matches are held on Sunday; check the papers (especially *Bola*, the daily football paper) or ask at the turismo. Tickets are cheap (from around 600$00) and are sold at the stadium on match day or you can buy them, for slightly inflated prices, at the ABEP ticket agency on Praça dos Restauradores.

SL Benfica plays at the recently upgraded Estádio da Luz (also called Estádio SL Benfica) in the north-western Benfica district (Map 1; metro: Colégio Militar-Luz). For ticket information call ☎ 217 266 129 or contact Benfica's inquiries office (☎ 217 276 961, fax 217 264 761). Its Web site is at www.slbenfica.pt.

Sporting plays at the Estádio José de Alvalade, just north of the Universidade de

euro currency converter 100$00 = €0.50

Lisboa (Map 1; metro: Campo Grande or take bus No 1 or 36 from Rossio). For any information call ☎ 217 589 021 or fax 217 599 391. A new stadium here (along with the Estádio da Luz) will host Euro 2004 matches.

The Estádio Nacional (National Stadium; ☎ 214 197 241), which hosts the national Taça de Portugal (Cup Final) in May, is in Cruz Quebrada, west of Lisbon (take the train from Cais do Sodré).

Bullfighting

Bullfighting is still quite popular in Portugal, despite pressure from international animal-rights activists. Lisbon, like nearly every town in the country, has its own *praça de touros* (bullring) – an eye-catching Moorish-style building across Avenida da República from Campo Pequeno metro station.

Fights traditionally take place from April through October, usually on Thursday (and occasionally Sunday). Tickets, on sale outside the bullring, range from 3000$00 to 11,000$00, depending on whether you want a *sol* (sunny), *sol e sombra* (sunny and shady) or *sombra* (shady) seat. You can also buy tickets from the ABEP ticket agency on Praça dos Restauradores.

You can see more traditional bullfights in bull-breeding Ribatejo province, especially in Santarém during its June agricultural fair and in Vila Franca de Xira during the town's July and October festivals. See the Treatment of Animals section in the Facts about Lisbon chapter for more on the background of bullfighting, and the boxed text 'Man, Bull & Horse' earlier in this chapter for a description of a typical Portuguese *tourada*.

Shopping

Lisbon is a tempting place to shop, if only because street life moves slowly enough to make browsing a pleasure. And although modern shopping centres are increasingly in vogue you can still find plenty of traditional and specialist shops. Prices, too, are generally attractive – among the lowest in Europe, particularly for shoes and leather items. During the summer sales many clothes shops – even designer outlets – offer discounts of up to 50%.

Most city centre shops are open 9 am to 1 pm and 3 to 7 pm on weekdays and close at 1 pm on Saturday. Shopping mall shops often stay open as late as 10 or 11 pm daily. A chain of small grocery stores, Select Shops, is open until 2 am daily (a relatively central one is at Avenida Miguel Bombarda 59-B; Map 2). During the month of August, many shopkeepers take a break *para férias* (for holidays) for a week or so.

If you live outside the EU and spend more than 11,700$00 at a shop that's a member of the Europe Tax-Free Shopping Portugal scheme, your purchase will be eligible for a VAT refund of 17%. See Taxes & Refunds under Money in the Facts for the Visitor chapter for details.

Most major stores (but not the smaller, more traditional ones) can arrange the shipping of goods home, though it's likely to take a minimum of three weeks.

WHAT TO BUY

Some of the best buys are the uniquely Portuguese products such as azulejos, ceramics and handicrafts and, of course, port wine. If you're into haute couture, this is a great place to find all the latest bank-breaking fashions by leading Portuguese designers.

Antiques

For upmarket antiques, trawl Rua de São Bento (west of Bairro Alto; Map 4) or Rua Dom Pedro V (north of Bairro Alto; Map 6), where you'll find everything from porcelain and crystal to Indo-Portuguese furniture.

Get Your Discounts Here!

Turismo de Lisboa's Shopping Card guarantees holders discounts of up to 20% in over 200 selected shops in the best shopping districts in the city area (Baixa, Chiado and Avenida da Liberdade). Available at all Turismo de Lisboa outlets, the card costs 500/900$00 for 24/72-hour versions.

More down-to-earth (though not necessarily cheaper) are the shops in Campo de Santa Clara, near Igreja de São Vincente de Fora (Map 8). Especially busy on days when the adjacent flea market is in full swing (see the boxed text 'Markets' later in this chapter), they offer everything from glass, ceramics and religious statuettes to furniture, silver and jewellery.

Keep an eye out for the occasional antique shop to be found in the Alfama district, too, eg, Casa Domingues (Map 8), Rua de Santa Marinha 3, and the posher Antiguidades Outro Era (Map 8) at Largo Santo António de Sé 15. In Bairro Alto, the tiny O Velho Sapateiro (Map 6) at Travessa da Queimada 46 has some intriguing items, including old postcards of Portugal and Spain.

Beyond Lisbon, Sintra's São Pedro district is renowned for its antique shops; its twice-monthly fair also hosts a few stalls of the flea-market variety.

Azulejos & Ceramics

Lisbon has many azulejos factories and showrooms. One of the finest (and priciest) is Fábrica Sant'Ana (Map 7), the pink building at Rua do Alecrim 95. The street-level showroom is open 9 am to 7 pm weekdays and 10 am to 2 pm on Saturday. The factory is upstairs, along with what look to be the offices of azulejo-makers' guilds. More affordable azulejo souvenirs can be found at the attractive Museu Nacional dos Azulejo (see the Things to See & Do chapter).

Other good outlets include the following:

Cerâmica Viúva Lamego (Map 5; ☎ 218 852 402) Largo do Intendente Pina Manique 25; azulejos (including made-to-order items) and other ceramic ware

Olaria do Desterros (Map 5; ☎ 218 850 329) Rua Nova do Desterro 14; venerable, family-run pottery factory in a neighbourhood of warehouses and hospitals; the entrance is at entry F in an alley, seemingly within the grounds of the Hospital do Desterro

Ratton (Map 5; ☎ 213 460 948) Rua da Academia Ciências; more of a gallery than a shop, both displaying and selling some of the best hand-made contemporary azulejo creations in the country, by such leading names as Jorge Martins and Paula Rego

Vista Alegre (Map 7; ☎ 213 428 612) Rua Ivens 53 and Largo do Chiado 20; the most famous name in ceramic manufacturers, with finely crafted products at a number of stores around the city

Modern Art & Sculpture

Lisbon has around 100 art galleries, most holding occasional exhibitions by individual artists whose work they may offer for sale exclusively. Contemporary Portuguese art represents some intriguing and good-value buys, especially in the avant-garde movement. If you're more interested in modern sculpture, check out the art gallery in the Estoril Casino, which displays and sells the compositions of around 50 contemporary sculptors who often work with Portuguese white marble.

When buying any artwork, be sure to ask for a certificate guaranteeing authenticity, signed by both the gallery owner and artist. Any gallery can arrange packing and shipping of your purchase.

Galeria III (Map 1) Campo Grande 111; the most internationally famous gallery in Lisbon, representing big-name artists such as Paula Rego; some prints available too

Galeria Arte Periférica (Map 10) at the Centro Cultural de Belém; particular emphasis on the work of younger artists

Novo Século (Map 5) Rua do Século 23; specialises in modernist art

Books

With the boom in tourism to Lisbon – and in megastores stocking everything from music to literature – there's an increasingly wide range of English (and some French and German) books available. The swanky FNAC store (see under Music) has a particularly good selection of translated Portuguese literature on offer.

The older, traditional *livrarias* (book-shops) have limited foreign-language titles, mostly guidebooks and a few translated Portuguese classics. The exception is the city's biggest bookseller, Livraria Bertrand, which stocks books in English, French and German (plus an impressive range of kids' titles in both English and Portuguese). Its main store (Map 7; ☎ 213 421 941) is at Rua Garrett 73 but there are at least half a dozen other branches, including one in the Centro Comercial Colombo (Map 1).

For second-hand books, check out several enticing shops along Calçada do Carmo (behind Rossio train station; Map 6) and a couple of stalls in the arcade near the Praça do Comércio end of Rua Augusta (Map 7). Other bookshops are listed below.

Editorial Notícias (Map 6) Rossio 23; some French and English-language books including guidebooks and coffee-table books

Livraria Britânica (Map 5) Rua de São Marça 83, opposite the British Council; exclusively English-language books (including for kids)

Speciality Shops

Searching for a satin glove? A trilby hat with a red silk band? Or a made-to-measure shirt? You won't have to go very far to find them. Camisaria Pitta, at Rua Augusta 195, in the Baixa district, is one of the oldest shirt makers in Lisbon, with quality men's and women's clothes as well as superb made-to-measure shirts. At nearby Rossio 69 you'll find Azevedo Rua, the hat fanatic's haven, stocked with mostly men's hats for every occasion. And for elegant gloves in leather or lace, satin or silk, head for Luvaria Ulisses, at Rua do Carmo 87, the smallest and most exquisite little Art Deco shop in Lisbon. All these shops can be found on Map 6.

Livraria Buchholz (Map 2) Rua Duque de Palmela 4; a huge literature collection in Portuguese, English, French and German

Librairie Française (Map 2) Avenida Marquês de Tomar 38; Lisbon's only exclusively French bookshop

Livraria Municipal (Map 2) Avenida da República 21-A; elegant shop devoted entirely to Lisbon, with books on city history, art and architecture (including a few titles in English), and easy chairs

Livraria Portugal (Map 6) Rua do Carmo 70; limited range of French and English-language books, especially art and history

Valentim de Carvalho Megastore (Map 6) Edifício Grandella, Rua do Carmo; best known for its CDs and cassettes, but a fair range of books on the 1st floor, too.

Clothes

Except during the summer sales, or at the outdoor markets, you won't necessarily find great clothing bargains, but the range is impressive. Some of the best souvenirs are Portugal T-shirts (Sintra has its own range of attractive designs).

Popular high-street Spanish chains selling stylish women's clothes are Zara (see below for details of some stores) and Mango at Rua Augusta 43. Mango's menswear equivalent is the good-value Massimo Dutti (Map) at 5 Avenida da Liberdade 114. All of these have branches at Centro Comercial Colombo shopping mall.

Children's Clothes Thanks to the attention lavished on Portuguese kids, children's clothes shops seem to be everywhere. The following are some of the best:

Cenoura (Map 6) Rua Augusta 221 and Centro Vasco da Gama (Map 9); famous chain of children's shops, with zany designs for teenagers

Maison Louvre (Map 6) Rossio 106; gear for toddlers to 10-year-olds

O Palhaço (Map 7) Rua Augusta 97; upmarket range of items for babies and toddlers

Rabimos (Map 6) Rossio 94; trendy stuff for toddlers to teenagers

Zara (Map 7) Rua Garrett 1-9 (and several other branches in and around Lisbon including Rua Augusta 71, CascaiShopping and Centro Vasco da Gama); highly popular, good-value Spanish chain of stylish shops selling bright, casual cotton clothes for all ages

Designer Clothes Worth a look, even if you're not digging deep enough into your pocket to actually buy anything, are some of the imaginative designs by leading Portuguese designers. These are now gaining international prestige, and attracting increasing attention at the twice-annual ModaLisboa fashion trade shows. The main Turismo de Lisboa centre, CRIA, in Praça do Comércio, displays a sample at its ModaLisboa shop. Or visit Gardenia (Map 7), at Rua Garrett 54, which stocks a selection of both national and international contemporary designs. You can also check out the latest Lisbon looks at the following specific designer outlets:

Ana Salazer (Map 6) Rua do Carmo 87; very feminine and distinctive designs, sold here and in Paris *21.347.2289*

Augustus (Map 7) Rua Augusta 55 and Centro Vasco da Gama; famous stylist of women's clothes

Fátima Lopes (Map 6) Rua da Atalaia 36; internationally successful collections displayed in funky shop-cum-disco

José António Tenente (Map 6) Travessa do Carmo 8; classy wear and accessories for both men and women

Lena Aires (Map 6) Rua da Atalaia 96; leading name for women's fashions, mainly *prêt-a-porter*

Loja Branca (Map 5) Praça das Flores 48; daring women's clothes, often in natural materials, by Manuela Gonçalves

Shoes

Lisbon, as elsewhere in Portugal, abounds i* *sapaterias* (shoe shops), although you m have a hard time finding big sizes. *T* Avenida de Roma in the north of *t*

...ıap 1; metro: Roma) to check out renowned shops such as Hera at No 37-A, Mocci at No 61-A or Stivali at nearby Avenida João XXI 11. Amoreiras and Centro Vasco da Gama shopping malls have branches of these shops, too (plus the popular Pablo Fuster Spanish shoe shops). You'll also find dozens of shoe shops in the Baixa district, especially along Rua Augusta (Map 6).

Handicrafts & Textiles

A fascinating (if rather overpublicised) *artesanato* is Santos Ofícios (Map 7) at Rua da Madalena 87, with an eclectic range of folk art from all around Portugal. It's open 10 am to 8 pm daily, except Sunday. Another very good source of select, high-quality handicrafts from all over Portugal including straw dolls, hand-woven cotton and linen clothes, and ceramic and wooden objects is Rua do Teixeira 25. Casa Regional (Map 7), at Rua Paiva Andrade 4, specialises in handicrafts and embroideries from the Azores.

For hand-embroidered linen from its most famous source, Madeira, head for Madeira House (Map 7), at Rua Augusta 131, or Príncipe Real (Map 5) at Rua da Escola Politécnica 12. An unnamed shop (Map 5) at Avenida da Liberdade 159 stocks a wide selection of traditional Portuguese handicrafts, souvenirs and T-shirts.

If you're around in July or August, you'll find a sizable handicrafts fair at Estoril (see the Excursions chapter) where you can pick up unique items handcrafted locally. The following shops are also worth checking out:

Arte Rústica (Map 6) Rua Áurea 246; quality T-shirts, hand-painted ceramics, hand-embroidered tablecloths, and other items from Madeira
Casa Achilles (Map 5) Rua de São Marçal 194; bronzeware
Casa das Corticas (Map 5) Rua da Escola Politécnica 4; cork items, especially from cork's homeland, the Alentejo region
Caza das Vellas Loreto (Map 7) Rua do Loreto
~~...orable~~ candle shop that has been around
    ~~...~~es

~~...~~st-established outlet for CDs
~~...~~ covering the whole spectrum
~~...~~m pop-rock, alternative and

Brazilian strains to fado, jazz and classical music is Valentim de Carvalho, whose Megastore (☎ 213 241 570) is in Edifício Granella (Map 6), Rua do Carmo. It's open 10 am to 8 pm weekdays (to midnight Friday and Saturday) and noon to 8 pm Sunday.

There's a Virgin Megastore (Map 6) in the fabulous Art Deco Teatro Eden building in Praça dos Restauradores and also a well-stocked FNAC store (Map 7) in the Armazéns do Chiado, Rua Nova do Almeida 110, plus a branch in Centro Comercial Colombo (Map 1), which sells a vast array of audiovisual gear and music. The following outlets are more specialised:

Discoteca Amália (Map 6) Rua Áurea 272; strong on fado and other traditional Portuguese music
Discoteca Opus (Map 6) Loja 222, Centro Mouraria Martim Moniz, Largo Martim Moniz; African music, techno and zouk sounds
Illegal (Map 6) Rua 1 de Dezembro; hip, groovy clothes as well as the latest hip hop and techno CDs
raveman records (Map 6) Travessa da Queimada 33; house, techno and other dance music
Violino (Map 6) Calçada do Sacramento; the place for fado guitars and other musical instruments

Contemporary Furniture & Jewellery

Emporio Casa (Map 5) at Rua da Escola Politécnica 42 showcases the best in contemporary furniture and accessories. Even if you're not in the market for a designer teapot, this beautiful three-storey store is well worth a browse both for the modern Portuguese design on show as well as the hip lisboêtas who buy it.

The Dom Pedro V Joias shop (Map 6) at Rua Dom Pedro V 9 is a trendy outlet for pricey, modern jewellery.

Wine & Port

Portuguese wine of any variety – red, white or rosé; *maduro* (mature) or semisparkling young *vinho verde* – offers very good value. And you needn't hunt for specialist shops; most supermarkets stock decent stuff (from as little as 1000$00), which should please the snobbiest amateur taste buds.

If it's port wine you're after, have a taste at the Solar do Vinho do Porto, Rua de São

Pedro de Alcântara 45 in Bairro Alto (Map 6; see the boxed text in the Entertainment chapter). Then head for the supermarket or one of the following shops which have an enormous array of both wine and port. It helps if you know roughly what you want, but staff can usually offer recommendations. Don't despair if you leave your port purchase till the last minute: there's a shop that's run by the Instituto do Vinho do Porto in the international departures concourse at the airport.

Refer to the Drinks section in the Places to Eat chapter to learn more about Portuguese wines.

Casa Macário (Map 6) Rua Augusta 272; attractive little shop dating from 1913, specialising in vintage ports plus coffee and confectionery

Coisas do Arco do Vinho (Map 10) Centro Cultural de Belém; not just wine and port here but also wine books and all kinds of accessories plus regular wine-tasting sessions and even 'wine dinners'

Manuel Tavares (Map 6) Rua Betesga 1-A; lovely Art Deco shop crammed with wine, port and delicatessen items

Napoleão (Map 7) Rua dos Franqueiros 70; wide selection of port, wine and champagne, and excellent service from staff who really know – and love – their port; samples of the 10-year vintage are cheerfully dispensed

O Espírito do Vinho (Map 4) Rua Ferreira Borges 94-B; smart new shop aimed at an informed wine-loving public; wide range of wines and accoutrements (including collectors' corkscrews) plus wine-tasting courses

WHERE TO SHOP

The main shopping areas are in the Baixa, especially the pedestrianised Rua Augusta (for clothes, shoes and luxury goods from the likes of Louis Vuitton and La Perla) and the Chiado and Bairro Alto (especially Rua Garrett for clothes and linen and neighbouring streets for ceramics, young designer fashions and haute couture). Avenida da Liberdade hosts big name fashion such as Calvin Klein and Emporio Armani.

Swanky new shopping malls are becoming increasingly popular; favourites are the awe-inspiring Centro Comercial Colombo

Markets

For one of Lisbon's most entertaining shopping experiences, browse the sprawling Feira da Ladra which materialises every Tuesday morning and all day Saturday at Campo de Santa Clara, beside the Igreja de São Vincent de Fora in the Alfama district (Map 8). In addition to cheap clothes and shoes and second-hand books, you'll also find a motley array of junk, from nuts and bolts to old buttons and brassware, second-hand spectacles to 78-rpm records. Pricier antiques and furniture are available in a cluster of shops at the centre of the market.

Popularly translated as 'Thieves' Market' (*ladra* means thief), the name is actually believed to come from *lada*, meaning margin, a reference to when the market moved, centuries ago, to the margin of the Rio Tejo.

Market fans might also like to check out the following:

- A rough-and-ready complex of market stalls selling cheap shoes, clothes, toys, CDs and electrical wares daily except Sunday on the north-west corner of Praça de Espanha (Map 2)
- Themed markets, 10 am to 7 pm every Sunday near the Garcia de Orta gardens in the Parque das Nações (Map 9; metro: Gare do Oriente); the first Sunday of the month features stamps and coins, the second is a general collectors fair, the third is antiques, and the fourth features second-hand books

Markets outside Lisbon include the Feira de São Pedro, held in São Pedro (an outer district of Sintra) on the second and fourth Sunday of the month; and, along the Estoril Coast, the Feira de Cascais every Wednesday morning; the Feira de Carcavelos every Thursday morning (great for cheap clothes); and the Feira de Oeiras on the last Sunday of the month (for bric-a-brac and antiques).

and the Complexo das Amoreiras (see the following Shopping Malls section for more about these).

Trawl along Rua da Escola Politécnica for specialist art, craft and trendy stores and Rua do Alecrim or Rua Dom Pedro V for pricey antique ones. If you're after anything African or Asian (including food and music), delve into the quite scruffy Centro Mouraria Martim Moniz in Largo Martim Moniz, a popular, lively rendezvous for Lisbon's ethnic communities.

Delightful just to look at are the Art Deco shops of the kind your grandmother would recognise, dealing exclusively in shirts, hats or gloves (see the boxed text 'Speciality Shops'). Cheaper and tackier – but a lot of fun – are the open-air markets in and around Lisbon (see the boxed text 'Markets') where you can pick up anything from a souvenir T-shirt or embroidered tablecloth to a cow bell or gilded wooden angel.

Shopping Malls

The trend in booming Lisbon is for huge indoor shopping malls; not really the most atmospheric of retail experiences but easy to find and negotiate. As well as a dose of retail therapy, Lisbon likes to rendezvous at the numerous cafes in the complexes.

The colossal Centro Comercial Colombo, at Avenida Colégio Militar (Map 1; metro: Colégio Militar/Luz), is the largest shopping centre in the Iberian peninsula. With 500 shops plus cinemas, restaurants and a Playcenter with bowling alley (see Activities in the Things to See & Do chapter), it has well and truly stolen the limelight from the other giant, the Complexo das Amoreiras (Map 2).

The chrome-plated Amoreiras, Lisbon's first big shopping centre, designed by architect Tomás Taveira, is still very popular. It dominates the north-west of the city centre on its hilltop site on Avenida Engenheiro Duarte Pacheco. To get here, take almost any bus west from Parque metro station or bus No 11 from Praça do Comércio.

Swankiest of the newer city centre malls are Atrium Saldanha and its neighbour, the Galerias Monumental, on Praça Duque de Saldanha (Map 2). The modernist Centro Vasco da Gama (Map 9) bags a popular spot, right between Gare do Oriente and Parque das Nações.

Winning the prize for aesthetics are the Edifício Granella (Map 6) and Armazéns do Chiado (Map 7) in Bairro Alto, the grand department stores destroyed by a fire in 1988 and redesigned by leading architect, Álvaro Siza Vieira.

Biggest and best mall outside Lisbon is CascaiShopping, between Sintra and Cascais, with 130 shops (including Toys 'R Us and C&A) and dozens of restaurants, plus cinemas and a games area for kids. Bus No 417 from Sintra/Cascais goes past regularly.

Excursions

Portugal is one of Europe's smallest countries (only 560km north to south and 220km east to west) and has an efficient public transport system, so it doesn't take long to get to places from Lisbon, the hub of the transport network. An express coach to Porto in the north takes around 3½ hours, to the southern Algarve coast it's four to five hours, and two hours east is the delightful town of Évora. But you don't even have to go this far to discover some great destinations. The following places can all be reached in under an hour, although Sintra and Setúbal warrant at least an overnight stay.

SINTRA
pop 20,600

If you're planning to make only one trip out of Lisbon, Sintra, just 28km north-west, should receive top priority. Cool and verdant, it's also a worthwhile destination in its own right for several days of exploration or relaxation. You could even base yourself here and see Lisbon on day trips.

On the northern slopes of the craggy Serra de Sintra, Sintra's lush vegetation and spectacular mountaintop views have lured admirers since the times of the earliest Iberians, who found the ridge so mystical they called it the Mountain of the Moon and made it a centre of cult worship (some of its strange effects are actually caused by massive deposits of iron ore). The Romans and the Moors were equally captivated by Sintra – the remains of a Moorish castle overlook the town. For 500 years the kings of Portugal chose Sintra as their summer resort, and the nobility built extravagant villas and surrealist palaces on its wooded hillsides.

Poets – especially the romantic English – were enraptured by its natural beauty. Even Lord Byron (who had few nice things to say about Portugal) managed to be charmed: 'Lo! Cintra's glorious Eden intervenes, in variegated maze of mount and glen', he wrote in his famous travel epic, *Childe Harold*.

Monastic Masterpieces

Two of Portugal's most outstanding architectural gems (both Unesco World Heritage Sites) lie just over 130km north of Lisbon. The Mosteiro de Santa Maria da Vitória – usually known as Mosteiro da Batalha (Battle Abbey) – is an awesome Dominican monastery dating from 1434. Fundamentally Gothic in style, it's memorable for its additional 15th-century Manueline flourishes.

Some 20km to the south-west of Batalha is the 12th-century Mosteiro de Santa Maria de Alcobaça. One of Europe's most significant medieval Cistercian monuments, it once housed 1000 monks, its vast kitchen were described as 'the most distinguished temple of gluttony in all Europe'.

Six express buses daily run from Lisbon to Alcobaça (1250$00, two hours) from where there are regular runs to Batalha (370$00, 40 minutes). Accommodation is available in both towns; the seaside resort of Nazaré (14km west of Alcobaça) also makes a tempting overnight stop.

Despite hordes of summer tourists, especially in July when the town hosts a major music festival, Sintra still has a bewitching atmosphere and offers some fantastic walks and day trips: the Parque Natural de Sintra-Cascais encompasses both Serra de Sintra and nearby coastal attractions (including Cabo da Roca, Europe's most westerly point). Try to avoid weekends and public holidays, when the place is packed.

Designated a Unesco World Heritage Site in 1995, Sintra is now linked in tourist promotions with Cascais, Estoril and Mafra. Local authorities aim to make Sintra 'the cultural capital of Portugal' and have some grand plans, including a cable car to the Palácio Nacional da Pena and a theme park on the maritime discoveries. The most recent ecofriendly development, likely to happen

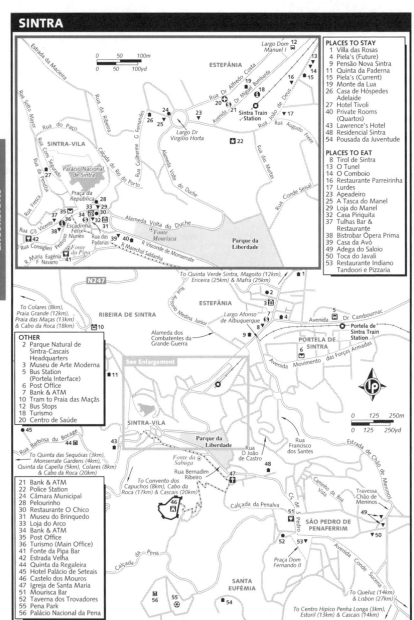

SINTRA

PLACES TO STAY
1 Villa das Rosas
4 Piela's (Future)
9 Pensão Nova Sintra
11 Quinta da Paderna
15 Piela's (Current)
19 Monte da Lua
26 Casa de Hóspedes Adelaide
27 Hotel Tivoli
40 Private Rooms (Quartos)
43 Lawrence's Hotel
48 Residencial Sintra
54 Pousada da Juventude

PLACES TO EAT
8 Tirol de Sintra
13 O Tunel
14 O Comboio
16 Restaurante Parreirinha
17 Lurdes
23 Apeadeiro
25 A Tasca do Manel
31 Loja do Manel
32 Casa Piriquita
37 Tulhas Bar & Restaurante
38 Bistrobar Ópera Prima
39 Casa da Avó
49 Adega do Saloio
50 Toca do Javali
53 Restaurante Indiano Tandoori e Pizzaria

OTHER
2 Parque Natural de Sintra-Cascais Headquarters
3 Museu de Arte Moderna
5 Bus Station (Portela Interface)
6 Post Office
7 Bank & ATM
10 Tram to Praia das Maçãs
12 Bus Stops
18 Turismo
20 Centro de Saúde
21 Bank & ATM
22 Police Station
24 Câmara Municipal
28 Pelourinho
30 Restaurante O Chico
31 Museu do Brinquedo
33 Loja do Arco
34 Bank & ATM
35 Post Office
36 Turismo (Main Office)
41 Fonte da Pipa Bar
42 Estrada Velha
44 Quinta da Regaleira
45 Hotel Palácio de Seteais
46 Castelo dos Mouros
47 Igreja de Santa Maria
51 Mourisca Bar
52 Taverna dos Trovadores
55 Pena Park
56 Palácio Nacional da Pena

by late 2001, is restricted vehicle access to the congested historic centre.

Orientation

There are four parts to Sintra: the historic centre (Centro Histórico), called Sintra-Vila (or Vila Velha: 'old town'); the new-town district of Estefânia, 1.5km north-east, where the Lisbon-Sintra railway terminates and where you'll find most cheap accommodation; and the new town's extension, Portela de Sintra, 1km farther east, where you'll find Sintra's new bus station (opposite the Portela de Sintra train station). The fourth area, the district of São Pedro de Penaferrim, 2km south-east of Sintra-Vila, hosts several good antique shops and restaurants and an excellent fortnightly market, the Feira de São Pedro, held on the second and fourth Sunday of the month.

Buses run to Sintra-Vila from the bus terminal via Sintra station. Note that you can't drive up to Palácio Nacional da Pena and that parking in Sintra-Vila is severely restricted. Be sure to lock your vehicle and keep valuables with you if you park at Castelo dos Mouros or the Monserrate Gardens.

Information

Tourist Offices There are two turismos, one at Sintra train station (☎ 219 241 623), and the main office (☎ 219 231 157, fax 219 235 176, e cm.sintra@mail.telepac.pt) at 23 Praça da República in Sintra-Vila, near Palácio Nacional de Sintra. Both are open 9 am to 7 pm daily (until 8 pm from June to September) and can provide a free map, packed with information, as well as help with accommodation. The Web site is www.cm-sintra.pt.

Money There's a bank with an ATM on Rua das Padarias in Sintra-Vila and several others in Estefânia, including on Avenida Dr Miguel Bombarda.

Post & Communications There are post offices both in Sintra-Vila and Estefânia, open until 6 pm weekdays. You can connect to the Internet (at 500$00 per half-hour) at Loja do Arco at Rua do Arco do Teixeira 2.

It's open 11 am to 7.30 pm daily and also stocks a wide range of Portuguese literature (including English and French translations) and Portuguese music. Hotel Tivoli (see Places to Stay later) has a credit-card fax and Internet facility available to all.

Medical Services & Emergency The *centro de saúde* (medical centre; ☎ 219 232 122) is at Rua Dr Alfredo Costa 34, and the police station (☎ 219 230 761) at Rua João de Deus 6, both in Estefânia.

Palácio Nacional de Sintra

The Sintra National Palace (also known as the Paço Real or Palácio da Vila) dominates the town with its two huge white conical chimneys. Of Moorish origins, the palace was greatly enlarged by João I in the early 15th century, adorned with Manueline additions by Manuel I in the following century, and repeatedly restored and redecorated right up to the present day.

It's connected with a treasury of notable occasions: João I planned his 1415 Ceuta campaign here; the three-year-old Sebastião was crowned king in the palace in 1557; and Afonso VI, who was effectively imprisoned in the palace by his brother Pedro II for six years, died of apoplexy in 1683 while listening to Mass in the chapel gallery.

Interior highlights include an unrivalled display of 15th- and 16th-century **azulejos** (especially in the Sala dos Árabes, or Arab Room), which are some of the oldest in Portugal; the **Sala das Armas** (Armoury Room, also called the Sala dos Brasões or Coat of Arms Room), with the heraldic shields of 74 leading 16th-century families on its wooden coffered ceiling; and the delightful **Sala dos Cisnes** (Swan Room), which has a polychrome ceiling adorned with 27 gold-collared swans.

Most memorable of all is the ground-floor **Sala das Pêgas** (Magpie Room), its ceiling thick with painted magpies, each holding in its beak a scroll with the words *por bem* (in honour). The story goes that João I commissioned the cheeky decoration to represent the court gossip about his advances towards one of the ladies-in-waiting.

EXCURSIONS

Caught red-handed by his queen, 'por bem' was the king's allegedly innocent response.

The palace is open 10 am to 5.30 pm daily except Wednesday; admission costs 600$00 (students 300$00). The last tickets are sold 30 minutes before closing. At weekends and public holidays the palace is crammed with tour groups.

Castelo dos Mouros

The battlements of this ruined castle snake over the craggy mountainside 3km above Sintra-Vila. First built by the Moors, the castle was captured by Christian forces under Afonso Henriques in 1147. Much restored in the 19th century, it offers some wonderful panoramas. The castle is open 9 am to 7 pm daily (admission free).

Palácio Nacional da Pena

The Pena National Palace is the most bizarre building in Sintra. This extraordinary architectural confection, which rivals the best Disneyland castle, was cooked up by the fertile imagination of Ferdinand of Saxe Coburg-Gotha (the artist-husband of Queen Maria II) and the Prussian architect Ludwig von Eschwege. Commissioned in 1840 to build a 'romantic' or 'Gothick' baronial castle from the ruins of a 16th-century Jeronimite monastery that stood on the site, Eschwege delivered a Bavarian-Manueline fantasy of embellishments, turrets and battlements (and even added a statue of himself in armour, overlooking the palace from a nearby peak).

The interior is just as mind-boggling. The rooms have been left as they were when the royal family fled the country on the eve of the revolution in 1910. There is Eiffel-designed furniture, Ferdinand-designed china as well as a whole room of naughty nude paintings. More serious works of art include a 16th-century, carved-alabaster altarpiece by Nicolas Chanterène in the original monastery chapel.

The palace is open 10 am to 6.30 pm daily except Monday (to 5 pm in winter); admission costs 600$00 (under-26s and seniors 300$00). Last tickets are sold 30 minutes before closing time.

Intricate window detail of the
Palácio Nacional da Pena

Below the palace, en route from the castle if you're walking, is the enchanting **Pena Park**, open 9.30 am to 7 pm daily (to 5.30 pm from October to May); admission is free. It's redolent with lakes and exotic plants, huge redwoods and fern trees, camellias and rhododendrons. There's an old-fashioned shuttle bus from the park entrance to the palace for 200$00 return.

Convento dos Capuchos

If Palácio Nacional da Pena monastery, 8km south-west of town, leaves you aghast at its silly extravagance, try this atmospheric Capuchin monastery for the greatest contrast imaginable.

A tiny troglodyte hermitage, buttressed by huge boulders and darkened by surrounding trees, the monastery was built in 1560 to house 12 monks. Their child-sized cells (some little more than hollows in the rock) are lined with cork, hence the monastery's popular name, Cork Convent. Visiting the place is an Alice-in-Wonderland experience as you squeeze through low, narrow doorways to explore the warren of cells, chapels, kitchen and cavern where one recluse, Honorius, spent an astonishing but obviously healthy 36 years (he was 95 when he died in 1596). Hermits hid away here right up until 1834 when the monastery was finally abandoned.

Closed at the time of research, there was no indication if the monastery would re-open; check with the turismo. There's no bus service; a taxi will charge around 2000$00 one way from Sintra-Vila.

Monserrate Gardens

Four kilometres west of Sintra-Vila are the Monserrate Gardens. Rambling and romantic, the gardens cover 30 hectares of wooded hillside and feature flora ranging from roses and conifers to tropical tree ferns, eucalypts, Himalayan rhododendrons and at least 24 species of palms.

First created in the 18th century by wealthy English merchant, Gerard de Visme, the gardens were enlarged in the 1850s by the painter William Stockdale (with help from London's Kew Gardens), who imported many plants from Australasia and Mexico. Neglected for many years (the site was sold to the Portuguese government in 1949 and practically forgotten), the garden is still a sad mess but the tangled pathways and aura of wild abandon can be very appealing.

At the heart of the garden is a bizarre Moorish-looking **quinta** (mansion), which was constructed in the late 1850s by James Knowles for another wealthy Englishman, Sir Francis Cook. Its previous incarnation was as a Gothic-style villa rented by the rich and infamous British writer William Beckford in 1794 after he fled Britain in the wake of a homosexual scandal. Beckford, who loved Monserrate, added his own touch of landscaping and even imported a flock of sheep from his estate in England. The villa was left derelict for years, but there are now plans to turn it into a museum.

The gardens are open 10 am to 5 pm daily (admission free).

Museu do Brinquedo

Sintra has several art museums of rather specialist interest, but this toy museum – in a spacious modern building – is a delightful international collection of clockwork trains, lead soldiers, Dinky toys, porcelain dolls and much more, including a couple of computers on which visitors can play games. João Arbués Moreira, an engineer by profession, began this collection (now over 20,000 pieces) more than 50 years ago when he was 14. Often to be found in the museum, the wheelchair-bound João is still fascinated by the toys and the history they represent, and the collection continues to grow.

The museum (wheelchair-accessible, of course) also has a cafe and a small shop, and is open 10 am to 6 pm daily except Monday; admission costs 500$00 (300$00 children and students).

Museu de Arte Moderna

Sintra put itself on the international art map when this museum opened in 1997 in the neoclassical former casino in Estefânia. Some of the world's best postwar art (including a particularly strong selection of pop art) was collected by business tycoon José Berardo and his associate Francisco Capelo. Among the 350 or so pieces displayed are works by Warhol, Lichtenstein, Pollock and Kossoff. Check out the top-floor cafe, too, with its open-air terrace and good views.

The museum is open 10 am to 6 pm Tuesday to Sunday; admission costs 600$00 (students 300$00). On Thursday, admission is free for those under 18 and over 65 years.

Quinta da Regaleira

This fairy-tale villa is a collection of pseudo-Manueline buildings created in the early 20th century by stage designer, Luigi Manini for António Carvalho Monteiro, a Brazilian mining millionaire. Now belonging to the town council and open to the public, the mansion's showpiece is the Palácio dos Milhões (so called because it cost so many millions to build). Also in the extensive grounds are a chapel, the Capela da Santíssima Trindade, and an initiation well, the Poço

EXCURSIONS

Parque Natural de Sintra-Cascais

The Sintra-Cascais Natural Park is one of the most delightful areas in Portugal. Easily accessible from Lisbon, its terrain ranges from the verdant lushness of Sintra itself to the crashing coastline of Praia do Guincho (a champion site for surfers), and the wild and rugged Cabo da Roca, Europe's most westerly point. Sintra's mountains experience exceptional climatic conditions, which are enjoyed by dozens of plant and tree species; a large number of exotic species were also introduced to Pena Park and Monserrate Gardens during the 18th and 19th centuries. There are plenty of walking routes (though no official trails). See Activities in the Sintra section for details of organised jeep safaris, walking and biking tours.

At the park's headquarters (☎ 219 235 116, fax 219 235 141), Rua General Alves Roçadas 10, Sintra, you can pick up English or French-language brochures on Monserrate Gardens or Pena Park (150$00 each) or the more informative *Guide of the Protected Areas near Lisbon* (750$00).

Iniciáto, which spirals down 30m to a labyrinth of underground galleries. The mansion (☎ 219 106 650) is open for guided 90-minute visits 10 am to 6 pm daily (to 4 pm in winter), but admission is a s teep 2000$00 (1000$00 for seniors and under-26s).

Activities

The Sintra region is increasingly popular for mountain biking and hiking. A favourite walking trail (see the Sintra map) is from Sintra-Vila to Castelo dos Mouros, a relatively easy 50-minute hike. The energetic can continue to Palácio Nacional da Pena (another 20 minutes) and up to the Serra de Sintra's highest point, the 529m Cruz Alta, which offers spectacular views.

Sintraventura, an operation run by the Sintra town council's sporting division (☎ 219 106 432, fax 219 242 805), offers regular day-long mountain-biking or walking trips costing 350$00 per person; reserve a place six working days in advance.

With a few days' notice, Wild Side Tours company (☎ 919 869 010, fax 214 433 744, 🖻 wild-side@clix.pt) can organise day-long hiking trips (from April to June and September to October) costing around 4000$00 per person. Wild Side also does mountain biking in the Peninha region of Sintra, Cabo da Roca or Guincho (6000$00), and kayaking along the Estoril Coast (6000$00). A minimum of three people is usually required.

Specialising in biking, hiking and canoeing is Cabra Montêz (☎ 917 446 668, fax

214 382 285, 🖻 cabramontez@ip.pt). Half-day biking trips in the area cost 7000$00 including bike rental, or 4000$00 with your own bike (including a snack lunch). Prices are considerably cheaper for groups of 10 or more; call ahead to see if you can join a group (weekends are best).

Two outfits arrange jeep safaris. Ozono Mais offers a day's 'guided adventure' costing 9900$00 per person including lunch. Planeta Terra runs 'Ecotour' jeep safaris. See the Setúbal Activities section later in this chapter for contact details.

Special Events

Sintra's big cultural event is the classical Festival de Música, held from mid-June to mid-July in the palaces and other posh venues here and at Estoril and Cascais. It's followed by the equally international Noites de Bailado, a classical and contemporary dance festival continuing until the end of August and held in the gardens of the luxurious Hotel Palácio de Seteais. Contact the turismo for details.

Places to Stay – Budget

The nearest camping ground is *Camping Praia Grande* (see the West of Sintra section later), on the coast 12km from Sintra.

The *pousada da juventude (☎ 219 241 210)* is in Santa Eufémia, 4km from Sintra-Vila and 2km south-west of São Pedro, which is the closest you'll get by bus; in the high season, dorm beds cost 1900$00 and doubles without/with bathroom cost 4200/4600$00. Advance booking is essential.

Some of the cheapest accommodation in Sintra itself can be found in the 80 or so *quartos* (private rooms); doubles usually cost about 5000/3500$00 with/without bathroom. The cheapest – and dampest – are probably the *quartos (☎ 219 233 463)* at Rua Visconde de Monserrate 60. The turismo also has details of private apartments with kitchens costing from 8000$00.

Casa de Hóspedes Adelaide (☎ 219 230 873, Rua Guilherme Gomes Fernandes 11) is the kind of place where rooms are rented by the hour, but if you don't mind that you'll find clean, simple doubles (without bathroom) costing 4000$00. The long-popular *Piela's (☎ 219 241 691, Rua João de Deus 70)* is due to move to a converted old house at Avenida Desiderio Cambournac 1-3 in 2001. Its new doubles (all with private bathroom) will cost from 6000$00 to 7500$00.

Places to Stay – Mid-Range & Top End

Monte da Lua (☎/fax 219 241 029, Avenida Dr Miguel Bombarda 51) offers tastefully decorated doubles with bathroom costing 10,000$00. Try to get one of the quieter rooms at the back that overlook the wooded valley. Similarly priced, rooms at the popular *Quinta da Paderna (☎ 219 235 053, 919 461 261, Rua da Paderna 4)* also have lovely views.

In an enviably picturesque position on the high road between Sintra-Vila and São Pedro, *Residencial Sintra (☎ 219 230 738, Travessa dos Avelares 12)* is a big old mansion with 10 high-ceilinged, spacious rooms costing 15,000$00. It's perfect for families, with a rambling garden, outdoor patio and swimming pool.

Among several Turihab properties in the area, the 19th-century *Villa das Rosas (☎/fax 219 234 216, Rua António Cunha 2-4)* boasts some splendid decor, with azulejos in the hall and dining room. There's also a tennis court in the grounds for guests. Doubles cost 20,000$00, including breakfast. The *Pensão Nova Sintra (☎/fax 219 230 220, Largo Afonso de Albuquerque 25)* offers

deluxe doubles for 12,000$00. Its outdoor patio is a big plus.

Top-end accommodation includes the modern *Hotel Tivoli (☎ 219 233 505, fax 219 231 572, Praça da República)* where deluxe doubles cost 24,000$00. For considerably more style and real atmosphere, head for the former hostelry of Lord Byron, *Lawrence's Hotel (☎ 219 105 500, fax 219 105 505, [e] lawrence's@mail.telepac.pt, Rua Consigliéri Pedroso 38)*. Restored in exquisite taste by a Dutch couple, it has doubles costing 34,000$00 (suites 53,000$00), many overlooking the wooded valley behind, and worth every escudo.

Rural alternatives nearby include *Quinta Verde Sintra (☎/fax 219 616 069, Estrada de Magoito 84)* near Magoito, which has doubles for 13,000$00, an apartment for 15,000$00 and a swimming pool; *Quinta das Sequóias (☎ 219 243 821, fax 219 230 342)*, a superb manor house en route to the Monserrate Gardens, with doubles costing 25,000$00; and in a wooded valley nearby, the 16th-century former farmhouse, *Quinta da Capella (☎ 219 290 170, fax 219 293 425)*, where doubles cost 28,000$00.

Places to Eat

Estefânia Rua João de Deus has several good dining choices, including *Restaurante Parreirinha (☎ 219 231 207)* at No 41, which serves great grilled fish (try the succulent grilled dourada) plus proper vegetables (a rarity); the humble *O Comboio (☎ 219 241 187)* at No 84 where huge servings cost less than 1000$00; and the smarter *O Tunel (☎ 219 231 386)* next door. There's also a good cafe at *Piela's* (see Places to Stay) and a tiny snack bar, *Lurdes (☎ 219 241 657)* at No 38, with daily lunchtime specials for 800$00.

The unpretentious *A Tasca do Manel (☎ 219 230 215, Largo Dr Virgílio Horta 5)* offers daily specials for an appetising 900$00. Nearby *Apeadeiro (☎ 219 231 804, Avenida Dr Miguel Bombarda 3-A)* is a pricier but long-established favourite where you'll eat well for under 1500$00. For cheap pizzas (800$00) and lunchtime snacks, head for the big and busy *Tirol de Sintra (Largo Afonso de Albuquerque 9)*.

EXCURSIONS

Sintra-Vila The cafes and restaurants here are inevitably geared for the passing tourist trade, but *Tulhas Bar & Restaurante (☎ 219 232 378, Rua Gil Vicente 4)*, a converted grain warehouse, has maintained its character and quality, with tasty dishes mostly under 1300$00. It's closed Wednesday. *Casa da Avó (☎ 219 231 280, Rua Visconde de Monserrate 46)* is simpler but similarly priced.

Chic and cavernous *Bistrobar Ópera Prima (☎ 219 244 518, Rua Consiglieri Pedroso 2-A)* serves snacks as well as main meals and is open until 2 am. There's live music here, too (see the Entertainment section for details).

For Sintra's famous *queijadas* (sweet cheese cakes) and *travesseiros* (almond pastries), head for the popular pastelaria *Casa Piriquita (Rua das Padarias 1–5)*. Picnic supplies can be bought nearby in *Loja do Manel* grocery store on Rua do Arco do Teixeira.

São Pedro Meat-lovers will like *Toca do Javali (☎ 219 233 503, Rua 1 de Dezembro 12)* where you can get your teeth into a chunk of wild boar for about 2500$00. Go early to get one of the few outdoor tables in the garden. It's closed Wednesday. Down the road, at Travessa Chão de Meninos, two outlets of *Adega do Saloio (☎ 219 231 422)* specialise in grills. Dishes cost from 1600$00 to 2000$00 but some cheaper half-portions are also available.

Restaurante Indiano Tandoori e Pizzaria (☎ 219 244 667, Praça Dom Fernando II) offers some refreshingly different dishes at reasonable prices.

Entertainment

Fonte da Pipa (☎ 219 234 437, Rua Fonte da Pipa 11-13) is a cosy bar with snacks and inexpensive drinks; it's open from around 9 pm nightly. *Estrada Velha (☎ 219 234 355, Rua Consiglieri Pedroso 16)* is another popular bar, usually open until about 2 am.

Check out *Bistrobar Ópera Prima* (see Places to Eat earlier) for its live jazz, soul and blues music from around 10.30 pm to 1 am on Tuesday, Wednesday and Thursday nights. Some rather touristy fado playing

happens nightly from July to September at *Restaurante O Chico (☎ 219 231 526, Rua do Arco do Teixeira)*. There's no admission charge but meals are pricey.

Taverna dos Trovadores (☎ 219 233 548) in São Pedro is an upmarket tavern, which also has live Portuguese music from Thursday to Saturday nights. A more casual dive popular with locals is *Mourisca Bar (☎ 219 235 253, Calçada de São Pedro 56)*, where you can play snooker, darts or chess.

Getting There & Away

Buses operated by Stagecoach (☎ 214 867 681) or Mafrense (☎ 219 230 971) leave from Sintra regularly (fewer on Sunday) for Cascais (440$00 direct/510$00 via Cabo da Roca, 45/60 minutes), Estoril (440$00, 40 minutes), Mafra (405$00, 45 minutes) and Ericeira (405$00, 45 minutes). Some services leave from the new Portela Interface terminal at Portela de Sintra, others from the old bus stops outside Sintra train station. Check with the turismo. The Stagecoach Web site is www.stagecoachplc.com. See under Cascais for a useful bus service to the airport.

Train services (210$00, 45 minutes) run every 15 minutes between Sintra and Lisbon (Rossio station or Entrecampos).

Getting Around

Bus Stagecoach bus No 435 runs regularly to São Pedro via Sintra-Vila. To get to the Palácio Nacional da Pena (600$00), catch Stagecoach bus No 434, via the turismo in Sintra-Vila every 20 minutes from 10.20 am to 5.15 pm daily. All these services start at the new terminal at Portela de Sintra.

For 1250$00 you can buy a Day Rover Ticket which allows unlimited bus travel on the Stagecoach network.

Taxi & Car Rental You can pick up a taxi at the train station and also outside Palácio Nacional de Sintra. They aren't metered so check the fares first with the turismo. For a return trip to the Palácio Nacional da Pena, Castelo dos Mouros or Monserrate Gardens, figure on about 2000$00 (including an hour's waiting time). There's a 20% supplement at weekends and on holidays.

Diller (☎ 219 271 225, fax 219 271 122), based in nearby Pêro Pinheiro, will deliver rental cars to Sintra for no extra charge.

Horse & Carriage Getting around by horse and carriage is the most romantic option. They clip-clop all over the place, even as far as Monserrate (10,00$00 return). The turismo has a full list of prices. The carriages wait outside Parque da Liberdade or by the *pelourinho* (pillory) immediately below Palácio Nacional de Sintra.

WEST OF SINTRA

The most alluring day trips from Sintra are to the **beaches** of Praia das Maçãs and Praia Grande, about 12km west. Praia Grande, as its name suggests, is a big sandy beach with ripping breakers, that hosts heats of the European Surfing Championships. It also boasts a 102m-long ocean-water swimming pool, reputedly the largest in Europe, open from May to September (1000/600$00 per adult/child per day). Praia das Maçãs has a smaller and cosier beach and a trio of popular discos in the village. Azenhas do Mar has an even smaller beach, with a spectacular clifftop location for its village.

En route to the beaches, 8km west of Sintra, is the ancient village of **Colares** atop a ridge (not to be confused with traffic-clogged Várzea de Colares on the main road below). It's a quiet spot with spectacular views, which has been famous for its wines since the 13th century. These are made from the only vines in Europe to survive the 19th-century phylloxera plague, thanks to their deep roots and the local sandy soil. Call in advance to arrange a visit to the Adega Regional de Colares (☎ 219 291 210) and taste some of the velvety reds.

Attracting all of the tour buses, however, is **Cabo da Roca** (Rock Cape), about 18km west of Sintra. This sheer cliff, rising 150m above the roaring sea, is Europe's westernmost point. A wild and rugged spot, it's surprisingly uncommercialised, perhaps because it feels too uncomfortably remote; there are only a couple of stalls, a cafe and a tourist office where you can buy a certificate to show you've been here.

Touch Rugby

This popular game has become a big hit on beaches along the Estoril Coast and west of Sintra. If you see huge crowds gathered at Cascais' Praia da Ribeira, chances are they're watching a touch rugby tournament. If you're in Praia Grande around noon on 23 August, you can join in one of the biggest tournaments in the area. It's open to anyone over nine years old and the only rule is to have fun!

Places to Stay & Eat

Praia Grande's often crowded *Camping Praia Grande* (☎ 219 290 581, fax 219 291 834, Avenida Maestro Frederico de Freitas 28) is 600m from the beach (500m from the Sintra-Praia das Maçãs road). It charges 570/535/420$00 per person/tent/car and also has bungalows and luxury quartos available.

At No 19 on the same road, 1km before the beach, the delightful quartos of *Sra Maria Pereira* (☎/fax 219 290 319) overlook a large rambling garden (including BBQ facility) and cost 8000/10,000$00 a double/triple, including breakfast. Three self-catering apartments are also available (12,000$00 to 15,000$00). You need to book well ahead in summer.

Deluxe *Hotel Arribas* (☎ 219 292 145, fax 219 292 420, **e** hotel.arribas@mail.telepac.pt), overlooking Praia Grande beach and swimming pool, has doubles costing 18,000$00.

In Praia das Maçãs, the run-down but spacious *Residencial Real* (☎ 219 292 002) at the northern end of the village has expansive ocean views and doubles costing 10,000$00. *Residencial Oceano* (☎ 219 292 399, fax 219 292 123, Avenida Eugénio Levy 52), right by the tram terminal, has neat modern rooms for 12,000$00. Both prices include breakfast.

Both beaches have cafes and restaurants. In Praia das Maçãs, *Cervejaria Búzio* (☎/fax 219 292 172), beside Residencial Oceano, is recommended for its seafood. The *Café Cervejaria Dolomite* opposite is considerably cheaper, with dishes for around 1000$00.

EXCURSIONS

Entertainment

Three popular nightclubs at Praia das Maçãs are *Concha* (☎ 219 292 067), on the left near the GALP petrol station; *Casino Monumental* (☎ 219 292 024) in the centre; and *Quivuvi* (☎ 219 291 217) farther along on the right, in a modern shopping mall. They all bop till at least 4 am at weekends.

Getting There & Away

Bus No 441 from Sintra goes frequently via Colares to Praia das Maçãs (340$00, 25 minutes) and on to Azenhas do Mar (340$00, 35 minutes). In summer it also runs frequently via Praia Grande (at other times, hop off at the Ponte Ridizio junction, just before Praia das Maçãs, from where it's a 1.2km walk along Avenida Maestro Frederico de Freitas to Praia Grande).

The century-old tram service that was established to connect Sintra with the bathing resort of Praia das Maçãs was recently revived. Taken over by the town council in 2000, its services were in some doubt. It should run from Ribeira de Sintra (1.5km from Sintra-Vila; take bus No 441 or 403) three to four times daily, except Monday and Tuesday (500$00). Check at the turismo for the latest details.

Bus No 403 runs regularly to Cabo da Roca (440$00, 45 minutes).

CASCAIS

pop 30,000

This former fishing village ('Kush-KAISH') has been tuned in to tourism since 1870, when the royal court first came here for the summer, bringing a train of nobility in its wake. It's now the liveliest beach resort on the Estoril Coast, attracting a young and international crowd. If you like to have your home comforts (eg, British-style pubs and McDonald's), you'll be happy in the touristy pedestrianised centre, but there's a surprisingly unspoilt old-town area that provides a pleasant afternoon's meander.

Orientation

Everything of interest is within easy walking distance. The train station (where buses also terminate) is a few minutes' walk north of the main pedestrianised Rua Frederico Arouca. Car drivers are advised to head for the free parking areas around the Parque Municipal da Gandarinha.

Information

Tourist Offices The turismo (☎ 214 868 204, fax 214 672 280), at Rua Visconde da Luz 14, is open 9 am to 8 pm weekdays and 10 am to 6 pm weekends (to 7 pm on weekdays between October and May).

Money There are several banks with ATMs on and near Alameda Combatentes da Grande Guerra. A private exchange bureau, Empório, operates 10 am to 7.30 pm Monday to Saturday, from the basement of a shopping centre at Rua Frederico Arouca 45.

Post & Communications The post office on Avenida Marginal is open until 6 pm weekdays only.

You can connect to the Internet and send and receive emails from Smartprint (☎ 214 866 776) in the basement of the shopping centre at Rua Frederico Arouca 45. It's open 10 am to 6 pm weekdays and charges 155$00 per five minutes.

Medical Services & Emergency Cascais Hospital (☎ 214 827 700) is on Rua Padre Loureiro. The main police station (☎ 214 861 217) is on Rua Afonso Sanches.

Cascais has a small but growing reputation for violent crime, some involving tourists. A tourist police post (☎ 214 863 929) inside the Cascais turismo operates 10 am to 8 pm daily (to 10 pm in summer).

Old Cascais

For a hint of Cascais' former life as a fishing village, head for the **fish market**, between Praia da Ribeira and Praia da Rainha, where an auctioneer sells off the day's catch in an unintelligible rapid-fire lingo at about 6 pm daily except Sunday.

The atmospheric back lanes and alleys to the west of the *câmara municipal* (town hall) are also worth exploring. In a shady square south-west of the câmara municipal is **Igreja de Nossa Senhora da Assunção**,

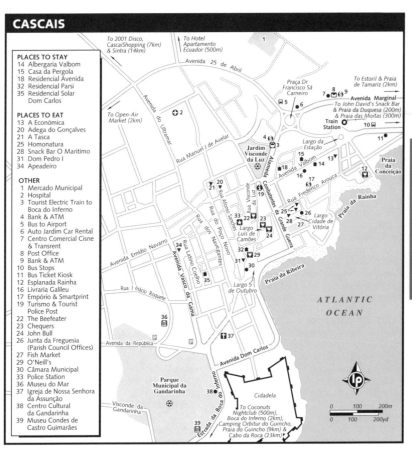

CASCAIS

PLACES TO STAY
14 Albergaria Valbom
15 Casa da Pergola
18 Residencial Avenida
32 Residencial Parsi
35 Residencial Solar
   Dom Carlos

PLACES TO EAT
13 A Económica
20 Adega do Gonçalves
21 A Tasca
25 Homonatura
28 Snack Bar O Marítimo
31 Dom Pedro I
34 Apeadeiro

OTHER
1 Mercado Municipal
2 Hospital
3 Tourist Electric Train to
   Boca do Inferno
4 Bank & ATM
5 Bus to Airport
6 Auto Jardim Car Rental
7 Centro Comercial Cisne
   & Transrent
8 Post Office
9 Bank & ATM
10 Bus Stops
11 Bus Ticket Kiosk
16 Esplanada Rainha
16 Livraria Galileu
17 Empório & Smartprint
19 Turismo & Tourist
   Police Post
22 The Beefeater
23 Chequers
24 John Bull
26 Junta da Freguesia
   (Parish Council Offices)
27 Fish Market
29 O'Neill's
30 Câmara Municipal
33 Police Station
36 Museu do Mar
37 Igreja de Nossa Senhora
   da Assunção
38 Centro Cultural
   da Gandarinha
39 Museu Condes de
   Castro Guimarães

decorated with azulejos predating the 1755 earthquake that destroyed most of the town.

The town hall organises monthly three-hour guided tours of old Cascais for small groups. Call ☎ 214 825 408 for details.

Museums

The large and leafy Parque Municipal da Gandarinha is great for kids with its aviaries, duck ponds and playground; it also contains the delightful **Museu Condes de Castro Guimarães** (☎ 214 825 407). The mansion of the Counts of Castro Guimarães, built in the late 19th century, displays the family's furnishings and *objets d'art* from the 17th and 18th centuries, including some striking Indo-Portuguese furniture and Oriental silk tapestries; its walls are liberally adorned with early azulejos. Downstairs is a small display of archaeological finds from the area. The museum is open 10 am to 5 pm daily except Monday; admission (with guided tours only, every half-hour) costs 250$00.

The excellent **Museu do Mar** (☎ 214 825 400) in Jardim da Parada has a small but high-quality display of model boats, fish, dolphins and whales, traditional fisherfolk's clothing and other marine artefacts. The museum is open 10 am to 5 pm daily except Monday and is wheelchair-accessible; admission costs 250$00.

Close to the Museu Condes de Castro Guimarães, the new **Centro Cultural de Gandarinha** was due to open at the time of research to host changing exhibitions and other cultural events.

Beaches

Cascais has three sandy bits of beach (**Praia da Ribeira** is the largest and closest) tucked into little bays just a few minutes' walk south of the main drag. They're nothing to write home about (nor is the water quality) but they make pleasant suntraps if you can find an empty patch.

Far more exciting waves break at **Praia do Guincho**, 9km north-west of Cascais. This long, wild beach is a surfer's and windsurfer's paradise with its massive crashing rollers. Beware of the strong undertow which can be dangerous for swimmers and novice surfers.

Boca do Inferno

Cascais' most famous tourist attraction, 2km west, is Boca do Inferno (literally, 'Mouth of Hell'), where the sea roars into an abyss in the coast. You can walk there in about 20 minutes, but don't expect anything dramatic unless there's a storm raging.

Activities

There are horse-riding facilities (around 4000$00 per hour) at the Centro Hípico da Quinta da Marinha (☎ 214 869 282), 2km inland from Praia do Guincho.

John David's Snack Bar & Watersports Centre (☎ 214 830 455), which is at Praia da Duquesa midway between Cascais and Estoril, has windsurfing boards for rent.

Special Events

Summertime musical events include the Estoril Festival de Jazz and the Festival de Música da Costa do Estoril, held in both Cascais and Estoril during July. From July to mid-September, you can enjoy a Verão de Cascais (Cascais Summer) program of free outdoor entertainment (eg, live bands) at

10.30 pm nightly, usually at Estoril's Praia de Tamariz and/or Cascais' Praia de Moitas (en route to Estoril).

Sometime between July and September (there's no fixed date), Cascais honours the patron saint of its fisherfolk, the Senhora dos Navegantes, with a day-long procession through the streets.

Places to Stay

Advance reservations are essential for summer. The prices listed here are for July (prices are higher in August).

Camping Orbitur do Guincho (☎ 214 870 450, fax 214 872 167) is in Areia, about 1km inland from Praia do Guincho and 9km from Cascais. Rates are 750/620/670$00 per person/tent/car. Hourly buses run to Guincho from Cascais.

The best budget bets are quartos, costing from 6000$00 to 7000$00 a double. The turismo will contact the owners for you.

Popular *Residencial Avenida* (☎ 214 864 417, Rua da Palmeira 14) has just four prettily decorated doubles without bathroom costing 6000$00. *Residencial Parsi* (☎ 214 845 744, fax 214 837 150, Rua Afonso Sanches 8) is a crumbling old building overlooking the waterfront; doubles without/with bathroom cost 7000/9000$00.

Casa da Pergola (☎ 214 840 040, fax 214 834 791, e pergolahouse@netc.pt, Avenida Valbom 13) is a very pretty Turihab establishment with an ornate facade and a gorgeous garden. Doubles with bathroom start at 17,500$00, including breakfast. More modern and less inspired accommodation can be found at *Albergaria Valbom* (☎ 214 865 801, fax 214 865 805) opposite, at No 14, where comfortable doubles cost 13,000$00. Similarly priced but in a quieter location is *Residencial Solar Dom Carlos* (☎ 214 828 115, fax 214 865 155, Rua Latino Coelho 8), a 16th-century former royal residence featuring a chapel where Dom Carlos used to pray.

One of the most reasonably priced *hotel apartamentos* (apartment hotels) is *Hotel Apartamento Ecuador* (☎ 214 840 524, fax 214 840 703, e hotelequador@mail .telepac.pt, Alto da Pampilheira). A double with kitchen in this high-rise complex on the northern outskirts of town will cost 13,400$00 (18,700$00 after mid-July), including breakfast.

Places to Eat

A cluster of pleasant places with outdoor seating are in the cobbled Largo Cidade de Vitória including the low-key **Snack Bar O Marítimo** (☎ 214 843 988), which has a small lunch menu for under 1000$00. Behind the adjacent fish market is a string of good fish restaurants.

True to its name, the *casa de pasto A* **Económica** (☎ 214 833 524, *Rua Sebastião JC Melo, 11)* serves economically priced standard fare (though watch for overpriced *couvert* extras). **Dom Pedro I** (☎ 214 833 734, *Beco dos Invalides 5)* is a quieter, more upmarket nook, serving tasty and reasonably priced dishes; go early to grab one of the prized outdoor tables on the cobbled steps.

Apeadeiro (☎ 214 832 731, *Avenida Vasco da Gama 32)* is renowned locally for its grilled fish. Another popular haunt is **Adega do Gonçalves** (☎ 214 830 287, *Rua Afonso Sanches 54)*, where hearty servings cost around 1200$00. Cheaper and simpler is *A* **Tasca** at No 61.

There's a rare vegetarian restaurant, **Homonatura** (☎ 214 837 382, *Largo Cidade de Vitória 32 and Rua Frederico Arouca 24)*, which also offers Hatha yoga and alternative medicine courses.

Entertainment

There's no lack of bars to keep the nights buzzing, especially in Largo Luís de Camões, where the bars triple as cafes, restaurants and discos. Check out **John Bull** *(Praça Costa Pinto 32)*, **Chequers** (☎ 214 830 926, *Largo Luís de Camões)*, **The Beefeater** (☎ 214 840 696, *Rua Visconde da Luz 1)* or the Irish **O'Neill's** (☎ 214 868 230, *Largo 5 de Outubro)*. For a sea view with drinks, head for outdoor **Esplanada Rainha**, which overlooks the Praia da Rainha.

The most popular nightclub is **Coconuts** (☎ 214 844 109, *Avenida Rei Humberto II de Itália 7)*, with seven bars, two dance floors and an esplanade by the sea. It's

open 11 pm to 4 am nightly. Wednesday is Ladies' Night, featuring a male stripper. The long-established **2001** (☎ 214 690 550) rock music disco is about 7km north of town.

Shopping

A good source of second-hand books in English, Spanish, Italian, German and French is Livraria Galileu, Avenida Valbom 24-A. Really serious shoppers should head for CascaiShopping, a massive shopping complex en route to Sintra. Bus No 417 passes by regularly.

The town's mercado municipal, on the northern outskirts of town, is best on Wednesday and Saturday morning, while an open-air market fills the area next to the former bullring (now being converted into shops), 2km west of town, on the first and third Sunday of the month.

Getting There & Away

Trains from Lisbon's Cais do Sodré station run frequently to Cascais (25 minutes) via Estoril (30 minutes). It costs 210$00 to both places. Buses, operated by Stagecoach (☎ 214 832 055), run regularly from both Estoril and Cascais to Sintra (420$00 to 490$00, 40 to 70 minutes) and Cabo da Roca (320$00, 30 minutes), and seven times daily from Cascais to Praia do Guincho (320$00, 20 minutes). Bus tickets cost less when prepurchased from the bus station kiosk. Plans to move the bus terminal to near the post office had yet to be finalised at the time of research.

There's a direct hourly service to Lisbon airport (1250$00, 50 minutes) from Cascais (Avenida 25 de Abril) via Estoril bus station.

EXCURSIONS

At weekends some services continue to Lisbon's Parque das Nações. Since the ticket is equivalent to a Day Rover Ticket (see under Sintra earlier for details), you could sightsee en route.

Both Cascais and Estoril are included in most regional bus tours from Lisbon (see the Organised Tours section in the Getting Around chapter).

Getting Around

Daily throughout the summer a free electric tourist 'train' does a 45-minute round trip to Boca do Inferno, leaving every hour between 7 am and 10 pm from the Jardim Visconde da Luz. Also often waiting at the garden are a couple of horse carriages that do half-hour trips to Boca do Inferno for about 4000$00 return.

Among the many car rental agencies are Auto Jardim (☎ 214 831 073) and Transrent (☎ 214 864 566) in the basement of Centro Comercial Cisne. Transrent also rents mountain bikes/scooters/motorbikes from 1500/4000/7000$00 per day.

For taxis, call ☎ 214 660 101.

ESTORIL
pop 24,800

Long a favoured haunt of the rich and famous (and also a well known nest of spies during WWII), the genteel resort of Estoril ('Sh-to-REEL') is nowadays very much in the shadow of its much livelier neighbour, Cascais, 2km to the west. Its special draw is Europe's biggest casino. It also has a pleasant beach and several nearby golf courses.

Orientation & Information

The bus and adjacent train stations are on Avenida Marginal, opposite Estoril's shady Parque do Estoril, with the casino at the top.

The turismo (☎ 214 663 813, fax 214 672 280, e estorilcoast@mail.telepac.pt) is almost opposite the train station. This is the main office for both Estoril and Cascais. It's open 9 am to 8 pm Monday to Saturday (to 7 pm in winter) and 10 am to 6 pm on Sunday. You can find more information about the Estoril-Cascais area on its Web site at www.estorilcoast-tourism.com.

Golf on the Estoril Coast

If you're a gambler or golfer (and preferably rich) you'll be in seventh heaven in Estoril. This elegant beach resort not only has Europe's biggest casino, it also has half a dozen spectacular golf courses within 25km.

The closest is just 2km to the north. Golf do Estoril is one of the best known courses in Portugal, having hosted the Portuguese Open Championship several times. The Quinta da Marinha course, 9km to the west, was designed by Robert Trent Jones to give both high handicappers and scratch golfers a challenge, with the course rolling over windblown dunes and rocky outcrops.

Ten kilometres to the north-west is the Penha Longa golf club, a well-equipped Trent Jones Jr creation with superb views of the Serra de Sintra. Nearby are Estoril-Sol, with one of the country's best practice areas; and the Quinta da Beloura, designed by Rocky Roquemore, who's also responsible for the Belas Clube de Campo, 22km north-east of Estoril in the Carregueira Hills. Estoril's turismo has full details of all courses.

Casino

The casino (☎ 214 667 700) is open 3 pm to 3 am daily. There's an admission charge of 1000$00 (passport required) for the gaming room (everything from roulette to baccarat, French bank and blackjack), though it's free to play the slot machines and bingo. The vast Black & White Room theatre-restaurant (☎ 214 684 521), attached to the casino, puts on an international floor show nightly at 11 pm. Tickets cost around 9000$00 with dinner, 5000$00 without.

If you're interested in modern art and sculpture, check out the casino's 1st-floor art gallery.

Beach

Estoril's small, pleasant Praia de Tamariz has cafes and beachside bars as well as an ocean swimming pool, open 10 am to 8.30 pm daily in summer. A pedestrian underpass links the beach with the park.

Special Events

A *feira do artesanato* (handicrafts fair) takes place in Estoril, in an area beside the casino, 6 pm to midnight daily throughout July and August.

Early in October, Estoril Casino's art gallery is the venue for an International Naïve Painting Salon, acknowledged as the biggest and best such exhibition in Iberia.

Racing fanatics might like to check if the Formula 1 Grand Prix is back on track at the Autodromo do Estoril, 9km north of Estoril. Usually held in late September or early October, the race wasn't held for several years due to track repairs, which were completed in 2000.

See the Cascais section for details on shared music festivals, the Estoril de Jazz and Festival de Música da Costa do Estoril.

Places to Stay & Eat

The cheapest pensões are *Pensão Costa* (☎ 214 681 699, Rua de Olivença 2), near the train station, where doubles without/with bathroom cost 5000/6000$00, and *Pensão Maryluz* (☎ 214 682 740, Rua Maestro Lacerda) near Pensão Smart (see later in this section) with similar doubles costing 6000/7000$00.

The long-popular *Pensão Smart* (☎ 468 21 64, Rua José Viana 3), in a quiet residential area about 10 minutes' walk north-east of the train station, was undergoing long-term renovations at the time of research; doubles will probably be at least 10,000$00.

More upmarket guesthouses along busy Avenida Marginal, a few minutes' walk uphill from (east of) the station, include *Residencial São Cristóvão* (☎/fax 214 680 913), at No 7029, where doubles/triples cost 11,000/16,000$00 (including bathroom and breakfast).

For old-world looks and charm, *Hôtel Inglaterra* (☎ 214 684 461, fax 214 682 108, e hotelinglaterra@mail.telepac.pt, Rua do Porto 1) fits the bill, with doubles costing 21,300$00.

Restaurants are pricey here. The most tempting is the seaside *Praia de Tamariz* (☎ 214 681 010), which has a slightly cheaper snack bar next door. On the western edge of town, the *English Bar* (☎ 214 680 413, Avenida Sabóia 9), near Monte Estoril train station, is popular for its seafood.

Getting There & Away

For details of train and bus services, see under Cascais.

Palácio de Queluz

The pink-hued palace at Queluz, 5km north-west of Lisbon, is the most elegant example of rococo architecture in Portugal, a miniature Versailles with feminine charm and formal gardens of whimsical fancy. It was converted in the late 18th century from a hunting lodge to a summer residence for the royal family and designed by the Portuguese architect Mateus Vicente de Oliveira and French artist Jean-Baptiste Robillon.

One wing of the palace is often used to accommodate state guests, an annexe is now a deluxe *Pousada de Dona Maria I* (☎ 214 356 158, fax 214 356 189) and the vast kitchens have been converted into an expensive restaurant, *Cozinha Velha* (☎ 214 36 158). But the rest is open to the public 10 am to 1 pm daily except Tuesday and Wednesday; admission costs 400$00.

The easiest way to get here is by train from Lisbon's Rossio station to the Queluz-Belas station (180$00, 20 minutes). From here, it's a 15-minute downhill walk (follow the signs).

Just a part of the formal gardens of the palace

MAFRA
pop 10,000

This low-key town, 39km north-west of Lisbon, is famous for the massive Palácio Nacional de Mafra, the most awesome of the many extravagant monuments created during the reign of Dom João V in the 18th century, when money was no problem. The former royal park, Tapada de Mafra, is an additional attraction. Mafra doesn't have much accommodation, but it's an easy day trip from Lisbon, Sintra or Ericeira.

Orientation

You can't miss the palace; its massive, recently restored facade dominates the town. Opposite is a pleasant little square, Largo da República, where you can find cafes, restaurants and taxis. Mafra's bus terminal is opposite the Parque Desportivo (see the Information section) but buses also stop by the palace (called 'convent' on timetables).

Information

Tourist Offices The turismo (☎ 261 812 023, fax 261 815 104, e turismo@ cm.mafra.pt) is 300m north of the palace on the main Avenida 25 de Abril. It's open 9.30 am to 12.30 pm and 2 to 6 pm weekdays and 9.30 am to 1 pm and 2.30 to 6 pm weekends (to 7 pm daily in summer). You can search its Web site, www.cm-mafra.pt, on the office computer.

Email & Internet Access The vast Parque Desportivo Municipal Engenheiro Ministro dos Santos, on Avenida Dr Francisco Sá Carneiro, 1.5km north-west of the turismo, has an Espaço Jovem, or youth centre (☎ 261 819 200), where you can surf the Internet or send and receive emails free of charge, for limited periods and by prior appointment. It's open 9.30 am to 12.30 pm and 2.30 to 5.30 pm weekdays.

Palácio Nacional de Mafra

The Mafra National Palace is a combination of palace, monastery and basilica, a huge baroque and neoclassical monument covering 10 hectares. It was begun in 1717, six years after Dom João V promised to build a monastery if he received an heir. A daughter, Dona Maria, was fortuitously born the same year. As the king's coffers filled with newly discovered gold from Brazil, the initial design – meant for 13 monks – was expanded to house 280 monks and 140 novices, and to incorporate two royal wings. No expense was spared to build its 880 halls and rooms, 5200 doorways, 2500 windows and two bell towers boasting the world's largest collection of bells (57 in each). Indeed, when the Flemish bell-founders queried the extravagant order for a carillon of bells, Dom João is said to have doubled the order and to have sent the money in advance.

If you have read *Memorial do Convento*, the magical novel by Nobel Laureate José Saramago (translated into English under the title *Baltasar & Blimunda*), which is based around the building of the palace, you'll appreciate the incredible effort involved in its construction (for more on Saramago, see the boxed text 'José Saramago's Lisbon' in the Facts about Lisbon chapter).

Under the supervision of German architect Friedrich Ludwig, up to 20,000 artisans (including Italian carpenters and masons) worked on the monument, with a mind-boggling 45,000 in the last two years of its construction, all of them kept in order by 7000 soldiers. The presence of so many outstanding artists spurred João V to establish a school of sculpture in the palace; open from 1753 to 1770, it employed many of Portugal's most important sculptors. Though the building may have been an artistic coup, the expense of its construction and the use of such a large workforce helped destroy the country's economy.

The palace was only briefly used as a royal residence. In 1799, as the French prepared to invade Portugal, Dom João VI and the royal family fled to Brazil, taking most of Mafra's furniture with them. In 1807, General Junot billeted his troops in the monastery, followed by the Duke of Wellington and his men. From then on, the palace became a favourite military haven. Even today, most of it is used as a military academy.

On the one-hour tours it's very easy to become dazed by the 230m-long corridors and interminable salons and apartments, but a few things stand out, eg, the amusing 18th-century pinball machines in the games room. Most impressive is the magnificent 88m-long, barrel-vaulted baroque library, with 40,000 books dating from the 15th century.

The central basilica, with its two bell towers, is wonderfully restrained by comparison, featuring multihued marble floors and panelling and Carrara marble statues.

The palace-monastery is open 10 am to 5 pm daily, except Tuesday and public holidays; admission costs 400$00 (free on Sunday morning). English-language tours usually take place at 11 am and 2.30 pm.

Tapada de Mafra

The palace's 819-hectare park and hunting ground, Tapada de Mafra, was originally created in 1747 and is still partly enclosed by its 21km-long perimeter wall. There are 90-minute tours by minibus or electric tourist train at 10.15 am and 3 pm on Saturday and Sunday (1250/600$00 per adult/child under 10), which take you to see the park's deer, wild boar and half-dozen wolves, plus its falcon-recuperation centre. For weekday tours (at 10 am and 2 pm daily) you must call ☎ 261 817 050, or email ⓔ tapada.mafra@clix.pt, to reserve a place.

There are a number of well-signposted *percurso pedestres* (walkers' trails) through the park. A leaflet (in Portuguese only) available at the park entrance illustrates the animal footprints you might come across – along with their *excremento*.

The park opens its gates only at 10 am and 2 pm daily; you can stay until 5 pm. Admission costs 600/1000/2000$00 for walkers/cyclists/horse riders. The park entrance is about 6km north of Mafra, along the road to Gradil (look for the *Patrimonio do Estadio* sign at the gate). By taxi it costs roughly 1000$00 one way from Mafra.

Activities

Walking & Cycling The admirable Câmara Municipal de Mafra organises a program of walking/biking trips one weekend a month between March and December. The 10km trips (which last from 9.30 am to 1 pm) visit nearby areas of interest, and

EXCURSIONS

VITOR VIEIRA

Traditional white-and-blue windmills can still be seen in the countryside around Mafra.
euro currency converter 100$00 = €0.50

EXCURSIONS

Safe Haven for Wolves

Some 10km north-east of Mafra is the Centro de Recuperação de Lobo Ibérico (Iberian Wolf Recovery Centre; ☎ 261 785 037), established in 1989 to provide a home for wolves that have been trapped, snared or kept in dire conditions. The centre's 17 hectares of secluded woodland provide a refuge for some 26 wolves, all from the north of the country where Portugal's last 200 or so Iberian wolves roam. Its Web site is at www.duartevieira.com/lobo.

You can visit the low-profile centre from 4 to 8 pm at weekends or on holidays (2.30 to 6 pm in winter). Admission is free. The best time is around 5 pm when the wolves emerge in the cool of the dusk, though even then sightings are never guaranteed.

To support the centre's activities, you can 'adopt' a wolf for about 5000$00 a year. For more information, write to CRLI, Apartado 61, 2669-909 Malveira.

To get to the (unsignposted) centre, head to Malveira then take the Torres Vedras road for 3km, and turn off to Picão just after Vale da Guarda. At the end of the village (opposite Picão's only cafe) there's a steep, cobbled track to the left (badly potholed in places). Buses run frequently from Mafra to Malveira (210$00, 20 minutes) where you have to change to a Torres Vedras bus to reach Vale da Guarda. The centre is 2km from the Picão turn-off.

MARTIN HARRIS

cost 400/600$00 per person if you register at the Espaço Jovem in Mafra or Ericeira a day before (see Information under Mafra and Ericeira), or are 700/1000$00 without prior registration.

Getting There & Away

There are regular buses to Mafra from the Campo Grande terminal in Lisbon (520$00, 75 minutes), Ericeira (210$00, 20 minutes) and Sintra (380$00, 45 minutes). Contact Mafra's bus terminal on ☎ 261 816 152 to check on departure times.

ERICEIRA
pop 6000

This pretty, but rapidly developing seaside town, 10km west of Mafra, is a firm summertime favourite with the young Lisbon and European crowd thanks to its great surf and beaches, reasonably priced accommodation, lively bars and restaurants. At weekends,

especially, it's also got an appealing family atmosphere, with the pedestrianised streets perfect for romping kids. Many lisboêtas have holiday homes in the Ericeira area so it can get crowded.

Orientation

The town sits high above the sea, its old town clustered around the central Praça da República. Rua Dr Eduardo Burnay leads south of here to a newer part of town, focused on Praça das Navegantes. The bus terminal is 800m north of the centre, off the N247 highway.

There are three sandy beaches just 15 minutes' walk away: Praia do Sul (also called Praia da Baleia) to the south and Praia do Norte and Praia de São Sebastião to the north. A few kilometres farther north is the unspoilt Praia de São Lourenço, while Praia Foz do Lizandro is the same distance to the south.

Information
Tourist Offices The amazingly gung-ho turismo (☎ 261 863 122, fax 261 865 909, [e] jteric@mail.telepac.pt), Rua Dr Eduardo Burnay 33-A, is open 9 am to midnight daily in summer (9 am to 8 pm Monday to Thursday and 9 am to 10 pm on Friday and Saturday in winter). It has phones for public use and a computer for searching its bilingual Web site, www.ericeira.net.

Email & Internet Access At the Espaço Jovem (☎/fax 261 860 555), in the beautiful Casa da Cultura Jaime Lobo e Silva on Rua Mendes Leal, you can surf the Internet or send or receive emails free of charge, by prior appointment. It's open 10 am to 1 pm and 2.30 to 6.30 pm on weekdays, and 10 am to 1 pm Saturday.

Clube de Video (☎ 261 865 743), Praça da República, also has Internet facilities (600$00 per hour). It's open 11 am to 1 am daily.

Surfing
Ericeira's big attraction is surfing. Praia da Ribeira de Ilhas, a World Championship site, is just a few kilometres north, though the waves at the nearer Praia de São Sebastião are challenging enough for most amateurs.

Ultimar (☎ 261 862 371), at Rua 5 de Outubro 37A, rents boards for 2500$00 a day. It's open 9.30 am to 1 pm and 3 to 7.30 pm Monday to Saturday (closed Saturday morning and Sunday).

Places to Stay
Camping *Parque de Campismo Municipal de Mil Regos (☎ 261 862 706)*, north-east of Praia de São Sebastião but close to the noisy main road, charges 300/250/100$00 per person/tent/car; there is a municipal swimming pool next door. *Clube Estrela (☎ 261 815 525)* at Sobreiro, 5km east of Ericeira, is open to visitors with a Camping Card International for 550/410/350$00.

Private Rooms & Apartments There are plenty of quartos and apartamentos costing around 6500/9000$00 in summer (cheaper the longer you stay). Ask at the turismo or look for signs in shops and pensões.

Pensões & Residenciais Along Rua Prudéncio Franco da Trindade (just up from Praça da República), *Hospedaria Bernardo (☎/fax 261 862 378)* at No 17 has spacious doubles costing 5000/7000$00 without/with bathroom. At No 25, *Hospedaria Vinnu's (☎ 261 863 830, fax 261 866 298)* has bright, modern rooms (including triples with refrigerator) from 6000$00 to 8000$00.

At the more modern *Hotel Pedro O Pescador (☎ 261 869 121, [e] hotel.pedro@mail.telepac.pt, Rua Dr Eduardo Burnay 22)*, doubles cost 9000$00. At No 7 on the same street, *Residencial Fortunato (☎/fax 261 862 829)* offers good-value doubles costing 7500$00, including breakfast.

Prices escalate in August.

Places to Eat
For pizzas and pastas under 1000$00, try *Ristorante Pão d'Alho (☎ 261 863 762, Estrada de Sintra 2)*. Rua Dr Eduardo Burnay has several other budget choices, including the no-frills *Cervejaria O Caniço (☎ 261 862 364)* at No 11.

Restaurante Gabriel (☎ 261 863 349, Avenida da Horta) offers great grilled fish. For something classier, the sea-view *O Barco (☎ 261 862 759, Avenida Marginal 14)* fits the (pricey) bill, with its excellent seafood specialities.

Entertainment
Among Ericeira's 20-odd nightclubs and bars, the biggest place is *Discoteca SA – Sociedade Anonima (☎ 261 862 325)*, that's housed in a cavernous former *adega* (winery) just off the N247, 3km south of town above Praia Foz do Lizandro. On the beach itself are several bars including *Limipicos*.

More central options include *Disco-Bar Ouriço (☎ 261 862 138, Avenida Marginal 10)* and cafe-bars in Praça das Navegantes, notably *La Luna (☎ 965 216 400)*.

Getting There & Away
Express buses to/from Lisbon's Campo Grande terminal (690$00, 80 minutes) via Mafra run every 30 to 60 minutes. Services to/from Sintra (390$00, 45 minutes) depart every hour. The turismo has timetables.

SETÚBAL PENINSULA

The Setúbal Peninsula is the northern spur of the region the tourist board calls the Costa Azul and easily accessible from Lisbon. You can laze on the vast beaches of the Costa da Caparica, join trendy lisboêtas in the beach resort of Sesimbra farther south or eat great seafood in nearby Setúbal, where express bus connections make it a convenient stopover if you're heading south or east.

There are two major nature reserves as well – Reserva Natural do Estuário do Sado and Parque Natural da Arrábida – and plenty of activities including surfing, dolphin-watching, mountain biking and hiking trips.

Cacilhas

This suburb across the Rio Tejo from Lisbon is famous for its fish restaurants and the **Cristo Rei**, the immense statue of Christ with outstretched hands visible from almost everywhere in Lisbon. The 28m-high statue (a smaller version of the one in Rio de Janeiro) was built in 1959 and partly paid for by Portuguese women grateful for the country having been spared the horrors of WWII. A lift (operating 9 am to 7 pm in summer; 250$00) takes you right to the top from where you can gasp at the panoramic views.

Getting There & Away Ferries to Cacilhas (110$00, 10 minutes) run frequently from Lisbon's Cais da Alfândega terminal by Praça do Comércio. To reach the statue, take Bus No 101 from the bus station opposite Cacilhas ferry terminal.

Costa da Caparica

This 8km-long stretch of beach on the west coast of the peninsula is Lisbon's favourite weekend escape, with cafes, restaurants and bars catering for every age group. During the summer a narrow-gauge railway runs along the entire length of the beach from Costa da Caparica town (which shares the same name as the coastline itself), giving you the option of jumping off at any one of 20 stops.

Orientation & Information Praça da Liberdade is the focus of Costa da Caparica town. Immediately west of the praça, the

---

Stressed Out?

If you're stressed out from too much sight-seeing in Lisbon, there's an unusual cure at hand: thalassotherapy. A treatment using minerals from the sea, including iodine, calcium and sulphur, thalassotherapy helps alleviate stress, fatigue and insomnia as well as rheumatism, circulatory problems and obesity.

The Centro de Talassoterapia (☎ 212 905 655, fax 212 912 657), at Avenida 1 de Maio 25-A, Costa de Caparica, offers various treatments including hydromassage (in a bath of seaweed), marine hydrotherapy and aqua-gymnastics as well as a straightforward sauna, massage and solarium. Prices range from 1600/2500$00 for the solarium/sauna to 8500$00 for two treatments per day for a two to 11-day treatment. The centre is open 10 am to 2 pm and 3 to 7 pm Monday to Saturday.

CLINT CURÉ

---

pedestrianised Rua dos Pescadores leads directly to the beach. The bus terminal is 400m north-west of the square on Avenida General Humberto Delgado; additional stops are by the square and beach.

The turismo (☎ 212 900 071, fax 212 900 210), Avenida da República 18 (near the square), is open 9.30 am to 1 pm and 2 to 6 pm Monday to Saturday (closing at 5.30 pm weekdays and 1 pm Saturday in winter).

Beaches & Surfing The long beach has distinctive characteristics. The northern part attracts families, while Praia do Castelo (stop No 11 on the train) and Praia Bela Vista (No 17) are recognised gay and nudist havens.

A particularly good spot for surfers is at São João da Caparica. Fonte da Telha (where the train stops) is best for windsurfing. Check the handy *Tabela de Marés* booklet (available at the turismo) listing tide times, surf shops and clubs. Aerial (☎ 212 912 292), in the shopping complex on Avenida 1 de Maio, rents boards.

Places to Stay Orbitur's *Costa da Caparica (☎ 212 903 894, fax 212 900 661)* camping ground, 1km north of town, charges 790/650/680$00 per adult/tent/car. *Clube de Campismo de Lisboa (☎ 212 900 100, fax 212 902 848)*, just north of Orbitur, charges 640/675/640$00 to Camping Card International (CCI) holders.

Costa da Caparica town has many pensões and apartments but in summer or midseason weekends, they fill quickly and prices escalate. *Pensão Capa-Rica (☎ 212 900 242, Rua dos Pescadores 9)*, a modern complex near the beach, has small doubles without/ with bathroom that cost 5000/8000$00. Slightly pricier is *Residencial Copacabana (☎ 212 900 103)* at No 34.

At Fonte da Telha, the *Friendship Hostel and Health Centre (☎ 217 975 870, fax 217 975 057)*, run by a former wrestling champion, has some doubles for 5000$00 and a communal kitchen. Modern *Residencial Lareira (☎ 212 978 230, fax 212 978 239, Avenida Mar, Lote 204)*, 1km above the beach (opposite the turn-off to Golf da Aroeira golf course), has doubles costing around 9000$00, with breakfast.

Places to Eat In Costa da Caparica town, pricey seafood and other restaurants line Rua dos Pescadores. On the beach itself, *Carolina do Aires (☎ 212 900 124, Avenida General Humberto Delgado)* has a good reputation.

In Fonte da Telha, the friendly *Manuel dos Frangos (☎ 212 961 819)* offers a relaxed atmosphere and great fish dishes.

Getting There & Away Transportes Sul do Tejo (☎ 217 262 740) run regular services to Costa da Caparica from Lisbon's Praça de Espanha (services may eventually shift to Gare do Oriente) taking about an hour, depending on traffic (420$00). During the summer, Carris bus No 75 does a special weekend-only Costa da Caparica run every 15 minutes from the Campo Grande metro station (500$00 return).

Alternatively, catch a ferry from Lisbon's Cais d'Alfândega to Cacilhas from where buses run every 15 to 30 minutes to Costa da Caparica town (320$00, about 45 minutes). You can also take the new Fertagus train which runs from Entrecampos to Fogueteiro via the Ponte 25 de Abril. At Pragal (265$00, 17 minutes from Entrecampos), the stop nearest Costa da Caparica, buses run to town every 20 minutes (320$00, around 25 minutes). These services operate on a reduced scedule at weekends.

Getting Around The train along the beach operates daily during summer (weekends only from Easter until around May) and costs 600$00 return to Fonte da Telha (or 380$00 return to stop No 9).

Setúbal
pop 80,000

Once an important Roman settlement, Setúbal ('STOO-bahl') is now the largest town on the Setúbal Peninsula and Portugal's third-largest port (after Lisbon and Porto). Situated on the northern bank of the Sado Estuary 50km south of Lisbon, the town has a relaxed, untouristy atmosphere, nearby beaches and excellent fish restaurants. It's also the base for a number of adventure activities, notably trips to see the famous dolphins in the estuary and explorations of the Parque Natural da Arrábida and the Reserva Natural do Estuário do Sado.

Orientation The extensively pedestrianised centre focuses on Praça de Bocage and Largo da Misericórdia, with most places of interest within easy walking distance. The main bus station is about five minutes' walk from the municipal turismo.

Drivers should save themselves headaches (and meter charges) by heading for the free parking in Largo José Afonso (follow signs to the 'Albergaria' nearby).

EXCURSIONS

Information The municipal turismo (☎/fax 265 534 402) on Praça do Quebedo is open 9 am to 7 pm on weekdays and 9 am to 12.30 pm and 2 to 5.30 pm weekends in summer (weekdays only during winter).

The Costa Azul regional turismo (☎ 265 539 120, fax 265 539 127) at Travessa Frei Gaspar 10 is open 9 am to 7 pm daily during the summer months (closing at 12.30 pm on Sunday). It opens 9 am to 12.30 pm and 2 to 6 pm on Monday and Saturday and 9 am to 6 pm Tuesday to Friday (closed Sunday) during winter.

Money There are several banks with ATMs along Avenida Luísa Todi, including at No 290.

Email & Internet Access At the Instituto Português da Juventude (IPJ; ☎ 265 532 707) on Largo José Afonso, you can surf the Internet or send emails at slack times (no charge). This service is available 10 am to 1 pm on Monday, Wednesday and Friday and 2 to 5 pm on Tuesday and Thursday.

At Ciber Centro (☎ 265 234 800, fax 265 234 437, e ciber.centro@mail.telepac.pt), Avenida Bento Gonçalves 21-A, charges are 250$00 per 15 minutes. It's open 9 am to 11 pm weekdays.

Medical Services & Emergencies The police station (☎ 265 522 022) is at Avenida Luísa Todi 350; and the hospital (☎ 265 522 133) is near the bullring off Avenida Dom João II.

Igreja de Jesus The striking Igreja de Jesus on Praça Miguel Bombarda was designed in 1491 by Diogo de Boitac, better known for his later work on Belém's Mosteiro dos Jerónimos. Walk inside the small, late-Gothic church and you'll see the earliest examples of Manueline decoration: extraordinary twisted pillars like writhing snakes, which are made from delicately coloured Arrábida marble. Walls of the nave and chancel are decorated with fine 18th-century azulejos. The church is open 9 am to 12.30 pm and 2 to 5.30 pm Tuesday to Saturday.

Galeria da Pintura Quinhentista While the Museu de Setúbal still plans its long-awaited renovations, its renowned Gallery of 16th Century Paintings – displaying some of the finest Renaissance art in the country – can be found around the corner from the Igreja de Jesus, on Rua do Balneário Paula Borba. The set of 14 panels from the Lisbon school of Jorge Afonso (sometimes attributed to the anonymous 'Master of Setúbal') and four other later panels attributed to Gregório Lopes show extraordinarily rich colours and detail.

The gallery is open 9 am to noon and 2 to 5 pm Tuesday to Saturday (admission free).

Museu do Trabalho Michel Giacometti A Museum of Work doesn't sound too enthralling, but the setting of this museum – a huge, cavernous former sardine-canning factory – is itself intriguing. Not only is there a realistic display of the former canning

Reserva Natural do Estuário do Sado

The Sado Estuary Natural Reserve encompasses a vast coastal area around the Sado River and Estuary, stretching from Setúbal at the northern end to near Alcácer do Sal in the south-east. Its mud banks and marshes, lagoons, dunes and former salt pans are a vitally important habitat for mammals, molluscs and migrating birds. The mammal species that attracts the most attention is the bottlenose dolphin (*Tursiops truncatus*; known in Portuguese as Roaz-Corvineiro); about 30 of them survive in these coastal waters. Among the 100 or so notable bird species are flamingos (more than 1000 regularly winter here), white storks (spring and summer) and resident marsh harriers and little egrets.

The park's headquarters in Setúbal (see the boxed text 'Parque Natural da Arrábida') has multilingual information about the park plus a Portuguese-only publication on walks (*Caminhos*). See Activities in the Setúbal section for details of some organised tours.

factory's activities, there's also an upper-floor display of rural crafts and professions, collected in northern and central Portugal in 1975 by the famous Corsican ethnographer Michel Giacometti with the assistance of 100 youngsters.

The museum, at Largo Defensores da República, is open 9.30 am to 6 pm Tuesday to Saturday (admission free). There's a pleasant cafe upstairs.

Museu de Arqueologia e Etnografia

At Avenida Luísa Todi 162, the Museum of Archaeology & Ethnography, houses an impressive collection of Roman remains. Setúbal was founded by the Romans after their fishing port of Cetobriga (now Tróia), on the opposite side of the river mouth, was destroyed by an earthquake in AD 412. The museum is open 9 am to 12.30 pm and 2 to 5 pm Tuesday to Saturday (admission free).

Castelo São Filipe
Worth the half-hour stroll to the west of town is this castle built by Filipe I in 1590 to fend off an English attack on the invincible Armada. Converted into a *pousada* (upmarket inn) in the 1960s, its ramparts are still huge and impressive and its chapel boasts 18th-century azulejos depicting the life of São Filipe.

Beaches
For good beaches, head west (ignoring the cement works en route) until you reach Figuerinha, Galapos or Portinho da Arrábida. Buses from Setúbal run regularly in the summer to Figuerinha (about 200$00).

Special Events
A major international film festival, the Festival Internacional de Cinema de Tróia, takes place in Setúbal in early June.

Activities
There is a wealth of activities and organised tours in Setúbal and the surrounding area.

Walking & Cycling
Sistemas de Ar Livre (SAL; ☎/fax 265 227 685, ☎ 919 361 725, e sal@cpsi.pt), Avenida Manuel Maria Portela 40, organises two-hour guided tours (in Portuguese) of Setúbal every Saturday for 1000$00 per person (2000$00 out of

Parque Natural da Arrábida

The Arrábida Natural Park stretches along the south-eastern coast of the Setúbal Peninsula from Setúbal to Sesimbra. Covering the 35km-long Serra da Arrábida mountain ridge, this is an area rich in Mediterranean thickets and plants, butterflies, beetles and birds, especially birds of prey. Even seaweed comes in 70 different varieties.

The variety of flora makes for great local honey, especially in the gardens of the Convento da Arrábida, a 16th-century former convent overlooking the sea just north of Portinho (call ☎ 218 527 002 to arrange a visit).

Public transport through the middle of the park is nonexistent. Your best option is to rent a car or motorcycle or take one of the organised trips (see Activities in the Setúbal section).

The headquarters for both Parque Natural da Arrábida and Reserva Natural do Estuário do Sado (☎ 265 541 140, fax 265 541 155) is on Praça da República, Setúbal. Open weekday office hours, it has multilingual brochures on the park but no detailed maps.

EXCURSIONS

season) and Sunday trips to a different area regionally. Its Web site, www.sal.jgc.pt, has details in Portuguese only.

Planeta Terra company (☎ 919 471 871 or 874, e planeta.terra@mail.telepac.pt), Praça General Luís Domingues 9, organises hiking and cycling trips in the Serra da Arrábida, costing from 4000$00 to 5000$00 per person per half-day (minimum of four people per group).

US-based Easy Rider Tours (see the Organised Tours section in the Getting There & Away chapter) runs a Costa Azul biking tour that includes a day's biking through the Serra da Arrábida.

Hot-Air Balloon Trips
Contact Hemisférios (☎ 265 612 714, 919 445 868, fax 254 612 776, e hemisferios@mail.telepac.pt) for balloon trips over the beautiful landscape of nearby Alcácer do Sal. The 25,000$00 charge includes an after-flight celebration with champagne, Alentejan bread and sausage.

Jeep Safaris Half-day 4WD tours through the Tróia Peninsula to Alcácer do Sal, or around the Setúbal Peninsula via Palmela, are offered by Mil Andanças (☎ 265 532 996) for 4900$00 per person.

Cruises, Canoes & Dolphin-Watching
Another unusual way to experience the area is aboard a modern galleon, the *Riquitum*, which sails along the Sado Estuary on two-hour trips (2000$00 per person). For details contact Troiacruze (☎ 265 228 482). Cruises on a remodelled fishing vessel are also offered by Nautur (☎ 265 532 914, e nautur@mail.telepac.pt). They cost about 6500$00 per person (including lunch) for a seven-hour trip to the Sado Estuary and Arrábida (7500$00 to Sesimbra).

Vertigem Azul (☎ 265 238 000, fax 265 238 001, e vertigemazul@mail.telepac.pt), Avenida Luísa Todi 375, offers three to four-hour dolphin-watching tours in the Sado Estuary (with a stop for snorkelling) for 5500/2750$00 per adult/child. This price includes a pretrip slide presentation about the dolphins held at the company's Café-Bar at Avenida Luísa Todi 305. It also has half-day canoeing trips in the estuary costing 5000$00 per person and also a combination dolphin-watching and canoe trip for 7000$00.

Lisbon's Dolphins

Lisbon is one of the world's few capital cities that can boast bottlenose dolphins (*golfinhos* in Portuguese) in its nearby waters. Up until the 1950s they were fairly common in the Tejo Estuary, appearing even close to the Terreiro do Paço ferry terminal. Increasing pollution brought this playground to a close. But in recent years – with stricter legislation ensuring cleaner waters – the dolphins have started to reappear. In 1997, a group of about 20 were spotted off Carcavelos, along the Estoril Coast.

The most steadfast community, numbering around 30, is in the Sado Estuary off Setúbal. Dolphin-spotting tours are arranged from there (see the Setúbal section for details)

Wine Tours Wine buffs may be interested in the free wine-cellar tours of the José Maria da Fonseca adega and museum (☎ 212 198 940, fax 212 198 942, e info@jmf.pt) at Rua José Augusto Coelho 11 in nearby Vila Nogueira de Azeitão, home of the famous *moscatel* wine of Setúbal. From Setúbal, buses leave frequently for Vila Nogueira de Azeitão (240$00, 20 minutes). The adega is open 9 am to noon and 2.30 to 4 pm weekdays.

Places to Stay – Camping & Hostel The adequate *Toca do Pai Lopes* (☎ 265 522 475) municipal camping ground is 1.5km west of town on Rua Praia da Saúde (near the shipyards); it costs 300/270/270$00 per person/tent/car. Another *parque de campismo* (☎ 265 238 318), 3km farther along the coast at Outão, charges 470/550/315$00. The summer-only Covas & Filhas bus to Figuerinha beach passes close by both sites.

The *pousada da juventude* (☎ 265 534 431, fax 265 532 963), attached to the IPJ (see Information earlier), has dorm beds/doubles with bathroom costing 1900/4600$00.

Places to Stay – Pensões & Residenciais Friendly, dowdy *Residencial Todi* (☎ 265 220 592, Avenida Luísa Todi 244) has doubles with/without bathroom costing from 4000/3000$00; a triple costs 5000$00. Overlooking the pleasant Praça de Bocage is the comfortable *Casa de Hóspedes Bom Amigo* (☎ 265 526 290), which has thin-walled doubles without bathroom (but hair dryers!), costing around 5000$00.

Residencial Bocage (☎ 265 543 080, fax 265 543 089, Rua São Cristovão 14) offers smart doubles for 7500$00. Convenient for drivers (free parking is available nearby) is *Albergaria Solaris* (☎ 265 541 770, fax 265 522 070, Praça Marquês de Pombal 12) where doubles cost 10,000$00.

Most luxurious of all is the *Pousada de São Filipe* (☎ 265 523 844, fax 265 532 538), within the town's hilltop castle. Doubles will set you back a tidy 31,600$00.

Places to Eat There are lots of cheap eateries in the lanes east of the regional turismo including **Neca's Snack Bar** (☎ *265 237 713, Rua Dr António Joaquim Granjo 10)*, which serves bargain daily specials costing around 800$00.

Along the western end of Avenida Luísa Todi is a string of seafood restaurants. Typically, prices are per kilogram, according to the day's catch; expect to pay around 1500$00 for a fresh dourada, grilled on the street outside and served with potatoes and salad. **Casa do Chico** (☎ *265 239 502)* at No 490 is small, friendly and less touristy than most. It's closed Monday.

Getting There & Away Buses leave frequently from Lisbon's Praça de Espanha or Gare do Oriente (550$00, 45 minutes to one hour) or from Cacilhas (490$00, 50 minutes), a quick ferry-hop from Lisbon's Cais de Alfândega terminal. From Setúbal, buses to Lisbon leave at least every 15 minutes.

Buses from Setúbal to Sesimbra (420$00) leave nine times daily from outside the office of the Covas & Filhos bus company on Avenida Alexandre Herculano 5-A.

From Lisbon, trains leave from Barreiro station (take the ferry from Lisbon's Terreiro do Paço terminal) to Setúbal every 30 to 60 minutes (200$00). They arrive at Setúbal's main train station, 700m north of the centre. There's a local station (serving only Praia da Sado, by the Rio Sado) at the eastern end of Avenida 5 de Outubro.

Ferries to Tróia depart every 30 to 45 minutes daily. The fare is 160/700$00 per person/car.

Getting Around You can rent a bicycle for 1500/3000$00 per day/three days from Planeta Terra (see Activities the section).

Car rental agencies include Avis (☎ 265 538 710) and Alucar (☎ 265 538 320).

Sesimbra
pop 8100

This former fishing village sheltering under the Serra da Arrábida, at the western edge of the Parque Natural da Arrábida, 30km west of Setúbal, has become a favourite seaside resort with lisboêtas. At weekends and in the high season the traffic, jet-skis and bar music hardly provide a tonic of tranquillity but if you like your beaches to buzz, this little resort may fit the bill. Cruises, guided walks or scuba-diving activities are also on offer, including trips to Capo Espichel where dinosaurs once roamed.

Orientation & Information The bus station is on Avenida da Liberdade, just five minutes' walk north of the seafront. Turn right when you reach the bottom of the avenue, pass the small 17th-century Forte de Santiago (now a GNR police station) and you'll reach the turismo (☎ 212 235 743, fax 212 233 855) at Largo da Marinho, in an arcade off seafront Avenida dos Náfragos. It's open 9 am to 8 pm daily between June and September (9 am to 12.30 pm and 2 to 5.30 pm in winter).

Castelo The imposing ruined Moorish castle above the resort was taken from the Moors by Dom Afonso Henriques in the 12th century, retaken by the Moors, and finally snatched back by the Christians under Dom Sancho I in the 13th century. Perched 200m above the town, it's a great spot for coastal panoramas. Allow at least an hour to reach it on foot.

Porto de Abrigo Porto de Abrigo, around 3km west of the centre, is increasingly a centre for tourist cruises and activities. Early morning and late afternoon, when fishermen auction off their catch, is still a good time to catch a more traditional fishing atmosphere.

Activities There are activities here for both land and sea enthusiasts.

Land The Setúbal-based SAL (see the Activities section under Setúbal) organise short 'nature tours' from here every Sunday (1000$00 per person).

Jeep Arrábida (☎ 212 280 104, 966 024 417) offers a five-hour jeep tour of the Serra da Arrábida (7000/5000$00 per adult/child) including the Cabo Espichel.

Speleology or rock-climbing fans should contact Núcleo de Espeleologia da Costa

EXCURSIONS

Azul (☎ 934 538 079) for details of its activities and courses.

Sea Clube Naval de Sesimbra (☎ 212 233 451), near Porto de Abrigo, runs three-hour coastal cruises (3000$00 per person) at 9.30 am every Tuesday and six-hour coastal fishing trips (8000$00) at 7 am every Saturday.

Sersub (☎ 212 280 604, 962 375 309) at Porto de Abrigo runs scuba-diving courses; a day's outing for experienced divers costs around 12,000$00 (including equipment).

Places to Stay *Forte de Cavalo (☎ 212 233 694)* camping ground, 1km west of town, costs 240/370/120$00 per person/tent/car. *Valbom (☎ 212 687 545)* camping ground at Cotovia, which is 5km north (take any Lisbon or Setúbal bus), charges 545/475/475$00.

Quartos cost from 4000$00 to 6000$00 for a double room (ask the turismo). The well-advertised central ones belonging to *Senhora Garcia (☎ 212 233 227, Travessa Xavier da Silva 1)* are nice but even pricier, at around 7000$00.

Residencial Nautico (☎ 212 233 233, Bairro Infante Dom Henrique 3) is a 10-minute walk uphill, but it has comfortable doubles costing 9000$00 to 15,000$00, including breakfast.

Places to Eat Fish restaurants abound on the waterfront of Sesimbra. For cheaper fare, try *Restaurante A Sesimbrense (☎ 212 230 148, Rua Jorge Nunes 19)* just off the Largo do Município (near the market). *Restaurante Chic (Travessa Xavier da Silva 6)*, a bar-restaurant favoured by resident expats, serves pizzas and salads.

For evening snacks and late-night drinks, trawl Avenida dos Náfragos. *Sereia (☎ 223 20 90)*, at No 20, attracts a lively crowd and is open until at least 2 am.

Getting There & Away Buses depart from Lisbon's Praça de Espanha three or four times daily (570$00) and at least nine times daily from Setúbal (420$00) and Cacilhas (450$00). Services may eventually move from Praça de Espanha to Gare do Oriente, so check with the turismo.

Language

Like French, Italian, Romanian and Spanish, Portuguese is a Romance language, derived from Latin. It's spoken by 10 million Portuguese and 130 million Brazilians, and is the official language of five African nations (Angola, Cape Verde, Guinea-Bissau, Mozambique and São Tomé e Príncipe). In Asia you'll hear it in the former Portuguese territories of Macau and East Timor, and in enclaves around Malacca, Goa, Damão and Diu.

Foreigners are often struck by the strangeness of the spoken language, but those who understand French or Spanish will see how similar written Portuguese is to the other Romance languages.

The pre-Roman inhabitants of the Iberian Peninsula are responsible for the most striking traits of the Portuguese language. The vulgar Latin of Roman soldiers and merchants gradually took over indigenous languages and a strong neo-Latin character evolved.

After the Arab invasion in AD 711, Arabic became the prestige cultural language in the Iberian Peninsula. Its influence on the Portuguese language ended with the expulsion of the Moors in 1249.

During the Middle Ages, the Portuguese language underwent several changes, mostly influenced by French and Provençal (another Romance language). In the 16th and 17th centuries, Italian and Spanish were responsible for innovations in vocabulary.

For a more detailed practical guide, get a copy of the new edition of Lonely Planet's *Portuguese phrasebook*.

Pronunciation

Pronunciation of Portuguese is difficult; as with English, vowels and consonants have more than one possible sound depending on position and stress. The following list should give you a rough idea of pronunciation, but listening to how local people speak will be your best guide.

Vowels

a	short, as the 'u' in 'cut'; long, as the 'e' in 'her'
e	short, as in 'bet'; longer, as the 'air' in Scottish *laird*; silent at the end of a word and in unstressed syllables
é	short, as in 'bet'
ê	long, as the 'a' in 'gate'
i	long, as in 'marine'; short, as in 'ring'
o	short, as in 'off'; long, as in 'note', or as the 'oo' in 'good'
ô	long, as in 'note'
u	as the 'oo' in 'good'

Nasal Vowels

Nasalisation is represented by **n** or **m** after a vowel, or by a tilde over it (eg, **ã**). The nasal **i** exists only approximately in English, such as the 'ing' in 'sing'. Try to pronounce nasal vowels with your nasal passages open, creating a similar sound to when you hold your nose.

Diphthongs

au	as the 'ow' in 'now'
ai	as the 'ie' in 'pie'
ei	as the 'ay' in 'day'
eu	pronounced together
oi	similar to the 'oy' in 'boy'

Nasal Diphthongs

Try the same technique as for nasal vowels. To say *não*, pronounce 'now' through your nose.

ão	nasal 'now' (owng)
ãe	nasal 'day' (eing)
õe	nasal 'boy' (oing)
ui	similar to the 'uing' in 'ensuing'

Consonants

c	before **a**, **o** or **u**, hard as in 'cat'; before **e** or **i**, soft as in 'cell'
ç	as in 'cell'
ch	as the 'sh' in 'ship' (variable)
g	before **a**, **o** or **u**, hard as in 'game'; before **e** or **i**, soft as the 's' in 'treasure'

153

h	never pronounced at the beginning of a word
nh	as the 'ni' in 'onion'
lh	as the 'll' in 'million'
j	as the 's' in 'treasure'
m, n	not pronounced when word-final; it simply nasalises the previous vowel
qu	before **a** or **o**, as the 'qu' in 'quad' before **e** or **i**, as the 'k' in 'key'
r	at the beginning of a word (or **rr** in the middle of a word) a harsh, guttural sound similar to the 'ch' in Scottish *loch*. In some areas of Portugal it's strongly rolled rather than guttural; in the middle or at the end of a word it's a rolled sound stronger than English 'r'
s	at the beginning of a word, as in 'see'; between vowels, as the 'z' in 'zeal'; before another consonant or at the end of a word, as the 'sh' in 'ship'
ss	as in 'see' (in the middle of a word)
x	as the 'sh' in 'ship', the 'z' in 'zeal', or the 'ks' sound in 'taxi'
z	as the 's' in 'treasure' (before another consonant, or at the end of a word)

Word Stress

Word stress is important in Portuguese, as it can change the meaning of the word. In Portuguese words with a written accent, the stress always falls on the accented syllable.

Gender

In Portuguese, things (as well as people) can be either masculine or feminine, with most masculine nouns ending in -**o** and most feminine ones ending in -**a**. This applies also to words or phrases about a person, with the ending agreeing with the person's gender – for example, *Obrigado/a* (Thank you), or *É casado/a?* (Are you married?).

The only single numbers with gender are 'one' or 'a' (*um* is masculine, *uma* feminine) and 'two' (*dois* is masculine, *duas* feminine).

Endings denoted as -**o/a** in the following sections indicate a choice based on the gender of the speaker or subject.

Basics

Yes/No.	*Sim/Não.*
Maybe.	*Talvez.*
Please.	*Se faz favor/Por favor.*
Thank you.	*Obrigado/a.*
That's fine/ You're welcome.	*De nada.*
Excuse me.	*Desculpe/Com licença.*
Sorry/Forgive me.	*Desculpe.*

Greetings

Hello.	*Bom dia.*
Hi. (informal, among friends)	*Olá/Chao.*
Good morning.	*Bom dia.*
Good evening.	*Boa tarde.*
Goodbye.	*Adeus.*
Bye. (informal)	*Chao.*
See you later.	*Até logo.*

Small Talk

How are you?	*Como está?*
I'm fine, thanks.	*Bem, obrigado/a.*
What's your name?	*Como se chama?*
My name is ...	*Chamo-me ...*
Where are you from?	*De onde é?*

I'm from ...	*Sou de ...*
Australia	*Austrália*
Japan	*Japão*
the UK	*o Reino Unido*
the USA	*os Estados Unidos*

How old are you?	*Quantos anos tem?*
I'm ... years old.	*Tenho ... anos.*
Are you married?	*É casado/a?*
Not yet.	*Aindo não.*
How many children do you have?	*Quantos filhos tem?*
daughter	*filha*
son	*filho*

Useful Adjectives & Adverbs

angry	*zangado*
beautiful	*belo*
better	*melhor*
delicious	*delicioso*

excellent	*excelente*
good	*bom/boa*
happy	*feliz*
hungry	*faminto*
ill	*doente*
lovely	*lindo*
married	*casado/a*
next (in time)	*seguinte or próximo*
one more/another	*mais um(a)*

Language Difficulties

I understand.	*Percebo/Entendo.*
I don't understand.	*Não percebo/entendo.*
Do you speak English?	*Fala inglês?*
Could you please write it down?	*Pode escrever isso, por favor?*

Getting Around

What time does ... leave/arrive?	*A que horas parte/ chega ...?*
the boat	*o barco*
the bus (city)	*o autocarro*
the bus (intercity)	*a camioneta*
the metro	*o metro*
the train	*o combóio*
the tram	*o eléctrico*

Where is the ...?	*Onde é a ...?*
bus stop	*paragem de autocarro*
metro station	*estação de metro*
train station	*estação ferroviária*
tram stop	*paragem de eléctrico*

I want to go to ...	*Quero ir a ...*
How long does it take?	*Quanto tempo leva isso?*
Is this the bus/train to ...?	*E este o autocarro/ combóio para ...?*

I'd like a ... ticket.	*Queria um bilhete ...*
one-way	*simples/de ida*
return	*de ida e volta*
1st class	*de primeira classe*
2nd class	*de segunda classe*

left-luggage office	*o depósito de bagagem*
platform	*cais*
timetable	*horário*

I'd like to hire ...	*Queria alugar ...*
a bicycle	*uma bicicleta*
a car	*um carro*
a motorcycle	*uma motocicleta*
a tour guide	*uma guia intérprete*

Fill it up, please. (ie, the tank)	*Encha a déposito, por favor.*

Directions

How do I get to ...?	*Como vou para ...?*
Is it near/far?	*É perto/longe?*
Go straight ahead.	*Siga sempre a direito/ sempre em frente.*

Turn left ...	*Vire à esquerda ...*
Turn right ...	*Vire à direita ...*
at the traffic lights	*no semáforo/nos sinais de trânsito*
at the next corner	*na próxima esquina*

What ... is this?	*O que ... é isto/ista?*
street/road	*rua/estrada*
suburb	*subúrbia*
town	*cidade/vila*

north	*norte*
south	*sul*
east	*leste/este*
west	*oeste*

Around Town

Where is (a/the) ...?	*Onde é ...?*
(nearest) bank	*o banco (mais próximo)*
city centre	*o centro da cidade/ da baixa*
... embassy	*a embaixada de ...*
exchange office	*um câmbio*
hospital	*o hospital*
hotel	*um hotel*
market	*o mercado*
police station	*o posto da polícia*
post office	*os correios*
public toilet	*os sanitários*
telephone office	*a central de telefones*
toilet	*os lavabos*
tourist office	*o turismo*

Signs

Entrada	Entrance
Saída	Exit
Empurre/Puxe	Push/Pull
Entrada Gratis	Free Entry
Turismo	Tourist Office
Quartos Livres	Rooms Available
Informações	Information
Aberto	Open
Encerrado (para Obras/Ferias)	Closed (for Repairs/Holidays)
Não Fumadores	No Smoking
Posto da Polícia	Police Station
Proíbido	Prohibited
Lavabos/WC	Toilets
Homens (H)	Men
Senhoras (S)	Women

What time does it open/close?	A que horas abre/fecha?
I'd like to make a telephone call.	Quero usar o telefone.
I'd like to change ...	Queria trocar ...
some money	dinheiro
travellers cheques	uns cheques de viagem

Accommodation

I'm looking for ...	Procuro ...
a camping ground	um parque de campismo
a youth hostel	uma pousada da juventude
a guesthouse	uma pensão (pl pensões)
a hotel	uma hotel (pl hotéis)
Do you have any rooms available?	Tem quartos livres?
I'd like to book ...	Quero fazer una reserva para ...
a bed	uma cama
a cheap room	um quarto barato
a single room	um quarto individual
a double room	um quarto de casal/ um quarto de matrimonial
a twin-bed room	um quarto de duplo

a room with a bathroom	um quarto com casa de banho
a dormitory bed	uma cama de dormitório
for one night	para uma noite
for two nights	para duas noites
How much is it ...?	Quanto é ...?
per night	por noite
per person	por pessoa
Is breakfast included?	O pequeno almoço está incluído?
May I see the room?	Posso ver o quarto?
Where is the toilet?	Onde ficam os lavabos (as casas de banho)?
It's very dirty/ noisy/expensive.	É muito sujo/ ruidoso/caro.

Shopping

How much is it?	Quanto custa?
May I look at it?	Posso ver?
It's too expensive.	É muito caro.
bookshop	livraria
chemist/pharmacy	farmácia
clothing store	boutique/confecções
department store	magazine
laundrette	lavandaria
market	mercado
newsagents	papelaria
open/closed (shop or office)	aberto/encerrado

Time & Dates

What time is it?	Que horas são?
At what time?	A que horas?
When?	Quando?
today	hoje
tonight	hoje à noite
tomorrow	amanhã
yesterday	ontem
morning/afternoon	manhã/tarde
Monday	segunda-feira
Tuesday	terça-feira
Wednesday	quarta-feira
Thursday	quinta-feira
Friday	sexta-feira
Saturday	sábado
Sunday	domingo

Emergencies

Help!	*Socorro!*
Call a doctor!	*Chame um médico!*
Call the police!	*Chame a polícia!*
Go away!	*Deixe-me em paz!/*
	Vai-te embora! (inf)
I've been robbed.	*Fui roubado/a.*
I've been raped.	*Fui violada/*
	Violarem-me.
I'm lost.	*Estou perdido/a.*

Numbers

1	*um/uma*
2	*dois/duas*
3	*três*
4	*quatro*
5	*cinco*
6	*seis*
7	*sete*
8	*oito*
9	*nove*
10	*dez*
11	*onze*
12	*doze*
13	*treze*
14	*catorze*
15	*quinze*
16	*dezasseis*
17	*dezassete*
18	*dezoito*
19	*dezanove*
20	*vint*
21	*vint e um*
22	*vint e dois*
30	*trinta*
40	*quarenta*
50	*cinquenta*
60	*sessenta*
70	*setenta*
80	*oitenta*
90	*noventa*
100	*cem*
101	*cento e um*
123	*cento e vinte e três*
200	*duzentos*
300	*trezentos*
1000	*mil*
2000	*dois mil*
one million	*um milhão (de)*

Health

Where is ...?	*Onde é ...?*
a hospital	*um hospital*
medical clinic	*um centro de saúde*
I'm ...	*Sou ...*
diabetic	*diabético/a*
epileptic	*epiléptico/a*
asthmatic	*asmático/a*
I'm allergic to ...	*Sou alérgico/a a ...*
antibiotics	*antibióticos*
penicillin	*penicilina*
I need a doctor.	*Preciso um médico.*
I'm pregnant.	*Estou grávida.*
antiseptic	*antiséptico*
aspirin	*aspirina*
condoms	*preservativo*
constipation	*constpaçao*
contraceptive	*anticoncepcional*
diarrhoea	*diarreia*
dizzy	*vertiginoso*
medicine	*remédio/medicamento*
nausea	*náusea*
sanitary napkins	*pensos higiénicos*
tampons	*tampões*

FOOD

I'm looking for ...	*Ando à procura ...*
food stall	*quiosque de comida/*
	bancada
grocery	*mercearia/*
	minimercado
market	*mercado*
restaurant	*restaurante*
supermarket	*supermercado*
Is service included	*O serviço está incluído*
in the bill?	*na conta?*
I'm a vegetarian.	*Sou vegeteriano/a.*
breakfast	*pequeno almoço*
evening dinner	*jantar*
lunch	*almoço*
counter in bar	*balcão*
or cafe	
bill (check)	*conta*

LANGUAGE

cover charge for service	*couvert*
prepayment required	*pré-pagamento*
menu	*ementa*
tourist menu	*ementa turística*
half-portion of a dish	*meia dose*
dish of the day	*prato do dia*

Places to Eat

casa/salão de chá – teahouse
casa de pasto – a casual eatery with cheap, simple meals
cervejaria – (lit: a beer house); also serves food
churrasqueira – (lit: a barbecue or grill); usually a restaurant serving grilled foods
marisqueira – seafood restaurant
pastelaria – pastry and cake shop
tasca – simple tavern, often with rustic decor

Entradas (Starters)

cocktail de gambas	prawn cocktail
salada de atum	tuna salad
omeleta de ...	...omelette
marisco	shellfish
presunto	smoked ham
cogumelos	mushroom

Sopa (Soup)

caldo verde	potato and shredded cabbage broth
gazpacho	refreshing cold vegetable soup
canja de galinha	chicken broth and rice
sopa à alentejana	bread soup with garlic and poached egg
sopa de legumes	vegetable soup
sopa de feijão verde	green-bean soup

Peixe/Mariscos (Fish/Shellfish)

ameijoas	clams
atum	tuna
bacalhau	dried, salted cod
camarões	shrimp
carapau	mackerel
chocos	cuttlefish
enguia	eel
espadarte	swordfish
gambas	prawns
lagostins	crayfish
lampreia	lamprey (like eel)
linguada	sole
lulas	squid
pargo	sea bream
peixe espada	scabbard fish
pescada	hake
polvo	octopus
robalo	sea bass
salmão	salmon
sardinhas	sardines
savel	shad
truta	trout

arroz de marisco – rich seafood and rice stew
caldeirada – fish stew with onions, potatoes and tomatoes
cataplana – a combination of shellfish and ham cooked in a sealed wok-style pan and typical of the Algarve region

Carne e Aves (Meat & Poultry)

borrego	lamb
bife	steak (not always beef)
cabrito	kid
carne de vaca (assada)	(roast) beef
carneiro	mutton
chouriço	spicy sausage
coelho	rabbit
costeleta	chop
entrecosto	rump steak
fiambre	ham
fígado	liver
frango	young chicken
galinha	chicken
javadi	wild boar
leitão	suckling pig
lombo	fillet of pork
pato	duck
perú	turkey
presunto	smoked ham
salsicha	sausage
tripas	tripe
vaca	beef
vitela	veal

Ethnic Dishes

cachupa – pork, corn and bean stew (Cape Verdean)

moamba da galinha – chicken stew (Angolan)

muzongué – fish broth with sweet potatoes (Angolan)

picanha – thin slices of grilled beef accompanied by beans and salad (Brazilian)

Legumes (Vegetables)

alface	lettuce
alho	garlic
arroz	rice
batatas	potatoes
cebolas	onions
cenouras	carrots
cogumelos	mushrooms
couve	cabbage
couve-flor	cauliflower
ervilhas	green peas
espargos	asparagus
espinafres	spinach
favas	broad beans
feijão	beans
lentilhas	lentils
pepino	cucumber
pimentos	peppers
salada	salad
salada mista	mixed salad

Ovos (Eggs)

cozido	hard boiled
escalfado	poached
estrelado	fried
mexido	scrambled
omeleta	omelette
quente	boiled

Frutas (Fruit)

alperces	apricots
ameixas	plums
amêndoas	almonds
ananás	pineapple
bananas	bananas
figos	figs
framboesas	raspberries
laranjas	oranges
limões	lemons
maças	apples
melões	melons
morangos	strawberries
pêras	pears
pêssegos	peaches
uvas	grapes

Condiments, Sauces & Appetisers

azeite	olive oil
azeitonas	olives
manteiga	butter
pimenta	pepper
piri-piri	chilli sauce
sal	salt

Snacks & Supplements

batatas fritas	French fries
gelado	ice cream
pão	bread
pão integral	wholemeal bread
queijo	cheese
sandes	sandwiches
uma torrada	an order (two pieces) of toast

Cooking Methods

assado	roasted
cozido	boiled
ensopada de ...	stew of ...
estufado	stewed
frito	fried
grelhado	grilled
na brasa	braised
no carvão	on coals (charcoal grilled)
no espeto	on the spit
no forno	in the oven (baked)

Drinks

água mineral	mineral water
(com gás)	(sparkling)
(sem gás)	(still)
aguardente	firewater
café	coffee
chá	tea
(com leite)	(with milk)
(com limão)	(with lemon)
sumo de fruta	fruit juice
vinho da casa	house wine
(branco)	(white)
(tinto)	(red)
vinho verde	semi-sparkling young wine

Glossary

See the Food section at the end of the Language chapter for words to do with food and drink.

aberto – open
adega – a cellar, especially a wine cellar; also means a traditional wine bar
Age of Discoveries – the period during the 15th and 16th centuries when Portuguese sailors explored the coast of Africa and finally charted a sea route to India
albergaria – an upmarket inn
arco – arch
armazém – riverside warehouse or store (many in Lisbon now being converted into restaurants or clubs)
artesanato – handicraft shop
ATM – automated teller machine
auto-da-fe – public sentencing ceremony of the Inquisition period
aviação – airline
azulejos – hand-painted tiles, often blue and white, used to decorate buildings

bagagem – baggage office
bairro – town district
balcão – counter in a bar or cafe
beco – cul de sac, alleyway
biblioteca – library
bicyclete tudo terrano (BTT) – mountain bike
bombeiros – fire services

câmara municipal – town hall
cartão/cartões telefónicos – plastic phonecard/s
casa de banho – public toilet
casa de fado fado house; a place (usually a restaurant) where people gather to hear *fado* music
casa de hóspedes – boarding house
centro de alojamento – accommodation centre
centro de comércio – shopping centre
centro de saúde – state-administered medical centre
chafariz – fountain

chegada – arrival (of bus, train etc)
churrasqueira or **churrascaria** – restaurant serving grilled foods, especially chicken
cidade – city
claustro – cloisters
concelho – council, municipality
consumo mínimo – minimum consumption charge (eg, at clubs)
correio normal – ordinary post
correio azul – priority post
Correios – post office
CP – Caminhos de Ferro Portugueses (the Portuguese state railway company)
Credifone – card-operated public phone

direita – right (direction); abbreviated as D, dir or Dta
Dom, Dona – honorific titles (Sir, Madam) traditionally given to kings, queens and other nobles now used more generally as a very polite form of address
duplo – room with twin beds

elevador – lift (elevator) or funicular
ementa – menu
encerrado – closed, shut down (eg, for repairs)
entrada – entrance (also starter, entrée)
esplanada – terrace or seafront promenade
esquerda – left; abbreviated as E, esq or Esqa
estação – station (usually train station)
estacionamento – parking
estalagem – inn; more expensive than an *albergaria*

fadista – *fado* singer
fado – traditional, melancholy Portuguese style of singing
farmácia – pharmacy
fechado – closed (eg, for the day/weekend/holiday)
feira – fair
férias – holidays
festa – festival
fortaleza – fort
freguesia – parish

GNR – Guarda Nacional Republicana, the national guard (the acting police force in towns without PSP police)
guitarra – 12-stringed, pear-chapted guitar used to accompany *fado*

hipermercado – hypermarket
horário – timetable
hospedaria – boarding house

IC (Intercidade) – express intercity train
ICEP – Investimentos, Comércio e Turismo de Portugal, the government's umbrella organisation for tourism and commerce
igreja – church
igreja matriz – parish church
IR (Interregional) – fairly fast train without too many stops
IVA (Imposto sobre Valor Acrescentado) – VAT (value added tax)

jardim – garden
judiaria – quarter in a town where Jews were once segregated
junta de turismo – see *turismo*

largo – small square
lavabo – toilet
lavandaria – laundry
limpar/limpeza a seco – dry-cleaning
lisboêtas – name for the inhabitants of Lisbon
lista – see *ementa*
livraria – bookshop
loja – shop

Manueline – a unique and elaborate style of art and architecture that emerged during the reign of Dom Manuel I in the 16th century
marranos – converted Jews or New Christians
meia dose – half-portion (food)
mercado municipal – municipal market
minimercado – grocery or small supermarket
miradouro – lookout
morna – melancholic music from Cape Verde
mosteiro – monastery
mouraria – Moorish quarter where Moors

were segregated after the Christian Reconquista
museu – museum
música popular – modern folk music

obras – repairs
open-air markets – huge outdoor markets specialising in cheap clothes and shoes, usually with many Roma stall-holders

paço – palace
paços de concelho – town hall (an older name for a *câmara municipal*)
papelaria – stationery shop
parque de campismo – camping ground
parque infantil – children's playground
partida – departure (of bus, train etc)
passar a ferro – ironing
pelourinho – stone pillory, often ornately carved; erected in the 13th to 18th centuries as symbols of justice and sometimes as places where criminals were punished
pensão (s), **pensões** (pl) – guesthouse; the Portuguese equivalent of a bed and breakfast (B&B), but breakfast is not always included
percuso pedestres – walkers' trails
portagem – toll road
posto de turismo – see *turismo*
pousada – government-run hotel (in a program called Pousadas de Portugal) offering upmarket accommodation, often in a converted castle, convent or palace
pousada da juventude – youth hostel
praça – square
praça de touros – bullring
praia – beach
pré-pagamento – prepayment required (as in some cafes or restaurants)
PSP – Polícia de Segurança Pública; the local police force

quarto de casal – room with a double bed
quarto individual – single room
quarto particular (or simply **quarto**) – room in a private house

R (Regional) – slow train
Reconquista – Christian reconquest of Portugal begun in 718 and completed in 1249

rés do chão – ground floor; abbreviated as R/C

residencial (s), **residenciais** (pl) – guest-house; slightly more expensive than a *pensão* and usually serving breakfast

retournados – refugees from Portugal's former African colonies

rio – river

romaria – religious pilgrimage

sanitários or **casas de banho** – public toilets

sapateria – shoe shop

sé – cathedral, from the Latin for 'seat' *(sedes)*, implying an episcopal seat

selos – stamps

semba – Angolan music

sem chumbo – unleaded petrol

serviço service charge

serviço de urgência – emergency ward

supermercado – supermarket

talha dourada – gilded woodwork

telemóvel – mobile phone

tourada – bullfight

Turihab – short for Turismo de Habitação, an association marketing private accommodation in country cottages, historic buildings and manor houses

turismo – tourist office

vila – town

LONELY PLANET

You already know that Lonely Planet produces more than this one guidebook, but you might not be aware of the other products we have on this region. Here is a selection of titles that you may want to check out as well:

Portugal
ISBN 1 86450 193 6
US$19.99 • UK£12.99

Portuguese phrasebook
ISBN 0 86442 589 9
US$7.95 • UK£4.50

Western Europe
ISBN 1 86450 163 4
US$27.99 • UK£15.99

Mediterranean Europe
ISBN 1 86450 154 5
US$27.99 • UK£15.99

Europe on a shoestring
ISBN 1 86450 150 2
US$24.99 • UK£14.99

Read This First: Europe
ISBN 1 86450 136 7
US$14.99 • UK£8.99

Europe phrasebook
ISBN 1 86450 224 X
US$8.99 • UK£4.99

Available wherever books are sold

LONELY PLANET

Guides by Region

Lonely Planet is known worldwide for publishing practical, reliable and no-nonsense travel information in our guides and on our Web site. The Lonely Planet list covers just about every accessible part of the world. Currently there are 16 series: Travel guides, Shoestring guides, Condensed guides, Phrasebooks, Read This First, Healthy Travel, Walking guides, Cycling guides, Watching Wildlife guides, Pisces Diving & Snorkeling guides, City Maps, Road Atlases, Out to Eat, World Food, Journeys travel literature and Pictorials.

AFRICA Africa on a shoestring • Cairo • Cairo City Map • Cape Town • Cape Town City Map • East Africa • Egypt • Egyptian Arabic phrasebook • Ethiopia, Eritrea & Djibouti • Ethiopian (Amharic) phrasebook • The Gambia & Senegal • Healthy Travel Africa • Kenya • Malawi • Morocco • Moroccan Arabic phrasebook • Mozambique • Read This First: Africa • South Africa, Lesotho & Swaziland • Southern Africa • Southern Africa Road Atlas • Swahili phrasebook • Tanzania, Zanzibar & Pemba • Trekking in East Africa • Tunisia • Watching Wildlife East Africa • Watching Wildlife Southern Africa • West Africa • World Food Morocco • Zimbabwe, Botswana & Namibia
Travel Literature: Mali Blues: Traveling to an African Beat • The Rainbird: A Central African Journey • Songs to an African Sunset: A Zimbabwean Story

AUSTRALIA & THE PACIFIC Auckland • Australia • Australian phrasebook • Australia Road Atlas • Cycling Australia • Cycling New Zealand • Fiji • Fijian phrasebook • Healthy Travel Australia, NZ and the Pacific • Islands of Australia's Great Barrier Reef • Melbourne • Melbourne City Map • Micronesia • New Caledonia • New South Wales • New Zealand • Northern Territory • Outback Australia • Out to Eat – Melbourne • Out to Eat – Sydney • Papua New Guinea • Pidgin phrasebook • Queensland • Rarotonga & the Cook Islands • Samoa • Solomon Islands • South Australia • South Pacific • South Pacific phrasebook • Sydney • Sydney City Map • Sydney Condensed • Tahiti & French Polynesia • Tasmania • Tonga • Tramping in New Zealand • Vanuatu • Victoria • Walking in Australia • Watching Wildlife Australia • Western Australia
Travel Literature: Islands in the Clouds: Travels in the Highlands of New Guinea • Kiwi Tracks: A New Zealand Journey • Sean & David's Long Drive

CENTRAL AMERICA & THE CARIBBEAN Bahamas, Turks & Caicos • Baja California • Bermuda • Central America on a shoestring • Costa Rica • Costa Rica Spanish phrasebook • Cuba • Dominican Republic & Haiti • Eastern Caribbean • Guatemala • Guatemala, Belize & Yucatán: La Ruta Maya • Healthy Travel Central & South America • Jamaica • Mexico • Mexico City • Panama • Puerto Rico • Read This First: Central & South America • World Food Mexico • Yucatán
Travel Literature: Green Dreams: Travels in Central America

EUROPE Amsterdam • Amsterdam City Map • Amsterdam Condensed • Andalucía • Austria • Baltic States phrasebook • Barcelona • Barcelona City Map • Berlin • Berlin City Map • Britain • British phrasebook • Brussels, Bruges & Antwerp • Brussels City Map • Budapest • Budapest City Map • Canary Islands • Central Europe • Central Europe phrasebook • Corfu & the Ionians • Corsica • Crete • Crete Condensed • Croatia • Cycling Britain • Cycling France • Cyprus • Czech & Slovak Republics • Denmark • Dublin • Dublin City Map • Eastern Europe • Eastern Europe phrasebook • Edinburgh • Estonia, Latvia & Lithuania • Europe on a shoestring • Europe phrasebook • Finland • Florence • France • Frankfurt Condensed • French phrasebook • Georgia, Armenia & Azerbaijan • Germany • German phrasebook • Greece • Greek Islands • Greek phrasebook • Hungary • Iceland, Greenland & the Faroe Islands • Ireland • Italian phrasebook • Italy • Krakow • Lisbon • The Loire • London • London City Map • London Condensed • Madrid • Malta • Mediterranean Europe • Mediterranean Europe phrasebook • Moscow • Mozambique • Munich • Netherlands • Norway • Out to Eat – London • Out to Eat – Paris • Paris • Paris City Map • Paris Condensed • Poland • Portugal • Portuguese phrasebook • Prague • Prague City Map • Provence & the Côte d'Azur • Read This First: Europe • Romania & Moldova • Rome • Rome City Map • Russia, Ukraine & Belarus • Russian phrasebook • Scandinavian & Baltic Europe • Scandinavian phrasebook • Scotland • Sicily • Slovenia • South-West France • Spain • Spanish phrasebook • St Petersburg • St Petersburg City Map • Sweden • Switzerland • Tuscany • Ukrainian phrasebook • Venice • Vienna • Walking in Britain • Walking in France • Walking in Ireland • Walking in Italy • Walking in Spain • Walking in Switzerland • Western Europe • World Food France • World Food Ireland • World Food Italy • World Food Spain
Travel Literature: Love and War in the Apennines • The Olive Grove: Travels in Greece • On the Shores of the Mediterranean • Round Ireland in Low Gear • A Small Place in Italy • After Yugoslavia

LONELY PLANET

Mail Order

Lonely Planet products are distributed worldwide. They are also available by mail order from Lonely Planet, so if you have difficulty finding a title please write to us. North and South American residents should write to 150 Linden St, Oakland, CA 94607, USA; European and African residents should write to 10a Spring Place, London NW5 3BH, UK; and residents of other countries to Locked Bag 1, Footscray, Victoria 3011, Australia.

INDIAN SUBCONTINENT Bangladesh • Bengali phrasebook • Bhutan • Delhi • Goa • Healthy Travel Asia & India • Hindi & Urdu phrasebook • India • Indian Himalaya • Karakoram Highway • Kerala • Mumbai (Bombay) • Nepal • Nepali phrasebook • Pakistan • Rajasthan • Read This First: Asia & India • South India • Sri Lanka • Sri Lanka phrasebook • Tibet • Tibetan phrasebook • Trekking in the Indian Himalaya • Trekking in the Karakoram & Hindukush • Trekking in the Nepal Himalaya
Travel Literature: The Age of Kali: Indian Travels and Encounters • Hello Goodnight: A Life of Goa • In Rajasthan • A Season in Heaven: True Tales from the Road to Kathmandu • Shopping for Buddhas • A Short Walk in the Hindu Kush • Slowly Down the Ganges

ISLANDS OF THE INDIAN OCEAN Madagascar & Comoros • Maldives • Mauritius, Réunion & Seychelles

MIDDLE EAST & CENTRAL ASIA Bahrain, Kuwait & Qatar • Central Asia • Central Asia phrasebook • Dubai • Farsi (Persian) phrasebook • Hebrew phrasebook • Iran • Israel & the Palestinian Territories • Istanbul • Istanbul City Map • Istanbul to Cairo on a shoestring • Jerusalem • Jerusalem City Map • Jordan • Lebanon • Middle East • Oman & the United Arab Emirates • Syria • Turkey • Turkish phrasebook • World Food Turkey • Yemen
Travel Literature: Black on Black: Iran Revisited • The Gates of Damascus • Kingdom of the Film Stars: Journey into Jordan

NORTH AMERICA Alaska • Boston • Boston City Map • California & Nevada • California Condensed • Canada • Chicago • Chicago City Map • Deep South • Florida • Great Lakes • Hawaii • Hiking in Alaska • Hiking in the USA • Las Vegas • Los Angeles • Los Angeles City Map • Miami • Miami City Map • New England • New Orleans • New York City • New York City City Map • New York City Condensed • New York, New Jersey & Pennsylvania • Oahu • Out to Eat – San Francisco • Pacific Northwest • Rocky Mountains • San Francisco • San Francisco City Map • Seattle • Southwest • Texas • USA • USA phrasebook • Vancouver • Virginia & the Capital Region • Washington, DC • Washington, DC City Map • World Food Deep South, USA
Travel Literature: Caught Inside: A Surfer's Year on the California Coast • Drive Thru America

NORTH-EAST ASIA Beijing • Beijing City Map • Cantonese phrasebook • China • Hiking in Japan • Hong Kong • Hong Kong City Map • Hong Kong Condensed • Hong Kong, Macau & Guangzhou • Japan • Japanese phrasebook • Korea • Korean phrasebook • Kyoto • Mandarin phrasebook • Mongolia • Mongolian phrasebook • Seoul • Shanghai • South-West China • Taiwan • Tokyo
Travel Literature: In Xanadu: A Quest • Lost Japan

SOUTH AMERICA Argentina, Uruguay & Paraguay • Bolivia • Brazil • Brazilian phrasebook • Buenos Aires • Chile & Easter Island • Colombia • Ecuador & the Galapagos Islands • Healthy Travel Central & South America • Latin American Spanish phrasebook • Peru • Quechua phrasebook • Read This First: Central & South America • Rio de Janeiro • Rio de Janeiro City Map • South America on a shoestring • Trekking in the Patagonian Andes • Venezuela
Travel Literature: Full Circle: A South American Journey

SOUTH-EAST ASIA Bali & Lombok • Bangkok • Bangkok City Map • Burmese phrasebook • Cambodia • Hanoi • Healthy Travel Asia & India • Hill Tribes phrasebook • Ho Chi Minh City • Indonesia • Indonesian phrasebook • Indonesia's Eastern Islands • Java • Lao phrasebook • Laos • Malay phrasebook • Malaysia, Singapore & Brunei • Myanmar (Burma) • Philippines • Pilipino (Tagalog) phrasebook • Read This First: Asia & India • Singapore • Singapore City Map • South-East Asia on a shoestring • South-East Asia phrasebook • Thailand • Thailand's Islands & Beaches • Thailand, Vietnam, Laos & Cambodia Road Atlas • Thai phrasebook • Vietnam • Vietnamese phrasebook • World Food Thailand • World Food Vietnam

ALSO AVAILABLE: Antarctica • The Arctic • The Blue Man: Tales of Travel, Love and Coffee • Brief Encounters: Stories of Love, Sex & Travel • Chasing Rickshaws • The Last Grain Race • Lonely Planet Unpacked • Not the Only Planet: Science Fiction Travel Stories • On the Edge: Extreme Travel • Sacred India • Travel with Children • Travel Photography: A Guide to Taking Better Pictures

Index

Text

A

ACARTE 83
accommodation 91-7
  camping 91, 93
  costs 91
  guesthouses 92, 94
  hostels 91-2, 93-4
  hotels 92-3, 94-7
  long-term rentals 97
activities 48, 89-90, 132,
  see also individual entries
Afonso, Jorge 21
Age of Discoveries 10-11, 20
air travel 51-5
  airport taxes 52
  airports 51, 65
  airline booking numbers 52
  disabled travellers 52
  international 53-5
  to/from other parts of
    Portugal 52-3
Ajuda 88-9
Alfama 72-3, 76-9
animals, treatment of 24
Antunes, António 20
Aqueduto das Águas Livres 84
architecture 20-1
  Manueline 86-7, 127, 129-
    30
  modern 86
Arco da Vitória 73
Arco do Cego 56
Armazéns do Chiado 126
Arraial Gay e Lésbico 41
art galleries
  Centro de Arte Moderna
    82-3
  Estoril casino 140
  metro 68
  Museu Calouste Gulbenkian
    81-2
  Museu de Arte Moderna
    (Sintra) 131
  Museu do Trabalho Michel
    Giacometti 148
  Museu Nacional de Arte
    Antiga 81

Bold indicates maps.

Museu-Escola de Artes
  Decorativas 77-8
Parque das Nações 86
artesanatos, see handicrafts
As Janelas Verdes 96
ascensors, see funicular
Atrium Saldanha 126
Azenhas do Mar 135
azulejos 22, 73, 80, 121-2,
  see also handicrafts

B

bacalhau 99-100
Bairro Alto 75-6
BaixAnima Festival 88
ballet 23, 117-18
Basílica da Estrela 72, 80
Basílica da Nossa Senhora dos
  Mártires 71
beaches 46, 135, 138, 146,
  149, see also individual
  entries under praia
Beco da Cardosa 73
Beco das Cruzes 73
beer 104
Belém 86-8
Biaxa 73-4
bicycle travel, see cycling
bird-watching 15, 148
boat travel 62
Boca do Inferno 138
books 37, 122-3
border crossings 51
Botelho, João 23
bowling 90
bullfighting 24, 119, 120
bus travel
  bus stations 55-7
  international 57-8
  to/from other parts of
    Portugal 55
  within Lisbon 65-6
business
  hours 46
  services 48-50
Byron, Lord 127, 133

C

Cabo da Roca 13, 132, 135
Cabo Espichel 151

Cacilhas 146
Café A Brasileira 71
Cais do Sodré 72, 74
caldo verde 99
Câmara Escura 78
camping 91, 93
  Camping Card International
    29-30
canoeing 132, 150
Capela de São João Baptista 76
car travel
  assistance 60-1
  drinking & driving 61
  driving licence 29
  fuel 61
  highways 60
  insurance 61
  international 61-2
  International Driving Permit
    29
  rental 68-70
  rules 61
  to/from other parts of
    Portugal 60-1
  traffic congestion 46
  within Lisbon 68
Carnaval 47
Casa do Fado e da Guitarra
  Portuguesa 77
Casa dos Bicos 76
Casa Museu de Fernando
  Pessoa 81
Cascais 136-40, **137**
  accommodation 138
  activities 138
  attractions 136-8
  beaches 138
  Boca do Inferno 138
  Centro Cultural de Gandar-
    inha 138
  entertainment 139
  Estoril Festival de
    Jazz 138
  Festival de Música da Costa
    do Estoril 138
  fish market 136-7
  food 139
  Igreja de Nossa Senhora da
    Assunção 136-7
  Museu Condes de Castro
    Guimarães 137

171

Boxed Text

Lisbon Maps

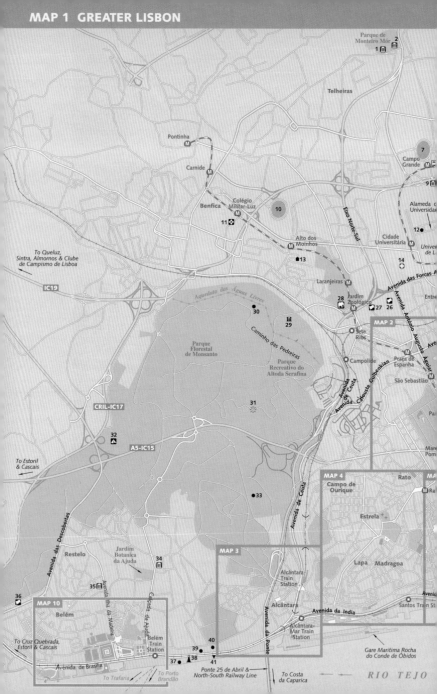

MAP 1 GREATER LISBON

Parque de
Monteiro Mór
1 🏛 2 🏛

Telheiras

Pontinha Ⓜ

Carnide Ⓜ

Campo
Grande Ⓜ 7

9 🏛

Colégio
Militar-Luz Ⓜ
Benfica Ⓜ
10

Alameda c
Universidae

11 ✠

12 ●

Alto dos
Moinhos Ⓜ

Cidade
Universitária Ⓜ

To Queluz,
Sintra, Almornos & Clube
de Campismo de Lisboa

13 🏛

14 🏛

Univers
de L

Laranjeiras Ⓜ

Aqueduto das Águas Livres

IC19

Avenida das Forças A

Jardim
Zoológico Ⓜ
28 27 26

30 ●

29 🏛

MAP 2

Caminho das Pedreiras

Seta
Rio

Parque
Florestal
de Monsanto

Parque
Recreativo do
Alto da Serafina

Campolide Ⓜ

Praça de
Espanha

São Sebastião

CRIL-IC17

31 ☀

Pa

32 🏛

Mare
Pom

A5-IC15

To Estoril
& Cascais

MAP 4

Rato

M Ra

Campo de
Ourique

33 ●

Estrela ✝

To Cruz Quebrada,
Estoril & Cascais

Lapa   Madragoa

Restelo

Jardim
Botânico
da Ajuda

34 🏛

MAP 3

Alcântara
Train Station

Avenida das Descobertas

Santos Train St

35 🏛

36 🏛

Alcântara

Avenida da Índia

Alcântara-
Mar Train
Station

MAP 10

Belém

Belém Train
Station

Avenida Ilha da Madeira

Calçada da Ajuda

39 ● 40 ▲

Gare Marítima Rocha
do Conde de Óbidos

To Trafaria

Avenida de Brasília

37 ● 38 ▲ 41 ▲

To Porto
Brandão

Ponte 25 de Abril &
North-South Railway Line

To Costa
da Caparica

RIO TEJO

Charneca

Aeroporto
de Lisboa

Avenida Marechal Craveiro Lopes

Alvalade

Entrecampos

Avenida dos Estados

Areeiro

Olaias

Chelas

Poço do
Bispo

Marvila

Xabregas

RIO TEJO

Parque do
Tejo e do
Trancão

MAP 9

Olivais
Norte

Gare do Oriente
Train, Bus &
Metro Station

Cabo Ruivo

Olivais

Olivais
Sul

PLACES TO STAY & EAT
4 Casa da Juventude
13 Quinta Nova da Conceição
32 Lisboa Camping - Parque Municipal
41 Café In

OTHER
1 Museu Nacional do Teatro
2 Museu Nacional do Traje
3 Instituto Geográfico do Exército
5 Olivais Swimming Pool
6 Lisboa Racket Centre
7 Estádio José de Alvalade
8 Campo Grande Bus Station
9 Museu da Cidade
10 Estádio da Luz (SL Benfica)
11 Centro Comercial
   Colombo & Play Center
12 Aula Magna da Reitoria
14 Santa Maria Hospital School
15 Galeria III
16 Biblioteca Nacional
17 Cooperativa Nacional
   Apoio Deficientes (CNAD)
18 Teatro Municipal Maria Matos;
   Teatro Infantil de Lisboa
19 Areeiro Swimming Pool
20 Federação Portuguesa de Campismo
21 Museu Nacional do Azulejo
22 Praça de Touros
23 Angolan Embassy
24 Banque Nationale de Paris
25 Feira Popular
26 US Embassy & Consulate
27 Brazilian Embassy
28 Jardim Zoológico
29 Quinta dos Marquêses da Fronteira
30 Parque Ecológico de Monsanto
31 Highest Point in Lisbon
33 Instalações de Ténis de Monsanto
34 Museu do Palácio Nacional da Ajuda
35 Museu Nacional de Etnologia
36 Moroccan Embassy
37 Tejo Bike
38 Monument to Amália Rodrigues
39 Cordoaria Nacional
40 Centro de Congressos de
   Lisboa (Parque Junqueira)

To Cacilhas   To Seixal   To Barreiro   To Montijo

OTHER
1 Market
2 Bus Station for Costa
   da Caparica & Sesimbra
3 Teatro Aberto
4 Mozambique Embassy
5 Barclays Bank
6 Biblioteca Municipal
7 Culturgest
8 Usit Tagus
10 Comissão para a Igualdade e
   para os Direitos das Mulheres
11 CIAL - Centro de Línguas
12 Planet Megastore
13 Select
14 ICEP (Investimentos, Comércio e
   Turismo de Portugal) Head Office
15 Librairie Française
16 Secretariado Nacional de Rehabilitação
17 Centro Artístico Infantil
   (Children's Art Centre); ACARTE
18 Museu Calouste Gulbenkian
19 Centro de Arte Moderna
20 Associação Portuguesa de
   Mulheres Empresárias
21 Livraria Municipal
23 Movijovem
25 Arco do Cego Bus Station;
   Intercentro (Eurolines) Ticket Office
26 Associação Opus Gay
27 American Chamber of Commerce
28 Tinturaria
29 Atrium Saldanha
30 Galerias Monumental
32 Instiut Franco-Portugais de
   Lisbonne & Alliance Française
37 Estufas (Greenhouses)
38 Clube VII
39 PostNet
43 Serviço de Estrangeiros e Fronteiras
   (Foreigners' Registration Service)
44 Mussolo
50 Polirent
51 Net Center
52 Intercentro (Eurolines) Ticket Office
55 Igreja de Penha de França
56 Jumbo Expresso Viagens
58 Instituto da Conservação da
   Natureza (ICN)
59 Top Tours
60 Crédit Lyonnais
61 Instituto Particular de Formação e
   Ensino de Línguas (IPFEL)
63 Usit Tagus
65 Lisboa Business Centre
66 Livraria Buchholz
68 Tour Bus Terminal
71 Instituto Português de
   Cartográfia e Cadastro
72 Complexo das Amoreiras
   (Amoreiras Shopping Centre)

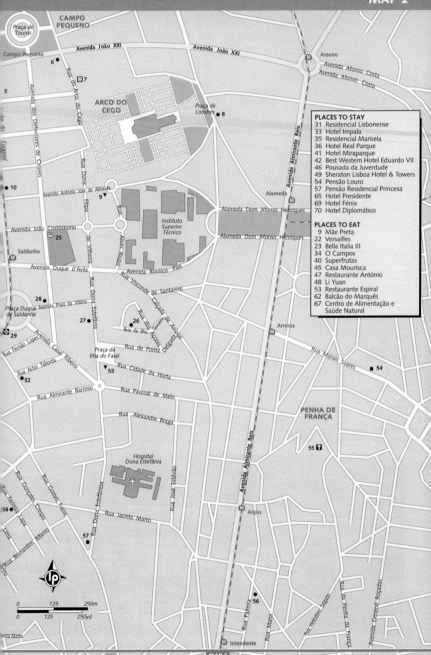

PLACES TO STAY
31 Residencial Lisbonense
33 Hotel Impala
35 Residencial Marisela
36 Hotel Real Parque
41 Hotel Miraparque
42 Best Western Hotel Eduardo VII
46 Pousada da Juventude
49 Sheraton Lisboa Hotel & Towers
54 Pensão Louro
57 Pensão Residencial Princesa
65 Hotel Presidente
69 Hotel Fénix
70 Hotel Diplomático

PLACES TO EAT
9 Mãe Preta
22 Versailles
23 Bella Italia III
34 O Campos
40 Superfrutas
44 Casa Mourisca
47 Restaurante António
48 Li Yuan
53 Restaurante Espiral
62 Balcão do Marquês
67 Centro de Alimentação e
   Saúde Natural

MAP 3

Tapada
da Ajuda

0   125   250m
0   125   250yd

Tapada da Ajuda

Avenida de Ceuta

Rua do Alvito

Acesso a Ponte

Avenida da Ponte

Calçada da Tapada

Alcântara
Train
Station

Rua dos Lusíadas
3

Rua de Alcântara

Rua das Fontainhas

Rua João de Oliveira Miguéns

4

5

Rua Prior do Crato

Rua Vieira da Silva

Rua Gilberto Rola

6

Rua do Arco

Largo do
Calvário

7

Rua de Cascais

Avenida 24 de

Travessa
Teixeira Júnior

Rua Maria
Luisa Holstein

8

Rua da Creche Florbela

9

Avenida da India

Alcântara-Mar
Train Station

Calçada da Tapada

Rua da Industria

Calçada da Tapada

SANTO
AMARO

Rua Jau

Rua Luis de Camões

Rua Cid Filinto Elísio

Rua Vicente

Rua Pedro Calmon

Rua dos Lusíadas

2

Calçada de Santo Amaro

Rua 1 de Maio

Avenida da Ponte

ALCÂNTARA

10

11

Doca de Alcânt

Rua da Junqueira

Avenida de Brasília

12

13

14

15

16 17

19 18

20

Doca de
Santo Amaro

21

Gare Marítima
de Alcântara

Rua General Gomes Aran

Avenida da India
Avenida de Brasília

Ponte 25
de Abril

North-South
Railway Line

RIO TEJO

PLACES TO EAT
8   Alcântara Café
12 Doca de Santo Esplanada
13 Havana
14 Tertúlia do Tejo
15 Cosmos
16 Celtas & Iberos
17 Zonadoca
18 Pasta Caffé

OTHER
1   Pilom
2   Kussunguila
3   Rotas do Vento
4   Paradise Garage
5   Gartejo
6   Timpanas
7   Luanda
9   Alcântara Mar
10 Museu da Carris
11 Museu de Cera
19 Hawaii
20 Café da Ponte
21 Salsa Latina

MARTIN MOOS

A night-time view of Castelo de São Jorge and Lisbon city centre from the Elevador de Santa Justa

MAP 4

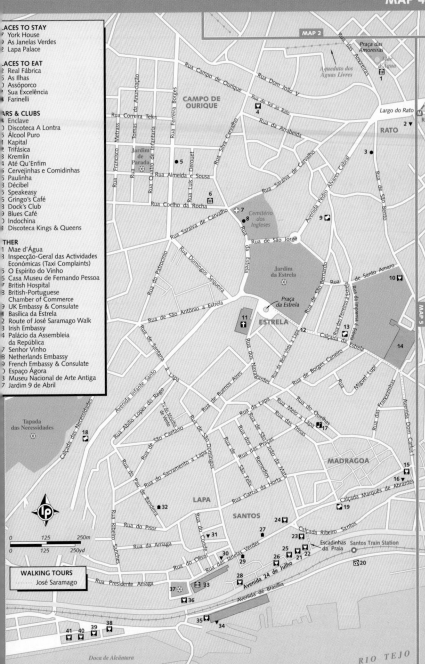

WALKING TOURS
.... José Saramago

MAP 5

RATO

Rua Alexandre Herculano

Rua da Escola Politécnica

Rua da São Mamede

Rua da Imprensa Nacional

Jardim Botânico

Avenida da Liberdade

Rua de Santa Marta

Rua do Passadiço

Rua de Santo António

Rato

Campo dos Mártires da Pátria

Rua de São Lázaro

Rua do Salitre

Rua da Alegria

Praça da Alegria

Avenida

Rua de São José

Elevador da Lavra

Praça do Príncipe Real

MAP 6

Praça das Flores

Rua Eduardo Coelho

Rua do Século

BAIRRO ALTO

Restauradores

Rossio Train Station

Rua Academia Ciências

Largo de Jesus

Rossio

Rua Betesga

BAIXA

Rua Aurea

Rua da Prata

Rua dos Poiais de São Bento

Calçada do Combro

MAP 7

Largo do Chiado

Baixa Chiado

Baixa Chiado

Rua Augusta

SANTA CATARINA

Rua da Boavista

Largo do Corde Barão

CHIADO

Rua do Arsenal

Rua Dom Luís I

Avenida 24 de Julho

Praça Dom Luís I

Cais do Sodré Train & Metro Station

Av. de Brasília

RIO TEJO

To Cacilhas

WALKING TOURS
José Saramago
Fernando Pessoa

MAP 5

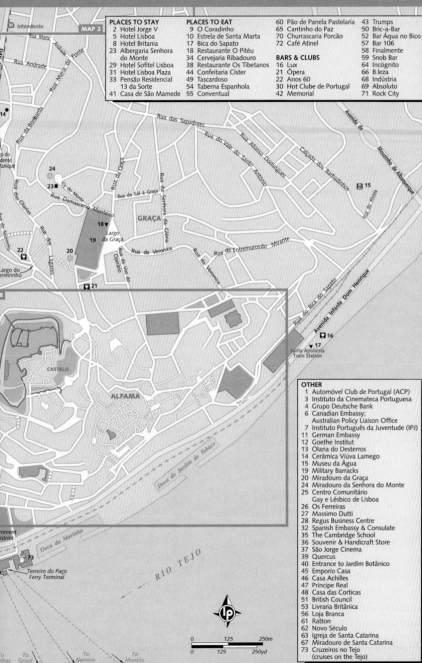

PLACES TO STAY
2 Hotel Jorge V
5 Hotel Lisboa
8 Hotel Britania
23 Albergaria Senhora do Monte
29 Hotel Sofitel Lisboa
31 Hotel Lisboa Plaza
33 Pensão Residencial 13 da Sorte
41 Casa de São Mamede

PLACES TO EAT
9 O Coradinho
10 Estrela de Santa Marta
17 Bica do Sapato
18 Restaurante O Pitéu
34 Cervejaria Ribadouro
38 Restaurante Os Tibetanos
44 Confeitaria Cister
49 Tascardoso
54 Taberna Espanhola
55 Conventual
60 Pão de Panela Pastelaria
65 Cantinho do Paz
70 Churrascaria Porcão
72 Café Atinel

BARS & CLUBS
16 Lux
21 Ópera
22 Anos 60
30 Hot Clube de Portugal
42 Memorial
43 Trumps
50 Bric-a-Bar
52 Bar Áqua no Bico
57 Bar 106
58 Finalmente
59 Snob Bar
64 Incógnito
66 B.leza
68 Indústria
69 Absoluto
71 Rock City

OTHER
1 Automóvel Club de Portugal (ACP)
3 Instituto da Cinemateca Portuguesa
4 Grupo Deutsche Bank
6 Canadian Embassy; Australian Policy Liaison Office
7 Instituto Português da Juventude (IPJ)
11 German Embassy
12 Goethe Institut
13 Olaria do Desterros
14 Cerâmica Viúva Lamego
15 Museu da Água
19 Military Barracks
20 Miradouro da Graça
24 Miradouro da Senhora do Monte
25 Centro Comunitário Gay e Lésbico de Lisboa
26 Os Ferreiras
27 Massimo Dutti
28 Regus Business Centre
32 Spanish Embassy & Consulate
35 The Cambridge School
36 Souvenir & Handicraft Store
37 São Jorge Cinema
39 Quercus
40 Entrance to Jardim Botânico
45 Emporio Casa
46 Casa Achilles
47 Príncipe Real
48 Casa das Corticas
51 British Council
53 Livraria Britânica
56 Loja Branca
61 Ratton
62 Novo Século
63 Igreja de Santa Catarina
67 Miradouro de Santa Catarina
73 Cruzeiros no Tejo (cruises on the Tejo)

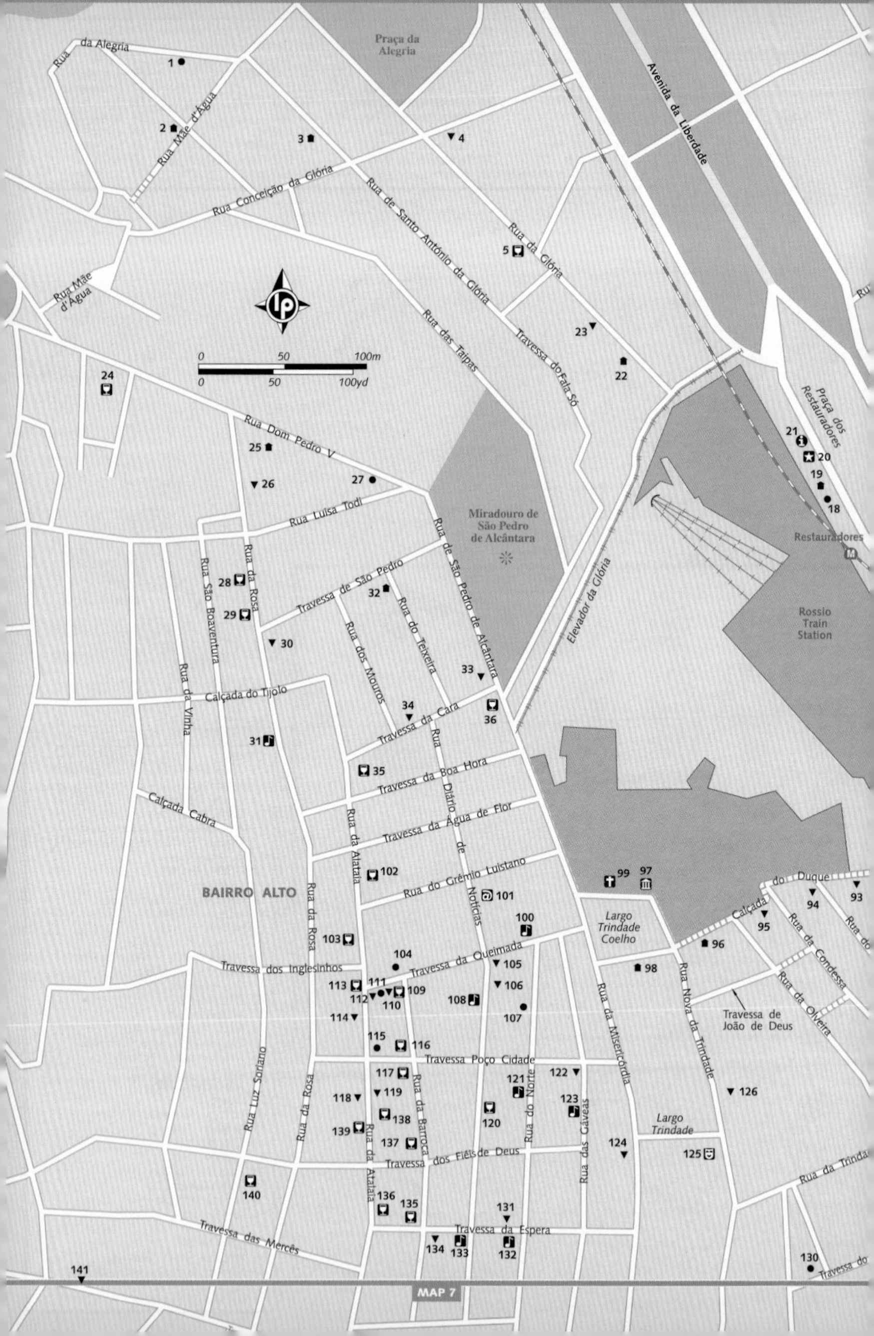

MAP 6

Rua da Alegria

Praça da
Alegria

Rua Mãe d'Água

Rua Conceição da Glória

Rua de Santo António da Glória

Rua da Glória

Avenida da Liberdade

Rua Mãe d'Água

Rua das Taipas

Travessa do Fala Só

Praça dos
Restauradores

Restauradores

Elevador da Glória

Rossio
Train
Station

Rua Dom Pedro V

Rua Luísa Todi

Miradouro de
São Pedro
de Alcântara

Rua da Rosa

Rua São Boaventura

Travessa de São Pedro

Rua de São Pedro de Alcântara

Rua do Teixeira

Rua da Vinha

Calçada do Tijolo

Rua dos Mouros

Travessa da Cara

Calçada Cabra

Travessa da Boa Hora

Rua do Diário de Notícias

Travessa da Água de Flor

BAIRRO ALTO

Rua da Atalaia

Travessa do Grémio Luisitano

Largo
Trindade
Coelho

Calçada do Duque

Travessa dos Inglesinhos

Rua da Rosa

Travessa da Queimada

Rua Nova da Trindade

Travessa de
João de Deus

Rua da Oliveira

Rua da Condessa

Rua da Misericórdia

Travessa Poço Cidade

Rua do Norte

Rua da Barroca

Rua das Gáveas

Largo
Trindade

Rua da Trindade

Travessa dos Fiéis de Deus

Rua do Século

Rua da Atalaia

Travessa das Mercês

Travessa da Espera

Travessa do

MAP 7

0   50   100m
0   50   100yd

MAP 6

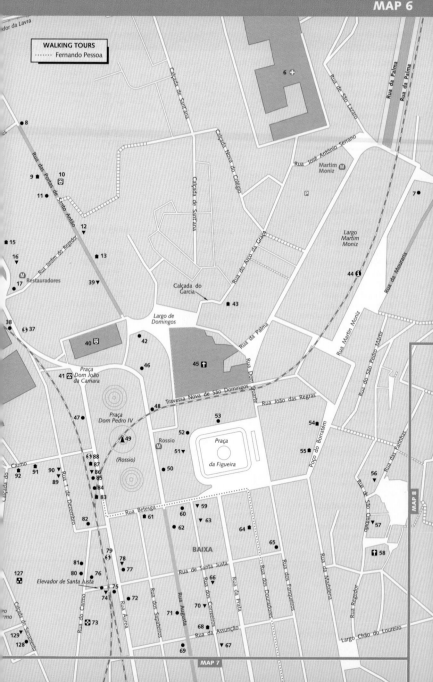

WALKING TOURS
.... Fernando Pessoa

dor da Lavra

8

Rua das Portas de Santo Antão

9
10
11

12

15
16
Restauradores
17

38
37

Carmo
92 91
90
89
88
87
86
85
84
83

82

127
Elevador de Santa Justa
81
80 76
79
78
77

75
74 72

129
128
73

Calçada de Santana

Calçada Nova do Colégio

Calçada de Santana

13

39

Rua Jardim do Regedor

Rua 1° de Dezembro

Calçada do Carmo

Rua do Carmo

Largo de Domingos

Calçada do Garcia

40
42
46
45
41
Praça Dom João da Camara
47
48
49
Rossio
(Rossio)
50
51
52
53

Praça Dom Pedro IV

Rua Betesga
59
61
60
62
63
64
65
66
70
71
68
69
67

BAIXA

Rua Áurea
Rua dos Sapateiros
Rua Augusta
Rua dos Correeiros
Rua da Prata
Rua da Assunção
Rua de Santa Justa

Rua dos Douradores
Rua da Madeira

6

Rua de São Lázaro

Rua José António Serrano

Rua da Palma
Rua da Palma

Martim Moniz

7

Largo Martim Moniz

44

Rua da Mouraria

Rua do Arco da Graça

43

Rua da Palma

Rua Dom Duarte

Travessa Nova de São Domingos
Rua João das Regras

Praça da Figueira

54
55
56
57
58

Poço do Borratém

Rua de São Pedro Mártir

Rua Martim Moniz

Rua das Farinhas

Rua de São Cristóvão

Rua dos Fanqueiros

Rua Regedor

Largo Chão do Loureiro

MAP 8

MAP 7

MAP 6

PLACES TO STAY
2 Hotel Botânico
3 Residencial Nova Avenida
9 Pensão Residencial Florescente
13 Pensão Lafonense
15 Pensão Imperial
19 Orion Eden Lisboa
22 Hotel Suiço-Atlântico
25 Pensão Londres
32 Pensão Globo
43 Pensão Residencial Gerês
54 Pensão Residencial Alcobia
55 Hotel Lisboa Tejo
61 Pensão Arco da Bandeira
64 Pensão Norte
68 Albergaria Insulana
83 Pensão Santo Tirso
87 Hotel Métropole
91 Pensão Estação Central
92 Hospedaria Bons Dias; Residencial Estrela do Mondego
96 Pensão Duque
98 Pensão Estrela de Ouro

PLACES TO EAT
4 O Fumeiro
12 Casa do Alentejo
16 Pinóquio
23 O Brinco da Glória
26 Restaurante Japanês Bonsai
30 O Cantinho da Rosa
33 Cafetaria Brasil
34 Mastiga na Tola
39 Gambrinus
51 Casa Suiça
56 Algures na Mouraria
57 São Cristóvão
59 Confeitaria Nacional
63 João do Grão
66 Ena Pãi
67 Restaurante Adega Regional da Beira
70 Lagosta Vermelha
74 Chiadomel
78 Casa Chineza
86 Café Nicola
89 Celeiro Supermarket
90 Celeiro
93 O Sol
94 Restaurante Solar do Duque
95 Casa Transmontana
105 Hau Lon
106 Vá e Volta
110 O Barrigas
112 Bota Alta
114 Ali-a-Papa
118 Pap' Açorda
119 Pedro das Arábias
122 Sinal Vermelho
124 Tavares Rico
126 Cervejaria da Trindade
129 Leitaria Académica
131 A Primavera
134 Tasca do Manel
141 Sinal Verde

SHOPPING
7 Centro Mouraria Martim Moniz
18 Virgin Megastore
27 Dom Pedro V Joias
38 Illegal
42 A Ginjinha
46 Azevedo Rua
48 Rabimos
50 Maison Louvre
53 Hospital das Bonecas (Dolls' Hospital)
60 Manuel Tavares
62 Casa Macário
69 Camisaria Pitta
71 Cenoura
72 Arte Rústica
73 Edifício Granella e Valentim de Carvalho Megastore
75 Papelaria Fernandes
76 Livraria Portugal
77 Discoteca Amália
80 Ana Salazer
81 Luvaria Ulisses
82 Tabacaria Adamastor
84 Tabacaria Mónaco
85 Editorial Notícias
104 O Velho Sapateiro
111 raveman records
115 Lena Aires
128 Violino
130 José António Tenente

BARS & CLUBS
5 Ritz Clube
24 Pavilhão Chinês
28 Play Bar
29 Nova
35 Primas
36 Solar do Vinho do Porto
102 Frágil
103 Arroz Doce
109 Sudoeste
113 Portas Largas
116 Os Três Pastorinhos
117 Cena de Copos
120 Tertúlia
135 Sétimo Céu
136 espaço fátima lopes
137 Clube da Esquina
138 Fremitus
139 A Capela
140 Café Be Pop

FADO HOUSES
31 O Forcado
100 Café Luso
108 Adega Mesquita
121 Adega do Machado
123 Lisboa à Noite
132 Nono
133 Adega do Ribatejo

MAP 6

OTHER
- 1 Lave Neve
- 6 São José Hospital
- 8 Piscina do Atenu
- 10 Coliseu dos Recreios
- 11 Portuguese Chamber of Commerce & Industry
- 14 Post Office
- 17 ABEP Ticket Agency
- 20 Tourist Police Post
- 21 ICEP Tourist Office
- 37 Bank & ATM
- 40 Teatro Nacional de Dona Maria II
- 41 Portugal Telecom Office
- 44 Turismo de Lisboa Kiosk
- 45 Igreja de São Domingos
- 47 Farmácia Estácio
- 49 Statue of Dom Pedro IV
- 52 Carris Ticket Kiosk
- 58 Igreja São Cristóvão
- 65 Farmácia Homeopática Santa Justa
- 79 Cota Câmbios
- 88 Cota Câmbios
- 97 Museu de Arte Sacra
- 99 Igreja de São Roque
- 101 Web Café
- 107 Agência 117 Theatre
- 125 Teatro da Trindade
- 127 Convento do Carmo

MAP 7

PLACES TO STAY & EAT
- 2 Restaurante Alto Minho
- 5 Tendinha da Atalaia
- 10 La Brasserie de l'Entrecôte
- 12 Café A Brasileira
- 13 Café Bénard
- 18 Belcanto
- 24 Caffé Rosso
- 28 Restaurante Múni
- 29 Residencial Duas Nações
- 36 Pensão Prata
- 38 Yin-Yang
- 45 Martinho da Arcada
- 51 Tagide
- 53 A Charcutaria
- 54 Cervejaria Alemã
- 56 Porto de Abrigo
- 60 Caneças
- 62 Cervejaria Solar do Kadete

SHOPPING
- 4 Caza das Vellas Loreto
- 9 Fábrica Sant'Ana
- 11 Vista Alegre
- 14 Casa Regional
- 21 Gardenia
- 22 Livraria Bertrand
- 23 Vista Alegre
- 25 Zara
- 26 Armazéns do Chiado & FNAC
- 31 Madeira House
- 33 O Palhaço
- 34 Santos Ofícios
- 35 Napoleão
- 40 Zara
- 42 Augustus
- 43 Mango
- 55 Mercado da Ribeira

BARS & CLUBS
- 1 Work in Progress
- 3 Ma Jong
- 6 Soul Factory Bar
- 7 Café Suave
- 57 Ó Gilíns Irish Pub
- 59 British Bar
- 61 Hennessy's Irish Pub
- 63 Bar do Rio

OTHER
- 8 Brazilian Consulate
- 15 Ciber Chiado; Café no Chiado
- 16 Teatro Municipal de São Luís; Teatro Estúdio Mário Viegas
- 17 Teatro Nacional de São Carlos
- 19 PSP Police Station
- 20 Basílica da Nossa Senhora dos Mártires
- 27 Fercopi
- 30 SPEA (Sociedade Portuguesa para o Estudo das Aves)
- 32 Barclays Bank
- 37 Núcleo Arqueológico
- 39 Banco Comércial Portuguesa
- 41 Turismo de Lisboa Kiosk
- 44 ATM & Cash Exchange Machine
- 46 Arco do Vitória
- 47 Equestrian Statue of Dom José I
- 48 Central Post Office
- 49 Turismo de Lisboa Main Office (CRIA)
- 50 Paços do Concelho (Town Hall)
- 52 Museu do Chiado
- 58 Jamaica
- 64 Cais do Sodré Car & Bike Ferry Terminal

MAP 7

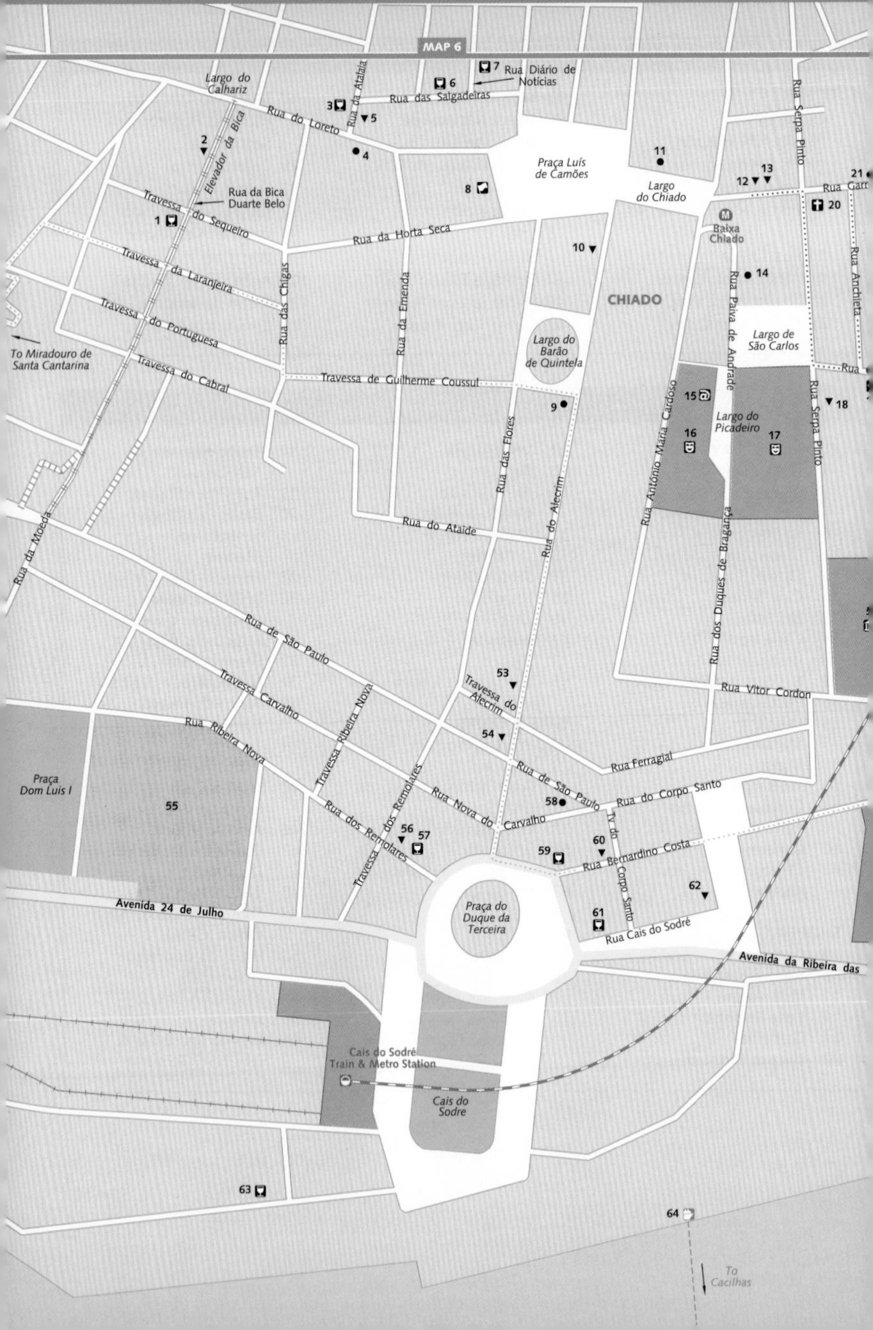
MAP 6
Rua Diário de Notícias
Largo do Calhariz
Rua das Salgadeiras
Rua da Atalaia
Rua do Loreto
Elevador da Bica
Rua da Bica Duarte Belo
Praça Luís de Camões
Largo do Chiado
Rua Serpa Pinto
Rua Garr
Baixa Chiado
Travessa do Sequeiro
Rua da Horta Seca
Travessa da Laranjeira
Travessa do Portuguesa
Rua das Chigas
Rua da Emenda
CHIADO
Rua Paiva de Andrade
Rua Anchieta
Largo de São Carlos
To Miradouro de Santa Cantarina
Travessa do Cabral
Travessa de Guilherme Coussul
Largo do Barão de Quintela
Rua António Maria Cardoso
Largo do Picadeiro
Rua das Flores
Rua do Alecrim
Rua do Ataide
Rua dos Duques de Bragança
Rua da Moeda
Rua de São Paulo
Travessa do Alecrim
Travessa Carvalho
Travessa Ribeira Nova
Rua Vitor Cordon
Rua Ribeira Nova
Rua Ferragial
Praça Dom Luis I
Travessa dos Remolares
Rua Nova do Carvalho
Rua do Corpo Santo
Rua dos Remolares
Tv do Corpo Santo
Rua Bernardino Costa
Avenida 24 de Julho
Praça do Duque da Terceira
Rua Cais do Sodré
Avenida da Ribeira das
Cais do Sodré Train & Metro Station
Cais do Sodre
To Cacilhas
1 2 3 4 5 6 7 8 9 10 11 12 13 14 15 16 17 18 20 21
53 54 55 56 57 58 59 60 61 62 63 64

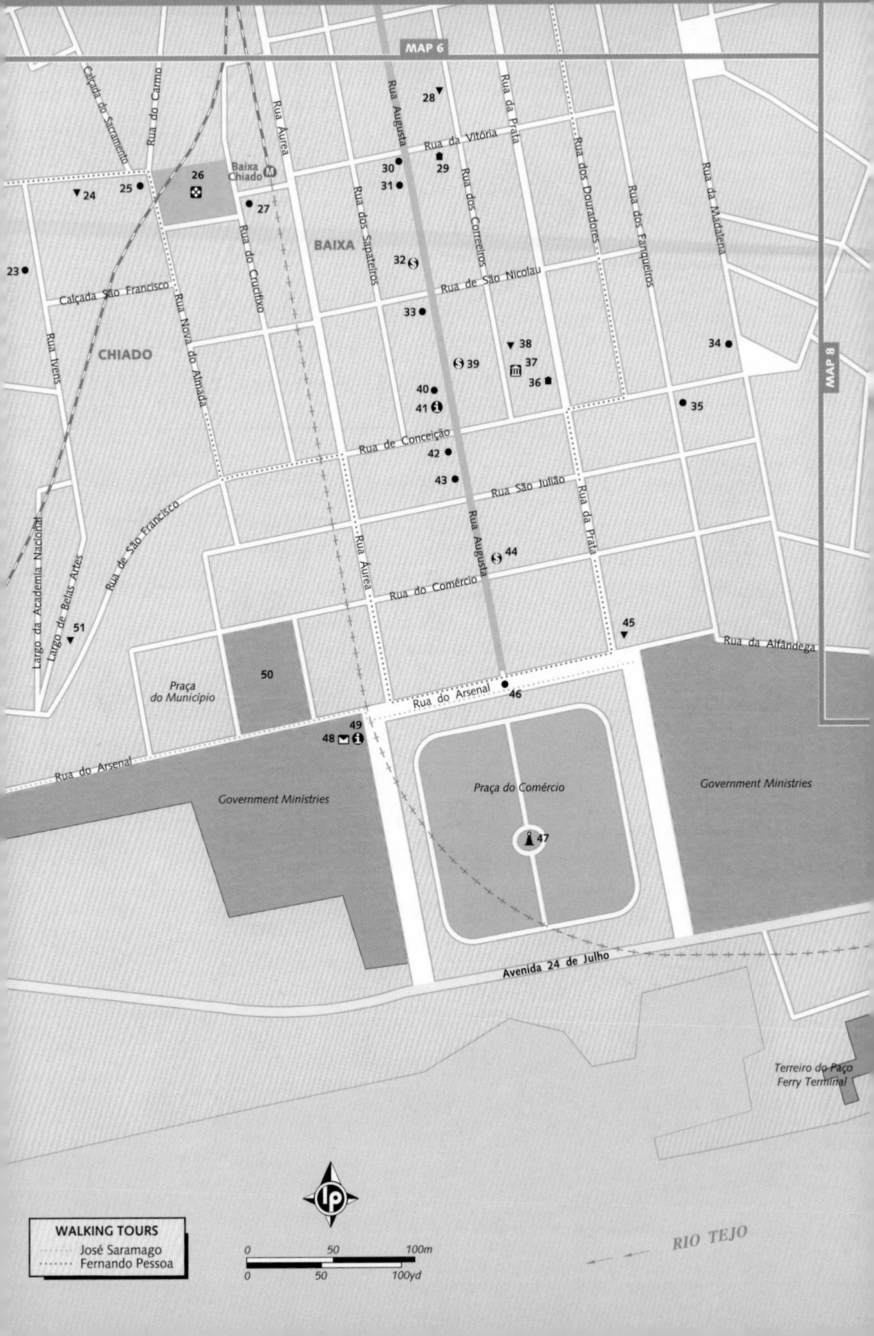

MAP 7

MAP 6

MAP 8

Rua Calçada do Sacramento

Rua do Carmo

Rua Áurea

Rua Augusta

Rua da Vitória

Rua da Prata

Rua dos Douradores

Rua dos Fanqueiros

Rua da Madalena

▼ 28

Baixa
Chiado Ⓜ

▼ 24   25 ●   ● 26
⊠

● 27

BAIXA

30 ●
31 ●

■ 29

Rua dos Sapateiros

Rua dos Correeiros

23 ●

Calçada São Francisco

Rua Nova do Almada

CHIADO

Rua Ivens

32 ⑤

Rua de São Nicolau

33 ●

34 ●

▼ 38
37 🏛
36 ■

⑤ 39

40 ●
41 🛈

35 ●

Largo da Academia Nacional

Largo de Belas Artes

Rua de São Francisco

Rua de Conceição

42 ●

43 ●

Rua São Julião

Rua Áurea

Rua Augusta

Rua da Prata

44 ●

▼ 51

Rua do Comércio

45
▼

Rua da Alfândega

Praça
do Município

50

Rua do Arsenal   46 ●

49
48 ✉ 🛈

Rua do Arsenal

Government Ministries

Praça do Comércio

Government Ministries

▲ 47

Avenida 24 de Julho

Terreiro do Paço
Ferry Terminal

RIO TEJO

WALKING TOURS
...... José Saramago
.... Fernando Pessoa

0   50   100m
0   50   100yd

MAP 8

PLACES TO STAY & EAT

1 Pensão Ninho das Águias
4 Monasterium Café
12 Casa do Leão
14 Castelo Mourisco
17 Gargalhada Geral
20 Bar Cerca Moura
25 Restaurante Tolan
27 Mestre André
29 Barracão de Alfama
30 Lautasco
32 Restaurante Cais d'Alfama
35 Malmequer Bemmequer
41 Snack-Bar Arco Iris
42 Pincho's
43 Jardim do Marisco
45 Pensão São João da Praça &
   Sé Guest House
46 Solar do Vez
48 Solar dos Bicos
50 Pensão Varandas
50 A Galera
51 Hua Ta Li

FADO HOUSES

3 Voz do Operário
28 O Bêco Restaurante Típico
31 Parreirinha de Alfama

OTHER

2 Teatro Taborda; Café.Com
5 Feira da Ladra
   (Flea Market)
6 Antiques & Furniture Market
7 Panteão Nacional
   (Igreja de Santa Engrácia)
8 Wasteels
9 Casa Domingues
10 Museu de Marioneta
11 Câmara Escura
13 Olissipónia
15 Miradouro de São Jorge
16 Costa do Castelo
18 Chapitô
19 Bus No 37
21 Museu-Escola de
   Artes Decorativas
22 Igreja da Santa Luzia
23 Miradouro de Santa Luzia
24 O Esboço
26 Museu Militar
33 Casa do Fado
36 Espaço Oikos
37 Antiguidades Outro Era
38 Ruins of Roman Theatre
39 Pé Sujo
40 Ruins of Moorish Tower

WALKING TOURS
...... Cathedral to Castle

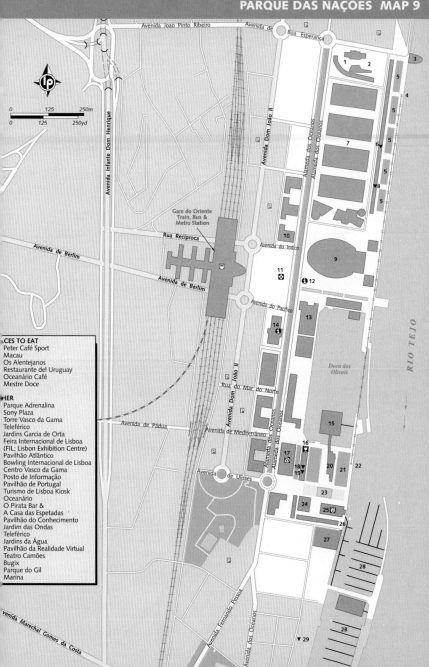

Avenida Joao Pinto Ribeiro

Avenida de Boa Esperança

1

2

3

5

4

5

5

Avenida Infante Dom Henrique

Avenida de Berlim

Avenida Dom João II

Alameda dos Oceanos

Alameda dos Oceanos

7

5

8

5

Gare do Oriente
Train, Bus &
Metro Station

Rua Recíproca

Avenida do Indico

10

9

Avenida de Berlim

11

12

Avenidas do Pacho

13

RIO TEJO

14

Doca dos
Olivais

Rua do Mar do Norte

Avenida Dom João II

15

Avenida de Pádua

Avenida de Mediterrâneo

Alameda dos Oceanos

Alameda dos Oceanos

16

17

18

19

20

21

22

Avenida de Ulisses

23

24

25

26

27

Avenida Fernando Pessoa

Avenida dos Oceanos

28

28

venida Marechal Gomes da Costa

29

0   125   250m
0   125   250yd

CES TO EAT
Peter Café Sport
Macau
Os Alentejanos
Restaurante del Uruguay
Oceanário Café
Mestre Doce

HER
Parque Adrenalina
Sony Plaza
Torre Vasco da Gama
Teleférico
Jardins Garcia de Orta
Feira Internacional de Lisboa
(FIL; Lisbon Exhibition Centre)
Pavilhão Atlântico
Bowling Internacional de Lisboa
Centro Vasco da Gama
Posto de Informação
Pavilhão de Portugal
Turismo de Lisboa Kiosk
Oceanário
O Pirata Bar &
A Casa das Espetadas
Pavilhão do Conhecimento
Jardim das Ondas
Teleférico
Jardins da Água
Pavilhão da Realidade Virtual
Teatro Camões
Bugix
Parque do Gil
Marina

MAP 10 BELÉM

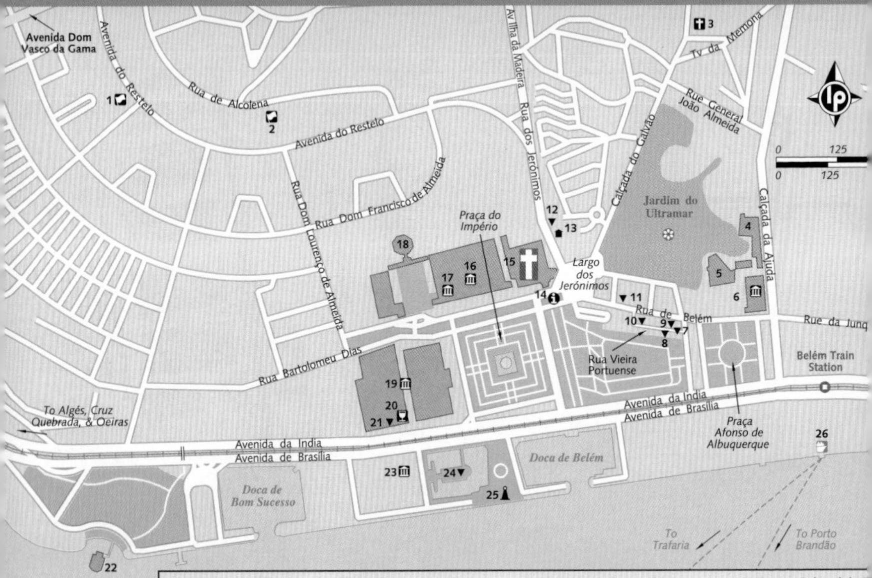

Avenida Dom Vasco da Gama

Avenida do Restelo

Rua de Alcolena

Avenida do Restelo

Rua Dom Francisco de Almeida

Rua Dom Lourenço de Almeida

Av Ilha da Madeira

Rua dos Jerónimos

Tv da Memória

Rua General João de Almeida

Calçada do Galvão

Jardim do Ultramar

Praça do Império

Largo dos Jerónimos

Rua Vieira Portuense

Rua de Belém

Rua Bartolomeu Dias

Belém Train Station

Rua da Jung

Avenida da India
Avenida de Brasilia

Praça Afonso de Albuquerque

To Algés, Cruz Quebrada, & Oeiras

Avenida da India
Avenida de Brasilia

Doca de Belém

Doca de Bom Sucesso

Calçada da Ajuda

To Trafaria

To Porto Brandão

PLACES TO STAY & EAT
7 Restaurante Floresta
8 A Cápsula
9 Nau de Belém
10 Adamastor
11 Pasteis de Belém
12 Restaurante São Jerónimo
13 Hotel da Torre

21 Cafetaria Quadrante
24 Portugália

OTHER
1 Cape Verdean Embassy
2 Guinea-Bissau Embassy
3 Igreja da Memória
4 Palácio Nacional de Belém

5 Presidência da República
6 Museu Nacional dos Coches
14 Turismo de Lisboa Kiosk
15 Mosteiro dos Jerónimos
16 Museu Nacional de Arqueologia
17 Museu de Marinha &
    Museu das Crianças
18 Planetário Calouste Gulbenkian

19 Centro Cultural de B
    Museu do Design
20 Bar Terraço
22 Torre de Belém
23 Museu de Arte Popu
25 Padrão dos
    Descobrimentos
26 Ferry Terminal

MAP 11 LISBON METRO

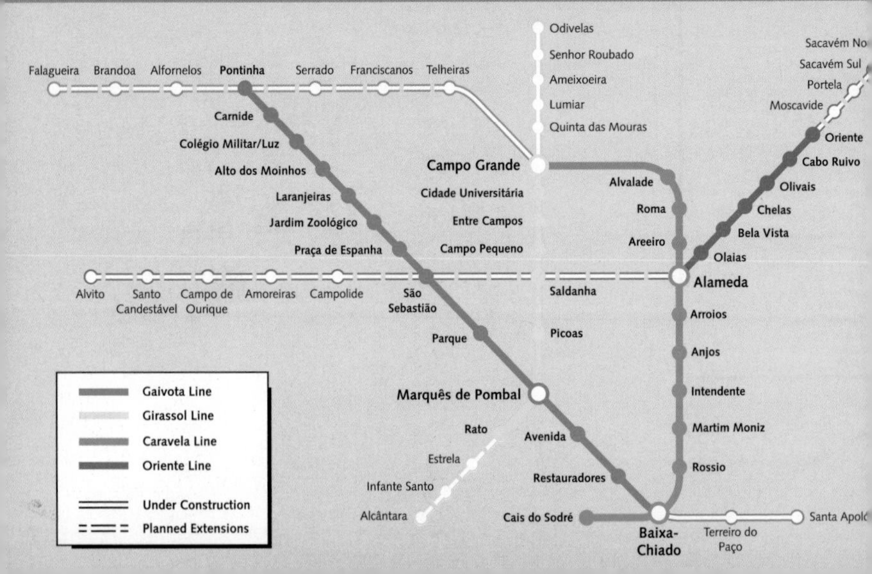

Falagueira Brandoa Alfornelos **Pontinha** Serrado Franciscanos Telheiras

Carnide

Colégio Militar/Luz

Alto dos Moinhos

Laranjeiras

Jardim Zoológico

Praça de Espanha

Alvito Santo Campo de Amoreiras Campolide São
        Candestável Ourique   Sebastião

Parque

Marquês de Pombal

Rato

Estrela

Infante Santo

Alcântara

Odivelas

Senhor Roubado

Ameixoeira

Lumiar

Quinta das Mouras

Campo Grande

Cidade Universitária

Entre Campos

Campo Pequeno

Saldanha

Picoas

Avenida

Restauradores

Cais do Sodré

Alvalade

Roma

Areeiro

Baixa-Chiado

Sacavém No

Sacavém Sul

Portela

Moscavide

Oriente

Cabo Ruivo

Olivais

Chelas

Bela Vista

Olaias

Alameda

Arroios

Anjos

Intendente

Martim Moniz

Rossio

Terreiro do Paço

Santa Apóló

Legend
Gaivota Line
Girassol Line
Caravela Line
Oriente Line

Under Construction
Planned Extensions

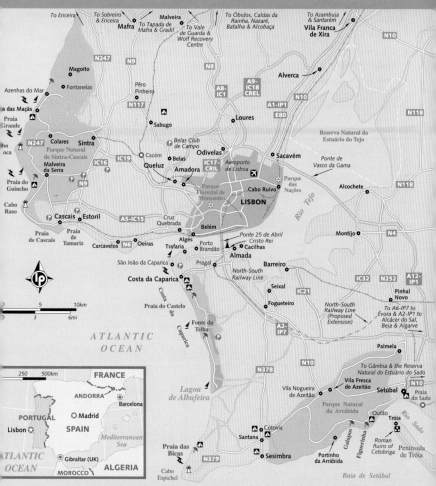

Colourful fishing boats docked at Setúbal harbour at the mouth of the Rio Sado

CARLOS COSTA

MAP LEGEND

CITY ROUTES

Freeway .... Freeway	_____ Unsealed Road
Highway .... Primary Road	_____ One Way Street
Road .... Secondary Road	_____ Pedestrian Street
Street .... Street	::::::::::: Stepped Street
Lane .... Lane	)= = = Tunnel
_____ On/Off Ramp	_____ Footbridge

REGIONAL ROUTES

.... Tollway, Freeway	.... Secondary Road
.... Primary Road	.... Unsealed Road

BOUNDARIES

— · — · — International
— · · — · · Autonomous Community
— · — · — Province
▄▄▄▄▄▄ Fortified Wall

HYDROGRAPHY

River, Creek
.... Lake
⊙ .... Spring; Rapids
⑤ →+← .... Waterfalls

TRANSPORT ROUTES & STATIONS

—O—.......... Local Railway	⊞ Funicular, Cable Car
- - -) .... Underground Rlwy	⊡ .... Ferry
Ⓜ .... Subway, Station	.... Walking Tour
- - -⊡- Lightrail Tram	Path

AREA FEATURES

Building	Market	Beach
Park, Gardens	Sports Ground	Cemetery

Plaza	
Swamp	

POPULATION SYMBOLS

✪ **CAPITAL** .... National Capital	● **City** .... City	● Village .... Village
◉ **CAPITAL** .... Provincial Capital	○ **Town** .... Town	Urban Area

MAP SYMBOLS

■ .... Place to Stay	▼ .... Place to Eat	● .... Point of Interest

❸ .... Bank	♫ .... Fado House	Ⓟ .... Parking	⊀ .... Surf Beach
⊟ .... Bus Terminal	⦿ .... Golf Course	➕ .... Police Station	🖼 .... Swimming Pool
🚠 Cable Car, Funicular	✛ .... Hospital	▬ .... Post Office	☎ .... Telephone
⬛ .... Camping Ground	🔲 .... Internet Cafe	🍺 .... Pub or Bar	🎭 .... Theatre
✚ Church	❄ .... Lookout	❌ .... Ruins	❶ Tourist Information
⊟ .... Cinema	♟ .... Monument	🏛 .... Stately Home	⚐ .... Windsurfing
◘ Embassy, Consulate	🏛 .... Museum	❌ Shopping Centre	🐘 .... Zoo

Note: not all symbols displayed above appear in this book

LONELY PLANET OFFICES

Australia
Locked Bag 1, Footscray, Victoria 3011
☎ 03 9689 4666 fax 03 9689 6833
email: talk2us@lonelyplanet.com.au

USA
150 Linden St, Oakland, CA 94607
☎ 510 893 8555 TOLL FREE: 800 275 8555
fax 510 893 8572
email: info@lonelyplanet.com

UK
10a Spring Place, London NW5 3BH
☎ 020 7428 4800 fax 020 7428 4828
email: go@lonelyplanet.co.uk

France
1 rue du Dahomey, 75011 Paris
☎ 01 55 25 33 00 fax 01 55 25 33 01
email: bip@lonelyplanet.fr
www.lonelyplanet.fr

World Wide Web: www.lonelyplanet.com *or* AOL keyword: lp
Lonely Planet Images: lpi@lonelyplanet.com.au